Legal Theory Today

Answering for Crime

Legal Theory Today

FOUNDING EDITOR

John Gardner, Professor of Jurisprudence, University College, Oxford

TITLES IN THIS SERIES

Law in its Own Right by Henrik Palmer Olsen and Stuart Toddington
Law and Aesthetics by Adam Gearey
Law as a Social Institution by Hamish Ross
Evaluation and Legal Theory by Julie Dickson
Risks and Legal Theory by Jenny Steele
A Sociology of Jurisprudence Richard Nobles and David Schiff
Costs and Cautionary Tales: Economic Insights for the Law by Anthony Ogus
Legal Norms and Normativity: An Essay in Genealogy by Sylvie Delacroix
Consent in the Law by Deryck Beyleveld and Roger Brownsword

Forthcoming titles:

Law after Modernity by Sionaidh Douglas-Scott
Law and Ethics by John Tasioulas
Law and Human Need by John Stanton-Ife

Answering for Crime

Responsibility and Liability in the Criminal Law

R A Duff

• HART •
PUBLISHING

OXFORD AND PORTLAND, OREGON
2009

Published in North America (US and Canada) by
Hart Publishing
c/o International Specialized Book Services
920 NE 58th Avenue, Suite 300
Portland, OR 97213–3786
USA
Tel: +1 503 287 3093 or toll-free: (1) 800 944 6190
Fax: +1 503 280 8832
E-mail: orders@isbs.com
Web Site: www.isbs.com

First published in 2007
Reprinted in paperback in 2009

Hart Publishing, 16c Worcester Place, Oxford, OX1 2JW
Telephone: +44 (0)1865 517530 Fax: +44 (0) 1865 510710
E-mail: mail@hartpub.co.uk
Website: http://www.hartpub.co.uk

British Library Cataloguing in Publication Data

Data Available

ISBN: 978–1-84113–753–7 (hardback)
ISBN: 978–1-84946–033–0 (paperback)

Typeset by Columns Ltd, Reading
Printed and bound in Great Britain by
TJ International Ltd, Padstow, Cornwall

Preface to Paperback Edition

I have taken the opportunity to correct a number of mistakes and omissions in footnote citations and in the list of references, but have not otherwise altered the text. The book has received a number of substantial and thoughtful critical discussions, for which I am grateful: in particular from Kim Ferzan (*Criminal Justice Ethics* 28 (2009)), Doug Husak (*Law and Philosophy* 28, (2009)), Nicola Lacey (*New Criminal Law Review* 12 (2009)), Victor Tadros (*Mind* 118 (2009) 465), and Peter Westen (*Oxford Journal of Legal Studies* 28 (2008) 563). I hope that its central claims can survive their various objections, and will respond to them in the near future; but my main hope is that the book can provoke new discussion and thought—even (or in more Socratic moods especially) if that discussion takes the form of vigorous disagreement and criticism.

RAD
July 2009

Acknowledgements

Much of the work on this book was done during my tenure of a Leverhulme Major Research Fellowship: I am very grateful to the Leverhulme Trust for this award, which gave me three invaluable years free from teaching and administration in which to think again about some of the questions on which I had been working for a number of years, and to make effectively a fresh start. I am also grateful to the University of Stirling for the support I have received, not just during the writing of this book, but throughout my academic career; and especially to my colleagues in the Department of Philosophy, who (apart from offering helpful comments on many aspects of the book) have through the years provided an ideally collegial, friendly, enthusiastic and constructively critical environment in which to pursue research.

I also owe debts to many other groups and individuals (and apologies to any whose help I fail to acknowledge here): to participants in seminars, conferences and workshops at which I have tried out much of the material in this book—at the universities of Athens, Cambridge, Copenhagen, Cyprus, Dundee, London and Oxford; at Queen's University (Ontario), Louisiana State University, Ohio State University and Rutgers University; at the Aristotelian Society, and at the IVR World Congress in Lund in 2003. Special mention must be made of three people—Lindsay Farmer, Sandra Marshall and Victor Tadros—with whom I worked for three years on a related project on the criminal trial: discussions with them, apart from being enormously enjoyable, have made a significant difference to this book, and I have benefited in particular from Victor Tadros's enthusiastic critiques of many of my ideas and arguments (on some issues, he even managed to persuade me that I was wrong). Special mention is also due to Doug Husak, from whom I have learned (and enjoyed learning) much in conversations over the years. I am also grateful to an anonymous referee for Hart Publishing. Finally, for this, as for my previous books, my thanks go to Sandra Marshall, whose support and companionship, both philosophical and personal, have been the cornerstone of my life.

I have drawn on material from several previously published articles and book chapters, and am grateful to the following publishers for permission to do so: The Aristotelian Society, ('Answering for Crime' (2005) 106 *Proceedings of the Aristotelian Society* 85); Blackwell Publishing ('Crime, Prohibition and Punishment' (2002) 19 *Journal of Applied Philosophy* 97); Buffalo Criminal Law Center ('Harms and Wrongs' (2001) 5 *Buffalo Criminal Law Review* 13); Cambridge University Press ('Action, the Act Requirement and Criminal Liability' in J Hyman and HC Steward (eds),

Agency and Action (2004) at 69); Michael E Moritz College of Law, Ohio State University ('"I Might be Guilty, but You Can't Try Me": Estoppel and Other Bars to Trial' (2003) 1 *Ohio State Journal of Criminal Law* 245; 'Who is Responsible, for What, to Whom?' (2005) 2 *Ohio State Journal of Criminal Law* 441); Oxford University Press ('Criminalizing Endangerment' in RA Duff and SP Green (eds), *Defining Crimes: Essays on the Special Part of the Criminal Law* (2005) at 43; 'Strict Liability, Legal Presumptions and the Presumption of Innocence' in AP Simester (ed), *Appraising Strict Liability* (2005) at 125); University of Tulsa College of Law ('Rethinking Justifications' (2004) 39 *Tulsa Law Review* 829).

Contents

Table of Cases

England and Wales

Scotland

European Court of Human Rights

USA

Table of Legislation

USA

Introduction

1. The 'General Part' and the 'Special Part'

'Wounding with intent' is a criminal offence in English law: it is committed by someone who causes a wound or grievous bodily harm to another, intending to cause grievous bodily harm or to resist or prevent a lawful arrest;[1] but a person who commits that offence can still gain an acquittal by offering a defence—for instance of self-defence or duress.

It is a criminal offence in English law for someone aged 18 or over intentionally to touch a person who is under 16 if the touching is sexual, and if either the other person is under 13 or the toucher does not reasonably believe that the other person is 16 or over: the prosecution need not prove that the touching was unwelcome to the person touched, or that it had any deleterious consequences, or that the toucher realised that the other person was or might be under 16.[2]

It is a criminal offence in English law to drive a car in a manner that 'falls far below what would be expected of a competent and careful driver', if 'it would be obvious to a competent and careful driver that driving in that way would be dangerous' to persons or to property: the prosecution need not prove that the driver was aware that he was driving incompetently or dangerously, or that any person or property was actually harmed.[3]

A trader who sells groceries by imperial rather than metric weight, or who has equipment for such sales in her possession 'for use for trade', commits a criminal offence in English law: it need not be proved that any customers were deceived, or received less than they had wanted, or that any material harm was caused.[4]

I am guilty of a criminal offence in English law if I possess 'an article in circumstances which give rise to a reasonable suspicion that [my] possession is for a purpose connected with the commission, preparation or instigation of an act of terrorism'—though I have a defence if I can prove

[1] Offences Against the Person Act 1861, s 18.

[2] Sexual Offences Act 2003, s 9.

[3] Road Traffic Act 1988, ss 2–2A.

[4] Weights and Measures Act 1985, s 8: see *Thoburn v Sunderland City Council* [2003] QB 151.

that my possession was not for any such purpose;[5] the prosecution need not prove that I intended to use the article to assist a terrorist purpose.

I commit an offence in English law if I have an uncertificated firearm in my possession, unless it counts as an antique: I am guilty of the offence even if I mistakenly believe, on reasonable grounds, that it counts as an antique or do not realise that it counts as a firearm.[6]

I commit an offence in English law if I am involved as a driver in a road accident in which someone is injured and fail to report the accident;[7] or if I use my car on a public road without displaying its excise licence in the right place;[8] or if, as director of a company, I fail to take 'all reasonable steps' to ensure that it files annual returns.[9]

These few examples of criminal offences in English law, for which people are convicted and punished by English courts, indicate the diversity of criminal offences in English law—a diversity that will be found in a random selection from any developed system of criminal law. That diversity presents an obvious problem for anyone embarking on a book about criminal responsibility and liability. Such a book must be something more than an undifferentiated list of the many different ways in which or grounds on which one can be held criminally liable in this or that system: it must say something general about the structure and grounds of criminal responsibility and liability. But what can we hope to say that is both general and useful about a collection of offences as disparate as these examples show our laws to contain?

The obvious answer to this question is that we should look to the 'general' rather than to the 'special' part of the criminal law: to the rules, principles and doctrines that apply more or less generally to the range of specific offences, rather than to the diverse definitions of those offences. Some such distinction between the 'general' and the 'special' parts is recognised more or less formally in criminal codes[10] and criminal law textbooks.[11] Its precise contours are, however, neither clear nor uncontroversial: there is continuing disagreement about how the 'general' part

[5] Terrorism Act 2000, s 57: furthermore, given proof that an article was in the same building as me, the court is allowed to assume that I possessed it, unless I can prove that I did not know it was there or that I had no control over it. See also the s 58 offence of collecting or having information 'of a kind likely to be useful to a person committing or preparing an act of terrorism'.

[6] Firearms Act 1968, ss 1(1), 58.

[7] Road Traffic Act 1988 s 170.

[8] Vehicle Excise and Registration Act 1994, s 33.

[9] Companies Act 1985, s 363.

[10] See the formal divisions of the German *Strafgesetzbuch* into the *Allgemeiner Teil* and the *Besonderer Teil*; of the Model Penal Code into 'General Provisions' and 'Definition of Specific Crimes'; and of the English Draft Criminal Code into 'General Principles' and 'Specific Offences' (Law Commission, 1989a).

[11] German publishers typically produce separate textbooks on the general and the special parts, something that Anglo-American publishers have not done since 1961 (see G Williams,

should be defined; about how doctrines and rules that are agreed to belong to the criminal law should be allocated as between the two parts;[12] about the extent to which and the ways in which offence definitions should be governed by principles or rules falling within a general part.[13] I will not have much to say directly about these controversies in what follows: they are liable to be unrewarding if they rest on an assumption that we must be able to draw a sharp distinction between general and special parts, and firmly allocate every doctrine or rule to one or the other. I should comment briefly, however, on what kind of distinction we should hope to draw, before explaining the way in which this book will be concerned with the 'general' principles of criminal responsibility and liability.

We cannot define the general part as consisting in those doctrines and rules that apply to every offence in the special part; that would leave too many doctrines and rules in limbo. But if we then say that it consists in those doctrines and rules that apply to some, or to a range of, special part offences, we replace the untenably precise by the unhelpfully vague. Some such vagueness is inevitable, and unproblematic if we do not place too much substantive weight on the distinction; but we can reduce it by saying that the general part consists in those doctrines, rules and definitions that are not essentially tied to any specific offence or set of offences. A brief look at the doctrine of provocation will clarify this suggestion, and explain 'essentially'.

In English and American criminal law, the doctrine of provocation formally applies only to homicide. By the criterion suggested here, however, it nonetheless belongs to the general part, since there is nothing intrinsic to the doctrine that makes it applicable only to homicide. The doctrine is that an offender's culpability is significantly reduced if he acted in response to a provocation that caused him to lose self-control and 'was enough to make a reasonable man do as he did',[14] or 'under the influence of extreme mental or emotional disturbance for which there [was] reasonable explanation or excuse'.[15] That doctrine could in principle be applied to a wide range of offences: it is not *essentially* tied to any specific offence or set of offences, and therefore belongs to the general part; the legislature must decide whether it should formally apply to all offences, as a general partial defence, or only to some (or one). Since provocation can be informally adduced as a mitigating factor in sentencing for other offences,

1961), but the distinction is also drawn, explicitly or implicitly, in Anglo-American textbooks: see eg LaFave, 2003; Ormerod, 2005; Dressler, 2006; Ashworth, 2006.

[12] See generally Fletcher, 1978: 393–408; Moore, 1997: 30–5; Tadros, 2002; Horder, 2005. See also Lacey, 1998, for an interesting discussion of changing conceptions of the scope and significance of the general part in Anglo-American legal thought.

[13] See Gardner, 1998a.

[14] Homicide Act 1957, s 3; but see Law Commission, 2004: Part 3, and 2006: Part 5.

[15] Model Penal Code, s 210.3(1)(b); see Commentary to s 210.3, at 53–73.

the decision to limit the formal doctrine, as one that bears on conviction, to murder cannot reflect the view that the defence is substantively apt only in that context: it implies, rather, that for expressive or pragmatic reasons (the special importance of 'fair labelling' in homicide, for instance;[16] or the mandatory sentence for murder in England) the defence need only be formally recognised in that context.

This account of what belongs to the general part is of course still either untenably precise or ineliminably vague. If it allocates to the general part any doctrine, rule or definition that is not essentially tied to a single specific offence, then (quite apart from problems about offence individuation) it would locate the definition of 'firearm' in section 57 of the Firearms Act 1968 in the general part, since that definition explicitly applies to all offences under that Act—which is hardly a plausible result. If we instead talk of doctrines, rules and definitions that are not essentially tied to any specific set, or family, of offences, we need to ask how we can identify and individuate sets or families of offences—and cannot expect a determinate answer.[17] The best way forward might be to abandon any attempt to distinguish the general from the special part for other than purely presentational purposes to do with the clearest and most convenient way to explicate the law; and to recognise that in place of the two distinct categories that talk of 'the general part' and 'the special part' suggests, the law exhibits a spectrum of doctrines, rules and definitions ranging from the most specific (or 'special'), in particular those defining offences, to the most general.

This book will be focused on issues at the 'general' end of this spectrum, but it will also reflect another distinction that seems both important and uncertain: that between the general part of the criminal law and whatever underlying moral or political values may be relevant to the normative appraisal of the criminal law.

Consider for instance the supposed principle that criminal liability requires an act.[18] That principle could be an explicit part of the criminal law, if it was included in the criminal code and applied by courts in interpreting the law.[19] Or it might be a part of the political morality of the society whose law is under discussion—if, although courts did not explicitly appeal to it, it figured regularly and effectively in public debates about what the law ought to be, and in legislative decision-making. Or it might be a feature of the 'critical' morality that normative theorists mobilise in arguing about what the criminal law ought to be:[20] they do not claim to

[16] On fair labelling generally see Ashworth, 2006: 88–90.
[17] See Gardner 1998a: 247–9.
[18] See Husak, 1998a.
[19] Cp Model Penal Code s 2.01(1).
[20] On 'critical' as against 'positive' morality, see Hart, 1963: 17–20.

find it either in the existing criminal law, or in the existing political morality, of the society whose law it is, but argue that it ought to be a part of their political morality. Natural Law theorists might also argue that, even if it is not in fact part of the law, it is a principle that the criminal law ought, given its nature and proper purpose, to respect—that there is something intrinsically illegitimate about a positive law that does not respect it.[21] But a more interesting possibility is that it might be part of what we can call the implicit general part: that is, even if it does not figure explicitly in any criminal code or statute, or perhaps even (in general terms) in authoritative appellate court decisions, it might be a principle that helps us to make best sense of the decisions that courts make in interpreting and applying the law (and of the laws that they are interpreting and applying), and that we can therefore identify as implicit in the law. Such an identification would be the outcome of a process of 'rational reconstruction'—a process of analysis and interpretation that aims to make the best possible rational sense of the various materials with which it is dealing:[22] for present purposes two aspects of that process are important.

First, although it might seem that there should be a reasonably clear distinction between analytical (or descriptive) and normative theoretical inquiries, in the criminal law as in other contexts,[23] the enterprise of rational reconstruction undermines such a distinction. It involves the excavation and reconstruction of norms that can be shown to be implicit in the system of law as it is applied by the courts, but must also involve the identification of laws or doctrines that are in terms of the law's own values illegitimate; and whilst theorists might hope to have to make only the kinds of 'detached normative judgement' about the law that do not commit them to accepting the norms they identify,[24] it will be hard not to engage with those norms in one's own normative voice. Consider, for instance, the offences under sections 57 and 58 of the Terrorism Act 2000 noted above.[25] A purely descriptive inquiry would report that these offences exist in English law, and that they falsify any general claim that criminal liability requires either anything recognisable as an act (or omission), or anything identifiable as a *mens rea*, or indeed anything that could be portrayed as a moral wrong. But that is hardly satisfactory: we at least want to know whether such offences are consistent with such general principles as English law contains—principles that, even if they are not explicit in a

21 Compare Moore, 1993.

22 See MacCormick, 1990; such a process also clearly has much in common with the interpretive efforts of a Dworkinian Hercules: see R Dworkin, 1986.

23 See Husak, 1987: 20–6.

24 See Raz, 1979: 153–9.

25 See at n 5 above.

code or statute, a process of rational reconstruction will reveal. We might expect (indeed hope) that they will not be consistent—for instance that they will be impossible to reconcile with any plausible interpretation of the presumption of innocence:[26] but in determining what counts as a 'plausible' interpretation of that presumption, or of any other legal doctrine, we are asking what makes best or possible sense of it; and this must be in part the question of what could make normative sense of it—what could portray it as a norm that people could take seriously.

Secondly, such an enterprise of rational reconstruction cannot focus only on what is strictly internal to the system of law under examination: as soon as it starts (as it will have to start) to identify principles that are implicit rather than explicit in the law, it will become less clear—or utterly unclear—whether those principles should be counted as part of the law, or as part of the underlying political morality to which citizens, legislators and judges appeal. Of course theorists who insist that there must be a clear answer to the questions that divide 'natural law' theorists from legal positivists will reject what they will see as such defeatism about the very possibility of deciding what is or is not part of the law: but that need not concern us here. The focus of this book will be on the principles and values that do or should structure our criminal law, and I will not be too concerned with the question whether those principles and values should be seen as part of the law or as part of the underlying political morality on which the law must depend for its legitimacy.

2. A Normative Theory of Criminal Law?

The possibility of such a process of rational reconstruction is denied by those who regard the criminal law as rationally irredeemable. 'Critical' theorists of various kinds argue that the criminal law is so fissured by tensions and contradictions (which reflect deeper tensions or contradictions in the political structures that underpin the law) that no such reconstruction can amount to anything more than a doomed attempt to rationalise what is irremediably irrational or a-rational—or, worse, to conceal its true political character.[27] One response to such critics is to argue, with John Finnis, that they are 'disappointed metaphysical absolutist[s]': that their critique of the law's irrationality reflects not the law's inherent failing, but their exaggerated misconceptions of what rationality requires, and of what the law would need to be to count as rational or

[26] See Tadros and Tierney, 2004, and ch 9.1 below.

[27] For different versions of such critique (which also differ in the strength of their destructive, or in some cases modestly reconstructive, ambitions) see eg Kelman, 1981; Lacey, 1993; Norrie, 2001.

coherent.[28] A more adequate response would show how the kind of theorising that such critics reject can assist both an understanding of what the law is (which will include an understanding of what it purports or aspires to be, in terms of the principles and values that a rational reconstruction reveals), and a more useful discussion of what the law ought to be, by taking seriously the concepts and ideas in terms of which the law presents itself.

Whatever room there may be for rational reconstructions that remain normatively non-committal or detached, the aims of this book are normative. I do not deny that it is possible to preserve a 'detached normative' stance from the law that one is rationally reconstructing—although it will be hard to do so in relation to one's own legal system: for we can reconstruct norms that make sense of the law, norms that people could take seriously, without accepting those norms. But my stance is not thus detached. I will engage in a fair amount of rational reconstruction, and offer analyses and arguments that start from our existing criminal laws: for normative theorising about human practices must begin with the practices that we actually have. However, first, as I noted above, even a normatively modest rational reconstruction of a practice should reveal values and principles intrinsic to it which can then ground an internal, or 'immanent', critique of the practice in its own terms. Secondly, if we are to make normative sense of the law, we must look beyond it to the political-moral values on which it depends: in explicating such values, we will also be laying the ground for a more external critique of the law and its principles.

The ideal aim of such a process might be to produce a 'theory of criminal law'. That is not what will emerge from this book: the most I hope to achieve is to sketch the normative and logical structures that any such theory should embody—to provide the skeleton to which flesh would then need to be added and which could be fleshed out in a variety of ways. I will say a little more about the reasons for this relatively modest ambition shortly, but should first say something about the nature of a 'theory of criminal law'—understood here and hereafter as a normative theory of criminal law.

What needs to be said here forms the start of an answer to two questions: 'What kind of theory?', and 'A theory of what?'.

As to 'What kind of theory?', talk of a 'theory of criminal law' might suggest that we should be looking for a coherently structured, internally consistent normative framework for the criminal law: if not for a theory that posits a single unifying aim or purpose for criminal law,[29] at least for one that posits a mutually coherent and consistent set of aims, principles

[28] Finnis, 1987a: 160.

[29] Although some theorists do just that: for two very different examples see Braithwaite and Pettit, 1990; Moore, 1997: ch. 1.

and values by which the criminal law should be structured. Attractive though such a theory—one kind of 'grand theory'—might be, however, we should not assume in advance either that it will be possible, or that its impossibility will show the futility of any attempt to render the criminal law rational and principled. As far as the possibility of such a theory is concerned, if we think about the broad scope of the criminal law and the diverse types of conduct that it covers; if we think too about the implications of the by now familiar idea that we live in times of value pluralism and conflict, and that in our political (and thus also our legal) lives we face the competing demands of values and principles that cannot be reconciled into a single and mutually coherent whole: we will see how unlikely it is that we will be able to make plausible normative sense of the criminal law in terms of such a theory, and how much more likely it is that the criminal law will need to be portrayed as a site at which the competing demands of different values, goals and principles must be negotiated.[30] But the impossibility of any such unitary theory does not show that we cannot hope for a normatively plausible reconstruction of criminal law. To suppose that it showed this would be to reveal oneself as a disappointed metaphysical absolutist, or a disappointed normative monist, for whom reason can speak with only one voice, and for whom principles are acceptable only if they are mutually consistent: but if we accept what is a commonplace of liberal political and moral thought, that values can conflict in ways that are rationally irresoluble, we must also accept that practical reason can speak with conflicting voices, and that we may find ourselves rationally drawn by the claims of conflicting values. If that is indeed our normative situation, we can expect it to be reflected in the criminal law: but an adequate normative theory of criminal law must then recognise the conflicting values that bear on the law, and the need to find a tolerable compromise between them. This is not to say that there is no point in pursuing grand theory: even if the pursuit is doomed, its failure might be instructive. It is to say only that we should not assume that the law's claims to principled rationality depend on the possibility of such a grand theory.

As to 'A theory of what?', there are two issues to note. The first concerns the scope of 'criminal law'. Theories and textbooks of 'criminal law' often implicitly take it to consist in the substantive criminal law (the general and the special parts):[31] but any adequate 'theory of criminal law' would also need to deal with such matters as criminal punishment; the criminal process—including not just the trial, but all that precedes the trial

[30] See Ashworth, 2006: chs 1–3.

[31] And often focus on only a limited range of traditional offences: for critical discussion, and some salutary correctives, see eg Lacey *et al*, 2003; Green, 1997, 2006; Dubber, 2001, 2005; Husak, 2005a, 2005b.

in the way of investigation and preparation; policing; and issues concerning criminalisation.[32] This book is, however, focused on the substantive criminal law: although it will say something about criminalisation and about aspects of the criminal trial, it will say almost nothing about criminal punishment, or about policing and the criminal process. As far as punishment is concerned, my reason is that I have written about this extensively elsewhere;[33] although the prospect of punishment is always present (in part because, as we will see, one purpose of criminal law and the criminal process is to identify the kinds of wrong that, and the wrongdoers who, merit punishment), I will not discuss its rationale here. As far as other aspects of the criminal justice system are concerned, one justification for not attending to them here concerns the division of labour and the merits of shorter books: if a book is to stay within the bounds of readable length, it will be enough for it to deal with the structure of the substantive criminal law, leaving other aspects of the criminal justice system for other books or writers. There is also good reason to start with substantive criminal law, so long as we remember that it is not the whole of 'criminal law', since it is in an obvious sense the heart of criminal law, in terms of which other aspects must be theorised. There is of course room to argue about the logical relationship between the substantive criminal law and punishment: on some accounts,[34] the function of criminal law is precisely to ensure the punishment of culpable wrongdoers, in which case we can understand the proper structure and contents of the substantive criminal law only by understanding the rationale of criminal punishment. I comment on this issue in Chapter 4, but it is clear that any normative account of other aspects of the criminal process must depend on an account of the proper aims of the substantive criminal law, since it is that which the police must enforce, and alleged breaches of which are to be investigated and prosecuted.

The second issue captured by the 'A theory of what?' question concerns not the scope of 'criminal law', but the scope and ambitions of normative theory. Should normative theorists aspire to an a-historical, a-contextual universality that speaks of what the criminal law should be at all times and places—in any society, whenever and wherever it exists? Or should they recognise, as critics argue, that the historical and cultural contingency not only of systems of criminal law, but of normative theorising about the

[32] For an ambitious sketch of a theory with this broad scope see Braithwaite and Pettit, 1990. There has been an increase in serious theoretical work on many of these other aspects of criminal law: on the criminal trial (eg Burns, 1999; Duff *et al*, 2004, 2006, 2007) and its rules (eg Roberts and Zuckerman, 2004); on criminal justice and the criminal process (eg Lacey, 1994; Zedner, 2004; Ashworth and Redmayne, 2005); and on criminalisation (eg Schonsheck 1994; Husak, 2007).

[33] See Duff, 2001.

[34] See eg Moore, 1997: ch 1; see also (more modestly) Husak 2005b.

criminal law, undermines such ambitious universalist aspirations?[35] This is not the place to engage in the debate about the possibility of genuinely a priori normative reasoning: all I need do here is declare that I have no such grand ambitions, and to make clear that it does not follow from the impossibility of such theorising that we cannot properly aspire to a rational critique or normative theory of criminal law; nor does it follow that such critique and such theorising must be limited to the very local setting of a particular legal system. To suppose that the former follows would be, again, to show oneself to be a disappointed metaphysical absolutist for whom 'reason' is real only if it is a priori; to suppose that the latter follows would be to ignore the possibility (a possibility that a moment's reflection will show to be often actualised) that different societies and their legal systems may be sufficiently closely connected to permit rational mutual discussion and argument.

To deny the possibility of a priori normative theorising is not to deny the possibility of rational normative theorising: it is rather to insist that such theorising is possible only within some human practice. That practice, that 'form of life', provides the 'we' of and to whom we talk when we talk of what 'we' can or should say or think or do, and the language in which we can thus talk; but that 'we' can expand as we come to realise the porous character of the boundaries between different forms of life, and the possibilities of discussion between them. We need to recognise that any kind of normative theorising (indeed, any kind of theorising) constitutes not the detached and solitary contemplation of eternal truths to which Platonists might aspire,[36] but a conversation with an actual or imagined set of interlocutors that requires a shared background of understandings, values and expectations. The interlocutors to whom this book is addressed are initially those who share my own background as a member of what purports to be a contemporary liberal democracy, and the intellectual and legal traditions that belong with such polities; how far it can address a broader set of potential interlocutors must remain an open question.

When legal theorists ask what 'the criminal law' ought to be, they must be asking about 'our' criminal law, but the temporal and cultural scope of that 'our' is open for exploration and extension. We are asking, not what 'the criminal law' ought to be at all times and in all contexts, but what the criminal law ought to be in a modern liberal democracy: what kind of account could make normative sense of the criminal law in such a

[35] See eg Lacey, 1998, 2000, 2001a, 2001b.

[36] See eg Plato, *Republic*, Bk VII (although even Aristotle, who was generally such a scathing critic of Plato's yearnings for a metaphysical Good, saw solitary contemplation of eternal truths as the perfection of human practical reason—*Nicomachean Ethics*, Bk X).

context—normative sense to us, as inhabitants of that context? However, given the diversity of forms taken by liberal democracy, that context is a pretty broad one.[37]

One point that these comments on the character of normative legal theory reinforce is that any such theory depends on political theory—on an underlying normative conception of the state and its proper relationship to its inhabitants. The account of criminal law that I will offer depends on a liberal-communitarian conception of a polity of citizens whose common life is structured by such core liberal values as autonomy, freedom, privacy and pluralism, informed by a conception of each other as fellow citizens in the shared civic enterprise. I will try to say enough about this conception to show what it amounts to in the context of the criminal law, but will not have space to defend it in detail.[38]

Two further limits on the scope of this book should be noted here: both concern the scope of 'the criminal law'.

The first is that I will focus on 'the law in the books', whilst recognising the truth in the by now clichéd distinction between 'the law in the books' and 'the law in action': between the law as represented in statutes, codes, textbooks and treatises, and the law as applied and used by the police and other officials as they enforce the law and investigate and prosecute crimes. Theorists must of course recognise the extent to which, in any practicable human system, the officials whose responsibility it is to enforce and administer the law will have a quite extensive discretion in discharging that responsibility, in particular in deciding what efforts to make to enforce which laws, and where and on whom to focus their investigative and prosecutorial efforts.[39] Such features of the law in action often do not change the law's content, since there is a real distinction between the content of the law and how that law with that content is applied and enforced: if, for instance, a police force reduces the resources that it devotes to investigating burglaries, and decides to make more than a minimal effort only for those above a certain threshold of seriousness, we should not say that the definition of 'burglary' as a criminal offence has effectively been changed (assuming that the police would still intervene if they saw a less serious burglary in progress). But the ways in which officials exercise their discretion can effectively change the law's content as it applies to the citizens —especially when they adopt systematic policies of selective enforcement of the law in the books. If it is a policy to prosecute

[37] My comments here concern the identity and scope of the 'we' that must be presupposed in any normative theorising; as we will see later (see Chs 2.2, 8.3), there is an analogous question about the identity and scope of the 'we' that a liberal criminal law must presuppose.

[38] But see Duff 2001: ch 2.

[39] Braithwaite and Pettit (1990) make much of this point.

those who speed on motorways only if they are driving more than 10 mph above the formal speed limit (so that no prosecution would be brought even if proof was easily available that a driver was driving at 8 mph above the limit), it is tempting to say that the law 'really' criminalises only speeding that exceeds the formal limit by that amount. The same is true if it is made a policy not merely to caution rather than prosecute those who are found with small amounts of cannabis in their possession (unless there is evidence that they are dealing), but to do nothing even if users flaunt cannabis in a police officer's face: the possession of small amounts of cannabis would then have been effectively decriminalised.[40]

Furthermore, legislatures might rely on this kind of discretion to ease the task of offence definition. Rather than trying to provide definitions which accurately specify the conduct that should be criminal (the conduct that constitutes the 'mischief' at which the law is aimed) and the kind of culpability that makes one who commits such conduct deserving of condemnation and punishment, they define them in ways that are admitted to be too broad—typically because a more precise, less over-inclusive definition would create more loopholes through which the ('really') guilty might escape, or in other ways make it harder ('too hard') for prosecutors to prove guilt. Those who worry about the excessive breadth of the offence are then reassured by being told that police and prosecutors will of course exercise their discretion to prosecute only a sub-class of those who commit what the law in the books defines as the offence—the sub-class containing those who commit the 'real' offence or who are 'really' culpable. This is a common defence of strict liability offences, and might also be offered in defence of sections 57–58 of the Terrorism Act 2000:[41] of course the offences are defined in terms that are, on their face, absurdly broad, but we must trust the police to use these provisions only against those who are ('really') suspicious; and to define the offences in a less over-inclusive way would make it much too easy for those really involved in terrorism to avoid conviction. Or consider section 57 of the Civic Government (Scotland) Act 1982:

> Any person who, without lawful authority to be there, is found in or on a building or other premises … so that, in all the circumstances, it may reasonably be inferred that he intended to commit theft there shall be guilty of an offence.[42]

The section is headed 'Being in or on building etc. with intent to commit theft', which spells out the exact mischief at which the provision is aimed; and, given that 'all the circumstances' must include whatever explanations

[40] As was said by critics of the cautioning scheme first piloted in Lambeth; but a cautioning scheme still treats possession as a criminal offence, albeit as a very minor one.

[41] See at n 5 above.

[42] See *Fulton v Normand* 1995 SCCR 629; Tadros, 2007: 198–9.

the agent can offer at the time, in most cases those who are properly convicted of the offence will have committed that mischief.[43] But 'reasonably inferred' is weaker than 'proved beyond reasonable doubt': some who had no such intention, and who would have been acquitted if charged explicitly with being in a building with intent to commit theft, may thus be guilty of the offence; and, if the clause is read literally, someone who later offers evidence that rebuts the inference to an intention to steal is still guilty if 'in all the circumstances' at the time at which he was found that inference was reasonable. But—we might be assured—we can trust police and prosecutors not to bring a prosecution unless they are confident that the person intended to steal.

It is when 'the law in action' diverges in such systematic ways as these from 'the law in the books' that the ('real') content of the criminal law becomes doubtful: but such cases also raise two obvious worries. First, in allowing such extensive discretion to officials, we open the way not just to errors due to incompetence or carelessness, but to the oppressive use of discretion—to the selective enforcement of the law against particular groups, or to the use of threats of prosecution as a means of inducing compliance with officials' wishes or demands (for instance for information). Secondly, this mismatch between what the law formally says, in its statutes, and how it is actually applied must cast a shadow over the way it addresses the citizens (most of whom might well not realise this mismatch), since its actions now belie its words. We will see more clearly in Chapter 4 why this is so important.

The second limit to be noted here concerns the growing importance of what we might call the pseudo-non-criminal law: the use of legal techniques that are not formally aspects of the criminal law, but that are used in place of the ordinary criminal law to deal with matters that fall within the criminal law's proper remit. Two examples will clarify this phenomenon. The first is that of 'Anti-social Behaviour Orders': orders by a court, on the application of a local authority or chief police officer, that impose specified restrictions on someone who is proved to have acted 'in an anti-social manner'; the point of those restrictions is to prevent the future repetition of such anti-social behaviour.[44] The making of the orders themselves is not formally a criminal process. What must be proved is admittedly that the person against whom the order is sought 'has acted . . . in an anti-social manner', ie 'in a manner that caused or was likely to cause

[43] More precisely, the ultimate mischief is theft: but we need not tackle here the question of how far the law should reach back from that mischief to 'precursor' offences or preparatory conduct (see ch 7.2(a) below).

[44] See Crime and Disorder Act 1998, ss 1–4; Anti-Social Behaviour Act 2003, s 85 (see Padfield, 2004).

harassment, alarm or distress' to others outside his household,[45] which matches the conduct element of an offence under sections 4A–5 of the Public Order Act 1986. But no mens rea need be proved; and whilst the House of Lords has held that the relevant conduct must be proved to a criminal standard, 'beyond reasonable doubt', we must wonder whether this will be robust enough to resist erosion, given the Court's insistence that the proceedings are civil, not criminal.[46] But once an order is made (an order that could impose very severe restrictions), it is a criminal offence, punishable by up to five years' imprisonment, to breach it. We need not consider the well-rehearsed objections to ASBOs here:[47] their relevance is simply that they exemplify governments' efforts to bypass (or subvert) the criminal law by turning into a civil process (one freed from the demands that genuine guilt be proved and that punishments be proportionate to the offence) matters that should properly be dealt with by the criminal law—a criminal law that is still (ab)used to back up that process. We will see more clearly in later chapters what it means to say that such matters 'should properly be dealt with by the criminal law'.

The second example is provided by preventive measures aimed at those suspected of terrorist activities or involvement: measures that have controversially included, in Britain, indefinite detention without a criminal trial or conviction, as well as a whole range of less dramatically oppressive measures of restraint, supervision and control.[48] Were these procedures criminal, they would have to observe the normal rules for criminal trials, and would permit detention only as a (proportionate) punishment for those duly proved guilty of a criminal offence; apart from the provisions for detention for those awaiting trial and denied bail, responsible adult citizens are not normally liable to preventive detention on the basis of a prediction that they would otherwise commit even a serious offence.[49] Attempts to justify such provisions typically appeal to the seriousness of the danger that terrorism poses, but there is another, deeper issue at stake, which I will not have space to discuss in this book.

The criminal law is, we will see, a law for citizens and for visitors to the polity, to whom many of the rights of citizenship are extended: it addresses

[45] Crime and Disorder Act 1998, s 1(1)(a).

[46] See *McCann* [2003] AC 787 for all three of these points—that no mens rea need be proved, that proof of the conduct must be to the criminal standard, and that the proceedings are not criminal.

[47] See eg Ashworth, 2004; Padfield, 2004; Simester and von Hirsch 2006.

[48] See eg the detention provisions of s 23 of the Anti-Terrorism, Crime and Security Act 2001, which the House of Lords declared to be incompatible with the right to liberty declared in Art 5(1) of the European Convention on Human Rights in *A v Secretary of State for the Home Department* [2005] HRLR 1; those provisions have now been repealed by the Prevention of Terrorism Act 2005, which provides for a range of 'control orders' instead. See generally Zedner, 2003, 2005.

[49] For the principled rationale for this see Duff, 1986: 172–8.

those whom it binds, those whom it subjects to judgment and punishment, as members of the political community. Now such membership is not optional: the fact that someone denies membership, or denies that he is bound by these laws, does not exempt or exclude him from membership. However, it is not clear that we should treat terrorists as members of, or as visitors to, the political communities that they attack—rather than as enemies with whom we are engaged in a war. This is not to say that there are then no moral or legal constraints on how we may treat them: enemies are not outlaws, but are bound and protected by the international laws of war (though those laws are ill-adapted to deal with terrorism) and still claim our respect as our fellow human beings; one of the most repugnant features of much of the rhetoric (and reality) of the 'war on terror' is the way in which those against whom the war is being fought are portrayed and treated as utter outlaws. But it is to say that it may be unclear how far we should treat genuine terrorists as criminals, or as enemy combatants—which raises the question whether this should also affect our conduct towards those who are suspected of being involved in terrorism. I will not be able to discuss that question directly here: but as we explore the character of criminal law in a liberal democracy, we will be able to see more clearly why it is important that those who are citizens should be both bound and protected by such a law, and therefore why we should at least be very slow to declare that anyone falls outside its protection and authority.

I have spent some time explaining what this book will not try to do: it is time to provide a brief sketch of what it will aim to do.

3. Answering for Crime

The book's first aim also brings into view a further limitation on its scope: it is concerned not with criminal liability, but with criminal responsibility. Many criminal law theorists probably share the view with which Markus Dubber begins his book on the Model Penal Code: '[t]he criminal law … comes down to a single, basic question: who is liable for what?'.[50] My focus, however, is on a logically prior question: who is (or should be) criminally *responsible* for what—and to whom? I will argue that we should attend, more carefully than theorists often attend, to the distinction between liability and responsibility, and to the relational, practice-based dimensions of responsibility. We should understand responsibility as a matter of being responsible (ie answerable) *for* something, *to* some person or body, within a responsibility-ascribing practice. Liability—to criminal

[50] Dubber, 2002a: 5.

punishment or to moral blame—is grounded in responsibility: I can be liable to punishment or blame for *X* only if I am held responsible for *X*. But responsibility does not entail liability, since I can accept responsibility for *X* but avert liability by offering a suitably exculpatory answer.

I first explicate this conception of responsibility as answerability, and its application to criminal responsibility. Chapter 1 explains in more detail what it is to see responsibility as a relational, practice-based, matter, and why it is crucial to preserve the distinction between responsibility and liability. The following chapters then explore the central question that a relational conception of responsibility makes salient: 'Who can be responsible, for what, to whom?'. This question must be tackled both as a general question about responsibility of any kind, and as a particular question about criminal responsibility—and a recurring issue will be that of how much that is substantive we can say about responsibility in general or 'as such'.

Chapter 2 deals briefly with the general question of who can be, which is to say who can be held, responsible: what kinds of capacity or characteristic must a person have if she is to be legitimately held responsible? I deal with the general question briefly, since I do not have much to add to the familiar accounts of responsibility as a matter of reason-responsiveness; but I will need to say something about the capacities that criminal responsibility in particular requires. The chapter then tackles two further questions raised by the relational conception of responsibility: as what are we responsible, to whom? As we will see, there is little to be said by way of general answers to these questions, but I will answer the particular questions about criminal responsibility: in a liberal democracy we are criminally responsible, I will argue, as citizens and to our fellow citizens. This answer, banal though it may seem, will illuminate some significant aspects of criminal law and its claims on us.

Chapter 3 turns to the question of what we are, or can be properly held, responsible for. If we treat this as a general question about the possible objects of responsibility, we will see that only rather weak constraints can be set. The two often cited conditions of responsibility are a 'control condition' (I am responsible only for what lies within my control), and an 'epistemic condition' (I am responsible only for that of which I am, or could be, aware): but the control condition sets only weak limits on the possible objects of responsibility, whilst the epistemic condition is, I will argue, a condition of liability rather than of responsibility. In Chapters 4–7 I tackle the more particular issue of criminal responsibility and its possible objects: within the generous limits of what we can be held responsible for in general, for what is it legitimate to hold us criminally responsible? To try to answer this question, we must attend to the various principles and requirements that have been suggested to determine the proper scope of the criminal law: the Harm Principle, that we should criminalise conduct only if it causes or threatens harm (to others)—that we should not be held criminally responsible for conduct that is neither harmful nor harm-threatening, however objectionable it may be in other respects; the legal moralist principle, that we should criminalise, and should be criminally responsible for, conduct that is morally wrongful; and the 'act requirement', that criminal responsibility should always be for, or on the basis of, an 'act' or a 'voluntary act'. Although I will not be able to suggest a determinate set of principles or criteria by which we can decide what kinds of conduct should, in principle, be criminal (life and any plausible system of criminal law are far too messy for that), I will show what role these principles or requirements can, once suitably interpreted, play in deliberations about criminalisation; I will also show how we can clarify the issues involved by focusing on the relational question of what we should have to answer for, as citizens, to our fellow citizens, under the aegis of the criminal law, and on the idea of crimes as public wrongs.

We will also need to discuss different types of criminal offence, and different structures of criminal responsibility and liability that they reveal: I will be particularly concerned with the difference between attacks and endangerments as distinct species of criminal wrong; with the distinction between *mala in se* and *mala prohibita*, and the role of *mala prohibita* in the criminal law; and with the ways in which the criminal law can be extended beyond what we can see as the primary category of directly harmful or harm-threatening wrongs. These will be the topics of Chapter 7.

By the end of Chapter 7, I hope to have developed an illuminating sketch of the structure and shape of a liberal polity's criminal law, understood as a practice that defines the kinds of wrong for which citizens should answer to each other, on pain of formal condemnation and punishment if they cannot offer an adequately exculpatory answer; and of the principles and values in the light of which the criminal law's content should be determined. This is the start of a sketch of criminal responsibility, but it is a complete sketch neither of responsibility, nor of the contours of criminal liability. Chapters 8–11 complete the sketch of responsibility, and outline some of the key structural aspects of criminal liability as something grounded in, but more than, criminal responsibility, by looking at what it is to answer a criminal charge.

Chapters 1–7 do not offer a complete sketch of criminal responsibility because they do not say enough about the conditions under which citizens can or cannot be called to answer criminal charges in a criminal court. Chapter 8 examines a range of conditions that constitute legal or moral bars to trial—conditions given which we cannot legitimately hold a suspected offender criminally answerable. It is important to distinguish these trial-barring conditions from those that justify an acquittal at trial (the significance of this distinction is highlighted once we focus on responsibility, as distinct from liability, as a matter of answerability); by attending to such conditions we can clarify the grounds of criminal responsibility, and begin to remedy theorists' tendency to draw too sharp a distinction between substance and procedure.

The distinction between responsibility and liability is reflected in the distinction between offences and defences: proof that the defendant committed an offence is proof that there is something for which he is criminally responsible—something for which he must answer in a criminal court; but he can then avoid conviction, blocking the transition from responsibility to liability, by offering a defence. Chapter 9 accordingly tackles the question of how we should distinguish offences from defences, and shows why that distinction is indeed both possible and important; it also deals with the role and significance of the Presumption of Innocence.

Chapter 10 deals with legal doctrines that seem to undermine the orthodox understanding of offences as consisting in both 'actus reus' and 'mens rea', and the orthodox distinction between offences and defences. It discusses strict criminal liability, which seems to flout the demand that conviction of a criminal offence should depend on proof of fault, of mens rea, as to all aspects of the offence; but it also discusses doctrines of strict criminal responsibility, the importance of which the distinction between responsibility and liability brings into focus.

Chapter 11 offers a sketch of the logical structure of defences: we need to distinguish not only justifications from excuses, and excuses from exemptions (excuses admit responsibility, whereas exemptions negate it), but also justifications from warrants; this will enable us to dissolve some controversies about the structure and scope of legal justifications. Here again my interest is in the structure rather than the content of the criminal law, and in fleshing out the distinction between responsibility and liability.

(I should also make explicit here a further limitation on the scope of this book: that it will focus on the responsibilities of individual agents in relation to what they do as individuals. I will not discuss the prospective or retrospective responsibilities of corporations or other kinds of collective; nor will I discuss the ways in which we can collaborate or be complicit in each others' actions and the responsibilities that different modes of participation involve. Both sets of issues are important, but my present aim is to clarify the individual responsibility of individual agents: that must be, for liberal theorists, central to an understanding of criminal responsibility; it will also provide the foundations on which further discussions of complicity and of collective agency and responsibility must be built.)

The net result of these 11 chapters is not a theory of criminal law; but it is an account of the structure of criminal law as an institution (or set of institutions) through which a liberal polity can define a realm of public wrongdoing, and call those who perpetrate (or are accused of perpetrating) such wrongs to account.

1

Responsibility and Liability

In place of Markus Dubber's 'single, basic question: who is liable for what?',[1] I suggested that we should begin by asking 'who is (or should be) criminally *responsible* for what *to whom*?'. We should, that is, recognise the priority of responsibility over liability, and the relational dimensions of responsibility; and we should make the question explicitly normative. In this chapter, I explain the relational dimensions of responsibility, why they merit attention, and why it is important to distinguish responsibility from liability. The distinction that I draw here between responsibility and liability is admittedly to some degree stipulative: I do not claim that it precisely matches the standard usage of those terms (which are anyway used in several different ways), or that it captures their only proper meanings. I aim to show, however, that it is a significant distinction, and that by attending to it we can illuminate the logical structure of the criminal law and gain a better understanding of some familiar issues in criminal law theory. That will be the task of subsequent chapters: the task of this chapter is to provide an initial explanation of the distinction, and of the relational conception of responsibility which it involves.

1. Responsibility and Liability

Our concern here is with criminal liability and responsibility, and with their extra-legal moral analogues of responsibility for moral wrongdoing and liability to moral blame or criticism. There are of course other species of liability: as well as being criminally liable to conviction and punishment for the crimes that we commit, we may be liable to pay taxes on our income, to pay damages for harms that we cause, to pay maintenance for our children, and so on. Such other types of liability do not concern me here: my focus is on criminal liability to conviction and punishment, or moral liability to criticism and blame, and on the species of responsibility

[1] Dubber, 2002a: 5; see above, Introduction at n 50.

on which such liabilities depend. My focus is therefore also on responsibility for what was in some way untoward—for the harms or wrongs that I cause or commit. We are responsible too for the good and the right that we do or bring about: but we cannot explore the asymmetries between these two kinds of responsibility here.

The relationship between liability and responsibility can be simply stated: responsibility is a necessary but not a sufficient condition of liability. I am liable to conviction or blame for *X* only if I am responsible for *X*; but I can be responsible for *X* without being thus liable.

The phenomena of 'absolute' and 'vicarious' liability in criminal law might seem to cast doubt on the necessity of responsibility for liability. I can be convicted of being found drunk on a highway without proof that I could have avoided being there, even if I was carried there by the police;[2] an employer can be vicariously criminally liable for an employee's criminal conduct, even if that conduct was not authorised, expected or reasonably foreseeable by the employer:[3] in such cases the defendant seems to be criminally liable for the offence without proof that she was responsible for its commission. But there is equivocation here. Such laws make people *criminally* liable for something for which they might not be *morally* responsible. However, first, if they are not morally responsible for the action or state of affairs in question, they cannot be morally liable to blame or criticism for it—since moral liability requires moral responsibility. Secondly, they are criminally liable in such cases only because the law, rightly or wrongly, makes them criminally responsible. The law holds the person found drunk on a highway criminally responsible for being thus found—which implies a prospective criminal responsibility to make sure that one is not thus found;[4] it held a licensee whose employee sold drinks outside permitted hours criminally responsible for the employee's actions, even if the employee acted against her express instructions,[5] which implied a prospective responsibility to make sure that no drinks were sold in one's pub outside permitted hours. We might object that such responsibilities are unreasonably strict: the point here is that they are preconditions of the defendants' liability. Indeed, as we will see later, in Chapter 10, it might be reasonable to hold licensees criminally responsible for the sale of out-of-hours drinks in their pubs—to require them to answer for the commission

[2] See Licensing Act 1872, s 12; *Winzar v Chief Constable of Kent, The Times,* 28 Mar 1983. 'So far as responsibility for the offence is concerned, its commission ... was brought about by the police and had nothing to do with the defendant' (Simester and Sullivan, 2007: 113).

[3] See *ibid*: 247–56.

[4] On prospective responsibilities see sect 3 below.

[5] Licensing Act 1964, s 59.

of that offence in a criminal court: what is crucial is what kind of answer, if any, they can give that will avert a conviction; but that is a matter of liability rather than of responsibility.

To illustrate this point, suppose that the Licensing Act 1964 included a 'due diligence' defence of the kind that the Licensing Act 2003 provides for certain offences: that '[the] act was due ... to an act or omission by another person ... and [the licensee] took all reasonable precautions and exercised all due diligence to avoid committing the offence'.[6] Whether or not the law allows such a defence, the licensee is criminally responsible for her employee's actions; she must answer in court for those actions. If the law allows no such defence, she is also strictly liable; by contrast, if such a defence is allowed, she can admit responsibility, but avert liability by offering the defence.

The distinction between responsibility and liability is simply illustrated by justifications. If I wound an assailant, this being the only way to ward off his unlawful attack on me, I have a justification for what I do—a moral justification that saves me from moral condemnation for injuring him, and a legal justification that should save me from a criminal conviction for wounding.[7] In offering this justification, I do not deny responsibility for using violence on *V*, or for *V*'s wound. I admit responsibility for that action and its result, as something that I had reason not to do (for we always have reason not to use violence on fellow human beings, and to avoid acting in ways that will injure them). I thus admit that I must answer for my action and its result: I must answer morally to anyone whose business it is, and legally in a criminal court. But, I claim, I have an exculpatory answer: that my action was, in its context, justified as an act of self-defence.

This feature of justifications—that they admit responsibility while denying liability—also holds of excuses. If I commit perjury under the influence of a threat of harm which, while not sufficient to justify the commission of perjury, is sufficient to constitute an excuse, I am not criminally liable for committing perjury.[8] But I am criminally responsible for committing that offence: I must answer for it in court, and am liable to conviction and punishment if I cannot offer an exculpatory answer. My plea of duress functions, as does my plea of self-defence, to avert liability by blocking the transition from responsibility to liability.

[6] Licensing Act 2003, s 139.

[7] I assume here something that will be argued in more detail later (in Ch 9): that self-defence is a defence, as distinct from marking the absence of an element of the offence.

[8] Cp *Hudson and Taylor* [1971] 2 QB 202; I assume here that (*pace* Westen and Mangiafico, 2003) duress sometimes functions as an excuse rather than as a justification; see further Ch 11.5 below.

I am responsible for that for which I must answer, and I must answer for that which there was reason for me not to do: I must answer morally for doing what there was moral reason not to do, and criminally for doing what, according to the criminal law, there was legal reason for me not to do. I have both moral and legal reason not to use violence on others, and not to commit perjury: if I act in those ways, I must answer for so acting (and for the consequences—the injury to my assailant, the mistaken verdict—of those actions). If I can justify or excuse my actions by appealing to the context of the action and the reasons that motivated me to act thus,[9] I have an exculpatory answer that blocks the normal, presumptive transition from responsibility to liability. If, however, I can offer no such exculpatory answer, responsibility becomes liability.

If I am accused of wrongdoing, either formally in a criminal court or informally in moral discussion, I thus have two ways of averting conviction or blame. I can deny responsibility, claiming that I do not have to answer (in this forum) for that alleged wrong. In the simplest case, I deny responsibility by denying agency: I was not the person who broke your window. But, as we will see throughout this book, there are many other ways in which, and grounds on which, I can deny responsibility—even for my actions and their anticipated effects. Alternatively, however, I can admit responsibility, but avert liability by offering a defence: I must, I admit, answer for what I have done, but I offer an answer that, I claim, exculpates me.

Theorists often do not distinguish responsibility from liability;[10] one aim of this book is to show why the distinction matters. We will gain a clearer understanding (both analytical and critical) of the structure of the criminal law, and of the principles of criminal liability, if we distinguish two sets of questions: one concerns the conditions under which agents can be held criminally responsible, ie be called to answer in a criminal court; the other concerns the further conditions that must be satisfied if they are to be criminally liable for that for which they are criminally responsible. Someone who is summoned to answer a criminal charge can seek in various legitimate ways to avert a conviction, and it might be tempting to count them all as 'defences', on the ground that they all serve to defend a person against conviction.[11] I will argue, however, that it is important to distinguish conviction-averting pleas which deny responsibility from those which

[9] On the logic of justifications and excuses, see further Ch 11 below.

[10] But see Hart 1968a: 212–22, distinguishing 'role-responsibility' from 'liability-responsibility'.

[11] See eg Robinson, 1984: although he recognises that it is 'inappropriate ... to use this single term to refer to so many different matters' (i: 1), I will argue that he does not take this seriously enough.

admit responsibility but deny liability—and to distinguish between different kinds of responsibility-denial, depending on whether what is denied is that this person can be held responsible, or that she is responsible before this court, or that she is responsible for this alleged conduct.

Once we distinguish responsibility from liability, we can bring the relational dimensions of responsibility into clearer focus.

2. Responsibility as Relational

It is a commonplace that responsibility involves a dyadic relationship: an agent is responsible *for* something. The relational conception of responsibility that concerns us here is not merely dyadic, but triadic: I am responsible *for X*, *to S*—to a person or body who has the standing to call me to answer for *X*. I am also responsible for *X* to *S as* Φ—in virtue of satisfying some normatively laden description that makes me responsible (prospectively and retrospectively) for *X* to *S*. To be responsible is to be answerable; answerability is answerability to a person or body who has the right or standing to call me to account; and I am thus answerable in virtue of some normatively laden description, typically a description of a role, that I satisfy.[12]

(There are non-relational ideas of responsibility. We talk about responsible agency; we commend responsible parents or teachers. Such ideas can be explained in terms of relational responsibility. Responsible agency is a matter of having the capacities that are necessary if one is to answer for one's actions: a responsible agent is capable of responding to the reasons that bear on her actions, and of answering for her actions in the light of those reasons.[13] A responsible parent takes her responsibilities seriously and discharges them conscientiously: she pays due attention to the matters that concern her, and is therefore well placed to answer for her actions, ie to accept retrospective responsibility in relation to those matters.[14])

The 'for *X*' dimension of this triadic relationship is familiar: I can be held responsible for a wide range of 'objects of responsibility', including actions, omissions, thoughts, feelings and states of affairs.[15] The 'to *S*' and 'as Φ' dimensions require a little further explanation, in part to make clear how the objects and directions of responsibility can differ from one context to another: how I can be responsible as Φ for *X*, but not for *Y* (though

[12] Compare Hart, 1968a: 212–14; Lucas, 1993; Watson, 2001; contrast Tadros, 2005a: 24–31.

[13] See Ch 2.1 below, on responsibility as a matter of reasons-responsiveness.

[14] See further sect 3 below, on prospective responsibility.

[15] See Ch 3 below for a discussion of what general limits there are on the possible objects of responsibility.

both X and Y lie within my control); or responsible to S for X, but not for Y; or responsible for X to S, but not to T.

To illustrate. We can specify my responsibilities as a university teacher. That will involve an account of my prospective responsibilities:[16] it is my responsibility to keep up to date with my subject, plan courses that contribute suitably to the curriculum, prepare and conduct my classes in pedagogically effective ways, mark students' work, and so on. We might disagree about what falls, or should fall, within my responsibilities as a teacher, but any account will set some limits to them: as a teacher in a secular university, for instance, it is no part of my responsibility to attend church services; as a philosophy teacher it is not my responsibility to play football on Saturday for a local amateur team—though I may have such responsibilities as a member of a church or of that team. To say that these are my responsibilities as a teacher is to say that I may be called, and must be ready, to answer as a teacher for my conduct in relation to these matters—for how I discharge (or fail to discharge) these responsibilities.

A full specification of my responsibilities must also identify the people or bodies to whom I am responsible as a teacher—and thus by implication those to whom I am not responsible as a teacher. I am responsible as a teacher to my students, my colleagues and my employer: they can call me to account for the way in which I discharge my pedagogical responsibilities; they can call me to answer for failing to turn up to class or for giving an ill-prepared lecture. But, first, I am not responsible as a teacher to my aunt, or to a passing stranger, or to my fellow footballers: they have no standing to call me to account for missing the class or for giving a bad lecture; if they challenge me about it, or demand that I answer to them for it, I can reply that it is not their business. Secondly, I am not responsible to my students, my colleagues (qua academic colleagues) or my employer for my conduct as a member of a church or a football team. There will be someone to whom I am responsible, as a member of the church, for my religious practices—perhaps my priest, the other members of my congregation, or only God. There are people to whom I am responsible as a member of a football team—other members, our supporters if we have any: depending on the kind of team it is, I may be responsible to them not merely for how I play (and whether I turn up), but for keeping fit and joining in training. But I am not responsible to my academic colleagues for my footballing performance, any more than I am responsible to my fellow footballers for my performance as a teacher.

The responsibility-laden descriptions (teacher, parent, member of a church or team) that help to structure our lives determine the content and

[16] On the distinction between prospective and retrospective responsibilities see further sect 3 below.

the direction of our responsibilities: what we are responsible for and to whom. Such descriptions extend our responsibilities: as a member of a team I have responsibilities that I would not otherwise have, and am responsible to people to whom I would not otherwise be answerable. They also limit our responsibilities: there are matters within my control and knowledge, even matters that bear on my students' welfare, for which I may deny that I am responsible as a teacher (it is not my responsibility, I might say, to offer them advice on their sexual relationships); and there is only a limited range of people or bodies to whom I am responsible as a teacher.[17] Claims of the form '*A* is responsible for *X*' are therefore incomplete: they must be filled out by specifying as what and to whom *A* is responsible for *X*. That specification need not be explicit if it is obvious from the context; but it must be available.

John Gardner seems to deny this. Responsibility ('basic responsibility') does, he agrees, involve the ability to answer for ourselves, to 'assert ourselves as responsible beings', which requires an interlocutor to whom I can offer my account of myself:

> But why does it need a *particular* interlocutor? In respect of the same wrong or mistake, couldn't I assert my basic responsibility by offering the same account of myself to everyone I come across, from judges in the Old Bailey to friends in the pub to strangers on the bus?[18]

I could certainly *offer* my account of how I came to give such a bad lecture to 'everyone I come across', although I would probably receive some puzzled responses if I did so: an Old Bailey judge and a stranger on the bus might naturally reply that I do not have to answer to them for my performance as a teacher. More to the point, they have no right to demand that I answer to them for my lecture: if they tried to call me to account for it, I could properly refuse, on the ground that it is not their business.[19]

Some might argue that whilst such limitations hold for those responsibilities that are tied to particular social or institutional roles, they do not hold for our moral responsibilities—our responsibilities as moral agents. Surely, they might say, as moral agents we are responsible to every other moral agent; to recognise ourselves and others as members of the Kingdom of Ends is to recognise not only that we have duties towards all other members, but also that we must be ready to answer to them for our moral conduct or misconduct. The first response to this claim is that, even

[17] We may disagree about what I am responsible for, and to whom, as a teacher: but nothing in my argument depends on claiming that the content or direction of our responsibilities can be uncontroversially specified.

[18] Gardner, 2003: 165.

[19] It can sometimes be proper for me to see myself as answerable to *S* but not for *S* to demand that I answer to her (I owe this point to Maggie Little); but my responsibility is still specifiable as being to *S*.

if it is true, it does not undercut the relational account of responsibility: we must still ask not merely what we are responsible for, but to whom we are responsible; the claim about universal moral jurisdiction is the claim that in the case of moral wrongdoing the answer to the second question is 'Every moral agent'. The second response, however, is that the claim is anyway false: even if there are some wrongs for which any other moral agent can call us to account, for many we are answerable only to a limited range of people. Many of our role-responsibilities, for our discharge of which we are (as we have seen) responsible only to a limited range of people, are moral responsibilities: I have a moral as well as an institutional responsibility to my students to turn up for classes and to mark their work, but that does not give my aunt or an Old Bailey judge the standing to hold me responsible for my discharge of that responsibility; it is still not their business. Similarly, if I treat a friend badly (I let her down, or fail to respond sympathetically when she calls on me for help), I am responsible to her, and to our other friends, for that moral failure; but I am not responsible to the passing stranger or to the Old Bailey judge. If we have moral responsibilities simply as moral agents or as human beings, they are indeed owed to other moral agents or to other human beings, as such, in which case I am in principle answerable to any other moral agent or to any other human being for my failures to discharge them;[20] but not all our moral responsibilities are of that kind.

There are also, it is true, some things for which I am not responsible to anyone other than myself. If I set myself the self-improving project of learning the piano, no one else may have the standing to call me to account if I fail to practise as I should: but I am responsible for that failure—to myself. This is not simply an ad hoc attempt to preserve the relational character of responsibility, while making it less interesting, by positing oneself as the person to whom one is always answerable. For, first, responsibility to ourselves plays a substantive role in our lives: to take oneself and one's agency seriously is, in part, to hold oneself responsible for how one lives. Secondly, we must still ask who else (if anyone) has the standing to hold us responsible for different aspects of our lives; we must still explain what it is to be responsible for *X* partly by specifying to whom we are responsible for *X*.

It might still be argued that responsibility is not always to anyone. Suppose that someone vandalises the plants and trees on an uninhabited island that no one owns: surely we can say that he is responsible for that vandalism without being able to specify anyone to whom he is responsible,

[20] I leave open the question of whether the class of 'moral agents' to whom I would be answerable extends beyond the class of 'human beings'—though I think it does not (see Gaita, 1991: ch 3). I am answerable only 'in principle' because there are often good reasons why others should refrain from calling me to account.

and indeed without supposing that there must be someone who has the standing to call him to answer.[21] I could accept this objection, and defuse its force by arguing, first, that responsibility is still a matter of answerability in that if I am responsible for *X* I must be ready to answer for *X* if there is someone who has the standing to call me to account; and, secondly, that if we are told that *A* is responsible for *X*, we can always properly ask 'To whom is *A* responsible for *X*?', and normally expect an answer. This would allow that there might be unusual cases in which there was no one to whom *A* was responsible; since criminal responsibility is clearly not such a case, however, this would not undermine my claim that to understand the structures of criminal responsibility we must ask to whom, and as what, we are criminally responsible.

I am still inclined to stick to the stronger claim—that if I am responsible for *X*, there must be some person or body (which might be God, or myself) to whom I am responsible. If there really is no person or body to whom I must answer for *X*, no one who has a proper interest in *X* such that she can call me to account for it, the claim that I am responsible for *X* seems to lose its content. As for the vandal on the uninhabited island, we may (depending on how we understand our responsibilities in relation to the natural world) say that he is answerable to those who might visit the island; or to those who care for the aesthetic values that he violates; or to all of us, since we all share a responsibility to take respectful care of the environment; or only to his own conscience.[22] However, all that I require for the purposes of this book is the weaker thesis that we can always ask to whom *A* is responsible, together with the plausible claim that in the context of criminal law we can certainly expect an answer to that question.

We can see more clearly what this relational conception of responsibility involves by distinguishing it from two others that have also been called 'relational'.

The first can be discerned in Richard Rorty's remarks on the way in which 'justification is relative to an audience'.[23] To justify myself is one way of answering for what I have done, ie of accepting responsibility; to be called to justify myself is to be held responsible for that which I am called to justify. To call responsibility relational might then be taken to mean that I am responsible if, and only if, some person or body actually holds me responsible by calling me to answer; and that when I am thus called to

[21] Thanks to Henry Laycock, Mick Smith and Victor Tadros (who provided the example) for this objection.

[22] On some versions of 'deep ecology', we might owe that responsibility to the natural world, or to the eco-system, itself. This would then be one of a number of cases in which we are responsible to people or beings (responsibilities to infants and animals provide other examples) who cannot themselves call us to answer; in such cases, other people might claim the standing to act, and to call, on their behalf.

[23] Rorty, 1995: 283; see also Rorty, 1986. For criticism see Gardner, 2003: 164–6.

answer what I must look for is an answer that will satisfy the particular person or body that holds me responsible—which would indeed be to portray responsibility as strongly 'relative to an audience'. The relational conception that I offer here is not, however, so radically relativistic. As a matter of descriptive theory, we can note what people are or are not held responsible for in this or that forum, under the norms of this or that practice, and what kinds of answer do in fact satisfy, or according to the practice's norms should satisfy, the particular audience; our descriptive accounts are then relativised to particular fora and practices. As normative theorists, however, our interest is in what people *should* be held responsible for, by whom, and what kinds of answer *should* satisfy those who call them to account; and although we cannot provide entirely context-independent answers to such questions,[24] the relational conception of responsibility sketched here does not imply that we cannot take a critical rather than a purely descriptive stance towards existing practices and their responsibility-ascriptions.

This is as true of criminal responsibility as it is of other species of responsibility. We can note, in descriptive or analytical mode, that English law holds one who supplies equipment that he knows is to be used in a burglary criminally responsible not merely for supplying the equipment, but for the burglary;[25] and we can ask whether English courts should also, if they are to apply the law strictly, hold a doctor who prescribes contraceptives to a girl of 15, knowing that this will facilitate the commission of an offence of unlawful sexual intercourse, criminally responsible for the commission of that offence.[26] In normative mode, however, we must ask whether the law *should* be such that these agents are criminally responsible for such offences. Who should have the standing to call them to account? To whom should they have to justify or explain themselves, on pain of what kinds of sanction if they cannot do so? What kinds of explanation should be accepted as exculpatory? A central aim of this book is to show how we can set about answering these questions as questions about criminal responsibility: this will involve showing how criminal responsibility is related to moral responsibility, as to both its objects (what we should be held responsible for) and its direction (to whom we are or should be responsible).

[24] See above, Introduction, sect 2.

[25] See *Bainbridge* [1960] 1 QB 129, and Accessories and Abettors Act 1861, s 8.

[26] See *Gillick v West Norfolk and Wisbech Area Health Authority* [1986] AC 112. To hold that the doctor should be criminally *responsible* is not to say that she should be criminally *liable*: we may think that she has a suitable defence, such as necessity (see *Clarke* (1985) 80 Cr App R 344; Ormerod, 2005: 180).

The second 'relational' conception of responsibility from which that offered here must be distinguished is Alan Norrie's. Norrie espouses 'a relational theory of blame':

> Responsibility lies with individuals *and* with societies of which they are a part, so that, neither individualized nor denied, it is shared. It traverses a space *between* the individual and the social, constituting a blaming relation.[27]

Norrie draws on the metaphysics of 'entity relationism', according to which 'personal being is always being in relation to others', and 'individual responsibility' is 'constructed out of an interaction'.[28] However, to accept some version of social constructivism, according to which persons are constructed or constituted by their social relationships and by their roles in social practices, need not be to hold that responsibility is shared in Norrie's sense—that we should hold both individual offenders and the 'societies of which they are a part' co-responsible for their crimes: as far as the metaphysics of entity relationism or of social constructivism go, we could be constructed as individually responsible agents, whose identity-constituting relations include those of holding each other individually responsible. What really grounds Norrie's 'relational' account of responsibility is a normative claim that it is unjust to hold individuals responsible for their crimes without also holding co-responsible the societies which produced the conditions from which those crimes flowed. But neither kind of argument, metaphysical or normative, bears on our concerns here, since they do not bear on the analytical claim that to be responsible is to be answerable (ie liable to be held responsible) for something to some person or body. That claim is consistent both with relationist metaphysics and with a more individualist metaphysics, and implies nothing yet about who should be held responsible by whom for crimes committed in this or that social context. The relations that concern us here are not the metaphysical relationships that might part-constitute persons, nor the moral relationships that shared responsibility involves, but the logical relationships between the agents who are held responsible, that for which they are held responsible, and those who hold them responsible.

Responsibility does not always involve such relationships: purely causal responsibility, for instance, is responsibility for something (the storm was responsible for the damage to my house), but is not responsibility to anyone. But moral and criminal responsibility are, I claim, always relational in this way, as are other kinds of responsibility that are ascribed to human agents within human practices: the goal-keeper's responsibility for failing to save the penalty, and for the loss of the game, might not be a

[27] Norrie, 2000: 220–1.

[28] *Ibid*: 217–8, and see 197–235 generally: for Norrie's sources see Bhaskar, 1993; Harré, 1983.

matter of moral responsibility, in that no moral blame might be at stake: but he is still responsible to someone (most obviously, to his team-mates) for that failure and that loss.

This sketch of the logic of responsibility, understood relationally, can be completed by a brief examination of a distinction that has already been noted: that between prospective and retrospective responsibility.[29]

3. Prospective and Retrospective Responsibilities

The main focus of this book is on retrospective responsibility: on the ways in which and the grounds on which we can be called to answer for what we have done or not done, or for what happened or did not happen. We can be retrospectively responsible for our acts and omissions (and their outcomes); for events and states of affairs; for our beliefs, thoughts and emotions. I can be called to answer for lying to you (and for the effects of my lie) or for failing to prevent some harm; for the bath overflowing, or for the untidy state of the garden; for my belief that free will is compatible with determinism, for my sado-masochistic fantasy about a neighbour, or for the anger or irritation that I feel towards my children.[30] Retrospective responsibilities of all these kinds depend, however, both on there being someone to whom I must answer, and who has the standing to call me to answer, and on the prospective responsibilities that I have to those who can thus call me to answer. I may have to answer to my housemates (but not to passing strangers) for the bath overflowing or for the untidy garden; to my fellow philosophers (but not to my uncle) for my beliefs about free will; to my neighbour or to my partner (but not to my academic colleagues) for my sexual fantasy; to my partner and children (but not to my neighbour) for my anger or irritation towards them. Such claims about answerability must, however, be grounded in claims about my prospective responsibilities to those people. I must answer to my housemates for the bath or the garden only if and because I had a responsibility, as their housemate, to ensure that the bath did not overflow or that the garden was kept tidy; I must answer to my children for my anger only if and because I have a responsibility to them, as their parent, to control my emotions towards them.

My prospective responsibilities are those that I have as it were before the event: they are those matters that it is up to me (my responsibility) to

[29] On prospective responsibilities see generally Lucas, 1993; Casey, 1971; also Zimmerman, 1988: 1–5.

[30] On the 'control condition' of responsibility and its application to such cases see Ch 3.1 below.

attend to or to take care of. They may be tied to specific roles:[31] we talk of the responsibilities of teachers, doctors, parents, citizens. We also have responsibilities that are tied to roles, if at all, only in a looser sense—as friends, for instance, or simply as human beings (to respect the interests of others), or as inhabitants of this planet (to have some practical concern for its future). We have such responsibilities in virtue of our satisfaction of normatively significant descriptions—'teacher', 'parent', 'bus driver', 'neighbour', 'human being', and so on; by unpacking those descriptions (a task that will often involve normative disagreement), we can explain both what one's responsibilities are as a Φ, and to whom they are owed. Prospective responsibilities include moral duties that we have in virtue either of our humanity (a duty to help those in desperate need, perhaps) or of more specific moral roles that we fill (such as the duties of parenthood or friendship), but not all prospective responsibilities are either moral or duties: a goalkeeper's responsibilities as a member of the team are not moral responsibilities or duties; it may be a shop worker's responsibility to put up the poster advertising the day's bargains, but that responsibility is neither moral nor a duty.

The dependence of retrospective responsibility on prospective responsibility is clearest in the context of omissions. Your library book is not returned in time: you could have returned it but did not; I knew that it was due and could have reminded you to return it, but did not. You are responsible to the library staff and to other users for its non-return, because in borrowing the book you incurred a prospective responsibility to return or renew it by the due date; this was part of the set of responsibilities you took on in signing up as a user of the library. It is, however, not clear whether I am also responsible for the book's non-return, even if I knew it to be within my power to prevent it. If I am also a library user, the library staff or other users might claim that I should have intervened, and call me to account for failing to do so; if I am your friend, you might ask why I did not remind you—thus holding me responsible for failing to remind you. This would be implicitly to claim that I had a prospective responsibility as a library user, or as your friend, in relation not just to books that I borrowed, but to any of the library's books (as the library staff would be claiming) or to books that you had borrowed (as you would be claiming). Without some such implicit claim, I cannot be held responsible for the book's non-return or for my 'failure' to remind you to return it: if I am a stranger, neither you nor the library staff or other users could plausibly call me to account for not intervening, because, as I might

[31] Cp Hart, 1968a: 212–4, on 'role-responsibility'.

naturally say, your behaviour in relation to the library book was not my business—it did not fall within any of my prospective responsibilities.[32]

The same point applies to actions and their results, although there is often less room for disagreement about the scope of our prospective responsibilities in this sphere. If I lit a bonfire, realising that it would probably damage my neighbour's tree, there would normally be no room to deny my responsibility for endangering the tree, and for any damage to it.[33] What makes such denial difficult is not, however, the mere fact that I expected that outcome, but that it would be hard to deny that such likely damage to another's property was something to which I should attend as a reason against lighting the fire: that, in other words, that aspect of my conduct fell within my prospective responsibilities. I have a prospective responsibility to attend to harm that my actions might cause, as a reason against actions that might cause it; if I nonetheless act in a way that causes or threatens such harm, I must be ready to answer for it, since I will be retrospectively responsible for it. Even in such a simple case, we must ask to whom I am responsible:[34] certainly to my neighbour, but what of our other neighbours? Do they have the right to call me to answer for what I have done? Is it also their business? To say that it is their business (which would imply that they also had a prospective responsibility to urge me to desist if they saw what I was doing) would imply a normatively rich, and contestable, conception of 'neighbour'; on a more atomistically individualistic conception of social life, such matters would be the business only of those directly affected. As we move beyond such apparently simple cases, the room for disagreement about just what we are responsible for, and to whom, increases.

Consider other ways in which my conduct might have an impact on my neighbours. The noise of my music might annoy them; the colour I have painted my front door might offend their aesthetic sensibilities, as might my style of dress; the fact that I am living openly with my gay partner might offend their moral sensibilities. In each of these cases, they might hold me responsible for the actions that thus affect them, which would be to claim that the effect on them provided a reason against acting as I did, to which I should have attended, ie that those effects fell within my prospective responsibilities. In each of these cases, however, I might deny that I am responsible to them for such conduct—which would be to deny that I must explain, justify or apologise for such conduct to them. This

[32] This would also be to deny that I 'failed' to remind or urge you to return it: see Casey, 1971.

[33] If I light the fire *with the intention* of thereby damaging the tree, I clearly cannot deny responsibility for the risk or damage to the tree; as an agent, I make myself responsible for *X* by intending it.

[34] If I actually damage the tree, I am in principle criminally responsible; see Ch 2 for discussion of the direction of criminal responsibility.

would not be to deny that I am responsible for those actions altogether. I might admit that there is someone to whom I am responsible for them: for my noisy music to my grandmother who sleeps upstairs; for my dress style to my partner; for my cohabitation arrangements to my parents, in that I see the distress that they might suffer as a reason against cohabiting, and recognise a duty to explain myself to them. It would simply be to deny that I have any prospective responsibilities about such matters to my neighbours, ie that the effects on them give me any reason to modify my conduct. Such a denial is most plausible in the case of my cohabitation arrangements: I do not, I insist, need to justify or explain myself in this respect to my neighbours; it is simply not their business. It is less plausible in the case of noise, since it would be harder to deny that, at least if the noise is loud, persistent and made at times when others are trying to sleep, I am responsible to my neighbours—that I had a prospective responsibility to pay attention to the effects on them; but we may still think that there is a level of 'normal' noise, at 'normal' times, for which I do not need to answer to my neighbours even if they find it disturbing. As to the colour of my front door, we may find wide disagreement about my responsibilities—about whether I should consult my neighbours' sensibilities, or only those of others sharing the house with me.

That I deny responsibility to my neighbours does not of course make it true that I am not responsible to them for such actions: they might still insist that I am responsible, and we then have a normative disagreement about the scope and character of neighbourly responsibility. But any claim that I am responsible must be a claim that I am responsible to some specifiable person or body, and must be grounded in a conception of my prospective responsibilities to that person or body. Both retrospective and prospective responsibilities are relational: I am responsible as a Φ, for *X*, to *A* (I am responsible as a neighbour, for the loud music I play at night, to my neighbours).

We have prospective responsibilities in virtue of satisfying some normatively significant description: I have responsibilities as a Φ (a neighbour, teacher, friend, son, and so on), and my understanding of just what those responsibilities are will depend on my understanding of what it is to be a Φ. In specifying Φ, we typically also identify the people or body to whom I am responsible: as a neighbour, I am responsible to my neighbours; as a son I am responsible to my parents; as an employee I am responsible to my employer. But there is ample room for disagreement or uncertainty about such responsibility-implying descriptions and their precise implications.

There is room for uncertainty and disagreement about which descriptions are relevant as having this kind of normative significance. Employees in exploitative jobs might recognise that their employers ascribe various responsibilities to them, but deny that these are genuine responsibilities:

they might, that is, deny that 'employee [of *A*]' has responsibility-generating normative force, at least in this context. Likewise, people can disagree about the normative significance of biological parenthood: do 'parent' and 'child', understood biologically, imply mutual responsibilities?

There is room for uncertainty and disagreement about whom we owe responsibilities to. We may agree that teachers have responsibilities to their students, to their colleagues and to their employer, but do they also have responsibilities to the taxpayers who pay their salaries, or to members of the wider community in which they work? Do company directors have any responsibilities, not just to their employees and shareholders, and their customers, but to the wider community? Sometimes we can specify the legal responsibilities that they have, as a matter of positive law: but do they have moral responsibilities (which might justify such legal responsibilities, or ground an argument that they should be more extensive)?

There is, even more obviously, room for uncertainty and disagreement about the precise content of our prospective responsibilities. We might disagree, for instance, about just what responsibilities neighbours have to and for each other. If I hear what might be a burglary next door, do I have a responsibility to investigate or to phone the police? If I do nothing, must I answer to my neighbour for what would then count as a failure to act, accepting responsibility for that failure and (in part) for her loss if it was a burglary; or can I claim that it was none of my business, and so not my responsibility? We might disagree about the responsibilities of manufacturers. How far, for instance, should they attend (beyond what the law requires) to the impact their activities have on the physical or social environment? If a manufacturer is thinking about moving his production processes out of Britain to a country where labour is cheaper, he is of course responsible to his shareholders for the decision he makes, and for its impact on the firm's profits, and, surely, to his current employees for its effects on them. But is it also his responsibility to attend to the further effects of the move on the local economy, on his suppliers, on his competitors; or can he claim that such matters are not his business—not matters to which he should attend in deciding what to do? And so on, through a very wide range of cases in which people disagree about the scope and content of the responsibilities, prospective and thus also retrospective, of different kinds of agent.

It is not my purpose to explore such disagreements here. My aim is simply to clarify the logical structure of responsibility-ascriptions, as a prelude to the more substantive discussion of the character, scope and content of criminal responsibility that will occupy later chapters. I have so far done no more than illustrate the way in which responsibility is a matter of being answerable for something to someone; the way in which our retrospective responsibilities are determined by our prospective responsibilities—responsibilities that we have in virtue of our satisfaction of normatively relevant descriptions; and some of the ways in which people can disagree about the character, direction and content of our responsibilities.

One point worth emphasising here is the way in which conceptions of what it is to be Φ can limit our prospective responsibilities, and thus our retrospective responsibilities. Often, of course, they extend our responsibilities, making us responsible for things for which we would otherwise have no responsibility: as a parent, I have responsibilities for this child that I would not have were I not his father, and do not have towards children in general; as a friend, I have responsibilities towards my friends that I would not have were they not my friends, and that go beyond those I have to other people in general. Sometimes, however, an account of what it is to be a Φ sets limits on my responsibilities, allowing or requiring me to deny responsibility for things for which I would otherwise be responsible. Suppose we accept, for instance, that we have a responsibility, as citizens, not just to refrain from crime ourselves, but to refrain from acting in ways that we know will facilitate others' criminal actions: if I know that the person to whom I sell or lend a chisel plans to use it to commit a burglary, I have good reason not to give it to him; I cannot say that what he does with it is not my business. Now a doctor might know that by prescribing contraceptives to a girl of 15, she will be 'facilitating' the commission of unlawful sexual intercourse: the girl and her partner are more likely to have intercourse if they have this safeguard against pregnancy. Should we then hold the doctor responsible, morally or criminally, for assisting the commission of a crime?[35]

On one view, she is morally, and perhaps should therefore be criminally, responsible for assisting the commission of the offence. She may be able to avoid moral or criminal liability by offering a defence of necessity—that it was more important to protect her patient's health than to avoid facilitating the commission of the offence: but she must offer a defence if she is to avoid liability, since she acted as she had good moral and legal reason not to act; she must therefore answer for her action—but can avoid liability if she can show that she had reasons to act as she did which outweighed or defeated the reasons against acting thus. That would be to claim that it was her responsibility, as a doctor, to attend to such a foreseeable effect of her medical activity, as a reason against prescribing contraceptives. But we might instead argue that that is no part of her responsibility as a doctor: her concern should be with her patient's health, and her responsibility is simply to provide medically appropriate treatment.[36] On this view, the fact

[35] See *Gillick v West Norfolk and Wisbech Area Health Authority* [1986] AC 112, and n 26 above.

[36] Cp Lord Scarman's comments in *ibid*, at 190; see Duff, 1990a: 85–7.

that the medically appropriate treatment would also facilitate the commission of an offence is not something to which she should attend as a reason against providing that treatment; nor should she be called to answer, after the event, for assisting the commission of a crime. She would not then need a defence: rather than admitting responsibility and denying liability by offering a defence (as she would have to do on the first view), she would now be denying responsibility—denying that 'assisting the commission of a crime' is something for which she should be called to answer.

This chapter has sketched out the logic of responsibility as answerability. Responsibility, as something distinct from and prior to liability, is responsibility as Φ, to *S*, for *X*: to determine what we are responsible for in this or that context we must ask as what we are responsible, and to whom (or what) we are responsible. An answer to the 'as what' question will explicate the relevant normatively laden description that we satisfy, and the prospective responsibilities that that description implies. This will then enable us to answer both the 'to whom' and the 'for what' questions: to whom are those prospective responsibilities owed; who therefore has the right to call us to answer for our discharge of them; what is their content?

It is time now to turn to criminal responsibility as a particular species of responsibility, and to ask as what, to whom, and for what we should be criminally responsible.

2

Criminally Responsible as What, to Whom?

We are responsible for particular matters, to specifiable people or bodies, in virtue of our satisfaction of relevant normatively significant descriptions. Such descriptions locate us within the normative structures of particular institutions and practices, within which and in terms of whose constitutive values responsibilities—both prospective and retrospective—are recognised and attributed. I have responsibilities as a teacher to my students and colleagues; as a parent to my children, my partner, and others who have a proper interest in how I treat my children; as a footballer to my team-mates; as a neighbour to my neighbours, and so on. Those to whom I am responsible are those who have the right or standing to remind me of my prospective responsibilities and to call me to account (hold me retrospectively responsible) for the way in which I discharge or fail to discharge those responsibilities.

What then of criminal responsibility? We are criminally responsible under—ie in virtue of being bound by—the criminal law; we are called to account in criminal courts for that for which we are criminally responsible; if we cannot offer an adequately exculpatory answer we are liable to criminal conviction and punishment. One question then concerns the scope of our positive criminal responsibilities: we can ask, for instance, what those who fall within the jurisdiction of English criminal law are criminally responsible for under English law. But the question that concerns us here is normative: for what *should* we be criminally responsible? An answer to that question must be grounded in a normative conception of the criminal law as a particular kind of institutional practice, and central to that normative conception will be an account of what we are responsible as, and to whom or what we are thus responsible. We have parental responsibilities as parents, pedagogical responsibilities as teachers and moral responsibilities as moral agents; in each case, an answer to the 'as what?' question provides the start of an answer to the 'to whom?' question. So as what are we criminally responsible: what is the relevant normative description, whose satisfaction gives us our responsibilities under the criminal law; to whom, or what, are those responsibilities owed?

This question provides the main focus of this chapter, though the conception of criminal law on which its answer depends will be developed in Chapters 4–6. There is, however, a logically prior question to which we must first briefly attend.

1. Who Can Be Responsible?

We have responsibilities in virtue of satisfying any of a wide range of normatively significant descriptions—in virtue of our participation in that wide range of social practices within which such descriptions have their normative significance. We can have responsibilities as parents, as friends, as employees and as employers, as neighbours, as citizens, and so on: to determine what those responsibilities should be we must give an account of the normative structure of the relevant social practice—as I will do in relation to the criminal law. But the ascription of such description-relative responsibilities surely depends on a logically prior, more general species of responsibility. I can have responsibilities as a parent, or neighbour, or shopkeeper, or employer, only if I am a responsible agent—one who is capable of taking on such specific responsibilities, who can be expected to recognise and discharge them, who can be properly held responsible for his actions. Although the focus of this book is on criminal responsibility, rather than on this underlying idea of responsible agency, I should say something about what it is to be a responsible agent at all.

We do not, of course, suppose that responsible agents are responsible for every aspect of their lives and conduct: the question of what we can generally be responsible for is the topic of Chapter 3. More to the present point, we do not suppose that every person is a responsible agent: young children, or adults suffering from various severe, all-embracing kinds of mental disorder, are not responsible agents who should be left free to run their own lives or be held responsible for what they do; they are not candidates for either prospective or retrospective responsibility. What then distinguishes the responsible from the non-responsible: in virtue of what characteristics should a person count as a responsible agent?

The most useful way to answer this question is to try to identify the capacities on which participation in the range of responsibility-ascribing practices depends. What capacities must we have if we are to be able, in any of the wide range of contexts in which responsibility is at issue, to accept and discharge the responsibilities that are ascribed to us, or to answer for our own actions, or to hold others responsible for theirs? Particular practices require different specific capacities: but we should be able to say something about the basic, general capacities that define a basic, general notion of responsible agency. It is here that 'capacity' theories of responsibility have their place: they do not compete with 'choice' and 'character' theories,[1] which concern the objects of responsibility (what we are responsible for); capacity theories rather concern the conditions of responsible agency.

The capacities on which responsibility depends are best understood as a matter of reason-responsiveness:[2] a responsible agent is one who is capable of recognising and responding to the reasons that bear on his situation. A responsible agent is 'responsable' to reasons: which means not that he is responsible only when and insofar as he is actually responsive to reasons (since we can be responsible for our very failures to respond to relevant reasons), but that he is responsible insofar as he is capable of responding appropriately to relevant reasons. Those reasons may be, and in the context of criminal responsibility typically are, reasons for action; but responsibility can also be a matter of one's capacity to respond appropriately to reasons for belief, for emotion, and for other kinds of thought. We might say that what matters is the extent to which our actions, thoughts and feelings are under our rational control; but that is just to say that what matters is the extent to which we are responsable to reasons in acting, thinking and feeling as we do.

Responding appropriately to reasons is not simply a matter of acting, thinking or feeling in conformity to them. It involves recognising reasons as reasons, ie as considerations by which my actions and thoughts could be guided; having some grasp of their relevance (of the contexts in which they apply) and force; being able not simply to follow them, but to weigh them in deliberation and in relation to other reasons—and, when appropriate, to take a self-reflective, critical stance towards them and ask whether I should recognise them as reasons at all;[3] and, finally, being able to act or think as deliberation shows them to require or permit. It is a matter of rationality, both practical and theoretical—we are responsible agents insofar as we are rational agents. But rationality in this context involves more than purely intellectual capacities: a rational agent is one whose emotions and desires or other conative dispositions, as well as her beliefs, are responsable to reasons.[4]

[1] Contrast Horder, 1993; Wilson, 2002: 333–43.

[2] For different kinds of 'reason-responsiveness' theory see Wolf, 1987; Scanlon, 1988; Wallace, 1994; Pettit and Smith, 1996; Fischer and Ravizza 1998 (on which see Watson, 2001); Morse, 1998; Glannon, 2002. The differences between these different versions need not concern us here.

[3] On the importance of this self-reflective dimension, see eg Watson, 1975; Wolf, 1987; Scanlon, 1988.

[4] I cannot embark here on a discussion of the rationality of emotions and conative dispositions, or of the broadly Aristotelian conception of practical rationality through which we can understand these dimensions of reason: but see eg Watson, 1975; Wolf, 1987; Kahan and Nussbaum, 1996; and below, Ch 3.2.

The connection between responsibility and reason-responsiveness should now be clear. Our prospective responsibilities generate reasons—for action, thought, or feeling —to which we should attend. Given my parental responsibilities, the fact that my child is playing truant gives me reason to take steps to get her to school, whereas it does not give a passing stranger any such reason for action; given my responsibilities as a philosopher, the fact that a fellow philosopher has offered what she claims to be a refutation of a thesis that I propounded gives me reason to consider her arguments and re-examine my views; given my responsibilities as a human being, the fact that the person I pass in the street is obviously ill and in distress gives me reason to feel sympathy, and to stop and help. Our retrospective responsibilities are then for the ways in which we respond, or fail to respond, to those reasons. As the child's parent I am responsible (to the child, to the school, to the relevant legal authority) for the steps I take to get her to school, or for my failure to take such steps—whereas a passing stranger is not responsible to anyone for 'failing' to take such steps since, without prospective responsibility for the child's schooling, not taking such steps does not constitute a failure to take them. As a philosopher I am responsible to my fellow philosophers, for my response or lack of response to my critic's arguments. As a human being I am responsible to the person in distress (as my fellow human being), and to others for my response or lack of response to her need.

There is clearly much more to be said about responsibility as reason-responsiveness, and about the various capacities that reason-responsiveness requires, but it cannot be said here. I should, however, note two points that will be important in what follows.

First, there are two distinct moments of responsibility—two times at which the question whether this person is a responsible agent can arise. One moment is the time at which an agent acts as she has reason not to act: is she at that time a responsible agent—is she capable of responding appropriately to the relevant reasons? The other time is that at which the agent is called to answer for her actions: since responsibility is answerability, it matters whether she is now capable of answering for what she did. Usually the two moments match: a person who is reason-responsable at the time of her action is usually also capable of answering when she is called to account (which is often very shortly after the time of the action); a person who is non-responsible at the time of the action, who then lacks the rational capacities that reason-responsiveness requires, will usually also be incapable of responding rationally when she is later called to account. But they can diverge: someone who was non-responsible at the time of the action can be restored to rational competence, whilst someone who was responsible at the time of the action can become non-responsible. These two possibilities are illustrated by the provisions that the criminal law makes for mentally disordered offenders/defendants. It provides an insanity defence for those who were so disordered as to be non-responsible at the time of their commission of an offence;[5] and it precludes the trial of a defendant who, whilst she might have been rationally competent at the time of the (alleged) offence, is not now fit to be tried.[6] Someone who is unfit to plead might have committed the offence charged, and have been criminally responsible at the time of its commission (which is to say that she could *then* have been called to answer for it); but she is not *now* responsible for committing that offence, because she cannot now be called to answer for it. We will discuss such provisions in more detail later (in Chapter 8.2): we need simply note here that responsibility as answerability requires a capacity both to respond to reasons and then to answer for oneself.

Secondly, the reasons to which responsible agents must be able to respond are of different kinds in different contexts: although the capacities involved in reason-responsiveness are not peculiar to one kind of reason, we cannot assume that someone who is reason-responsable in one context will be reason-responsable in every context. The example of the so-called 'partial psychopath' illustrates this point. A complete psychopath is someone who is not responsable to any practical reasons that reach beyond the immediate moment and his current desires: he has no practical understanding of either morality or prudence; he is non-responsable both to moral reasons and to reasons flowing from his own long-term interests.[7] A partial psychopath is incapable of moral understanding, but capable of prudential deliberation and action; he is not responsable to moral reasons, but is responsable to prudential reasons.[8] Such a person is in principle prudentially responsible: he can have the kinds of prospective responsibility that normal adults have to attend to their own interests, short-term and long-term; he can be called to answer (by those with a legitimate interest in the matter) for his imprudent actions. But he is not morally responsible: he cannot be expected to recognise or to respond appropriately to moral reasons; nor, therefore, can he be called to account for his failures to do so—for his morally wrongful actions. If we then ask whether he should be held *criminally* responsible, we must first get clear about the kinds of

[5] See eg Simester and Sullivan, 2007: 643–56 (for English law); Model Penal Code, s 4.01. Given its effect, the insanity defence is hardly used outside murder cases, but it applies in principle to any offence.

[6] Criminal Procedure (Insanity) Act 1964, s 4 (as amended by Criminal Procedure (Insanity and Unfitness to Plead) Act 1991); Model Penal Code, s 4.04.

[7] The idea of psychopathy as a responsibility-negating condition is of course deeply controversial, but serves a purely illustrative purpose here: see further Duff, 1977.

[8] See Cleckley, 1964: 195–234. One might wonder how deep a conception of his own interests is available to a person who cannot understand moral or other non-self-oriented reasons (see Duff, 1977: 196–8); but we need not pursue that issue here.

reason that are relevant in that context—what kinds of reason the criminal law deals with, and whether such a person is capable of responding appropriately to such reasons. To what kind of reason is someone who commits an offence (without justification) unresponsive, or insufficiently responsive, in the eyes of the criminal law? If those reasons are moral reasons, a partial psychopath should not be held criminally responsible. If, instead, the criminal law offers us what are intended to be adequate prudential reasons for refraining from crime (threats of punishment), a partial psychopath is criminally responsible, since he is responsable to such reasons.[9] If the criminal law deals in distinctively legal reasons to which those who are bound by the law are supposed to be responsive, we must ask what kind of reason legal reasons are, what kind of rational force they are supposed to have, and what is required if we are to understand them as the kinds of reason they are.

We can begin that task, and the task of developing an account of criminal responsibility as a specific type of responsibility, by asking what we are criminally responsible as, and to whom (or what) we are criminally responsible; this will also help us towards an account of what we can properly be held criminally responsible for, by helping us towards an account of what kind of institution or practice the criminal law is.[10] However, one further preliminary point must be noted.

It might be thought that in explaining responsibility as a matter of reason-responsiveness, or the capacity to participate in a range of practices within which responsibilities are ascribed, accepted, discharged and argued, I have evaded the most basic question about responsibility —the question of free will, of whether anyone is ever a responsible agent at all. Philosophers have offered forceful arguments to show that our assumption that many of us are responsible agents who can justly be held responsible for much that we do would be undermined by the truth of a determinist thesis that we cannot show to be false; or that whether or not a version of determinism is true, that assumption is incoherent:[11] we must surely then ask whether any of us can be held responsible for anything before we ask about our criminal responsibilities.

However, one cannot tackle every important question at once; this is one question that I will not tackle in this book. I suspect anyway that once we are clear about the criteria and conditions of responsibility that obtain

[9] Compare Kenny, 1978: 42–4; he argues that prudential deterrability suffices for criminal responsibility.

[10] To which it might be replied that 'the criminal law' is not a single institution or practice, but a complex and often mutually conflicting collection of institutions and practices (see eg Braithwaite and Pettit, 1990). But, as I suggested earlier (see above, Introduction at nn 31–34), there is good reason to focus initially on the substantive criminal law, and to see whether we can say anything general about its character and purposes.

[11] See G Strawson, 1986.

within our responsibility-ascribing practices, and realise that we can—because we do—participate successfully in such practices, the general metaphysical problem of 'free will', even if it does not dissolve, will lose much of its force.[12] We are, at least very often, responsible agents who can properly be held responsible for what we do because we are capable of participating in these practices, of responding to the reasons that they generate, and of answering for our actions in terms of such reasons; that is all there is to responsible agency.

2. As What Are We Criminally Responsible?

The criminal law speaks to those whom it claims to bind: it speaks of what kinds of conduct constitute crimes, and of what will be demanded of us or imposed on us if we engage, or are accused of engaging, in such conduct—of our liability to be prosecuted, and to be convicted and punished if we are proved guilty. This is not to deny that we might distinguish 'rules for citizens' from 'rules for courts'.[13] It is to deny that the criminal law is addressed *solely* to the courts, as a set of norms about when and how they are to impose criminal liability.[14] But even without the communicative conception of law that I will offer, any liberal theorist must surely deny that: the familiar principle that those who are to be liable to the law's sanctions must be given fair notice of what would make them liable,[15] and a fair opportunity to avoid liability,[16] requires the law to be addressed to them. What we must now ask, however, is a set of crucial questions about the way in which the law addresses us: as what are we addressed, in what terms or tones, and by what or by whom? I begin with the 'as what?' question.

[12] My view is thus close in spirit to PF Strawson, 1962; see also Wallace, 1994.

[13] See, variously, Fletcher, 1978: chs 6.6–8, 7, 9–10; Dan-Cohen, 1984; Alldridge, 1990; Robinson, 1997. To say that aspects of the law are addressed to courts rather than to citizens should not be to say that they may be *concealed* from citizens (see Dan-Cohen 1984: 632–4, 637–43, 671; in response, see Singer, 1986: 84–100): citizens should at least be able to know the rules under which the courts will deal with them (see Robinson, 1997: 207–9). The claim should be only that rules for courts are not directly addressed to the citizens.

[14] Compare Kelsen, 1925/1945: 63—'Law is the primary norm which stipulates the sanction'; on which see Hart, 1994: 35–42.

[15] See Ashworth, 2006: 74–7; LaFave, 2003: 104–7; *US v Harriss* 347 US 612, 617 (1954)—the law must 'give a person of ordinary intelligence fair notice that his contemplated conduct is forbidden by the statute' (but I will argue later that 'forbidden' should not be the appropriate term).

[16] See eg Hart, 1968a: 46–50, 201; Moore, 1997: 549–62.

(a) Territories, Sovereigns and Subjects

If we ask as what, to whom, we are in fact criminally responsible, as a matter of positive law, the simplest answer is a territorial one: we are criminally responsible to a state as agents whose alleged criminal conduct occurs within its geographical territory. The jurisdiction of English criminal law is initially defined by the Principle of Territoriality; similar provisions are found elsewhere.[17] (The law's claim to jurisdiction over conduct committed within the territory of the state whose law it is involves two claims: that it can define such conduct as criminal; and that its courts have jurisdiction to try the alleged perpetrator of such conduct. Some count the first as a matter of 'ambit', and only the second as a matter of 'jurisdiction',[18] but for present purposes we can capture both aspects under the idea of 'jurisdiction'.)

However, whilst a Principle of Territoriality is central to any specification of our actual criminal responsibilities under positive law, it cannot help with the normative question—as what and to whom *should* we be criminally responsible? That principle might, subject to a variety of qualifications (some of which will be noted later), capture the *extension* of criminal responsibility, but not in a normatively illuminating way: 'acting within geographical area *X*' lacks the normative significance that an answer to the 'as what' question requires. We are to be answerable under a system of criminal law: but a system of criminal law and a state within which that system could exist require more than a collection of people who happen to live or act in the same geographical area; without a lot more than that, there would indeed be nothing recognisable as a human society, let alone a political or legal system.[19] That 'more' involves an idea of community: not necessarily a richly normative communitarian idea of the sort that eschews liberal individualism (and worries liberal individualists), but a metaphysical idea of the sort that even liberal individualists must presuppose;[20] an idea of people living together (as distinct from merely beside each other) in a society defined by some set of shared values and understandings that might be implicit, inchoate or disputed,[21] but without which society, politics and law would be impossible.

[17] See Hirst, 2003: ch 1, on English law; LaFave 2003: 193–229, on American law; German Criminal Code s 3, on the *Territorialitätsprinzip* in German law. I leave aside here issues about what counts as the criminal conduct occurring within a specified territory: see Hirst, 2003: ch 4; Moore 1993: 293–8.

[18] See eg Hirst, 2003: 9–10.

[19] See Winch, 1960.

[20] On the distinction between metaphysical and normative issues in this context (and some of its problems) see Rawls, 1985; Taylor, 1989; Mulhall and Swift, 1992: chs 5–6.

[21] And that might have as much to do with the procedures by which collective decisions are made as with the substantive content of those decisions, if proceduralist versions of liberalism are plausible: see eg Waldron 1999; Archard 2005.

A minimalist idea of political and legal community is provided by classical positivism, which offers a more substantive, though still normatively inadequate, answer to the 'as what, to whom?' question. If law consists in the commands of a sovereign, then we are responsible *as* that sovereign's subjects, and are responsible *to* the sovereign for our acts of disobedience to its commands; the relevant community consists of those who habitually obey a particular sovereign. That community will typically inhabit an identifiable geographical territory, since a sovereign's power to secure obedience is typically geographically delimited; that is why the Principle of Territoriality might roughly capture the extension of criminal responsibility. But what grounds that responsibility is sovereignty, not territory.

Classical positivism can thus provide an account of jurisdiction. It also offers a grounding for the 'practical difference' thesis—the thesis that if the law has authority, it must be able to make a practical difference to our deliberation and action.[22] For on this view the criminal law is a source of distinctive reasons for action: whatever reasons we may or may not have had in advance of the law for acting in the way that it now prescribes, the fact that such conduct is now commanded by the sovereign offers us a new and distinctive reason for action, grounded in the sovereign's authority (however we understand that authority). Any adequate account of criminal law and responsibility must be able to deal with both these issues; but the way in which classical positivism deals with them cannot serve the aims of normative theory.[23]

It is no doubt disturbingly often true that the tones in which the criminal law is heard to speak by those whom it claims to bind and to call to account are indeed those of an Austinian sovereign: it is heard (and not unreasonably heard) as the voice of an alien sovereign, a 'they' or 'it' set over against the 'us' who are constituted as its subjects, issuing commands backed by the threat of sanctions against disobedience. But that is not how the criminal law should speak or be heard in what aspires to be a liberal democracy, for two reasons.

First, whilst as members of such a polity we are of course subject to the law, this should not be subjection to a law that is imposed on us by another, separate power distinct from us: the law that binds us should be our law—a law to and by which we bind ourselves, not a law that is imposed on us by a sovereign; it should be in that sense a 'common' law.[24]

22 See Shapiro, 1998a, 1998b; in response, Coleman, 1998.

23 Nor was it intended to, given the classical distinction between analytical and censorial jurisprudence. But my discussion of positivism plays a purely heuristic role, to highlight the issues that a normative theory of criminal responsibility must address, which is why I ignore later more sophisticated versions of positivism.

24 Compare Cotterrell, 1995: ch 11, on the '*community*' as contrasted with the '*imperium*' model of law. On this idea of a common law see Postema, 1986: chs 1–2; Duff, 2001: 56–68.

This is not merely to say that the law must be subject to democratic control. It is also to say that it must be a law which we can recognise as reflecting values that we share as members of a political community: a law that we can make our own, because the voice in which it speaks is a voice that is, or that we can see should be, our collective voice.

Secondly, the reasons for action that law as a sovereign's commands offers are altogether too distinctive, too radically separated from the extra-legal (especially moral) reasons that we recognise. Of course we have, positivists will insist, sufficient extra-legal reasons to refrain from committing such wrongs as murder, theft and assault. But the criminal law, understood as the sovereign's commands, does not direct our attention to those reasons; it offers us new, content-independent reason—that the sovereign prohibits these actions. Now we will see later that the law can sometimes offer reasons for action that are not wholly content-dependent: sometimes 'because that's the law', if not 'because that's the criminal law', is a good reason for action.[25] But when the criminal law defines such familiar *mala in se* as assault or fraud, and calls us to account for our commission of such offences, it should address us in terms of the moral reasons in virtue of which such actions are criminalised, not of the commands of a sovereign who must be obeyed. This is partly a matter of 'transparency': the reasons that the law offers us for conforming to its demands should be the reasons that justify those demands themselves.[26] It is also a matter of the character of criminal wrongdoing: what the fraudster or assailant should be held criminally responsible for is not disobedience to a command, but the substantive wrong that he committed; the reasons for action to which he failed to respond (for which failure he is now called to answer in a criminal court) must concern that substantive wrong, not merely disobedience to an authoritative command.[27]

Criminal responsibility cannot be normatively grounded either in geographical location or in subjection to a sovereign's commands. In what then can it be grounded?

[25] The difference between 'because that's the law' and 'because that's the criminal law' will be important later: see Ch 4.4. The very idea of content-independence is more problematic than is often recognised, but its problems need not concern us here (see Markwick, 2000).

[26] See further Ch 4.3 below.

[27] That is why it is misleading to talk, as theorists often talk, of what the criminal law 'prohibits' or 'forbids' (see Model Penal Code, s 1.02(a)) in relation to *mala in se*: for it implies that the criminal law consists in something like commands or orders (see Ch 4.3 below). The problem here is the same as that faced by penal theorists who justify punishment as removing of the unfair advantage that was intrinsic to the crime: we distort the criminal wrongfulness of *mala in se* if we suggest that it consists in taking unfair advantage of the law-abiding—or in disobeying a sovereign's commands (see Murphy, 1973; Duff, 1986: ch 8).

(b) Moral Agents

A different answer to our question is offered by positivism's familiar opponent—natural law theory and the legal moralism that can flow from it. Consider for instance Moore's claim that the function of criminal law is 'to attain retributive justice', by 'punish[ing] all and only those who are morally culpable in the doing of some morally wrongful act'.[28] This suggests that we are criminally responsible *as* moral agents, since we are responsible for our failures to respond appropriately to the moral reasons with which criminal law is concerned: culpable responsibility *for* moral wrongdoing is responsibility *as* a moral agent. If we are responsible *as* moral agents, we are presumably also responsible *to* other moral agents, in virtue of our shared membership of the moral community.

Legal moralism does capture an important truth: the criminal law is properly concerned with moral wrongdoing. 'Moral wrongdoing' provides the start of an answer to the question 'For what should we be criminally responsible?'; the criminal law's purpose should be to identify and declare the public wrongfulness of certain kinds of moral wrongdoing, and to provide for an appropriate public response to them.[29] This claim will be defended in Chapter 4; our task here is to see why Moore's version of legal moralism does not provide a plausible answer to the 'as what and to whom?' question.

One familiar objection to legal moralism is that it is radically under-inclusive, since it cannot legitimise the extensive range of *mala prohibita* that we find in contemporary systems of criminal law: if the function of criminal law is to visit retribution on wrongdoing, we must be able to identify that wrongdoing independently of and prior to the criminal law that is to secure its punishment; if *mala prohibita* consist in conduct that is not wrongful independently of or prior to its criminalisation,[30] they cannot involve such punishable wrongdoing. If this objection holds, it also seems that legal moralism cannot accommodate the 'practical difference' thesis: if the law's function is to punish independently wrongful conduct, it cannot provide us with any reasons for refraining from such conduct that we did not already have. As we will see in Chapter 4.4, however, this objection can be met, once we define *mala prohibita* more appropriately as consisting in conduct that is not wrongful prior to its legal regulation.

The other familiar objection to legal moralism is that it is radically over-inclusive, since it implies that we have good reason to criminalise every kind of moral wrongdoing, even if other considerations often then

[28] Moore, 1997: 33–5.

[29] In saying this I do not commit myself to Moore's particular brand of metaphysical realism, which portrays criminal law as a 'functional kind'.

[30] See eg Gordon, 2000: 9; LaFave, 2003: 36; Simester and Sullivan, 2007: 3.

tip the balance against criminalisation.[31] We surely have no reason, not even one outweighed by countervailing reasons, to criminalise such undoubted and serious wrongs as the betrayal of a friend's confidence, or the demeaningly contemptuous dismissal of a colleague's ideas. I am of course answerable for such wrongs to those whose business they are—to my friends, or to my colleagues; but a central liberal claim is that such wrongs are, 'in brief and crude terms, not the law's business'.[32] I will defend this claim in Chapter 6, but we should note here another dimension to the over-inclusiveness of simple legal moralism: that as well as failing to recognise the realm of wrongs that are in principle 'private', it cannot deal adequately with the issue of jurisdiction.

If we are criminally responsible simply as moral agents, and if the function of criminal law is to provide for the retributive punishment of 'all ... those who are morally culpable in the doing of some morally wrongful act', English criminal law has reason to criminalise not merely theft (and other wrongs) committed in England, or by or against English citizens, but theft committed anywhere by or against anyone: to make it a crime under English law, triable by English courts (if they get the chance), for a German citizen to steal from a fellow German in Germany, for instance. But a German thief would rightly object that his wrongdoing is not the business of English criminal law or the English criminal courts: he is answerable for it in Germany, but not in England. Simple legal moralism seems to provide no normative basis for such jurisdictional limits to the criminal law of a nation state.

A legal moralist might try to deal with this issue of jurisdiction, whilst maintaining that a system of criminal law has plausible ground to claim jurisdiction over any culpable moral wrongdoing wherever and by and against whomever it is committed, by arguing, first, that there are practical reasons for operating with an explicit or implicit division of legislative, adjudicative and punitive labour: since we have a structure of nation states, it is pragmatically sensible for each to exercise criminal jurisdiction over wrongdoings within its reach—that is, primarily, wrongs committed within its territorial boundaries. Secondly, from respect for each other's sovereignty, states should respect the Principle of Territoriality. I have some reason to intervene if I see a child misbehaving, and to call her to account for her misconduct; but out of respect for the child's parents and their authority, I should normally leave it to them to deal with the child.

[31] See Moore, 1997: ch 18.
[32] Wolfenden, 1957: para 61.

So too, a state should normally respect another state's sovereignty by leaving it to deal with crimes committed by its own citizens within its own territory.[33]

On this view, a national legislature that took its responsibilities seriously would begin with a provisional claim to universal jurisdiction over moral wrongdoing—with the view that it should criminalise, and seek to provide for the punishment of, culpable moral wrongdoing wherever, and by and against whomever, it is committed; but then, in moving from the question of what it had in principle good reason to do to the question of what it should do, all things considered, it would see better reasons to limit its jurisdictional claims. That seems to me an implausibly imperialistic view of the responsibilities of a national legislature. When I become aware of a stranger's moral misconduct towards her friend or her parents, I do not think it my business to intervene, or to call her to answer for what she has done: my attitude is not that I have some reason to call her to account, since we are both moral agents, but better reason not to interfere; it is *ab initio* that that is not my business.[34] Analogously, national legislatures do not and should not begin with the thought that they have good reason to criminalise all moral wrongdoing, and then see reasons to limit their jurisdictional ambitions; they should, rather, recognise that only a certain range of wrongdoings are even in principle their business.[35]

How then can we begin to identify that range? The obvious answer, for liberal democrats, is that we should replace 'moral agent' by 'citizen': we are criminally responsible as citizens to our fellow citizens.

(c) Citizens

As members of a liberal democracy, we are related to each other, to the state and to the laws that bind us not as simply subjects (for we are meant to be self-governing), nor simply as moral agents (for membership is more limited than that), but as citizens of the polity. The law and the whole apparatus of the state supposedly speak and act in our name on our behalf: they are not the organs of a separate sovereign, but the formal institutional manifestations and instruments of our shared political lives—of the civic enterprise in which we are collectively engaged (just as the institutional structure and authorities of a properly functioning university are manifestations or instruments of the shared academic enterprise in which the university's members are collectively engaged). That is what makes the

[33] Compare Hirst, 2003: 10–11 on the 'unwarranted usurpation of [another state's] sovereignty'.

[34] On the limits of ordinary moral jurisdiction see above, Ch 1.2, at nn 19–20.

[35] I discuss below (at nn 45–49) cases in which states or their courts do claim a universal jurisdiction.

law, particularly the criminal law, a common law—a law that is our law as citizens: its voice is not (should not be) the voice of a sovereign who demands our obedience as subjects, but our own collective, civic voice; it is a voice in which we speak to ourselves, as citizens, of the shared values and goals by which our civic enterprise as a polity is constituted. That is also to say, however, that it is a voice in which we speak to ourselves, rather than to the whole world, or to moral agents at large.

As citizens who are both bound and protected by the values of our polity, we have both rights and responsibilities: we are answerable to each other for our conduct as citizens. What those rights and responsibilities are depends on the account we give of the civic enterprise—of the enterprise of living together as and in a polity: that is a central topic of political theory, which we need not pursue here, save to note two points that will be true of any liberal theory, whatever its precise character.

First, whether we give, for instance, a contractualist or communitarian account of liberal political association,[36] such political association will be partial and limited: it will be just one, often not the most significant, of the associations or communities in which its members lead their lives and find their goods; it will properly concern itself with only a limited dimension of their lives. We are not only citizens: we are parents, workers and colleagues in this or that job, friends, neighbours, members of a range of other associations, many of which may be more important and central to our lives than is our citizenship; our civic responsibilities often impinge only lightly, if at all, on these other dimensions of our lives.

Secondly, a primary reason for the partial, limited character of liberal political association is the central role that liberals give to the values of privacy, freedom and responsibility. Even liberals who deny that the state can or should be wholly neutral between different conceptions of human good will insist that it must leave its citizens the freedom to pursue any of a range of possible lives and goods; it must allow, indeed assist, them to take responsibility for their own lives (a responsibility that they will for the most part have not to the state or to the polity as a whole, but to other members of the more local associations in which they live most of their lives); it must, that is, allow them as extensive a 'private' realm as possible.

The idea of privacy in this context is clearly both strongly normative and context-relative. The private is not that which takes place in what can be factually described as 'private' (in the home, for instance): that can certainly be a public matter (as domestic violence is), whilst what takes place 'in public', outside the home, can be a private rather than a public matter—my choice of hair colour, for a trivial instance. The 'private', in

[36] I would myself advocate a republican liberal communitarianism: see Dagger, 1997; Duff, 2001: ch 2.

this context, is that which is not your business—you have no right to interfere, no standing to call me to account: but the scope of that 'you' depends on the context. My religious beliefs are 'private' in the context of my job (unless I am, for instance, a priest), in that my employer and my colleagues have no standing to question me about them or to call me to answer for them; but they may not be private in the context of a religious community to which I belong, since my fellow believers or my priest may have such standing. My shabby treatment of a friend might not be private in the context of the group of friends to which we both belong—it might be the business not only of me and the person I mistreat, but of our mutual friends collectively; but it is private in the context of the polity—it is not the business of my fellow citizens simply in virtue of our mutual citizenship. The realm of privacy that a liberal polity must respect is not a given; it is the outcome of a normative deliberation about what is whose business. Such a normative distinction between the 'public' and the 'private' can of course be abused, as feminist critics argue;[37] but rather than abandoning it we should try to draw it in a more appropriate way.

An account of the civic enterprise will include an account of our civic responsibilities: of what we owe to each other, and must answer for to each other, as citizens. To say that we are criminally responsible as citizens is not to say that we are criminally responsible for all our failures in our civic responsibilities: some of those responsibilities are not matters of law at all; others are not matters of criminal law. Criminal responsibility is just one dimension of civic responsibility; to grasp its proper scope, we must get clear about the proper role of the criminal law within a liberal polity, and about the particular responsibilities which concern it. That task will be taken up in Chapters 4–6, but something preliminary can be said here.

3. Civic Criminal Responsibility

The criminal law is concerned with moral wrongdoing: that is the truth in legal moralism that I noted above and will defend later. But it is not even in principle concerned with all kinds of wrongdoing (legal moralism's error is to suppose that it is). It is, as is often said, concerned with wrongs that are 'public' rather than 'private': but the task then is to explain this idea of 'public wrongs'. In Blackstone's classic formulation, whilst private or civil wrongs infringe 'the civil rights which belong to individuals, considered merely as individuals', crimes:

[37] See eg Olsen, 1983; Pateman, 1988. For a very good general discussion see Sypnowich, 2000.

> are breach and violation of the public rights and duties, due to the whole community, considered as community, in its social aggregate capacity. …[B]esides the injury done to individuals, [crimes] strike at the very being of society, which cannot possibly subsist, where actions of [that] sort are suffered to escape with impunity. In all cases the crime includes an injury: every public offence is also a private wrong, and somewhat more; it affects the individual, and it likewise affects the community.[38]

Now it might be tempting to suppose that a public wrong 'affects the community' only if it somehow harms or injures not just its individual victim (if there is one), but 'the community' as a whole. We are indeed familiar with attempts to explain the idea of crime in such terms: to argue, for instance, that the criminal wrongfulness of theft lies in the unfair advantage that the thief takes over all law-abiding citizens, or in the 'social volatility' or the loss of trust that it causes.[39] But this is not how we should understand the idea of a public wrong since, whilst there are some crimes that do indeed injure the public rather than identifiable individuals, to portray the criminal wrongfulness of such victimising crimes as murder, rape, wounding and fraud as consisting in the harm that they do to 'the public' is to distort the matter: they are wrongs because of what they do to their direct victims, and they are crimes or public wrongs, not because of some further injury that they do to 'the public', but because they are wrongs that properly concern 'the public', ie wrongs that properly concern us all as citizens. What the offender is called to answer for in such cases, what he is condemned for, should not be the unfair advantage he gained or the social volatility or mistrust he caused, but the wrong that he did to his victim.[40]

A central task for a normative theory of criminal law, as an account of what we should be criminally responsible for, is therefore to explain this notion of the public and to identify the principles, criteria or considerations that can help us determine which wrongs should count as being in this sense public. To say that we are criminally responsible as citizens, and to our fellow citizens, is only the first—but a crucial—step towards that goal: it shows us that what should count as public, and therefore as in principle criminal, wrongs are those that should concern all citizens, as wrongs, simply in virtue of their shared citizenship with the offender and with the victim. These are wrongs for which we must answer to our fellow citizens, and central to a system of criminal law is not only a substantive law that defines these wrongs, but a law of criminal procedure that creates and governs the institutions and processes through which we are to be called thus to answer. A defendant is summoned to trial: she is summoned

38 Blackstone 1765–9: Bk IV, ch 1, at 5.

39 See, respectively, Murphy, 1973; Becker, 1974; Dimock, 1997.

40 See further Marshall and Duff, 1998; and below, Ch 6.5.

by a court or a legal official, to answer to a criminal charge in a criminal court; she is to be judged 'Guilty' or 'Not Guilty' by a lay jury, or by a lay magistrate (or bench of magistrates), or by a professional judge; but the court and those who judge her are acting and speaking in the name and on behalf of the polity as a whole. This is concealed by the way in which cases are titled in English and Scottish criminal courts: to label the case as '*Regina v D*', or as '*HM Advocate v D*', rather suggests a positivist conception of being answerable to a sovereign. But it is made explicit in way in which cases are labelled in some American states, as '*People v D*', or '*Commonwealth v D*'.[41] As against the classical positivist, the liberal republican claim is therefore that we are criminally responsible not to a separate sovereign, but to ourselves; as against simple legal moralism, the claim is that we are criminally responsible not to the whole world of moral agents, but to our fellow citizens—that the criminal law is properly concerned not with moral wrongs as such, but with such public wrongs as are internal to the particular polity whose law it is.

(It is worth emphasising again that in thus relativising responsibility I am not relativising wrongfulness. We can be as non-relativistically universalistic as we like about morality, and insist that what is wrongful in England is also wrongful in America, in France, in Japan or in Korea.[42] The point at issue here concerns not what is or is not wrongful, but to whom or what we are responsible for the wrongs that we commit; and the claim is that when it is criminal responsibility that is at stake, we are responsible to our fellow citizens (whom we also have the collective standing to hold responsible). It is also of course true that different systems of criminal law differ in their content: what counts as a criminal wrong in one system might not count as a criminal wrong in another system. Such differences do not always reflect different underlying views of what is right or wrong: they might instead express different views about which wrongs are in the relevant sense 'public'; or relatively minor differences in the precise interpretation and definition of such public wrongs; or different systems of regulation, which then generate different *mala prohibita*. But for English criminal law not to claim jurisdiction over a theft committed in France by a French citizen is not for it to imply that such a theft is not wrong; it is simply to remain properly silent about something that is not its business.)

By grounding the criminal law's jurisdiction in citizenship rather than in territory, we can also make better sense of the ways in which states sometimes claim jurisdiction over wrongs committed by or against their

[41] For a developed account of the criminal trial as a process of calling to account see Duff *et al*, 2007; and see further below, Ch 8.

[42] See above, Ch 1 at nn 23–26.

citizens abroad.[43] Such provisions vary in scope, but their claim is, in relation to crimes against citizens, that the perpetrator is answerable to this polity for such wrongs against its members; and, in relation to crimes by citizens, that any member of the polity is responsible to the polity for any such wrongs that he commits. There is nothing puzzling about such claims. They may be controversial, since they rest on conceptions of the scope of the bonds of citizenship that may be disputed: but there is nothing puzzling in a claim that I am answerable to my fellow citizens for wrongs that I commit elsewhere, since I do not leave my status as citizen behind when I go abroad; or a claim that as citizens we have a proper interest in wrongs done to our fellow citizens, and the standing to call the wrongdoer to answer for them. This is not to say that a polity *should* claim jurisdiction over all crimes committed either by or against its citizens wherever they are committed: one could instead plausibly hold that we are not answerable to our fellow citizens for wrongs that we commit abroad, and that while we may expect our fellow citizens to have some collective concern at least for serious wrongs that we suffer abroad, that concern should not extend to calling the wrongdoers to account. The point is simply that claims to extra-territorial jurisdiction over crimes committed by or against the polity's members make straightforward sense if we take citizenship to be the basis of criminal responsibility—whereas if we start with a territorial criterion of jurisdiction they will seem much more puzzling.

The suggestion that criminal responsibility should be grounded in citizenship requires an immediate qualification, and raises a further issue that we cannot pursue here.

The qualification is that the criminal law of a decent polity covers temporary residents of, and visitors to, the polity as well as its citizens. We need not inquire here into the conditions under which people should be able to become citizens of a polity; the issue concerns those who find themselves for a time within the territory of a polity of which they are not citizens. Such visitors should, as guests, be accorded many of the rights and protections of citizenship, as well as being expected to accept some of its responsibilities and duties. In particular, they should be bound and protected by the polity's laws, including its criminal law. If they commit what the local law defines as a public wrong, they must answer for it to the polity whose law it is—just as anyone who commits such a wrong against them will have to answer for it as he would for a wrong committed against a fellow citizen. This is not to revert to a geographical principle that grounds jurisdiction in the territorial location of crime: what makes

[43] See eg the French *Code Penal*, Art 113.6–7 (see Hirst, 2003: 43); . German Criminal Code s 7.1–2; the English Sex Offenders Act 1997 s 7 (see Hirst, 2003: ch 5; Home Office, 1996); LaFave, 2003: 205–9.

normative sense of jurisdiction is still the law's identity as the law of a particular polity, whose members are its primary addressees. But given such a polity, whose members are responsible to each other for what their law defines as public wrongs, its laws can also bind and protect visitors to the polity and its territory.

The further issue concerns the various ways in which criminal jurisdiction can transcend the bounds both of national citizenship and of national territory. Such transcendence might simply involve some larger polity of which those paradigmatically bound by the law can still be seen as citizens: thus one can see the criminal law of the European Union, for instance, as aspiring to bind citizens of the Member States as citizens of Europe.[44] But sometimes what is claimed is a wholly unconstrained, universal jurisdiction. This is sometimes claimed by the law of particular nation states. Under section 134 of the Criminal Justice Act 1988, torture is an offence triable in English courts, wherever and against whomever it is committed:[45] English law thus claims a wholly universal jurisdiction over torture, independent of both citizenship and territory.[46] But it is also and more widely claimed by international criminal tribunals, and now by the International Criminal Court, whose founding statute gave it jurisdiction over 'the most serious crimes of international concern', namely 'genocide', 'crimes against humanity', 'war crimes' and 'the crime of aggression'.[47] How then should we understand international criminal responsibility: as what, and to what or whom, are defendants in such trials held to be answerable?

One response to this question is to deny that responsibility is thus relational at its core. What matters is that those who commit such wrongs must be punished; we then ask whose task it should be to punish them, and whether we should create international tribunals, either ad hoc or standing, to discharge this task.[48] Those who believe, as I do, that responsibility is fundamentally relational must then argue that the basic issue concerns not a non-relationally specified demand that such wrongdoers be punished, but the question 'To whom are such wrongdoers answerable?'. One answer to this question is that they are still answerable

[44] See eg Arts III. 271–5 of the Treaty Establishing a Constitution for Europe (available at http://europa.eu.int/constitution). Something similar is of course true of federal systems: Americans are bound both, as American citizens, by federal criminal law and, as citizens of their particular state, by the laws of that state.

[45] This gave effect to the UN Convention against Torture and other Cruel, Inhuman or Degrading Treatment or Punishment (1984): see *R v Bow Street Metropolitan Stipendiary Magistrate ex p Ugarte* [2000] 1 AC 147. It covers only torture committed by, or at the instigation or with the consent of, a 'public official or person acting in an official capacity'.

[46] See further Hirst, 2003: 54–5, 201–81; Cassese, 2003: 277–322; Reydams, 2003.

[47] Rome Statute of the International Criminal Court, arts. 1, 5: see Cassese, 2003: 340–405; also May, 2005.

[48] This seems to be the logic of Altman and Wellman, 2004.

to the national political communities within which they committed their crimes (when their crimes were thus geographically limited in scope): international tribunals should have jurisdiction only when the relevant national courts either no longer exist or cannot discharge that task, and such tribunals must still be seen to act on behalf and in the name of the members of the particular polity. Another, more ambitious, answer is that there are some crimes, crimes that are properly called 'crimes against humanity', for which the perpetrators must answer not just to this or that more local community, but to humanity itself:[49] this answer promises much, but those who offer it face the task of making sense of the idea of humanity as a community.

We cannot pursue the topic of international criminal law and criminal responsibility here; it will be enough if we can gain a clearer understanding of criminal responsibility within the kinds of domestic or municipal criminal law that impinge most directly on us. Such criminal responsibility is, I have argued, grounded in citizenship.

If we bear in mind (as those who preach the 'war on crime' are prone to forget) that both victims and offenders are citizens, we can see that grounding responsibility in citizenship will have significant implications, not only for the content and structure of the substantive criminal law (a topic to be discussed in later chapters), but also for the criminal process and criminal punishment. If the criminal process is to be a process through which citizens call each other to answer for their alleged public wrongdoings, we must ask what kind of process can serve that purpose and how it can treat defendants as citizens. If criminal punishment is to be something imposed on citizens by their fellow citizens, as an appropriate response to the wrongs that they have committed, we must ask how punishment could have that character: what kinds of punishment, for what purposes, could we with clear consciences impose on each other (on ourselves) as citizens? I say a little more about the criminal process in Chapter 8, but cannot discuss punishment further here;[50] my main concern is with the way in which the answer suggested to the 'as what, to whom?' question about criminal responsibility in this chapter can guide us in trying to answer the 'for what?' question in the following chapters.

[49] See eg Luban, 2004.
[50] On the criminal trial see Duff *et al*, 2007; on punishment see Duff, 2001.

3

Responsible For What?

Before we ask what we can be criminally responsible for, we must ask what we can be in any way or context responsible for. Are there limits, logical or normative, on the possible objects of responsibility, which constrain all kinds of responsibility-ascription? In this chapter I will discuss two general conditions of responsibility that theorists have found plausible: a control condition, concerning the agent's control over that for which she is to be held responsible; and an epistemic condition, concerning her actual or possible awareness of relevant facts.[1] Neither condition, we will see, sets strict limits on the possible objects of responsibility—a conclusion that need not disturb us if we remember the distinction between responsibility and liability drawn in Chapter 1.1: we are responsible for much for which we are not liable to be condemned because we can offer a justification or excuse that repels liability without denying responsibility. Some conditions that theorists portray as responsibility-negaters should rather be understood as liability-negaters.

1. Control as Necessary for Responsibility

I have control over *X*, an actual or potential state of affairs, or *X* is within my control, insofar as it is up to me whether or not *X* is the case: insofar as it is within my power both to bring it about that *X* is the case and to bring it about that *X* is not the case. Control is in part a matter of how far the world is responsive to me and my agency: can I bring about those results in the world that I intend and try to bring about? It is also a matter of my own capacities for thought and movement: how far can I think and move 'at will'? It is also, in relation to control over one's own conduct, a matter of reason-responsiveness: how far is my conduct guided by what I recognise as good reasons for action? Much would need to be said in an

[1] See Aristotle, *Nicomachean Ethics* III.1; Zimmerman, 1988; Fischer and Ravizza, 1998.

adequate account of control, especially of control over one's own conduct,[2] but that is not necessary for present purposes: my interest here is in the significance of control, as thus intuitively understood, as a necessary condition of responsibility.

It seems to be a logical rather than a normative matter that we can be morally responsible (ie properly held responsible) only for that over which we had or could have some control. I can hold you responsible for something over which you in fact exercised no control; but it is not clear that it would even make sense to hold you responsible for something over which I admit you had and could have had no control. 'But there was nothing I could have done about it' is an appropriate response to being held responsible: if the responsibility-ascription is to be sustained, that response must be rebutted. That is why responsibility is tied to agency: we can be held responsible, either retrospectively or prospectively, only for that in relation to which we could exercise some effective agency.[3]

It might seem that this logical point does not transfer to criminal responsibility. Criminal liability presupposes criminal responsibility: since we can in fact be held criminally liable for matters over which we had no control, we can be criminally responsible without control; any 'control requirement' on criminal responsibility must therefore be a normative rather than a logical requirement.[4] But we must treat this point carefully, as *Larsonneur* (often cited in this context) shows.[5] Ms Larsonneur, a Frenchwoman, was ordered to leave the UK; she went to the Irish Free State, but she was brought back to Liverpool by the police: she was convicted of the offence of being 'found' in the UK as 'an alien to whom leave to land in the United Kingdom has been refused'.[6] It might seem that, since the offence as thus specified required neither mens rea nor a voluntary act or omission, it imposed liability without control. But, first, the offence as fully specified is committed only by an alien who 'lands' in the UK, and it could have been argued that, had she been carried from the ship by the police, she would not have 'landed' in the UK;[7] if she did land,

[2] See generally Fischer and Ravizza, 1998; also Frankfurt, 1978; Simester, 1996a; Husak, 1998a.

[3] Some deny that control is necessary for responsibility: I can be responsible for bringing *X* about although it was not within my power to avoid doing so (see Frankfurt, 1969, on which see Fischer and Ravizza, 1998: ch 2; Widerker and McKenna, 2003). The kinds of example to which Frankfurt appeals can be dealt with either by distinguishing different types of 'control' ('guidance control' from 'regulative control', for instance); or, perhaps more usefully, by asking more carefully just what we can be held responsible for and just what we do or do not control: but I cannot pursue the details here.

[4] See eg Husak, 1998a; Simester, 1998.

[5] *Larsonneur* (1933) 24 Cr App R 74; see eg Ormerod, 2005: 73–4—but also Lanham, 1976.

[6] Aliens Order 1920.

[7] Compare *Hill v Baxter* [1958] 1 QB 277, on what can count as 'driving'.

if she walked down the gangplank herself, that was something over which she had control, since she could have refused to land. Secondly, she was brought back from Ireland because she had gone there (which did not count as leaving the UK) instead of going somewhere—France, for instance—that was clearly not part of the UK; and that was something that she did control. A similar point applies to *Winzar*:[8] although once the police picked Mr Winzar up he had no control over whether he was found in a highway, we have no reason to doubt that he had had control over whether he got drunk, and thus over whether he was found *drunk* in a highway. In neither case was the minimal 'control requirement' violated; neither defendant was held criminally liable for something over which she or he had no control.

I am not defending the law as it was interpreted and applied in these cases; nor do I deny that a statute could be so worded that it imposed criminal responsibility and liability without requiring the satisfaction of even a minimal control condition. My point is, rather, first, that such a statute would be inherently defective as a criminal statute; but, secondly, what is wrong with such cases as *Larsonneur* and *Winzar* is not that they impose criminal responsibility without control.

When the law defines a criminal offence, it declares that *this*—being found drunk in a public highway, for instance—is something that those bound by the law have good reason to avoid or not to do; and that they may be called to answer for it in a criminal court if they do it or do not avoid it. The retrospective criminal responsibilities that the criminal court seeks to determine are derived from the prospective responsibilities—to avoid being found drunk in a highway, for instance—that the criminal law defines.[9] Now it is a legitimate, and devastating, objection to any ascription of prospective responsibility that the person to whom it is ascribed has no control over the matter in question: if you are to maintain that it is my responsibility, ie that it is up to me, to do *X* or to avoid the occurrence of *Y*, you must be able to rebut any claim that it is not within my power to do *X* or to avoid the occurrence of *Y*. That is why, first, a law that imposed criminal responsibility without even a minimal control requirement would be inherently defective: it would impose prospective responsibilities that the agent lacked the power to discharge.[10] However, secondly, the law's ascriptions of prospective responsibilities must satisfy requirements of reasonableness as well as of possibility. To hold Mr Winzar criminally responsible for being found drunk on a public highway is to hold that the

[8] *Winzar v Chief Constable of Kent, The Times*, 28 Mar 1983; see above, Ch 1 n 2.

[9] On this relationship between prospective and retrospective responsibilities see Ch 1.3 above.

[10] Compare Fuller's requirement, as part of the 'internal morality of law', that the law not make demands that it is not possible for citizens to fulfil (Fuller, 1964: 70–9).

fact that the police might take him onto a highway gave him reason not to get drunk, whilst to hold Ms Larsonneur criminally responsible for being found in the UK is to hold that the fact that the police might take her back to Britain gave her reason to go somewhere other than the Irish Free State. What is objectionable about such holdings is not that they ascribe responsibility in the absence of control, as minimally understood here, but that it is unreasonable to hold such agents thus criminally responsible for the conduct of the police.[11]

The minimal control requirement, by itself, thus does little to limit the potential scope of our responsibility, either prospective or retrospective: the fact that at the time of the event that constituted the completion of the alleged offence (being found on a highway or in the UK) the agent lacked control over its occurrence might create a presumption that she could not properly be held responsible for it; but that presumption can be rebutted by showing that at an earlier time she could have acted in such a way that that event would not have ensued. The question then concerns not the control requirement itself, but whether it would be reasonable to hold that, at that earlier time, she had a prospective responsibility so to act.[12]

There is a further way in which the control requirement sets only very generous limits on the potential scope of criminal responsibility: we have control over far more than the kinds of action (or movement) that are traditionally supposed to be the only proper objects of criminal responsibility; what constrains the scope of our retrospective responsibility is more often the limited scope of our prospective responsibilities in relation to what we could control.

2. What Can We Control?

We exercise control over those bodily movements that are involved in our actions (and over such lack of movement as might be involved in omissions); I will say more about actions and omissions in Chapter 5. We

[11] Another possibility is that Mr Winzar and Ms Larsonneur could be held criminally responsible, but be able to avoid liability by offering a defence—that they were found where they should not have been found only because of the actions of the police. See Ch 10.2–3 below, on strict criminal responsibility..

[12] This provides the answer to the 'time frame' arguments of 'critical' theorists: that once we allow ourselves to look to earlier times at which the agent could have so acted that the criminal event would not occur, we deprive the control requirement (or the related requirement for a 'voluntary act') of any substantive force (see eg Kelman, 1981: 600–5, 618–20, 637–40; Norrie, 2001: 111–20; for a traditional response, see Moore, 1993: 35–7). What can do the substantive work is not the control requirement by itself, but that requirement coupled with a standard of reasonableness in ascriptions of prospective responsibility. Critical theorists will not, of course, find such an appeal to standards of reasonableness reassuring; they will argue that this does nothing to make criminal law rational or principled. We cannot pursue that issue here: see MacCormick, 1990; Duff 1998a.

also have, though we do not typically exercise, control over other bodily movements and processes. My breathing and blinking usually just go on, without my involvement as an agent, but I could control them, to a degree: I can 'at will' hold my breath (for a time) or breathe faster or slower; I can keep my eyes open (for a time), or blink faster or slower. I can also, less directly, control such processes as my digestion or my heart beating: I can act in such a way that, for instance, my heart beats faster or slower, or stops altogether. But of course we have control over, and can be held responsible for, much more than this.

(a) Thoughts, Emotions and Character

We have control over many of our thoughts. Thoughts often come unbidden to my mind, but the content and direction of my thoughts are often up to me; even if I cannot simply decide what to think about, I can try, sometimes successfully, to make myself think about *X*, or not think about *Y* (I set in place reminders of *X*, or hide any reminders of *Y*). We also have some control over our beliefs: although I cannot decide to believe that *p*, I can affect what I come to believe by the way in which I attend, or fail to attend, to the relevant evidence, and so on.[13]

We have some control over our emotions. I cannot feel a particular emotion simply by deciding to do so, but insofar as my emotions are rational, ie structured by or responsive to reasons, they are within my control, in that I can attend to the reasons for or against them: I can arouse my indignation by thinking about the injustice that someone suffered, or calm my anger by attending to the justified character of the action that initially provoked it; I can also adopt more indirect strategies for modifying my emotions, as when I try to avoid situations that might provoke anxiety.[14]

We have some control over the ways in which our characters develop, or do not develop, even if we had no control over their initial formation. We can identify failings and faults in ourselves, and set about trying to correct them—at least sometimes with some hope of at least partial success. This is not a matter of simply deciding to be different and at once making it so; it is rather a matter of finding methods and techniques (including especially the breaking of old habits and the inculcation of new habits) by which one can gradually alter the character and direction of some of one's existing dispositions of thought, feeling and conduct.

13 See B Williams, 1973a; Husak, 1998a: 86–90.

14 See generally B Williams, 1973b; Midgley, 1978; Solomon, 1993; Kahan and Nussbaum, 1996.

We can be held responsible for our thoughts, beliefs, emotions and character traits. My partner might hold me responsible for spending the morning thinking about this book rather than about how to pay my debts. A friend might hold me responsible for believing too readily that she had let me down, or call me to account for my unjustified anger against her. Others might hold me responsible for still being so aggressively bad-tempered, if I could have taken steps to improve that aspect of my character. In all these cases, to be held responsible is to be called to answer for thinking, believing, feeling or being as I had reason not to think, believe, feel or be; if I cannot (or will not) provide a suitably exculpatory answer (or show that those who call me to answer lack the standing to do so), I am liable to be blamed or criticised for that for which I am held responsible.

This is not to say that we can properly be held *criminally* responsible for our thoughts, beliefs, emotions or character traits—only that they can be objects of responsibility in some contexts. We will discuss the scope of criminal responsibility in Chapter 5, but should note here that we cannot rule out criminal responsibility for thoughts, emotions or character traits a priori. On some accounts of criminal attempts, for instance, it is the firm intention to commit a crime for which the offender is really held liable (and responsible); the conduct that attempt liability requires serves simply to provide appropriate evidence of that criminal intention.[15] As for emotions, mere emotion is not criminal, but criminal responsibility can sometimes be grounded partly in the emotions that motivate or are displayed in actions: if my assault on *V* is motivated by hostility towards his racial or religious group, or 'demonstrates' such hostility towards his group, I may be convicted of 'racially or religiously aggravated assault'[16]. Some theorists famously argue that criminal liability should be grounded in the defective character traits that the defendant's criminal conduct revealed, although it is not always clear whether they are portraying character as the object, or only as a condition, of liability.[17] We should not be criminally responsible, we will see, for thoughts, emotions or character

[15] See eg G Williams, 1955; Model Penal Code, Commentary to s 5.01, at 329–31; Husak, 1998a: 86–90. For discussion see Duff, 1996: ch 2.

[16] Crime and Disorder Act 1998, ss 28–29 (as amended by Anti-terrorism, Crime and Security Act 2001, s 39); Simester and Sullivan, 2007: 414–6. Those in the grip of a certain kind of Kantianism might argue that what I can be responsible for is not the hostility (as a 'pathological' emotion) as such, but displaying it in action (as a 'practical' emotion). As we will see in Ch 5, I should indeed be criminally responsible for an emotion only insofar as it is manifested in action: but that reflects constraints on the objects of *criminal* responsibility, not of responsibility as such (and Kant's discussion of pathological love in the *Metaphysics of Morals* shows that his distinction between 'pathological' and 'practical' emotions is more complicated than the *Groundwork of the Metaphysic of Morals* might suggest: see Wood, 2000).

[17] See eg Bayles, 1982; Lacey, 1988: ch 3. For discussion see Duff, 1996: ch 7; Ch 5.7 below.

traits as such: but this is not because we lack the control over them that responsibility requires—nor because we cannot be responsible for them at all.

(b) Intended and Expected Outcomes

We also, of course, have control over the intended and expected outcomes of our actions. Our control is often not complete, in that the success or failure of our action, the occurrence or non-occurrence of its expected side-effects, are often to some degree a matter of luck: but it is a confusion to think that what responsibility requires is a control so complete that *nothing* depends on luck or chance.[18] If I Φ with the intention of bringing *X* about, or realising that *X* will certainly ensue as a side-effect of my action, I have control over *X*'s occurrence in that it depends to a significant degree on me and on what I do; *X* will not ensue if I do not Φ.[19]

Given such control, we can be held responsible for the intended and anticipated outcomes of our actions. If I act with the intention of bringing *X* about, I cannot deny responsibility for its occurrence: I make myself responsible for it, for my action of bringing it about, by acting with that intention. This point is neatly captured by Anscombe's remark that intended actions are those 'to which a certain sense of the question "Why?" is given application', the relevant sense being 'of course that in which the answer, if positive, gives a reason for acting'.[20] To be held responsible for an action is to be called to answer for it—a call that might naturally take the form of asking (in challenging tones, if the action was one I had reason not to do) 'Why did you do that?':[21] if the action of which the question is asked was an intended action, I cannot deny that the

[18] That confusion about the ideas of control and luck, and the relationship between them, infects the familiar argument that criminal responsibility and liability should not depend on the actual outcomes of our actions, since we lack (complete) control over them. For a clear version of that argument see Ashworth, 1987; for criticism see Duff, 1996: ch 12; Moore, 1997: ch 5.

[19] There are of course cases of over-determination in which *X* will occur even if I do not Φ: I start a fire that I realise will burn down my neighbour's house; someone else has started a similar fire that would have the same effect (on the problems that such cases create for analyses of causation see J Thomson, 1987; Moore, 1997: 349–51). I do not then have control over whether the house burns down; but I still have control over whether I burn it down, ie whether it burns down as a result of my action. There are further complications, which we need not pursue here, in cases of multiple agency (whether coordinated or coincidental), when what is at issue is my shared responsibility for the outcome, or my responsibility for my contribution to it.

[20] Anscombe, 1963: 9.

[21] And my concern is only with responsibility for what is in some way untoward—with cases in which I am *held* responsible: see Ch 1.1 above.

question is appropriate, as one that I can and should answer by explaining my reasons for acting thus—unless I can deny that the questioner has the standing to ask it.

Matters are a little more complicated in relation to effects that are foreseen without being (directly) intended—effects that we are certain will ensue, but that form no part of our reason for action. Whatever significance the distinction between intended and foreseen effects might have,[22] the mere fact that an effect was foreseen rather than intended does nothing to negate or reduce the agent's responsibility for it. However, first, the structure of responsibility, the way in which I can answer for what I have done, is now different; secondly, we can sometimes deny responsibility for foreseen effects as we cannot for intended effects.

As to the first point, 'a certain sense of the question "Why?"' is also 'given application' in relation to foreseen side-effects. If I light a fire that burns down your tree, you might call me to answer for it in similar terms, whether I intended to burn your tree or simply foresaw its destruction as a side-effect of my action: 'Why did you do that?'. If I intended to burn it, my (honest) answer will explain my reasons for burning it, by specifying the 'desirability-characteristic', either instrumental or intrinsic, that I took burning your tree to have:[23] that it was blocking my view, for instance, or that I was taking revenge for a wrong you had done me. The intended outcomes of my actions are those that, as I see it, I have reason to pursue, and pursue for those reasons; I answer for them by explaining those reasons (in justificatory, excusatory or confessional tones, depending on whether I now seek to explain them as good, as understandable, or as inadequate reasons); that explanation opens the way to a discussion of whether my reasons were good reasons, as well as of the character and force of the reasons that, at least as you see it, militated against acting thus. If, however, your tree's destruction was simply a foreseen side-effect of an action the intended outcome of which was something else (perhaps my intention was to get rid of my own hedge by burning it, but I realised that the fire would spread to your tree), my answer will take a different form. I will not now explain the desirability-characteristics of burning your tree, since my action is not structured by the thought that there are any; I must rather explain my reasons for starting the fire *despite* the fact that it would destroy your tree. If I am to justify my action and thus avert your condemnation (not to mention conviction for criminal damage), I must argue either that my reasons for starting the fire were strong enough to outweigh the reason against starting it that the destruction of your tree

[22] On the distinction and its significance see further Ch 7.1 below.

[23] On 'desirability-characteristics' see Anscombe, 1963: s 37.

provided; or that at least in this context the admittedly certain destruction of your tree provided no reason against starting the fire.

This latter possibility leads us to the second point about responsibility for foreseen side-effects: that it is possible, and sometimes plausible, to deny such responsibility, given the way in which retrospective responsibility depends on prospective responsibility. Suppose that you planted the tree on my land, despite my warning you that you should not do so. I might now deny that I am responsible to you, that I must answer to you, for its destruction: once I had warned you as I did, I might argue, I had no further (prospective) responsibility for your tree; you planted it at your own risk; the fact that my actions might cause it harm now gives me no reason not to act thus—the effect of my actions on the tree is not something that I need consider as a source of reasons for me to act differently. You might of course disagree, either because you deny that the land is mine, or because you think I still have some responsibility in relation to your tree even if was planted on my land and despite my warnings: but this just shows that the question of whether I am responsible to you for destroying your tree as a side-effect of my action is a normative question, which can be answered only on the basis of some normative account of my prospective responsibilities.

To deny that I am responsible to you for destroying your tree need not be to claim that there is no one to whom I am responsible for that: perhaps I must answer to my partner for thus aggravating our ongoing dispute with you, or to others with a proper interest in the local environment for thus damaging it. Sometimes, however, we can plausibly deny responsibility altogether for untoward events that we know will ensue from our actions; we can deny that we need or should answer to anyone for such events, by denying that we had any prospective responsibility for them. Usually, of course, the fact that harm will ensue to others as a foreseen side-effect of my action gives me some reason not to act thus, which is to say that I have some prospective responsibility to avoid causing such harm: but sometimes we can plausibly deny prospective responsibility in relation to what we still admit to be a harmful or otherwise untoward event—and thus deny retrospective responsibility for bringing it about. Control is thus necessary, but not sufficient, for responsibility: I can admit that it was within my power to determine whether X occurred or not, but deny retrospective responsibility for X when it occurs by denying that I had any prospective responsibility to avert it.

This point was explained and illustrated in Chapter 1.3, but three further illustrations will clarify its significance for the criminal law. Sometimes the denial of responsibility rests upon the fact is that X will occur only in virtue of the actions of others which intervene between my action and the subsequent occurrence of X. If members of a religious group go ahead with a meeting in the knowledge that opponents plan to break it up violently, they foresee a breach of the peace as a side-effect of their action: but they might argue that they should not be held criminally responsible for that breach, or for acting in a way that was liable to cause it.[24] This denial might be expressed in causal terms—it was their opponents' conduct, not theirs, that would cause the breach: but what makes that denial of causation possible is precisely a denial of prospective responsibility. The fact that their opponents would try to break the meeting up might give them prudential reason not to hold it; or moral reason—for instance if they owed it to their families not to expose themselves to danger in this way: but, their argument could plausibly run, it did not give them a reason to which the criminal law should require them to attend, since the law should not require us to see the prospective criminal responses of others as giving us reason not to pursue our own lawful activities. So, too, a shopkeeper who sells glue and crisp packets to customers who will, he knows, use them to sniff glue might deny that he should be held criminally responsible for the danger or harm to which they are then exposed: he should, he might argue, have no criminal responsibility to attend to such effects of his lawful activity as giving him reason to refuse to sell the goods.[25]

My aim here is not to defend such claims about the agents' prospective responsibilities: it is simply to illustrate the point that if we are to hold an agent retrospectively responsible for a foreseen effect of her action, we must be able to claim that she had an appropriate prospective responsibility in relation to such effects, and that such claims are normative claims that might be plausibly contested. Sometimes the existing criminal law provides a clear ruling on such issues, most obviously when it defines an offence in terms of foresight of the relevant effect: if someone enters into 'an arrangement which he knows or suspects facilitates (by whatever means) the acquisition, retention, use or control of criminal property by ... another person', he commits an offence, and will not be heard (by the court) to argue that it was no part of his criminal responsibility, as a citizen or as a bank manager, to attend to such effects of what he did at a client's request;[26] normative debate then focuses on whether the criminal law *should* impose such a responsibility on citizens. Sometimes, however, the normative issue arises in interpreting the law: to decide whether the

[24] See *Beatty v Gillbanks* (1882) 9 QBD 308; G Williams, 1983a: 338–9.

[25] See *Khaliq v H M Advocate* 1984 SLT 137; *Ulhaq v H M Advocate* 1991 SLT 614 (when the court held that it did not matter whether the purchasers were juveniles, as in *Khaliq*, or adults). The question of what responsibilities shopkeepers should have in relation to the crimes that they know or suspect will be facilitated by the goods they sell more usually arises in connection with charges of aiding and abetting (see Duff, 1990b), but in these cases the charges were of endangerment.

[26] Proceeds of Crime Act 2002, s 328; see Ormerod, 2005: 863, and at n 34 below for a qualification to this.

defendants in *Khaliq* and *Ulhaq* were guilty of endangerment, the court had to decide whether shopkeepers should be seen as having such a prospective responsibility for what their customers would do with their purchases.

A second illustration is provided by cases in which the foreseen effect is constituted, or mediated, by the attitudes or sensibilities of others. You might be offended by my behaviour: by my style of dress, by the racist jokes I tell, by my kissing my lover in the street. You might blame me for the offence or distress for which I am, as you see it, thus responsible. Now if I acted with the intention of offending you, I cannot deny responsibility for that offence; but if it was simply a foreseen outcome of my behaviour, there is room for argument. I might argue that yours was an unreasonable reaction to behaviour that was itself reasonable, and 'private' (in the sense that it was not your business), and that the fact that my behaviour would arouse such a response therefore gave me no reason not to engage in it; this would be to argue that I am not retrospectively responsible for your offence since I had no prospective responsibility in relation to it. To settle the issue, we would have to embark on a normative debate about the reasonableness or otherwise of my behaviour and your reaction, and about whether we have any responsibility to attend to the predictably unreasonable reactions of others (I assume that we would in such a debate distinguish racist jokes from dress sense and from public kissing). Again, I have control over the relevant outcomes: I could avoid your distress by not behaving as I do. The question of my responsibility for that distress concerns not control, but the extent of my prospective responsibilities in relation to others' emotional reactions to my behaviour.

That question is sometimes relevant in criminal law. We may be criminally responsible for the effects of our actions on others' feelings—for instance for 'using threatening, abusive or insulting words or behaviour ... within the hearing or sight of a person likely to be caused harassment, alarm or distress thereby'.[27] I am criminally responsible for such 'harassment' even if my conduct was reasonable, since such reasonableness constitutes a 'defence': but the prosecution must first prove that my behaviour was 'threatening, abusive or insulting', which depends not on how others in fact react to it, but on how it would be reasonable for them to react. Someone with deeply racist attitudes might feel threatened by a young black man who approaches him, or insulted if addressed by him in familiar terms, but that does not make the man's behaviour 'threatening' or 'insulting', nor should he be responsible for such effects on racists' sensibilities.[28] *Masterson v Holden* shows the importance of this point. The

[27] Public Order Act 1986, s 5.

[28] Similarly, what makes conduct 'offensive' is not that it in fact offends others, but that they are reasonably offended by it: see Duff and Marshall, 2005: 62–4.

defendant was cuddling his male lover at a bus stop late one night in a manner that upset two passing women: the Court upheld his conviction for using 'insulting words or behaviour … whereby a breach of the peace may be occasioned'.[29] The women were certainly upset, and this might indeed have led to a breach of the peace: but to hold the defendant criminally responsible for that risk of a breach of the peace the court had to hold that his behaviour was 'insulting'—not just that the women felt insulted by it, but that this was a reasonable reaction. The court held just this: Mr Masterson's conduct was 'objectionable'; an observer ('particularly … a young woman') would reasonably think that it 'insults her by suggesting that she is somebody who would find such conduct in public acceptable'.[30] We might disagree with the court, and argue that others should not feel offended or insulted by conduct between lovers of the same sex if they would not find such conduct between heterosexual lovers offensive. That would also be to deny that Mr Masterson should be held criminally responsible for such effects on others: as we might put it, their reactions are their concern rather than his; the fact that he might offend others gave him no reason (or no reason that concerned the criminal law) to refrain from such conduct; he should not have to answer to them, or to his fellow citizens generally, for the way in which he expressed his affection for his lover.[31] This would not be to deny outright that he was responsible for offending others: he might accept, for instance, that he was responsible to his lover for acting in a way that might cause trouble for them. But it would be to deny that he was responsible to the passers by, or to his fellow citizens as such, for such conduct. Here again my aim is not to settle the issue, but to clarify its logic. Mr Masterson probably foresaw that others might react as they did, and certainly had control over that effect, in that he could have avoided it by not cuddling his lover: but that is not enough to make him responsible for it; it also needs to be shown that he had an appropriate prospective responsibility for it.

A third illustration is provided by cases in which an agent's particular role or profession could be argued to limit her responsibilities. One such case was discussed in Chapter 1. If a doctor prescribes contraceptives for a patient who is under 16, knowing that the girl and her partner are more likely to have intercourse if they have this safeguard against pregnancy,

[29] *Masterson v Holden* (1986) 83 Cr App R 302, applying Metropolitan Police Act 1839, s 54.

[30] *Ibid*, at 309, per Glidewell LJ. See also *Parkin v Norman* [1983] 1 QB 92, at 100.

[31] Compare also the case of Stephen Gough, who walked naked from Lands End to John O'Groats, and was arrested, and twice imprisoned, for conduct liable to cause a breach of the peace (*The Guardian*, 4 Oct 2003 and 23 Jan 2004, and *The Independent*, 23 Jan 2004): we have to ask whether he should have been thus held criminally responsible for the foreseeable effect of his conduct on others; and he might deny that he should be, on the ground that it is unreasonable to be upset by mere nudity.

should she be held responsible for facilitating the commission of unlawful sexual intercourse, in which case she could avoid conviction for aiding and abetting only by pleading a defence of necessity? Or can she argue that her responsibilities as a doctor do not include, indeed that they exclude, such admittedly foreseeable effects of her medical activity?[32] That would be to argue that her concern as a doctor should be with her patient's health: her responsibility is to provide medically appropriate treatment, and the fact that the medically appropriate treatment would facilitate the commission of an offence is not something to which she should attend as a reason against providing that treatment; nor therefore should she be called to answer, after the event, for assisting the commission of a crime. Again, what is at issue in determining her retrospective responsibilities here is not her control over, or her foresight of, the outcome in question: she knows that if she prescribes contraceptives the commission of the offence will be easier, and she could avoid thus making it easier by refusing to prescribe them. What is at issue is the scope, and the limits, of her prospective responsibilities as a doctor.[33]

Similarly, the Court of Appeal held that section 328 of the Proceeds of Crime Act 2002 was 'not intended to cover or affect the ordinary conduct of litigation by legal professionals' in 'determin[ing] or secure[ing] legal rights and remedies for their clients'.[34] The lawyer's role, that is to say, limits her prospective responsibilities: she need not attend, as other citizens are required by the criminal law to attend, to the possibility that her professional activities will facilitate another's 'acquisition, retention, use or control of criminal property'.

(c) Risks, Foreseen and Unforeseen

I have been talking so far about effects of an action which are either intended or foreseen as (virtually) certain; but similar points apply to effects which are foreseen as being likely or possible rather than certain. The minimal 'control' condition that is, I have argued, required for responsibility is satisfied: if I act in a way that, as I know, creates a risk of harm, I could have avoided creating that risk, and avoided causing that

[32] See *Gillick v West Norfolk and Wisbech Area Health Authority* [1986] AC 112; above, Ch 1 at nn 35–6.

[33] Similarly, if a doctor withdraws treatment that would prolong a patient's life, at the patient's request or (if he is irreversibly comatose) because it will not benefit him, she could argue that she is not responsible for the patient's death (which is foreseeable and within her control), because it is not a factor to which, in this context, she should attend as a reason against withdrawing treatment. Her responsibility is to give treatment only with the patient's consent, or only when it is in the patient's interests.

[34] *Bowman v Fels* [2005] 1 WLR 3083, paras 83–84; see at n 26 above.

harm, by not acting thus.[35] This is not to say that I am responsible for all such foreseen and avoidable risks. I am responsible for (and only for) those that I had reason not to create (those in relation to which I had a suitable prospective responsibility), and for the creation of which I must answer to someone; and I am in the same way responsible for the harm that ensues if the risk is actualised. If, however, I can claim that the risk is not my business, not something to which I should attend in deciding how to act, I can deny that I am responsible, answerable, for its creation or for the harm if it is actualised. Thus although I know that if the shop I plan to open does well, it is likely that your competing shop will lose business, I might deny that I must answer for that risk, or for your loss if the risk is actualised: as I understand the market economy, the possible effect of my lawful actions on competitors is not something to which I need attend; the risk to you is not my business, and I therefore deny that I am responsible to you for its creation. (Others might take a different view; there is plenty of room for normative disagreement about the responsibilities of players in a market economy.) If I persist with a diet that endangers my health, I must answer for that to my family, perhaps to my friends, perhaps to my doctor (and certainly to myself); but if a stranger who saw me start on my third doughnut challenged me, I would reply that it was none of her business.

When I am responsible for knowingly creating a risk, I will properly be criticised for creating it recklessly, and for causing the harm if the risk is actualised, unless I can defend myself by showing that I acted reasonably.[36] I might be blamed less harshly than I would have been had I caused the harm deliberately or knowingly; but that is a matter of culpability, ie of liability, rather than of responsibility.

Nor does the fact that I did not notice the risk I was creating, or foresee the harm I might cause, necessarily negate my responsibility for creating the risk or for causing the harm if it eventuates. Whether or not I can sometimes be held to have been reckless of a risk that I was not aware of taking or creating,[37] I can be held to have been negligent in taking or creating it, which is also to hold me responsible both for taking the risk and for the harm if it eventuates. Some theorists have notoriously argued that criminal liability for negligence, whilst it might be useful, cannot be

[35] I might not have been able to avoid the occurrence of the harm, but could have avoided causing it by that action: see n 19 above.

[36] As we will see in Ch 10, there is an important difference here between moral and criminal responsibility: I am morally responsible for creating a risk even if I acted reasonably in doing so (reasonableness constitutes a defence); but I am in many cases criminally responsible only for creating an unreasonable risk.

[37] A discussion on which we need not embark here: see Duff, 1990a: ch 7; Simester and Sullivan, 2007: 135–8.

just, since negligence is not a species of fault;[38] one motivation for such arguments might be the idea that I lack control over that of which I am unaware—in which case I cannot legitimately be held responsible for it.[39] But, as critics of such arguments have pointed out, this is simply wrong: I can be held responsible and be blamed for risks that I negligently create and for harm that I negligently cause, so long as I could have avoided that risk (and thus avoided causing that harm) by taking precautions (including paying attention) that I could and should have taken.[40]

The more important point to notice here, however, is that a denial of negligence is often, at least in moral contexts, a denial not of responsibility but of liability. If I have created a risk of harm, or actually caused the harm, I might be accused of carelessness or negligence. Now I might of course want to rebut that accusation, and would typically do so by insisting that I did take all due care, and paid as much attention to what I was doing and its possible effects as it would be reasonable to expect me to pay. I *could* have taken more care, I implicitly agree, or paid more attention; it was within my power to avoid creating that risk or causing that harm: but I acted reasonably in not taking more care or paying more attention—which is to say that I was justified in taking no more care and paying no more attention than I did, and therefore should be excused from blame or liability for creating the risk or causing the harm.[41] As we have seen, however, justifications and excuses constitute defences that admit responsibility, whilst denying liability.

This suggests that I can be held responsible not only for the risks that I knowingly create, and for harms that I realised I might cause, but also for risks that I take inadvertently, and for harms that I thereby inadvertently cause. Such risks and harms are still within my control, in the minimal sense that I have argued is required for responsibility: for I could have noticed, and averted, the risk (and thus avoided causing the harm), by paying more attention and by acting differently. What makes it unjust to hold me liable to blame, conviction or punishment for creating such risks or causing such harm is not that I cannot be held responsible for them, but that if I did take all due care I have a defence to the charge of negligence.[42]

[38] See eg G Williams, 1961: 122–4; Hall, 1963.

[39] See Hart, 1968b: 149–52, discussing Turner, 1945.

[40] See Hart, 1968b; Simester, 2000. See also Moore, 1990, and 1997: 411–9, 588–92: in the earlier article, he argued against liability grounded in negligence on the basis of a 'choice' theory of criminal liability; in the later, revised, version, he accepts that negligence can be portrayed as involving a distinctive and lesser kind of culpability—'the culpability of unexercised capacity' (1997: 591).

[41] Which is not to say that I could not be properly held liable to pay for the harm if it can be repaired: see above, at the beginning of Ch 1.1.

[42] Again (see n 36 above) there is a difference between moral and criminal responsibility here; as we will see, I am typically held criminally responsible only for *negligent* risk-creation.

The argument of this section so far is meant to suggest that the 'control' requirement sets only very weak limits on the possible scope of our responsibility; more limit-setting is done by normative constraints on our prospective responsibilities than by a 'control' requirement. I can be responsible for risks that my conduct actually creates, and for the harm that ensues if a risk is actualised, even if I am unaware of the risk. The 'control' requirement is still satisfied, in that it was within my power not to create that risk or to cause that harm, since it was within my power to act differently; since this is true of omissions as well as of actions, I can—as far as the 'control' requirement is concerned—be responsible not only for risks and harms that I actively create or cause, but also for those that I could but do not prevent. What the 'control' requirement therefore amounts to is only a requirement of agency—that I was active as an agent in causing the relevant outcome, and that I had the capacity to act in a way that would have prevented it. That capacity to act differently requires the physical capacities for control over one's movements (and the opportunity to exercise those capacities) in the absence of which one's movements (or lack of movement) are involuntary: if I fall onto you, causing you some injury, I can deny responsibility by pointing out that I suffered a fit, or was blown over by a sudden gale, or was thrown onto you by someone much stronger than me. The capacity to act differently also requires, if it is to ground responsibility, the rational capacities that, as we saw in Chapter 2.1, are necessary for responsible agency: if I am incapable of recognising and responding to reasons for action, I lack the control over my conduct that responsibility requires. So long as I have such rational capacities, however, and have and can exercise the requisite physical capacities, the control requirement for responsibility is satisfied.

But, many will argue, there is more to responsibility than 'control' as minimally specified here: there is also an epistemic condition of responsibility, which I have so far ignored.

3. The 'Epistemic Condition': A Condition of Responsibility or of Liability?

I suggested in the previous section that I can be held responsible for unforeseen effects of my actions, or for risks that I inadvertently create, even when I was not negligent or otherwise at fault in bringing those effects about or in creating those risks. But, it might be objected, this is to

But in moral contexts negligence is typically a condition of liability, not responsibility, and the reasons for making it a condition of criminal responsibility do not have to do with the control requirement: see Ch 10.1 below.

ignore a further necessary condition of responsibility—an epistemic condition. We can be held responsible for risks or consequences that we did not in fact foresee: responsibility does not require actual knowledge. But we surely cannot properly be held responsible for risks of consequences that we could not have foreseen, or could not reasonably have been expected to foresee: as Aristotle pointed out, 'voluntariness' is negated both by compulsion and by non-culpable ignorance.[43] It might indeed be tempting to see the epistemic condition as part of the control condition, since I can exercise control over *X* only if I know that I can do so: perhaps I could open this locked door by pressing a concealed button; but if I do not know this, and could not find it out, I cannot exercise control over whether the door opens. It is, however, better to distinguish the control condition from the epistemic condition: partly because, for the sake of analytical clarity, we should distinguish the question of whether *X* was within my control from the question of whether I had the opportunity to exercise that control;[44] partly because, as I will argue, the epistemic condition is a necessary condition of liability, not of responsibility.

The failure of the epistemic condition does render blame unjustified. If you accuse me of damaging your property, I can rebut the accusation and avert blame by showing that I did not realise and could not have been expected to realise that what I was doing might damage your property. But this shows only that the failure of the epistemic condition negates liability: we still need to know whether it does so by negating responsibility, or by blocking the transition from responsibility to liability. It can be used as a condition of responsibility: indeed, we will see in Chapter 10 that it often functions as a condition of criminal responsibility. But it is not a general necessary condition of responsibility in the way that the control condition is: we can legitimately be held responsible when the epistemic condition is not satisfied—this is indeed what typically happens in moral contexts.

I knock over your treasured vase, which breaks. This was, let us suppose, an accident in which I was in no way at fault: the vase was just behind the door that I opened, and I had no reason to believe that it had been moved there; or the doorknob unexpectedly fell off onto the vase as I opened the door. Nonetheless, when we see what has happened, you might properly hold me responsible for breaking the vase, and I should accept that responsibility. To see that and why this is so, consider three points.

First, I should apologise for breaking your vase. I should express not just the regret that a concerned observer might express, that your vase has been broken (a regret that could be the same whether the vase was broken

[43] *Nicomachean Ethics* III.1; see also Fischer and Ravizza, 1998: 12–13; Zimmerman, 1988: 74–91; Feinberg, 1986: 269–315; Ginet, 2000.

[44] If I find out that something is within my control, that discovery does not *bring* it within my control: rather, it gives me the opportunity to exercise the control that I already had.

by human agency or by natural causes), but the apologetic regret that an agent expresses at and for the harm he has done;[45] and such apologetic regret admits responsibility. You would be rightly annoyed if I simply denied responsibility for the damage, and expressed only a spectator's regret.

Secondly, a natural way to fill out my apology would be to explain how I came to break the vase, which would (in this case) involve explaining how it was not a matter of negligence. Or if you say, in challenging tones that accuse me of breaking you vase, 'Look what you did!', a proper response would not be to deny that I broke it, or to claim that I do not have to answer to you for breaking it. I should instead recognise that you have the right to call me to answer for breaking your vase, and offer the exculpatory answer that I have: that I was taking all due care (which is to say that it would have been unreasonable to expect me to take the kind of care that would have averted the harm), and broke the vase through non-culpable accident. But such explanations, such answers, admit responsibility: they mark an acceptance that I should answer to you, as the vase's owner, for what I have done; rather than denying responsibility, they seek to block the transition from responsibility to liability.[46]

Thirdly, what makes the apology necessary, what underpins the ascription and acceptance of responsibility, is that I did what I in fact had good reason not to do: the fact that my action (opening the door) would cause such damage constituted a good reason not to act thus. I did not realise that I had that reason, just as one who mistakenly believes a glass of petrol to be a glass of gin does not realise that she has reason not to drink from it;[47] but that I have reason to Φ does not depend on my knowledge of the facts that constitute or generate that reason. If I realise, as I open the door, that your vase is just behind it, I do not acquire a new reason for action (a reason to open the door less far or less fast) that I lacked before; I become aware of the reason that already existed.[48] Now responsibility is tied to reasons: I am responsible, and must answer, for acting as I had reason not to act—for not responding appropriately to the reasons that bore on my

[45] On agent regret see B Williams, 1981a: 27–31.

[46] Liability, that is, to criticism or blame; I might nonetheless recognise a moral liability to pay for the vase to be repaired or replaced (if it is not covered by your insurance).

[47] See B Williams, 1981b: 102–3.

[48] This is not to claim that reasons for action are 'external' rather than 'internal', ie that I can have reason to act even if the action has no appropriate relationship to my existing motivational set (see Williams, 1981b; for a good critical discussion see Dancy, 2000). Although the criminal law, as I will portray it, does appeal to external reasons, that is not what is at stake here: as Williams himself argues, in arguing that agents can be mistaken about the reasons for action that they have (1981b: 102–3), even if the truth of '*A* has reason to Φ' depends on a suitable relationship between Φ-ing and her existing motivational set, it does not depend on her knowledge of that relationship or of the facts in virtue of which it obtains.

action. I am therefore responsible for breaking your vase, though I can offer an explanation of why I did not respond to that reason which saves me from being blamed.

To say that I am morally (retrospectively) responsible for breaking your vase is to assume that I had a prospective responsibility not to break it; but surely, it might be argued, that is not plausible. I do indeed have a responsibility to exercise due care as I go about in the world: to pay due attention to what I am doing, to take suitable precautions against causing harm. But it would be absurd to say that my responsibility is not to cause harm *tout court*, if only because that would be a responsibility that I could not discharge and could not reasonably be expected to discharge. Consider a more extreme case of a kind loved by philosophers. Unknown to me, due to some electrical malfunction, flicking this light switch will cause a major explosion; I flick the switch to turn on the light, and so cause the explosion which kills someone. Suppose too that, given the nature of the malfunction and my lack of expertise, even if I had checked the switch (from, as it would have seemed at the time, a bizarrely over-cautious anxiety), I would not have been able to detect the malfunction. Should we not agree, not just that I am not to blame (not liable) for the death that I cause, but that I am not responsible for it, in any sense other than the causal sense of 'responsible' that has no implications for answerability?

But yet—surely I owe it to others, most obviously to the victim's family, to explain how I came to cause his death; and, whilst my explanation averts liability, it admits responsibility, in that it admits that I must answer to them for causing his death. For it is still true that I acted as I in fact had good reason not to act—that I flicked the switch when I should not have done so, even though, tragically, I did not realise that fact and could not have been expected to do so. If someone better informed than me had told me about the malfunction just as I was about to flick the switch, I would not have acquired a new reason not to flick the switch that I did not already have (although I would have acquired a new reason to believe that I had reason not to flick it);[49] I would rather have become aware of the reason that already existed.

The implication of the argument of this section is that I am strictly morally responsible—that is, I am responsible even if I am not at fault—for the harm that my actions actually cause, even if I did not realise and could not reasonably have been expected to realise that I might cause such harm.[50] We should note, however, that moral responsibility is not typically

[49] This distinction between having reason to act and having reason to believe that I have reason to act will be important later: see below, Ch 11.3.

[50] On strict responsibility see further Ch 10 below. My argument has obvious affinities with Honoré's defence of strict responsibility as something distinct from strict liability (Honoré, 1988). However (though I cannot pursue this here), his arguments for strict

taken to be thus generally strict for harms that we do not prevent. We are often responsible for such harms, and that responsibility can be strict if the relationship that grounds it is suitably close or demanding. A parent whose child is harmed because he did not see that she was in danger, a doctor whose patient is harmed because she does not spot the symptoms of an illness, may be held strictly responsible for those failures: they may have to answer for them, even if the answer they can give is wholly exculpatory—that they took all the care that they could have reasonably been expected to take. Generally, however, we suppose that our responsibilities to prevent harm are conditional on the harm being one of which we are, or could and should be, easily aware. If I walk by a person who is obviously in serious danger or distress, and whom I could easily help at little cost to myself, I am responsible for what now counts as my failure to help him, and must answer for that failure—although my answer might exculpate me if I can offer some justification or excuse. But if, unknown to me, someone is drowning in a river nearby and I could in fact reach him and save him, we do not suppose that I am responsible either for a failure to save him or for his death: for we do not suppose that my prospective responsibilities to prevent others from suffering harm are so extensive as to cover harms of which I could not reasonably be expected to be aware.

The extent of our general responsibilities (those that are not tied to such specific roles as parent or doctor) to prevent harm to others is, of course, a matter of continuing controversy. One model is provided by the good Samaritan, who happened to come across the man who had fallen among thieves and put himself to some cost and trouble to help him.[51] But we may now disagree about whether our responsibilities are merely to respond to those needs that we happen across, or also to look for those who might need our help (although, thanks to modern media and communications, we also 'happen across' very many more people who desperately need help and whom we could help than the Samaritan did); and strict consequentialists who deny that there is any significant moral difference between causing harm and not preventing harm that it is within one's power to prevent must thus hold that our prospective responsibilities to prevent harm are in principle just as extensive and stringent as are our responsibilities not to cause harm.[52] We need not pursue this issue here (though I

responsibility—that we will, on balance, benefit from a system that gives us credit when our actions luckily turn out well, though we also suffer discredit when they unluckily turn out badly; and that our very identities as agents depend on such strict responsibility—seem to me less plausible than the idea of strict responsibility itself; and he makes the transition from strict responsibility to strict criminal liability rather too easy.

[51] See St Luke's Gospel, x: 30–37: there is no suggestion that the Samaritan went out looking for people who might need his help; he simply responded to the person in need whom he happened to find by the road.

[52] See B Williams, 1973c: 93–100 on 'negative responsibility'; also Casey, 1971.

will say a little more about acts and omissions in Chapter 5.6); what matters for present purposes is that whilst, I have argued, moral responsibility for our actions and their effects is usually ascribed strictly, the epistemic condition being a condition of liability rather than of responsibility, moral responsibility need not be thus strict in relation to harms that we do not prevent. The key point remains that while a modest control condition is a general, necessary requirement for responsibility, there is no such general, necessary epistemic condition for responsibility: for some purposes and in some contexts an epistemic condition might be a condition of responsibility, but in other contexts it functions rather as a condition of liability.

The upshot of this chapter is therefore that there are only very weak general constraints on the possible objects of responsibility—on what we can be held responsible for. We are properly held responsible only for what is within our control: but once we interpret the idea of control in a way that allows us to be held responsible for the effects of our negligent actions, we must realise that it allows us to be held responsible for *all* the actual effects of our actions, since in moral contexts lack of negligence negates not responsibility, but liability. As for the epistemic condition, I have argued that it does not set a general or necessary limit on responsibility: it is often a condition, not of responsibility, but of liability.

There are further limits on the scope of our retrospective responsibilities, but these are set by our prospective responsibilities, within the generous limits that the control condition sets. Given the diversity of types of prospective responsibility, tied as they are to the diverse roles that we play, the diverse practices within which and the diverse descriptions under which we have responsibilities, we cannot hope to offer a more determinate *general* account of what we can or should be held retrospectively responsible for; we have instead to ask what we can be held responsible for as this or that, within this or that particular role or practice.

Since this book is concerned with criminal responsibility, we must therefore ask what we can properly be held criminally responsible for: for what (given the argument of Chapter 2) should we be answerable to our fellow citizens, through a criminal process that convicts and punishes us if we cannot offer an adequately exculpatory answer? That is the question to which we must now turn.

4

Criminally Responsible For What? (1) Crimes as Wrongs

1. Preliminaries

We have seen that two supposed general constraints on the objects of responsibility are less constraining than many suppose. A control requirement is a condition of responsibility—we are responsible only for what lies within our control; but this allows us to be held responsible for any outcome of our actions. An epistemic condition concerning what we knew or could reasonably have known sets closer limits, but is not a general condition of responsibility: we can be held responsible even for unforeseen and unforeseeable outcomes of our actions.

The scope of our retrospective responsibilities is of course in practice not as wide as this: but their scope is limited less by the control or epistemic conditions than by the scope of our prospective responsibilities, since they determine our retrospective responsibilities. We have such prospective responsibilities as inhabitants of particular roles, as satisfiers of particular normatively significant descriptions, as participants in specific practices: we therefore cannot offer a *general* account of the objects of responsibility. We can ask what we are responsible for in this or that practice, as fitting this or that description, to this or that institution or group; but we cannot ask what we are responsible for *tout court*.

Our concern here is with criminal responsibility, and I have argued that we are criminally responsible as citizens to our fellow citizens. That argument points us in the right direction, but does not take us far towards an account of criminal responsibility: however we define our civic responsibilities, they reach well beyond the matters for which we can plausibly be held criminally responsible. To make further progress, we must engage with two familiar debates that converge on this question about the objects of criminal responsibility. One focuses on the criminal agent, and on the aspects of the agent that could ground criminal responsibility: it is exemplified by debates between 'choice', 'character' and 'action' theorists—can we ground criminal responsibility in the choices we make, or in the character traits our conduct displays, or in our actions?[1] The other focuses on the impact of the agent's conduct on the social world in which he acts, and is exemplified by the debates surrounding the Harm Principle and legal moralism: can we determine the proper scope of the criminal law by appealing to principles that require us to criminalise (only) conduct that is harmful, or wrongful?[2] Though these two debates are often conducted separately, they concern the same general question: for what can we properly be called to answer as citizens, by our fellow citizens, through a criminal process that convicts and punishes us if we cannot offer an adequately exculpatory answer?

I begin (in this chapter) with an aspect of the second debate, arguing that wrongfulness is not just a necessary condition of criminalisation, but its proper focus: we should criminalise wrongful conduct because it is wrongful. However, as we saw in Chapter 2, we still need an account of the kinds of wrong that can properly concern the criminal law. I therefore turn (in Chapter 5) to the first debate, to argue that we can make plausible sense of the claim that the criminal law should focus on wrongful *action*: it is primarily for our actions (rather than for our choices or character traits, for instance) that we should be criminally responsible. But this is still too wide: many kinds of wrongful action are not even in principle apt candidates for criminalisation. We must therefore return (in Chapter 6) to the second debate, to discuss harm and other possible foci of criminal responsibility: I will argue that, whilst we should not hope to establish any neat set of determinate criteria to guide decisions about criminalisation, we can clarify the questions that must be asked and answered in debates about criminalisation by focusing on the familiar but unclear idea that crimes are 'public' wrongs.[3]

Throughout this discussion, I should note, my concern is only with the question of what we have, *in principle*, good reason to criminalise: that is, with the first of the three 'filters' that Schonsheck identifies on the route to criminalisation.[4] What passes the first filter must pass two others before it may be criminalised, but I am not concerned here with the questions that those further filters ask—questions about countervailing reasons against criminalisation, and about the practicality of criminalisation. My aim is only to get clear about the first filter: about the kinds of consideration that provide good reasons for criminalisation.

[1] For a useful overview of these debates see Wilson, 2002: 332–56; also Horder, 1993; Moore, 1997: ch 13.

[2] The classic formulations of the Harm Principle are Mill, 1859, and Feinberg, 1984. For legal moralism see Moore, 1997, especially at 68–75; also Feinberg, 1988.

[3] See, classically, Blackstone, 1765–9: Book IV, ch 1 (see above, Ch 2 at nn 38–40); see Lieberman, 2002.

[4] Schonsheck, 1994—an unjustly neglected book.

2. Crimes as Wrongs

Within the weak constraints set by the general conditions of responsibility, for what can we properly be held *criminally* responsible? We can begin with the familiar, intuitively plausible thought that crimes should be moral wrongs. That thought is implicitly assumed in debates about criminalisation: it is an obviously relevant objection to a proposed criminal statute that the conduct it criminalises is not wrongful. Indeed, it might be tempting to argue that this marks a necessary connection between law and morality: criminal law must at least claim to define as criminal only conduct that is morally wrong;[5] but we need not pursue that argument here.

This is, after all, what distinguishes criminal punishment from other measures. Criminal convictions and punishments do not merely penalise; they condemn. A tax may be intended to discourage the conduct taxed, but it does not condemn that conduct; a fine, by contrast, when imposed as a punishment, condemns the conduct as wrongful.[6] A system of 'administrative regulations', like the German system of *Ordnungswidrigkeiten*, attaches penalties to breaches of the regulations—penalties designed to discourage disobedience. What distinguishes it from a system of criminal law and criminal punishments is that it does not condemn the conduct it penalises as wrongful, or those who engage in such conduct as wrongdoers; they have simply broken the rules and must pay the appropriate penalty.[7] Many citizens might in fact see the criminal law, or some of its offence definitions, in this light—as regulations which they may have prudential reason to obey, but which have no moral claim on them. Such a view is sometimes reasonable, when the law lacks the moral authority that it claims to define criminal wrongs and to call those who commit them to account:[8] but what is distinctive of criminal law is still that it purports to define, and provide for the condemnation of, certain kinds of moral wrong; to justify the criminal law's content we must therefore show that what it defines as crimes are indeed wrongs of the appropriate kind.

That is why some abolitionist theorists object not just to criminal punishment, but to the criminal law itself: they object not to law as such,

[5] Compare Raz, 1979, on the normative claims that law must make (see Duff, 1986: ch 3); also Finkelstein, 2000; and Husak, 2005b: 70–2 on the connection between this thought and negative retributivism.

[6] Compare Hart, 1968a: 6–7, on taxation; Feinberg, 1970a, on the difference between penalty and punishment.

[7] On *Ordnungswidrigkeiten* see Weigend, 1988. (But the European Court of Human Rights has held that *Ordnungswidrigkeiten* are in substance criminal: *Öztürk v Germany* (1984) 6 EHRR 409.)

[8] See further Ch 8 below.

but to any law that claims the authority to define and condemn wrongdoing; they urge us to focus on harms and their repair, rather than on wrongs and their punishment.[9] Their objections may not be persuasive, and I will argue shortly that we do have good reason to preserve a legal institution that focuses in this way on wrongdoing; but they are right to see this as a defining feature of the criminal law.

An obvious response to the claim that crimes must be, or be portrayed as, moral wrongs is that whilst it may fit the familiar range of '*mala in se*', crimes consisting in conduct that is held to be morally wrong prior to its criminalisation, it cannot fit a much larger category of contemporary offences—that of '*mala prohibita*', consisting in conduct that is not (and is not portrayed as being) morally wrongful prior to its legal regulation. This is a serious challenge: if the conduct that constitutes *mala prohibita* is not even alleged to be morally wrongful, then we must either abandon that claim or condemn as unjustified large swathes of existing law.[10] I will show shortly how that challenge can be met in a way that enables us to justify some *mala prohibita*, and to clarify the distinction between *mala in se* and *mala prohibita*. First, however, we must clarify the role that wrongfulness can play as a criterion of criminalisation.

3. Moral Wrongfulness as Condition or as Object of Criminal Responsibility?

We must distinguish the *intentional objects* from the *conditions* of responsibility.[11] When I am held responsible, there is something for which I am held responsible. Within any practice of responsibility-ascription there are also conditions of responsibility, which must be satisfied if the ascription is to be justified, but which are not part of that for which the person is held responsible. It is a condition of being criminally responsible for any crime that I was not at the time of the crime, and am not now, disordered in a way that undermined my capacity to be guided by reasons or to answer for my actions: but I am not held criminally responsible *for* not being thus disordered.[12] If it is argued that criminal responsibility is grounded in 'choice', or in 'character', we must therefore ask whether that ground is taken to constitute the object, or a condition, of responsibility. Are we to be criminally responsible for our criminal choices, or for our defective character traits? Or are we to be held responsible for something else, for

[9] Eg Christie, 1977; Hulsman, 1986; Bianchi, 1994; Walgrave, 2001; for discussion see von Hirsch *et al*, 2003.

[10] See especially Husak 2005b.

[11] See Horder, 1993: 204–6; Husak, 1998a: 67–73; Duff, 2002b: 155–60. The distinction is analogous to Dancy's distinction between 'reasons' and 'enablers': Dancy, 2004: 38–52.

[12] See Ch 2.1 above.

instance for a criminal action, on condition that we chose to act thus, or on condition that the action flowed from a defective character trait? Likewise, if it is said that criminalisation must be grounded in harm, or in wrongfulness, we must ask whether the harm or the wrongfulness is the object or a condition of criminal responsibility: are we to be criminally responsible for the harm or wrong that we do; or are we to be responsible for something else, on condition that our conduct is harmful or wrongful? The former would give us a 'positive' version of the Harm Principle or of legal moralism, making harmfulness or wrongfulness the primary reason for criminalising the conduct. The latter would give us a 'negative' version of the Harm Principle or of legal moralism: harmfulness or wrongfulness would be only a necessary condition of criminalisation, the positive reasons for which would lie elsewhere.[13]

One way to interpret the idea that crimes should be moral wrongs is to make wrongness a condition of justified criminalisation. The positive reasons to criminalise a particular kind of conduct lie not in its wrongfulness, but elsewhere—for instance in its harmfulness; but justice requires that we criminalise harmful conduct only if it is also morally wrongful—else we will convict and punish those who have done no wrong, which would be unjust. On this reading the wrongfulness of the conduct does not give us reason to criminalise it (just as, for negative retributivists, the offender's desert does not give us reason to punish him); it rather removes what would otherwise have been a moral obstacle to criminalisation.

This is one way to read Feinberg's version of the Harm Principle. What properly grounds criminalisation, Feinberg argues, is not simply '$harm_1$' (any setback to interests), but '$harm_2$', a setback to interests which also wrongs those whose interests are set back.[14] One could read this as positing a unitary notion of $harm_2$ as the intentional object of criminal responsibility, and the positive ground of criminalisation: what the criminal law should focus on, what we have reason to criminalise, is wrongfully harmful conduct; we are criminally responsible for such conduct *because* it is wrongfully harmful. One could instead, however, take the positive justifying aim of criminalisation to be to prevent $harm_1$—the kind of 'harmed condition' that is conceptually 'fundamental', and that we can hope to analyse 'without mentioning causally contributory actions'.[15] The criminal law can prevent $harm_1$ by criminalising conduct that causes or

[13] Compare the distinction between the 'positive' retributivist thesis that guilt provides a central justifying reason for punishment, and the 'negative' retributivist thesis that guilt is a necessary condition of justified punishment, the positive 'justifying aim' of which lies elsewhere: see Dolinko, 1991: 539–43; Hart, 1968a.

[14] See Feinberg, 1984: 31–6; 1988: xxvii–xxix.

[15] Feinberg 1984: 31.

might cause it, but a side constraint of justice on our pursuit of that preventive aim is that we should criminalise only conduct that is also wrongful.[16]

Legal moralism provides a more ambitious interpretation of the idea that crimes should be moral wrongs. If, as Moore claims, the function of criminal law is 'is to attain retributive justice ... [by] punish[ing] all and only those who are morally culpable in the doing of some morally wrongful action', moral wrongdoing constitutes the intentional object of criminal responsibility and the positive ground for criminalisation:[17] we should criminalise conduct because it is morally wrongful, and be held criminally responsible for such wrongful conduct. Another type of legal moralism is found in ambitious forms of 'virtue jurisprudence'. If 'the aim of the law is to make citizens virtuous',[18] or 'to promote the greater good of humanity ... by promoting virtue',[19] then vice, or conduct that displays vice, should be the primary ground of criminalisation and the object of criminal responsibility. What identifies a legal moralist is thus not the claim that moral wrongfulness is a necessary condition of criminalisation and criminal responsibility (even Feinberg believes that), but the claim that moral wrongfulness is a good reason for criminalisation.[20] One could interpret this in consequentialist terms: the, or an, aim of the criminal law is to prevent such immorality, by criminalising and punishing it.[21] I will argue, however, that Moore is right to this extent: the primary reason for criminalising immorality of the appropriate kind is not to prevent it, but precisely to ensure that those who commit it are called to answer for it in a criminal court, and punished for it if they have no adequately exculpatory answer.

How could legal moralism, as thus interpreted, be consistent with the basic principles of a liberal society? Whilst Stephen (who made no claim to be a liberal) might have been happy to criminalise conduct precisely in

[16] This kind of side-constrained consequentialist structure is familiar in penal theory: see eg Scheid, 1997.

[17] Moore, 1997: 33–5; see above, Ch 2.2(b). On Moore's account, only moral wrong*doing* is even in principle apt for criminalisation (see Ch 5 below). See also Stephen 1873/1967: 152—criminal law was 'in the nature of a persecution of the grosser forms of vice', in order to gratify 'in a regular public and legal manner' the 'feeling of hatred—call it revenge, resentment or what you will—which the contemplation of such conduct excites in healthily constituted minds'.

[18] Solum, 2003: 181.

[19] Huigens, 1995: 1425 (compare too theories that portray punishment as moral education—eg Morris, 1981; Hampton, 1984). For criticism see Duff, 2002b.

[20] Compare Feinberg's initial definition of legal moralism ('in the usual narrow sense'): '[i]t can be morally legitimate to prohibit conduct on the ground that it is inherently immoral, even though it causes neither harm nor offense to the actor or to others': 1984: 27; 1988: xix–xx.

[21] Feinberg later (1988: 324) amends his initial definition of legal moralism into such a preventive mould.

order to ensure that it suffered punishment, contemporary liberals are more likely to accept Walker's principle that 'prohibitions should not be included in the criminal law for the sole purpose of ensuring that breaches of them are visited with retributive punishment'.[22] Walker offered this principle as part of a critique of retributivism, but even retributivists might accept it. It is one thing to argue, as retributivists do, that once we have a criminal law which defines certain kinds of conduct as wrong, those who commit such wrongs should be punished because they deserve it, but quite another to argue that we should define such conduct as criminal precisely to ensure that those who engage in it are punished; that might seem to express the kind of vindictive hatred of which retributivists are often accused by their critics.

Walker is right about 'prohibitions'. To 'prohibit' conduct is to *make* it wrong within the practice in which the prohibition operates; its wrongfulness consists in disobedience to that prohibition. But if that is what prohibition involves, it would be oppressively cruel to prohibit conduct simply in order to punish those who engage in it. Walker is not, however, right about the criminal law. I will argue later that his principle does not apply even to '*mala prohibita*', but will first show why it does not apply to '*mala in se*', since we should not see the criminal law's definitions of *mala in se* as 'prohibitions'.

The idea that the criminal law prohibits the actions it defines as criminal fits a positivist portrayal of law as a sovereign's commands:[23] a command not to Φ amounts to a prohibition on Φ-ing. On this view, the criminal law gives us new reasons for action: whatever reasons we already had to refrain from what the law defines as murder, rape or theft, its prohibitions give us further reason to refrain. That reason is content-independent: it lies not in the nature of the prohibited conduct viewed independently of the prohibition (for the prohibition would then add nothing), but in the fact that the conduct is prohibited by a law that claims authority over us. Nor, if the law is to have normative force, can that further reason consist *solely* in the sanctions threatened against those who disobey: for those sanctions must be justified by the offender's disobedience of a prohibition that he already, independently of the sanction, had reason to obey.[24] Now it is worth noting how odd it would be for a person to refrain from murder, not because she saw it to be wrongful independently of the criminal law, but from respect for the law that criminalises it:[25] what kind of person would

[22] Walker, 1969: 26, and 1980: 5; see Duff, 2002c.

[23] See Ch 2.2(a) above.

[24] Compare Hart 1994: 20: 'though it may be combined with threats of harm a command is primarily an appeal not to fear but to respect for authority' (and see 82–91 on being obligated and being obliged).

[25] See Raz, 1994: 343–4.

be willing, independently of the law, to attack another's life, but yet so respectful of the law's authority that she would refrain from the attack because the law prohibited it? This suggests that, while the sanctions that the law threatens provide prudential incentives to obedience for those unpersuaded by whatever reasons underpin its 'prohibitions', it is not clear what role the reasons provided by the prohibitions themselves could play in guiding conduct: if citizens do not already see good reason to refrain from the prohibited conduct, given its pre-legal wrongfulness, respect for the law that prohibits it is unlikely to move them.[26]

The more important point, however, is that whatever content-independent reasons such prohibitions offered citizens to refrain from *mala in se* would be the wrong kind of reason. If the law is to address us as citizens (not as subjects), it must address us in terms of the values that supposedly structure our polity and that are expressed in its own provisions. It must also address us honestly: the reasons it offers us for refraining from conduct it defines as criminal must at least in the first instance be the reasons that justify the demand that we refrain from it; even if it then offers us deterrent reasons for refraining from crime, they must be a last, not a first, resort. For *mala in se*, those reasons concern the conduct's pre-legal wrongfulness: we should refrain from murder, rape, theft and other such crimes not because the law prohibits them, but because they are wrongs. If the law is to reflect those reasons, and the values from which they flow, its definitions of central *mala in se* must thus be understood as declarations, rather than as prohibitions. Its role is not to make wrong what was not already wrong, but to declare that these pre-legal wrongs are public wrongs: to declare, that is, not merely that they are wrongs (we do not need the criminal law to tell us that), but that they are wrongs that properly concern the whole polity, which should call their perpetrators to public account through the criminal courts.[27]

Those who espouse some version of political proceduralism may object that what I have said does not adequately recognise the deep value pluralism that characterises modern liberal societies, and the way in which agreement on procedures can resolve the problems that such pluralism poses. We cannot expect to be able to reach genuine collective agreement

[26] Except, perhaps, in cases in which the citizen accepts as authoritative the law's interpretation of an extra-legal wrong, although it is not one that she accepts for herself: see n 27 below.

[27] The criminal law also provides precise determinations of wrongs which are extra-legally controversial or unclear (see Duff, 2001: 64–5, also 68–71, 121–5, 179–97). Note that this conception of criminal law as declaring rather than prohibiting *mala in se* is compatible with the 'practical difference' thesis (see above, Ch 2 at n 22). Even if the law makes no authoritative difference to citizens' deliberations about whether or not to do what it defines as criminal, it can make a difference to their deliberations and actions after the event: most significantly, if they are accused of committing a crime they are required to appear in court to answer to the charge.

amongst members of a liberal polity on matters of substantive value, given the diverse values to which different groups are committed; but we can hope to reach agreement on procedures by which we can decide such issues as must be decided collectively, including issues about what kinds of conduct should be criminalised. We can then see the criminal law as involving prohibitions whose authority derives not from their content, but from the procedures through which they were created; in addressing us, the law now appeals not to the pre-legal wrongfulness of the conduct that it prohibits (since it is not to assume that citizens should agree about that), but to the respect that we owe to laws produced by political procedures on which we agree or would rationally agree.[28] We cannot, however, plausibly ground the authority of central parts of the criminal law in this way. For if we are to agree on procedures to structure the polity, we must be able to count on some level of mutual respect between those who are to agree on and work within the procedures; that is one way in which even proceduralists must appeal to agreement on substantive values. But it is hard to imagine a respect that is robust enough to underpin the requisite procedures which would not also preclude murdering, raping or subjecting to other central *mala in se* those whom I respect. 'Respect for agreed procedures' is no more plausible than 'respect for the law' as a normative reason for refraining from *mala in se.*

To say that criminal law has a declaratory rather than a prohibitory meaning in relation to central *mala in se* is not yet to say that such wrongs are criminalised because they are wrongs, or (primarily or only) in order to ensure that their perpetrators receive retributive punishment. Surely, it might be said, the point of criminalisation must still be, as Walker argues, reductive rather than merely punitive: we criminalise such conduct in order to reduce its incidence.

It is indeed part of the state's responsibility to seek to reduce the incidence of the kinds of conduct that are properly criminalised, since it is a proper part of the state's responsibility to seek to protect its citizens from suffering such wrongs.[29] However, it is one thing to say that the state should aim to reduce the incidence of some type of conduct, partly by some system of legal regulation.[30] It is quite another to say that it should do so through the criminal law, rather than through other, non-criminal modes of legal regulation, such as 'administrative' regulations which do not purport to condemn wrongdoing. If we are to justify maintaining a system of criminal law, as a particular type of legal institution, we must

[28] For a useful discussion of proceduralism see Archard, 2005.

[29] And, someone with Socratic sympathies might add, from committing them, if one who commits a serious wrong harms himself as well as his victim (see Plato, *Gorgias*).

[30] Only partly because there are of course many other ways of preventing or discouraging such conduct than by legal regulation of any kind.

explain why the state should regulate certain kinds of conduct by defining them as wrongs, through a process that calls perpetrators to account for committing them, and then subjects them to condemnatory punishments.

Part of that explanation will consist in an account of why this approach is consistent—as for instance a purely deterrent system of penalties is not—with the respect that is due to those whose conduct the state seeks to regulate: in the argument that a system of criminal trials that call people to account for their wrongs, and of punishments that are justified in retributive terms as appropriate responses to those wrongs, shows proper respect for those who are punished as responsible moral agents, whereas deterrent systems do not; I will not rehearse that argument here.[31] The other part of the explanation will show why we should make wrongdoing salient in this way: why should we opt for a system of criminal law and punishment, rather than one of non-criminal regulation and non-punitive penalties? The answer to this question is simple, at least in initial outline. If we are serious about the values by which we define ourselves as a political community, and about the demand that we show each other appropriate respect and concern as fellow citizens, we will take breaches of such values and of that demand seriously, and mark and condemn them as such. This point is missed by 'restorative justice' advocates who want us to focus on harm and its repair rather than on wrongs and their punishment, or to think of 'conflicts' rather than of 'crimes'.[32] Sometimes, even when a wrong has been done, it is indeed more important to seek to repair harm, and unhelpful to focus on the wrong: but sometimes it matters that we recognise and respond to wrongs as wrongs, both in our private lives and as a polity; we owe this to their victims, to their perpetrators (if we are to treat them as responsible agents), and to ourselves as citizens of the polity.

To say this, however, is to say that we should define certain kinds of conduct as criminal, rather than subject them to non-criminal modes of legal regulation, precisely to ensure, as far as we reasonably can, that their perpetrators are brought to trial and subjected to retributive punishment—punishments that are distinguished from 'penalties' by their backward-looking, condemnatory meaning. This is a modified version of the principle that Walker rejects—that 'prohibitions should . . . be included in the criminal law for the sole purpose of ensuring that breaches of them are visited with retributive punishment'.[33] It is modified in that we now talk of defining crimes rather than of prohibiting conduct; in that the aim is only to ensure 'as far as we reasonably can' that they are punished (given the costs of criminal justice, it would be absurd to aim to ensure that they are

[31] See von Hirsch, 1993, especially ch 2; Duff, 2001, especially chs 2–3.
[32] See n 9 above.
[33] Walker 1969: 26; see at n 22 above.

all tried and punished);[34] and in that the aim is to bring wrongdoers to trial as well as to punish them—since it is important to call them to answer for their wrongdoings, independently of any punishment that they may also suffer.

This is only a partial defence of legal moralism, for reasons noted in Chapter 2.2(b). We should criminalise certain wrongs in order to mark them out as public wrongs, which must be condemned as such, and for which their perpetrators should be called to answer; but that is not to say that we have good reason to criminalise *every* kind of wrongdoing. We still need to fill the gap in traditional forms of legal moralism by identifying the kinds of wrong that can properly concern the criminal law; but we must first attend to another issue. The argument so far has concerned *mala in se*—wrongs that can be identified as wrongs, independently not only of the criminal law that defines them as crimes, but of legal regulation more generally: they would be wrong even if no part of the law took any interest in them.[35] An increasing proportion of the criminal law, however, deals not with *mala in se,* but with *mala prohibita,* involving conduct that is wrongful, if at all, only in virtue of its legal prohibition. Can even the modest version of legal moralism advocated here deal with such offences?

4. *Mala Prohibita* as Wrongs

On the orthodox view, *mala in se* are crimes that are 'wrong in themselves' or 'inherently evil'; *mala prohibita* are not 'inherently evil'—they are 'wrong only because prohibited by legislation'.[36] Some theorists would echo Bentham's scathing comment on:

> the acute distinction, between *mala in se*, and *mala prohibita*: which being so shrewd, and sounding so pretty, and being in Latin, has no sort of occasion to have any meaning to it: accordingly it has none.[37]

The traditional way of explicating *mala prohibita* is indeed misleading; but the distinction is a real one, and seems to create a serious problem for legal moralism. However, that problem can be resolved if we distinguish the question of legal regulation from that of criminalisation.

[34] We should not forget how small a proportion of offenders are actually tried and convicted: for provocative discussion of the implications of this point see Braithwaite and Pettit, 1990, especially chs 6, 9.

[35] This is over-simplified, since some moral categories are in part defined by the law; as with property (see Honoré, 1993): this complicates the picture, but does not undermine the basic claim that *mala in se* involve conduct the wrongfulness of which does not depend on its being legally wrongful.

[36] LaFave, 2003: 36. See also Simester and Sullivan, 2007: 3; Gordon, 2000: 9–11; Dressler, 2006: 157–8.

[37] Bentham, 1776/1977: 63. See Gray, 1995; also G Williams, 1961: 189.

The traditional account of *mala prohibita* is easily read as implying that *mala prohibita* consist in conduct that 'is not wrongful prior to or independent of the law that defined it as criminal'.[38] On that reading, legal moralism cannot justify *mala prohibita*: if what is to justify criminalisation is the moral wrongfulness of the conduct in question, we cannot criminalise conduct that is not morally wrong prior to its criminalisation. However, we would do better to define *mala prohibita* as offences consisting in conduct that is not wrongful prior to the legal *regulation* that prohibits it, whilst *mala in se* are (supposedly) wrongs prior to any such legal regulation.[39] This leaves a logical space within which legal moralists can justify the creation of some *mala prohibita*, by arguing that conduct that breaches a legal regulation, even if it is not wrongful prior to that regulation, can be wrongful as a breach of the regulation.

The distinction between *mala in se* and *mala prohibita* cannot always be clearly drawn: as we will see, many of what are traditionally classified as *mala prohibita* are better seen as 'hybrid' offences.[40] Theorists sometimes also classify as *mala prohibita* offences that even by their own criteria should straightforwardly count as *mala in se*. Dressler's examples of *mala prohibita* include traffic offences, environmental pollution offences and offences concerning the manufacture or sale of impure food or drugs:[41] but it is implausible to claim that there is nothing wrong, prior to any legal regulation, with selling impure food, or with polluting the environment or with many kinds of conduct that constitute traffic offences. Such wrongs may be less serious than paradigm *mala in se* such as murder and rape, since they do not typically involve an intention to harm: but we must not confuse the distinction between *mala in se* and *mala prohibita* with that between more and less serious offences, or think that the criminal law cannot condemn both more and less serious offences proportionately to their seriousness.

We will look at hybrid offences, at different types of *malum prohibitum*, and at the kinds of argument that can justify their inclusion in the criminal law, in more detail in Chapter 7.3. All I want to do here is show that legal moralists can in principle justify the creation of *mala prohibita*, and for that purpose a simple example will do.

There is nothing inherently wrong in driving down a street that is too narrow for two cars to pass each other: there is a risk that I will meet an oncoming car and have to back up; but so long as I drive carefully I do no

[38] Husak, 2005b: 66.

[39] Only 'supposedly' because, as a classificatory matter, an offence counts as a *malum in se* if it is criminalised because it is thought to be pre-legally wrongful: we can both insist that consensual homosexual activity is not morally wrong, and classify it as *malum in se* in a legal system that criminalises it because it is thought to be morally wrongful.

[40] See Husak, 2005b; and below, Ch 7.3.

[41] Dressler, 2006: 157. See also LaFave, 2003: 36–9.

wrong. Suppose, however, that the appropriate legislature makes it a one-way street, to reduce congestion and the risks of harm that such narrow streets create. Once the appropriate traffic signs are erected, it is legally prohibited to drive what is now the wrong way down this street; and I commit an offence under English law if I do so.[42] This offence is a *malum prohibitum*: conduct—driving, say, from north to south down this street—that was not wrongful prior to its legal prohibition becomes a criminal offence.[43] How can it be justified by a legal moralist who insists that only wrongs should be criminalised?

The key here is to separate two distinct questions in the process of criminalisation. First, the legislature must decide whether to regulate this type of conduct: does it have good reason, relating to the common good of the community, to regulate what was until now unregulated? If it decides to regulate, a second question then arises: how, if at all, should the regulation be enforced? Should there be a formal enforcement mechanism at all, or should citizens just be exhorted to obey? If it is to be formally enforced, should it be enforced as an 'administrative' regulation breaches of which attract penalties but not punishments;[44] or should it be given the force of criminal law, so that breaches of it attract conviction and punishment (at a level appropriate to the non-serious character of the offence)? The legal moralist's answer to this second question is that breaches of the regulation should be criminalised if and only if they are moral wrongs of a kind that merits public censure and punishment, and we can now see how this answer is possible: by distinguishing the two legislative questions, we can see how conduct that is not wrongful prior to or independently of its *legal regulation* can be wrongful prior to or independently of its *criminalisation*—and thus how legal moralists can see good reason to criminalise it.

What moral wrong is committed by driving the wrong way down a one-way street (or by ignoring other kinds of traffic sign; but we can focus here on the one-way street)? To identify the wrong, we must identify the reasons that citizens have (or that the legislature claims that they have) to obey the traffic sign: are they moral reasons, such that one who is not

[42] See Road Traffic Act 1988, s 36.

[43] The offence, strictly speaking, is not 'driving from north to south', but 'failing to comply with a lawfully placed traffic sign'. Here, as in other 'pure' *mala prohibita*, the conduct that constitutes the offence is in a sense not even possible, let alone wrongful, prior to its legal regulation.

[44] There is a further question about whether such systems of non-criminal regulation, whose penalties serve primarily as deterrents, can be justified. My suspicion is that they cannot be: breaches of legal regulations should be penalised only if they constitute wrongs—in which case they should be punished as criminal offences (see Duff *et al*, 2007: ch 6.5); but that is not an issue that we need settle here.

guided by them does wrong? Those reasons are to an extent content-independent: what makes it wrong to drive this way down the street is the fact that the law prohibits it; had the regulation made the street one-way in the other direction, it would instead have been wrong to drive along it from south to north. In the context of *mala prohibita*, unlike that of *mala in se*, 'because it is the law' is thus part of the citizen's reason for action:[45] but only a part, since we must also be able to see why we have reason to obey this regulation. Such reason is, however, not difficult to discern. The regulation, if it is obeyed, serves the convenience (and to a degree the safety) of drivers generally: it prevents congestion, and the difficulties caused when two cars try to go down the street in different directions; it gives drivers the assurance that, if they start to drive down the street in the right direction, they will not meet an oncoming car. Now drivers surely have a general responsibility to consider the convenience and the safety of other road users: a driver who flouts this regulation fails to discharge that responsibility, and thus acts wrongly. That wrong is also plausibly seen as a 'public' wrong that properly concerns us all; if we think that, although not a serious wrong, it is one that should be publicly marked and censured, we will see good reason to give this regulation (and others like it) the backing of the criminal law. Conduct that was not wrongful prior to its legal regulation can thus become wrongful as a breach of a justified legal regulation: wrongful in a way that in principle merits criminalisation.[46]

There is of course much more than this to be said about *mala prohibita*—some of it will be said in Chapter 7.3. My aim here has been only to show that, if we distinguish the question of whether to regulate from that of how the regulations should be enforced, and define *mala prohibita* as offences consisting in conduct that is not wrongful prior to its legal regulation, we can see how legal moralists who make wrongfulness a criterion of criminalisation can still justify some *mala prohibita*. What is crucial for them is that the conduct is wrongful prior to or independently of its criminalisation; and, as we have just seen, that can be true of conduct that is not wrongful prior to or independently of its legal regulation.

A further point is worth noting, about what we are criminally responsible for. In the case of *mala in se*, the argument offered above suggests that we are criminally responsible not for 'breaking the law', but for the substantive wrong that we commit, and that the law defines as a criminal

[45] See above, Ch 2 at n 25. Note that the reason is not 'because it's the criminal law', since we are not yet at the stage of criminalisation.

[46] This kind of justification of *mala prohibita* is relatively straightforward when the regulation is justified in the appropriate way, as serving some aspect of the common good; matters are more complicated when the regulation is not thus justified (although the legislature claims that it is); see further below, Ch 7 n 94.

wrong: the law's definition of it as a crime is a condition which must be satisfied if we are to be held criminally responsible for it, but the object of responsibility, that for which we are responsible, is the wrong. With *mala prohibita*, by contrast, the breach of regulation is an aspect of the object of responsibility: what we are criminally responsible for is committing a wrong that consists partly in breaking the relevant legal regulation.

In this chapter I have offered a partial defence of legal moralism: a defence, since I have argued that moral wrongfulness should be not merely a necessary condition of criminalisation but its object—we should be criminally responsible for the wrongs we commit, because they are wrongs that should be publicly marked and condemned; a partial defence, since, as I noted in Chapter 2.2(b), it is implausible to suggest that we have good reason to criminalise *every* kind of moral wrong. That is the issue to which I now turn: how can we set about identifying the particular kinds of moral wrong that are in principle apt for criminalisation?

It is worth emphasising the significance of this order of argument. Suppose that we came to adopt a version of the Harm Principle as the answer to this question: we should criminalise only wrongs that cause or threaten harm to others. Our position might then be extensionally equivalent to that of someone who starts with preventing harm as the aim of the criminal law, but argues that for reasons of justice we should criminalise harmful conduct only if it is also wrongful. Even if that were so, our understandings of the meaning and functions of criminal law would differ sharply. On one view, the criminal law is a moralised practice, which focuses on moral wrongs; on the other, it is a technique of harm-prevention which is constrained by the demands of justice or fairness.

5

Criminally Responsible For What? (2) Action and Crime

1. The 'Act Requirement'

A first step towards identifying the kinds of wrong that can properly concern the criminal law could be to appeal to the 'act requirement', that criminal responsibility must be grounded in a 'voluntary act'. Moral responsibility need not be for actions: it can be for thoughts, emotions, even character traits.[1] An act requirement might thus set substantial constraints on the reach of the criminal law and the scope of criminal responsibility—constraints in tune with liberal concerns for privacy.[2]

Some version of the act requirement is still widely asserted as a condition of criminal responsibility,[3] and seems intuitively plausible. We should not, surely, be held criminally responsible for mere thoughts (however evil) that are not translated into action; or for mere involuntary movements; or for mere conditions; or even for omissions as such—all of which an act requirement seems to preclude. We should, surely, be held criminally responsible only for what we *do*—not for what we are, or for what happens to us, or even (generally) for what we merely fail to do. But any attempt to posit an act requirement as a condition of criminal responsibility faces major problems. The central question is whether we can give an account of 'action' that sets plausible substantive constraints on the scope of criminal responsibility: the danger is that we will end up with an account that either sets substantive but implausible constraints or, having been adapted to fit some plausible contours of criminal responsibility, fails to set any substantive constraints at all. The former danger is exemplified by Moore's account, as we will see shortly; the latter is

[1] See Ch 3.2(a) above.

[2] For more detailed treatments of the main arguments of this section see Duff, 1996 chs 9–11; 2002b; 2004.

[3] See especially Moore, 1993; also (variously nuanced) Sistare, 1989: 45–67; Robinson, 1995: 250; Wilson, 2003: 72–94; Gordon, 2000: 60—81; LaFave, 2003: 301–10; Dressler, 2006: 91–109; Ormerod, 2005: 37–51.

exemplified by Gross's suggestion that 'an act consists of events or states of affairs for which a person might be held responsible', which makes it definitionally true that we are criminally responsible only for acts, but at the cost of making the 'act requirement' vacuous.[4]

Before we tackle that question, however, we must deal briefly with a prior question. Is the act requirement meant to specify a condition, or the object, of criminal responsibility?[5]

Theorists sometimes portray the act requirement as specifying a condition of criminal responsibility. Under the law of attempts, an intending criminal must commit a suitable act—one that is 'more than merely preparatory', perhaps, or one that constitutes a 'substantial step' towards the commission of the crime—before he is guilty of an attempt.[6] On some views, the object of criminal responsibility is the firm intention to commit the crime, and the role of the actus reus is to provide appropriate evidence of that intention; we are, that is, criminally responsible for the intention, on condition that we undertook a suitable act towards fulfilling it.[7] Similarly, those who ground criminal responsibility in character might argue that what we are criminally responsible for is a defective character trait, but (to ensure reliable proof) only on condition that it is manifested in a criminal action.[8] Now the problems that face the act requirement arise in the same way whether it is taken to specify a condition, or the object, of criminal responsibility; but since my interest is in the objects of criminal responsibility, I will focus in what follows on actions as objects of responsibility. I will argue that we cannot sustain the traditional act requirement, but can sustain an 'action presumption'.

2. The Failure of the Act Requirement[9]

Moore's account illustrates the difficulty of providing a tenable account of the concept of an act that sets plausible substantive constraints on the scope of criminal responsibility.[10] An act, Moore argues, is a 'bodily-movement-caused-by-a-volition': criminal liability is for acts which have the further properties specified in the law's definition of an actus reus; an

[4] Gross, 1979: 56; see Husak, 1987: 108; Moore, 1993: 20–1.

[5] See above, Ch 4 at nn 11–13; and Husak, 1998a: 65–72.

[6] See Criminal Attempts Act 1981, s 1(1); Model Penal Code, s 5.01(1)(c).

[7] See G Williams, 1961: 631; Morris, 1965; American Law Institute 1985, Commentary to s 5.01, 303–32; Husak, 1987: 93–7; Duff 1996: 63–4.

[8] See Duff, 2002b: 156–60.

[9] See Husak, 1987: ch 4; Hornsby, 1999; Ashworth, 2006: 105–13; Simester and Sullivan, 2007: 64–78.

[10] Moore, 1993; 1997: chs 1, 5, 6. See University of Pennsylvania Law Review, 1994; Duff, 1996: chs 9–10.

actus reus consists of an act plus whatever circumstances and consequences the offence definition specifies. The core of the actus reus of murder, for instance, is 'the complex action of killing another',[11] which consists in a bodily-movement-caused-by-a-volition that causes another's death. The act requirement is not absolute, since we can sometimes be justly held criminally responsible for omissions; but, subject to that exception, criminal liability is and ought to be for actions as he defines them.[12]

One objection to this account is that it is a philosophically untenable account of action, but that is not the objection that concerns me here. The relevant objection is that even if it is a viable account of a concept of action, it is not an account of the kind of agency that interests the criminal law (or the other practices within which we describe, explain and assess human actions, including morality, history, literature and sociology). If the act requirement requires an 'act' in that sense, it does not set a plausible constraint on the scope of the criminal law.[13]

The simplest way to see the force of this objection is to notice the many, unexceptional ways in which we can act, ie do things, without moving our bodies. I can insult someone by means that involve moving my body—by words or gestures. But I can also insult someone without moving, or by not moving in an appropriate way: by not rising from my chair when she enters the room, if politeness requires me to rise; by not acknowledging an acquaintance who greets me in the street. Breaking a promise often involves moving my body, but need not do so: I break my promise to meet you in the pub at 6.00 by not moving from my chair to go to the pub. Nor is there anything abnormal about the cases in which I insult someone or break a promise without moving. They may be statistically unusual, but their status as doings is not doubtful or secondary: given the appropriate conventions, it is as much an insult to fail to rise when the Queen enters the room as it is to make a rude gesture at her; just as straightforwardly a breach of promise to fail to turn up to a promised meeting as to enter a room that I promised not to enter. We can call these cases of 'commission by omission': I do something (insult the Queen, break my promise) by omitting to do something else (stand up; come to the meeting). The point is, however, that they are clear cases of commission: of doing, of agency, of acting.

[11] Moore, 1993: 46.

[12] Criminal law theorists often adopt some version of volitionism, if not Moore's particular version: see, eg, Williams, 1983a: 147–8; LaFave, 2003: 304–7; Dressler, 2006: 94–7; Ormerod, 2005: 44–5.

[13] See variously Hornsby, 1993, 1994, 1999; Fletcher, 1994; B Williams 1994; Husak, 1998a.

Criminal offences, offences of commission rather than of 'mere omission',[14] can also be committed without bodily movements. Theft, in English law,[15] requires the appropriation of another's property, and appropriation is partially defined as 'any assumption by a person of the rights of an owner'. Someone leaves a book in my house, and I decide to keep it myself. Even if that decision is not already an 'appropriation',[16] I certainly appropriate the book if I lend it to a friend; but lending it could, given appropriate understandings between us, involve nothing more than not saying 'Yes I do' when she says 'You don't mind if I borrow this?'. Similarly, I can commit reckless endangerment in ways that involve moving, but also in ways that require no bodily movement—for instance by doing nothing to stop a fire which starts in my house and threatens to spread next door.[17]

Such cases may be statistically unusual, but they are not normatively deviant: the fact that no bodily movement is essentially involved in the commission of a crime casts no doubt on the reality of that commission; nor is the presence or absence of bodily movement relevant to debates about criminalisation. If it were suggested that some insults or breaches of promise should be criminalised, there would be plenty of argument about the merits of the suggestion, and about the kinds of case that might be criminalised: but it would be implausible to suggest that only insults or promise-breakings that essentially involved bodily movements should be criminalised. We might agree that we should be criminally responsible only for what we do, but if someone who insulted another without moving pleads 'But I didn't *do* anything' the answer is simple: he did something, since he insulted someone—which is certainly a doing.

The kinds of exercise of human agency that interest the criminal law cannot be analysed through a conception of action as essentially involving bodily movement. It is not essential to their identity as doings that they involve bodily movement; the fact that I Φ without moving does not render Φ's status as a doing doubtful in comparison with Φ-ings that involve bodily movement, since what matters is the social meaning, not the physical realisation, of Φ-ing. Those who define action in terms of bodily movement focus on our exercises of our capacity to move, and to control our movements, as embodied beings. We exercise that capacity when we move, and when we control movements that normally go on without such control—when we control our breathing, or hold back a yawn. Given our nature and the world in which we live, we must usually exercise that capacity when we engage with the world as agents, since we cannot usually

[14] See Ormerod, 2005: 76–8.
[15] See Theft Act 1968, ss 1, 3.1.
[16] See Wilson, 2003: 415.
[17] See Model Penal Code, s 211.2; also *Miller* [1983] 2 AC 161; Ormerod, 2005: 79–81.

have an impact on the world without physically moving or controlling our movements. Our responsibility for much that we do or fail to do also depends on our having that capacity and the opportunity to exercise it. But none of this shows that our doings can be defined, or understood in their character as doings, in terms of our exercise of that capacity for movement: for their identity and character as doings do not logically require movement.

We must therefore reject the claim that criminal responsibility requires, or should require, an act, understood as necessarily involving bodily movement: even if criminal responsibility in most cases involves bodily movements, they are not *necessarily* involved either as objects or as conditions of liability; they are not what interests the criminal law.

One response to the failure of the act requirement, as thus understood, is to argue that we must abandon it. What matters is not action, but control: we should be criminally responsible only for what lies within our control.[18] A control requirement sets weaker constraints on the scope of criminal responsibility than does an act requirement interpreted as requiring bodily movement: it allows criminal responsibility for thoughts, and for any condition that we could have avoided acquiring or could now remove. But, its advocates will reply, the constraints set by the act-as-bodily-movement requirement are not plausible; the control requirement lets in forms of criminal responsibility (possession offences, for instance) that the act requirement makes needlessly problematic;[19] and we should just recognise that such general constraints as act or control requirements cannot do much to limit the scope of criminal responsibility.

I will argue, however, that we can justify a kind of act(ion) requirement, or presumption, as a constraint on the scope, and the objects, of criminal responsibility. We should normally be criminally responsible only for what we do, not for what we merely think (or intend) or feel, or are. (Responsibility for what we fail to do, for omissions, will be more problematic.) The challenge then is to provide an account of action that is both tenable itself and plausible as a constraint on the scope of the criminal law. We can meet that challenge by offering an account of action as a social, rather than a natural, phenomenon.

3. Social Agency and the 'Action Presumption'

Those who analyse action as a matter of willed bodily movements portray it as a natural, a-social phenomenon, which in its essence engages only with the material world in which we physically move and which we can

[18] See especially Husak, 1987: ch 4; 1998a; also Glazebrook, 1978; Simester, 1998.
[19] See Moore, 1993: 20–2; Husak, 1998a: 70–1.

causally affect by our movements. If we are to understand action as it interests the criminal law, we must instead see it as a social phenomenon, engaged with the social world in which we live (a world in which our actions have meanings as well as effects, and in which their effects often depend on their meanings); as involving not just the exercise of our capacities to move and control our bodies, but the exercise of our capacity (a complex set of capacities) to engage in practical reasoning and to actualise its results in ways that make a difference to the world in which we live.[20]

Our status as human, social agents depends essentially on our possession of this capacity; we actualise ourselves as agents in exercising it. Such actualisations of the results of practical reasoning often also depend on the exercise of our capacity for controlled movement; indeed, insofar as such actualisations involve having an impact on the world around us, that is usually the case, given our nature as embodied beings. But although we must usually rely, as agents, on that capacity for movement, its exercise does not constitute or display what is essential to our social agency. What is essential to such agency is the exercise of the capacity to actualise the results of our practical reasoning in ways that make a difference to the social and material world in which we exercise it.[21]

On this conception of agency, the counter-examples to accounts of action as essentially involving bodily movement are straightforward cases of action. Whether I insult someone or break my promise in ways that involve bodily movement or in ways that do not is irrelevant to the character of my action as an insult or a breach of promise.

Can this conception of action ground a plausible 'action requirement' as a constraint on the objects of criminal responsibility: should we be criminally responsible only for actions in this sense? We are now focusing on what might interest the criminal law. Whilst the criminal law is not interested in bodily movements as such, it is interested in and addresses citizens as agents who have and exercise the capacity to actualise the results of their practical reasoning in ways that make a difference to the world in which they live and the law operates. It offers, or reminds us of, reasons for acting in certain ways; those reasons should, it claims, figure in our practical reasoning and guide our actions.[22] It calls us to answer, in its courts, for doing what we had reason not to do; but we can answer only for

[20] For more details see Duff, 1996: ch 11, drawing on (among others) Melden, 1961; Gustafson, 1986.

[21] By 'practical reasoning' I do not mean only those rich kinds of reasoning that connect individual actions to larger conceptions of the good, nor only occurrent processes of deliberation; any action done for a reason actualises the results of practical reasoning, even if that reasoning is implicit rather than occurrent.

[22] Some of the law's reasons guide actions, not by figuring *in* our practical reasoning, but by determining its limits. The reasons not to commit murder do not typically figure in our

doings that fell within the reach of our capacity to actualise the results of our practical reasoning. What we are held criminally responsible for is also often an action in this sense; but we should distinguish two kinds of case.

Sometimes what we are criminally responsible for is precisely the actualisation of a result of practical reasoning, when a crime consists in successfully carrying out an intention to Φ: if I carry out an intention to wound someone, or to deceive them into giving me their money, I am criminally responsible for the actualisation of that criminal intention. In other cases, what we are responsible for is not the actualisation of the intention to Φ itself, but the wrong that we do in actualising that intention. I can be guilty of Ψ-ing (of criminal damage, for instance, or of handling stolen goods) if I Ψ in or by carrying out my intention to Φ—if I damage another's property in carrying out my intention to burn my rubbish, or handle stolen goods in carrying out my intention to buy a television.[23] I will have more to say later, in Chapter 7, about the significance of the distinction between what I do with intent and things that I do in carrying out my intentions: all we need notice here is that in both kinds of case what we are criminally responsible for is an action.

So can we then claim that criminal responsibility should *always* be for an action; or more modestly that even if we can be criminally responsible for things other than actions, an action is always required as a condition of responsibility? Or can we say no more than that criminal responsibility depends on our capacity for action—on our capacity to act for and to be guided by reasons? Such a 'control requirement' does set plausible, if generous, limits on the objects and subjects of criminal responsibility,[24] but falls well short of an action requirement, since it requires only the possibility of reason-guided action. Can we justify an action requirement?

I will argue in what follows that, whilst we cannot justify a stringent action requirement, we can find a place for a more modest 'action presumption'. To see what this means and what force it can have, we should look in turn at the various possible bases of responsibility that an act requirement was taken to exclude: thoughts, involuntary movements, conditions or states of affairs, omissions and character.

deliberations, to be weighed along with other reasons for and against contemplated actions: our recognition of those reasons is shown in the way that we do not even consider murder as an option.

[23] Compare Davidson, 1980: 45–6 on ascribing Ψ-ing to me as an action if I Ψ in intentionally Φ-ing.

[24] See Chs 2.1, 3.1–2 above.

4. Criminal Responsibility for Thoughts?

Thoughts are sometimes actions—exercises of our capacity to actualise the results of our practical reasoning. We can have reason to engage in thought—in deliberation, contemplation or imagination; we can act for such reasons by engaging in such thought; and we can be held responsible for engaging or for failing to engage in such thought. However, we also contrast 'action' with 'mere thought': in this context actions are exercises of that capacity that are apt by themselves to have an impact on the external world. But why should we not be criminally responsible for thoughts in which we exercise our capacity for agency?

We must distinguish two kinds of active thought. First, there are those the completion of which requires no world-impacting action: fantasising or contemplating, for instance, might lead to overt action but are not necessarily frustrated without it; they can be completed within the realm of thought. Secondly, there are kinds of thought the completion of which requires overt action. Decision and intention formation are obvious examples: whilst I can fail to do what I decide or intend to do, such lack of overt action frustrates my decision or intention;[25] such thinking demands overt action in a way that the first kind does not.

The first kind of thought can be wrongful, and we might even say that it can wrong other people (that, for instance, I wrong you if I make you the object of my sadistic fantasies);[26] but there are familiar, liberal reasons for not criminalising it. Even without appealing to the Harm Principle, any plausible account of the distinction between 'public' matters that concern the polity, and 'private' matters that concern only the individual and those with whom he chooses to share them, must count such thoughts, at least when not expressed to others, as 'private'.

The case of practical thought, thought oriented towards action, is less straightforward: for some argue that such thought, for instance the formation of a firm criminal intention, can be a proper object of criminal responsibility.[27] The first point to note is that an action requirement cannot by itself generate a plausible alternative to such views. That requirement would itself be satisfied by the most minimal 'first act' test for attempts, counting any overt action done in furtherance of a criminal intention as sufficient for attempt liability:[28] but those who object to criminalising mere intentions would hardly be satisfied to be told that, whilst a bare intention to commit forgery is not criminal, someone who

[25] Compare Aristotle, *Nicomachean Ethics* VII.3: the conclusion of practical reasoning is action.

[26] Contrast Moore: 1993, 49–54 on criminal responsibility as being for wrong*doing*.

[27] See at n 7 above.

[28] See *Scofield* [1784] Cald 397, at 403; Duff, 1996: 35–7.

opens a desk drawer to get a pen with which to commit forgery can be held criminally responsible for committing an action in furtherance of his intention. What they demand, whether as object or condition of criminal responsibility, is not *some* overt action, but an action that brings the agent far enough along the road towards the crime's completion; and the familiar disagreements about how far that should be cannot be settled simply by appealing to an 'action requirement'.[29]

We can generate a more substantial action requirement if, recalling that crimes must be wrongs, we require a *wrongful* action as the object of criminal liability: for opening a drawer to find a pen is surely not a wrongful action. To which it will be replied that whilst opening a drawer to find a pen might not wrong anyone (ie infringe anyone's rights), it has not been shown that crimes must be wrongs in that sense;[30] and that if the drawer is opened as part of a course of action designed to culminate in successful forgery, the action of opening it *is* wrong precisely as part of that planned course of action. It takes its wrongfulness from the intention that informs it and the completed wrong to which it is a means: but it is nonetheless wrong, as something that one should not do (for that reason or with that intention). To generate a more substantial action requirement, we would need to require not just a wrongful action, but one that is more substantially wrong than the first act in a criminal enterprise. When an intending wrongdoer begins to put her criminal intention into action, she begins to give determinate or concrete shape in the world (the world in which that crime is to be committed) to the intended wrong, but in the early stages of the venture that shape is still shadowy and insubstantial, and involves an aetiolated or derivative kind of wrongfulness; criminal responsibility, however, should attach only to actions which are more substantially wrongful, as giving the intended crime a more substantial form, than are such first acts.

We cannot pursue here the question of how far beyond such minimal 'first acts' intending criminals should progress before they come within the reach of the criminal law—the law of attempts or other offences of preparation.[31] What needs explanation is the claim that criminal responsibility should be for wrongful actions, in the sense of 'action' I am using here, and not for mere criminal intentions. One who intends to commit a crime is committed to wrongdoing that concerns the criminal law; he is open to moral criticism: why should he not be criminally responsible?

[29] See Duff, 1996: ch 2; and below, Ch 7 at nn 46–48.

[30] Contrast Feinberg, 1984: 32–6, interpreting the Harm Principle as requiring actions that are wrongful as violations of rights (as well as harmful); see Ch 6.1–2 below.

[31] See Duff, 1996: chs 2, 13.5; also Ch 7.2(a) below.

Does whatever force an action requirement may have depend purely on the difficulty of proving intentions in the absence of conduct that corroborates them?[32]

We can find stronger, principled grounds for insisting on substantially wrongful actions as objects of criminal responsibility in the core liberal values of privacy and autonomy. Privacy concerns not what is done 'in private', but what is not the business of some specified set of 'others': in this context, what is not the business of the criminal law, or of our fellow citizens simply in virtue of our shared citizenship.[33] A liberal polity must leave its members as broad as possible a realm of privacy within which they can both think and act free from the coercive interference of the state. It must count as 'public', as the business of the polity as a whole, as minimal a realm as possible. The commission of an appropriate kind of substantive wrong is a public matter; so too, we can say, is conduct that poses a relatively imminent threat of such a wrong—conduct that is therefore substantially wrongful in virtue of its close connection to the threatened wrong. But a liberal law should recognise as 'private' thought and action that is not yet so determinately or intimately connected to such a wrong.

It might be objected that privacy can only be a good when it is used for purposes that are not themselves wrongful;[34] and that, even if we are not answerable to our fellow citizens for our non-practical thoughts, we surely should be answerable for any practical thoughts that are directed towards the commission of public wrongs. If I happen to find out that someone else (a stranger) is planning a robbery, I might think it imprudent to 'interfere' myself: but if I did so (for instance warning him not to do it), he could not legitimately complain that it was none of my business. Whether or not I have an obligation to inform the police, I would be justified in doing so; and whatever limits we set on police powers of surveillance, the police would be justified in taking some interest in the person, and in warning him. So the requirement for a substantially wrong action would have to bear on the content of the substantive criminal law, rather than on what is the business of one's fellow citizens or of criminal justice officials. It is here that the other liberal value, of respect for autonomy or for responsible agency, becomes relevant.

If the state is to treat its citizens as responsible agents who can be guided (who can guide themselves) by reasons, it should be slow to coerce them on the ground that they are likely to commit a wrong if not thus coerced, since that is to treat them as if they will not be guided by the reasons that should dissuade them from such wrongdoing. This is most obviously true

[32] See Model Penal Code, s 5.01(2); Husak, 1998a: 89–90.

[33] See above, Ch 2 at nn 36–37.

[34] Compare G Dworkin, 1982; Raz, 1986: 373–81.

when the grounds for that prediction of wrongdoing do not include a present intention to do wrong, as when people are diagnosed as 'dangerous' on the basis of other indicators;[35] but it is also true when the prediction is grounded on the agent's present criminal intention. It is one thing for a fellow citizen or a police officer to warn him that he should abandon his plan: that is still to treat him as a responsible agent who can be moved by the reason for not committing the wrong of which we remind him. It is quite another thing to hold him guilty of a criminal offence at so early a stage in his intended criminal enterprise: that is to treat him as someone who will not be dissuaded, or dissuade himself, from carrying the wrong through. We cannot wait until he has completed his enterprise: but we should wait until he has more definitively constituted himself as a wrongdoer by coming closer to completing his plan.[36]

We can therefore find grounds for an 'action requirement': criminal responsibility should (normally) be for a substantially wrongful action that impinges on the world in which citizens live together. Legislators are often prone to weaken any such requirement by creating new offences (typically in response to perceived emergencies) that impose criminal responsibility for conduct that scarcely amounts even to determinate preparation for a crime. Such 'pre-preparatory' stages of joint criminal enterprises have long been criminal, since the mere agreement to commit an offence constitutes a criminal conspiracy,[37] but individual actions that fall a very long way short of criminal attempts are also increasingly being criminalised, especially if they might contribute to a collective enterprise, as with the offence of collecting information that is 'likely to be useful to a person committing or preparing an act of terrorism'.[38] I will have more to say about such extensions of the criminal law in Chapters 7.2–3 and 10.3.

5. Criminal Responsibility for Involuntary Movements and States of Affairs?

The contrast between (criminalisable) action and (supposedly not criminalisable) thought is one of the distinctions that the act requirement is standardly used to draw. Others are those between actions and merely involuntary movements, and between actions and conditions or states of affairs. We can treat these distinctions together, since they raise the same issues.

[35] Which is what is wrong with policies of 'selective incapacitation', even if they could resolve the problem of 'false positives': see Duff, 1998b.

[36] Hence the importance of the idea of a '*locus poenitentiae*': see Duff, 1996: 37–42, 386–93.

[37] See Simester and Sullivan, 2007: 279–304.

[38] Terrorism Act 2000, s 58.

The control requirement allows responsibility for involuntary movements, conditions and states of affairs if they were within the agent's control: if, that is, they either resulted from a prior action or could have been averted by a suitable action. An action requirement would be stricter, permitting responsibility only if the movement, condition or state of affairs could be characterised as an intended result or a side-effect of an action. We will turn in the following section to the question of whether we should bring the action requirement into line with the control requirement by turning it into an 'action or omission' requirement; but it is worth briefly noting here the way in which the action requirement as I have specified it differs from the traditional act requirement.

Consider three examples. First, as I sit in a chair, a child playfully swings my arm in a way that will clearly knock over your vase; I could easily stop my arm from being so moved, but do not do so. The control requirement would allow me to be held criminally responsible for the damage to your vase. The act requirement would preclude criminal responsibility; no willed bodily movement of mine caused the damage. The action requirement would permit criminal responsibility if my non-resistance actualised the results of my practical reasoning—if I intentionally did not resist, for instance because I wanted your vase to be broken, or (more charitably) because I did not want to spoil the child's pleasure and did not notice the vase; it would not permit criminal responsibility if I simply failed to resist.

Secondly, Mr Speck was convicted of 'an act of gross indecency with or towards a child'.[39] A child came up to him as he sat in a chair and put her hand on his flies: he did not remove her hand and had an erection. The court rejected his claim that he had committed no *act* of indecency. The act requirement would demand his acquittal: the state of affairs of her hand being on his flies was neither an act nor an effect of an act of his; the erection was not an act since it was neither a willed movement nor the effect of one. The action requirement would, by contrast, permit his conviction if his failure to remove the girl's hand actualised the result of his practical reasoning that this was a means of obtaining sexual pleasure—but not if he simply failed to remove her hand (whilst the control requirement would permit his conviction in either case).

Thirdly, theorists agree that criminal responsibility for possession should not be ruled out in principle—even if legislatures are too quick to create possession offences.[40] The standard way of allowing them is to turn the act requirement into an 'act or omission' requirement, at least in this context. Thus Moore argues that what is punished is not 'the *state* of possessing'

[39] *Speck* [1977] 2 All ER 859; Indecency with Children Act 1960, s 1(1).
[40] See Dubber, 2001, 2005; and below, at nn 68–70, and Ch 7 at nn 71–74.

but 'either the act of taking possession or … the omission to rid oneself of possession';[41] this in effect replaces the act requirement by the control requirement. The action requirement, by contrast, allows us to count some possessions as actions (not just as failures to divest), even if they do not involve bodily movement or result from prior acts of acquisition. Someone leaves a gun in my house, and I decide to keep it; keeping it might involve no movement on my part, but it actualises the results of my practical reasoning, and thus counts as an action, something I do.[42] In other cases, of course, 'possession' might consist in nothing more than the failure to divest oneself: someone leaves drugs in my pocket or my house, and I simply fail to remove or dispose of them. The control requirement does not distinguish these two kinds of case; for in both it is within my control either to retain or to dispose of the item in question. The action requirement does distinguish them, and permits criminalisation only of the former kind.

These three examples illuminate the differences between the traditional act requirement, understood as requiring some voluntary bodily movement; the action requirement as I have specified it, requiring an actualisation of the results of practical reasoning in a way that has an impact on the world; and the control requirement. They also show why an action requirement is more plausible than the act requirement, and highlight the key difference between an action requirement and a control requirement: the latter makes criminal responsibility for omissions unproblematic, the former makes it problematic. That is the issue to which we must now turn.

6. Criminal Responsibility for Omissions

The question of whether or under what conditions we can be legitimately held criminally responsible for involuntary movements, or for conditions or states of affairs, has turned out to be the question of whether or under what conditions we can legitimately be held criminally responsible for omissions. A control requirement does not distinguish action from omission: whether *X* is an outcome of my action or an event that I could but do not prevent, I can have the same degree of control over whether *X* ensues, and can thus be criminally responsible on just the same basis in both cases. An act requirement precludes criminal responsibility for omissions—although Moore allows that some omission-based criminal responsibilities

41 Moore, 1993: 21; see also Model Penal Code, s 2.01(4).

42 Such 'active' possession is distinct from 'possession with intent', when the possession is intended as a means to a further end (see eg Firearms Act 1968, s 16; Misuse of Drugs Act 1971, s 5(3)), but possession with intent is always in this sense 'active' possession: see further at nn 68–70 below.

can be justified as exceptions to the act requirement.[43] An action requirement initially makes matters more complicated, since we must now draw not simply one distinction, between actions and omissions, but several.

First, whether we focus on actions, on acts or on control, we must distinguish omissions or lettings happen from mere not doings. For it to be true that *A* failed or omitted to Φ, or let *X* happen or failed to prevent *X*, it must be true not just that *A* did not Φ or did not prevent *X*, but that *A* disappointed an expectation that he would Φ or prevent *X*; and that expectation is typically, particularly in the context of responsibility ascriptions, normative. More precisely, it must be true that A had some prospective responsibility to Φ or to prevent *X*; absent such a responsibility, his not doing or not preventing would not constitute an 'omission' or a 'letting happen'.[44] My neighbour leaves her book in the garden; it starts raining; I could take the book indoors to save it from being ruined by the rain; I do not do so. She could properly accuse me of 'failing' to save her book or of 'letting' it be ruined, ie of an omission, only if she could claim that I had a responsibility (as a neighbour; in virtue of a prior agreement; ...) to save it.

Secondly, just as we can draw a distinction between action and non-action (between active and non-active) within the realm of thought (as distinct from action in another sense), so we can, as we have seen, distinguish active from non-active within the realm of omissions as distinct from actions. An omission can actualise the results of practical reasoning, when the agent explicitly or implicitly decides not to Φ or not to prevent *X* (for a reason that she could specify if asked); or it can involve simply the failure to exercise one's capacity for practical reasoning and one's capacity to actualise the results of such reasoning in a way that would lead one to Φ or to prevent *X*.

Thirdly, as we have seen, we can distinguish cases of 'commission by omission' from those of 'mere' omission: I insult the Queen by not standing up when she enters the room, or break a promise by not coming to meet you. Such commissions are typically made possible either by social conventions that give my inaction a particular meaning (for instance as an insult or a breach of promise), or by some particularly stringent prospective responsibility that I bear. If a parent does not feed his child, we would talk not just of letting the child go hungry, but of starving the child (or killing the child if she dies);[45] if a doctor does not administer treatment

[43] See Moore, 1993: 22–34, 55–9.

[44] See Casey, 1971; above, Ch 1, text preceding n 32.

[45] Compare *Gibbins and Proctor* (1918) 13 Cr App Rep 134 (see Ormerod, 2005: 79–80). See also *People v Oliver* 258 Cal Rptr 138 (1989): D had taken V home, allowed (if not encouraged) him to inject heroin in her bathroom, and failed to summon medical help when he collapsed; the court upheld her conviction for involuntary manslaughter.

that is unproblematically necessary to save a patient's life, we might say not merely that she let the patient die or failed to save him, but that she killed him.

Fourthly, however, there is a category of cases falling between 'commissions by omission' and 'mere omissions'. A 'mere' omission is a failure to act or to prevent; what the person is explicitly held responsible for is that failure, not its further consequences. I can be guilty of failing to report an accident in which I was involved as a driver even if the accident is in fact (unknown to me) reported by someone else;[46] the offence consists not in bringing it about (by action or omission) that the accident is not reported, but in failing to discharge my particular responsibility, as the driver, to report it. Similarly, a 'Bad Samaritan' statute could define the offence simply in terms of a failure to give assistance that one could easily and safely give to someone in urgent need—so that the offence is committed even if the endangered person is not in fact injured or killed (because he luckily escapes, or because others then intervene).[47] We could, however, also hold an omitter responsible for an event that she fails to prevent (if it occurs), but distinguish her relationship to that event from that of one who actively brought it about. If *D* failed to intervene to help someone in fatal danger, we could (especially if she had some special responsibility) hold her responsible for his death if he dies (not just for her failure to help him), but distinguish the wrong that she commits from that committed by one who kills, as a lesser wrong.

There is therefore not just one question about whether, or when, criminal responsibility should attach to omissions, but several.[48] I will not try to answer these questions here, but it is important to clarify the differences between them, and the ways in which answers to them will depend on conceptions of agents' prospective responsibilities. (There are several questions once we reject the simplistic consequentialist claim that there is no intrinsically significant difference between action and omission—between actively doing harm and failing to prevent it.[49] Taken at face value, that claim implies that we are morally, and should therefore at least in principle be held criminally, responsible for every harm that we

[46] See Road Traffic Act 1988, s 170.

[47] See eg German Criminal Code s 323c (see Dubber and Kelman, 2005: 251–2). Some comparable American statutes (Vt Stat Ann § 519; Wis Stat § 940.34; contrast R I Gen Laws § 11–56–1) explicitly limit the duty to intervene to cases in which the necessary assistance is not being provided by others; but presumably the fact that others arrived and helped after *D* had walked away would not save *D* from liability. See generally Feinberg, 1984: ch 4; Dressler, 2000a, and 2006: 116–17; Law and Philosophy, 2000.

[48] See generally Ashworth, 1989; Moore, 1993: 22–34, and 1997: 262–86; Simester, 1995; Sistare, 1995 (also 1989: 54–63); P Smith, 2003; Simester and Sullivan, 2007: 64–78; Dubber and Kelman, 2005: ch 13.

[49] See eg Bennett, 1966 and 1995: ch 8; Rachels, 1975. For a useful general discussion see Quinn, 1989.

could but do not prevent, in just the same way as we are for harms that we cause. That would be true if, but only if, we had responsibilities to prevent harm as universal and stringent as are our responsibilities not to do harm; without pursuing the familiar arguments here, we can simply note just how implausible such a conception of our responsibilities is.[50])

The first question is whether the criminal law should enforce any general responsibility to prevent harm; this is where 'Bad Samaritan' statutes come to the fore. We can recognise a general moral responsibility to help others who are in serious need, in virtue of our common humanity; if I do not help someone whom I could easily help, that counts as a failure to help for which I am morally answerable to the victim and to others. That general responsibility is enforced indirectly by the law when some of the taxes that we are legally required to pay are spent on humanitarian aid: but should we also ever be legally required as individuals to assist others in need, on pain of being condemned as public wrongdoers if we do not? There are good reasons of principle in favour of Bad Samaritan statutes;[51] what matters here, however, is that the criminal responsibilities that they impose are in two ways more limited than our criminal responsibilities not to cause harm. First, they do not cover all the harms for which we would be criminally responsible if we actively brought them about: they typically cover only emergencies involving (serious) physical harm. Secondly, Bad Samaritan offences are distinct from, and much less serious (punished much less severely) than, offences of active harm: their creation as distinct and lesser offences reflects, rather than rejecting, the view that there is a crucial moral difference between actively harming and not preventing harm.[52]

Bad Samaritan statutes turn what would otherwise count in law as mere not doings into omissions—failures to assist. So too do statutes that impose more specific positive duties to act in virtue of particular roles, relationships or activities: the legal requirement that drivers report accidents in which they were involved, for instance, or the requirement that bankrupts disclose all their property to the official receiver, or the requirement that parents ensure that their children attend school, or the requirement that employers take reasonable steps to ensure the health and safety of their employees.[53] The second question concerns the proper scope of these more specific duties, and the more specific omission-based criminal responsibilities that they generate. Here again it would be

[50] See eg Casey, 1971; B Williams, 1973c.

[51] See eg Feinberg, 1984: ch 4; Menlowe and McCall Smith, 1993.

[52] Which is why it is so odd for Feinberg to ground his defence of such statutes on the claim that (in easy rescue cases) 'the distinction between harming and not-preventing is morally insignificant' (1984: 186).

[53] See, respectively, Road Traffic Act 1988, s 170; Insolvency Act 1986, s 353; Education Act 1996, s 444(1); Health and Safety at Work etc Act 1974, s 2.

implausible to deny that the criminal law can properly be used to define and enforce some such positive responsibilities that are imposed on citizens who fill particular roles or engage in particular activities—duties of care for others to whom those roles or activities connect them, duties to assist the proper functioning of the state and its institutions. Indeed, the criminal law also imposes what can be quite demanding positive duties of specific assistance on all citizens as such: it is an offence to refuse to assist a police officer who asks one for help in dealing with a breach of the peace,[54] or to fail to appear if summoned for jury duty.[55] The substantive issues concern the proper extent of such positive responsibilities.

The third question concerns 'commission by omission'. It arises in one way when we ask whether someone who fails to discharge a duty to assist should be held criminally responsible not just for that failure, but for the harm that he fails to prevent (if it does ensue).[56] It is hard to see why, in principle, he should not be, given the salient role that 'resulting harm' plays in the criminal law generally. The fact that my criminal attempt succeeds, or that my dangerous conduct actually causes harm, typically makes a significant difference to my legal fate, either as making me guilty of a more serious offence or as making me guilty of an offence at all; so why should not the same be true of my failures to prevent harm?[57] One answer might be that I should be held responsible only for harms that I cause, and that failures to prevent harm do not cause it:[58] but so long as it is true (as it often will be) that the harm occurred *because* I did not prevent it, that can justify holding me responsible for it—indeed, saying that I caused it in the sense of 'cause' that is relevant here. Another answer might be that the 'because' will often be harder to prove in cases of omission than it is in cases of action: how confident can we be that intervention would have been successful? That consideration speaks to whether it would be practicable to hold the omitter criminally responsible for the harm that he does not prevent, rather than to the question of principle that concerns us here.[59]

[54] See Ormerod, 2005: 223. Note, however, that the offence of obstructing a police officer 'in the execution of his duty' (Police Act 1996, s 89) requires an active obstruction, not merely a failure to answer questions or to divulge information (see Ormerod, 2005: 547–9).

[55] Juries Act 1974, s 20.

[56] See at nn 46–47 above.

[57] With both actions and omissions, the occurrence of the harm might of course be a matter of luck; this is not the place to rehearse the arguments that criminal responsibility can properly depend on what is in this sense a matter of luck (see Ch 3, n 18 above).

[58] See eg Mack, 1980; Moore, 1993: 267–76; on the other side see Feinberg, 1984: 171–86.

[59] It is also true that if more than one person fails to intervene, responsibility for the resulting harm will be shared among all those who thus fail; but such shared responsibility is not problematic.

The other way in which the question of commission by omission arises is more central to our present concerns. When should the criminal law recognise that a criminal action can be committed by an omission? Since commissions by omission typically depend either on social conventions of meaning (that in virtue of which not standing when the Queen enters the room counts as an insult, for instance), or on the ascription of stringent responsibilities (to parents or doctors, for instance),[60] the question is when the criminal law should take notice of such conventions and responsibilities: but that question does not permit a single or simple answer; nor will the difference between 'commission by omission' and 'commission by commission' always be relevant to the answer. We can ask whether we should ever criminalise insulting behaviour or breaches of promise: but the difference between insults or breaches of promise that consist in doing something and those that consist in failing to do something will not be significant in our discussion of such questions.[61] We can ask when different 'result crimes' can be committed by omission, which is to ask when the responsibilities of particular agents in relation to particular kinds of harm are so stringent, based on such tight normative bonds, that a failure to take appropriate steps to avert such harms makes them the agent of the harms if they occur:[62] but that question can only be answered on a case by case basis.

Where does all this leave the 'action requirement'? Such a requirement is not undermined by offences of 'commission by omission', since these require actions: a parent who commits murder by not feeding his child commits (from the point of view of the law of homicide) the same type of action—killing—as does one who poisons his child. It is, however, undermined by the wide range of cases in which omissions are criminalised as omissions: both the range of specific offences of omission tied to specific positive duties to act in virtue of particular roles, relationships or activities, and the less common general offences of omission that are exemplified by Bad Samaritan statutes. Such examples undermine the action requirement as a descriptive or analytical principle: our criminal laws do not in fact always require action as the object or as a condition of criminal responsibility. They also undermine it as a normative principle. It would be quite implausible to argue that the law should not both impose at least some such specific duties on those who occupy certain roles or relationships, or who engage in certain activities, and criminalise as public wrongs failures to discharge those duties.[63] It is also hard to deny that there are at least

[60] See at n 45 above.

[61] See text following n 17 above.

[62] See Ormerod, 2005: 77–85.

[63] See at nn 53–55 above. Such offences might be portrayed as involving action—as offences of engaging in specified activities without taking the required steps (Hughes, 1958:

good reasons of principle in favour of some kind of Bad Samaritan statute: the fact that we are dealing here with failures to prevent harm, rather than with active harmings, gives us reason to define the offence more narrowly and as a less serious offence, but does not give us principled reason not to criminalise such failure at all.[64]

We therefore cannot sustain an action requirement which requires action, as distinct from omission, as either the object or a necessary condition of criminal responsibility; the cases in which action is not required are too common, and too uncontroversial, to count either merely as special exceptions to such a requirement or as errors. Nonetheless, the distinction between action and omission, between intervening in the world to do harm and failing to intervene to prevent it, still has some moral significance:[65] it is eroded only in those special cases, like that of parent and child, in which the agent has peculiarly stringent responsibilities of care. The idea of action can thus still play a modest role in determining the proper structure and scope of criminal responsibility.

First, we can talk of a limited 'action presumption', that criminal responsibility in result crimes, those defined in terms of results that are identifiable independently of the defendant's agency,[66] should be for the action of bringing the relevant result about, not for a mere failure to prevent its occurrence. The law should not, as a general rule, criminalise failures to prevent any result that it is criminal actively to bring about, although it may impose special duties to prevent specific kinds of harm on those who fill particular relationships or roles, or engage in particular activities. Secondly, when the law does criminalise failures to prevent harm, it should normally distinguish them from active harm-doings, as distinct and lesser offences: it can do this either by criminalising only the failure to act, without assigning criminal responsibility for the actual harm, or by distinguishing omissive from active responsibility for the harm.[67]

598; Gross, 1979: 63ff; in response see Moore, 1993: 31–3). That kind of analysis is sometimes appropriate, most obviously for offences of negligence which can be analysed as involving Φ-ing (driving, for instance) without taking due care, and which are therefore consistent with the action requirement. But in other cases we can say only that the duty to act is tied to one's satisfying a particular, often avoidable, description, whether what is described is an activity or a relationship; what is criminalised is then still an omission.

[64] See at nn 51–52 above.

[65] See at nn 49–50 above. I have not tried here to specify the distinction more precisely or to deal with various difficult borderline cases that arise (see eg Moore, 1993: 24–31): for present purposes we can rest content with an informal and admittedly vague contrast between intervening in the world and failing to intervene, so long as we bear in mind that what counts as 'intervening' may itself be a normative question (I intervene by insulting the Queen). See also Katz, 1987: 143, on the idea that we are dealing with omission rather than with action if the outcome in question would still have occurred had the agent not existed.

[66] See Gordon, 2000: 59 for a slightly misleading specification of the distinction between 'result crimes' and 'conduct crimes'.

[67] See at nn 56–59 above.

Such an action presumption is clearly defeasible, in the ways indicated here; but it does mark the way in which, when our concern is with criminal responsibility for identifiable results, actions should be the law's primary or paradigm focus: criminal responsibility for failing to prevent harm should be the exception—an exception typically justified by the seriousness of the harm, as in Bad Samaritan statutes, or by the agent's special responsibilities—rather than the general rule. These two principles together mark the way in which our responsibilities not actively to do harm are typically more stringent, more general (less tied to particular roles) and wider (covering wider ranges of harms and evils) than are our responsibilities to prevent harm: such differences in the scope and character of prospective responsibilities are familiar, although in some theorists' eyes controversial, in our moral lives; they are properly reflected in the criminal law.

A final example will illustrate this point, and illustrate the difference between the action presumption and both the traditional act requirement and a control requirement. 'Possession' is typically understood in existing criminal law as requiring nothing more than knowledge that one has control over the item in question. Possession offences therefore typically require no more than a failure to divest oneself of the relevant item: if I know that someone has left drugs in my pocket, house or car, I can be guilty of possessing them just so long as I do not dispose of them.[68] The law could instead require active possession—possession as an active keeping rather than merely as a failure to divest. It does this when it criminalises possession with intent to do something with what is possessed—to use a firearm to endanger life, or to supply drugs:[69] to possess *X* with intent is to possess *X* as a means to a further intended end, which is to actualise the results of one's practical reasoning about how to achieve that end. It could do this more generally by defining possession offences in terms of an intention to retain the item in question, rather than merely of knowledge that one had it: in that case I would not be guilty of 'possessing' drugs if someone left them in my pocket, house or car, even if I knew they were there, unless I intended to keep them. Whether it should do so, either in general or in relation to particular possession offences, is

[68] See eg Model Penal Code, s 2.01(4); Law Commission, 1989a, s 182; Simester and Sullivan, 2007: 77–8, 113–4; Ashworth, 2006: 108–9; *Warner v Metropolitan Police Commissioner* [1969] 2 AC 256. English criminal law does not always require even knowledge of the criminal character of what is possessed (see Misuse of Drugs Act 1971, s 28: D is guilty unless he can 'prove . . . that he neither believed nor suspected nor had reason to suspect' that what he had was a controlled drug; and see *McNamara* (1988) 87 Cr App R 246; *Lewis* (1988) 87 Cr App R 270; Simester and Sullivan, 2007: 155–6). On the even broader scope of 'possession' in American Criminal Law see Dubber, 2001, 2005; for further discussion see below, Ch 7 at nn 71–74.

[69] See eg Firearms Act 1968, s 16; Misuse of Drugs Act 1971, s 5(3); n 42 above.

just one instantiation of the general question of whether or when we should criminalise omissions as well as actions. Neither the traditional act requirement nor the control requirement enables us to raise that question about possession offences, since they do not distinguish active from omissive possessing: according to the act requirement, both active keepings that do not involve bodily movement and failing to divest oneself count equally as omissions, and are therefore equally problematic bases for criminal responsibility, whilst according to the control requirement both are equally under the agent's control, and are therefore equally unproblematic as bases for criminal responsibility. But it is a real, substantive question.

More precisely, there are two questions we must ask about criminalising omissions, here and in other contexts. The first question concerns our civic responsibilities. If there is a social mischief involved in some kind of item (firearms, for instance, or certain kinds of drug) being under the unconstrained control of private individuals (and that there is such a mischief must be a presupposition of possession offences),[70] citizens clearly have a civic responsibility not actively to commit that mischief—not to acquire or keep such items. But do they also have a civic responsibility to prevent the occurrence of that mischief—or, more modestly, to prevent its occurrence when they are peculiarly well placed to do so, as when they know that an item of the relevant kind is under their control by being within their space (their pocket, or house, or car)? Secondly, if they do have such a civic responsibility, should it be given the backing of the criminal law: is it a responsibility of such a kind and seriousness that failures to discharge it merit public condemnation and punishment as public wrongs? The action presumption shows, as the act requirement and the control requirement do not, what these questions amount to and why they are important; for it embodies, as they do not, the conception of action that is relevant to the criminal law.

7. Action and Character

One role for an action presumption, as for the traditional act requirement, is to declare that criminal responsibility should normally require *at least* action—rather than 'mere' thought, condition or omission. But there is another role: to declare that criminal responsibility should focus on *nothing*

[70] It is unlikely that possession will be a primary or self-standing mischief: typically, it will be a mischief only derivatively or secondarily, as creating a risk of some primary mischief that would ensue from the (mis)use of the item; see further below, Ch 7.2–3.

more than action; it should not, in particular, be concerned with character traits or virtues or vices, except to the extent that they are directly manifested in our actions.

This would seem to preclude 'character' theories of criminal responsibility, which ground criminal responsibility in traits of character *rather than* in choice or action:[71] but how far this is true depends both on how we should understand the idea of character in this context and on whether character is posited as the object or as a condition of criminal responsibility. The latter question is not always clearly addressed by character theorists, but it is more plausible to make some aspect of character a condition of responsibility for something else (for, in line with the argument of this chapter, our actions or omissions) than to make it the object of criminal responsibility.

One reason for this is that we need not then worry about the extent to which we can be held responsible for our characters. Another reason is that the criminal law is not structured around vices or character traits. Types of crime are defined and individuated, not in terms of the vices of character that they reveal, but in terms of the actions (or omissions) they involve, or the interests they injure, or the harms or evils they cause. The same crime—murder, theft or criminal damage, for instance—could manifest any of a range of vices or character defects, and conviction for the crime does not depend on identifying any specific vice or defect; but if the vice or defect was the object of criminal responsibility, it would surely be identified at the point of conviction, and therefore in the definition of the crime. Character theorists could of course argue that we should be criminally responsible for our defective character traits only on condition that they are manifested in action (perhaps because only action provides reliable and legitimate evidence of character); but that still would not explain why crimes are defined and classified in terms of actions or of their impact on the world, rather than in terms of the vices or character traits that are on this view the true objects of criminal responsibility. The most familiar objection to positing character as the object of criminal responsibility, however, is the liberal thought that the law should regulate our dealings with each other as social agents in a social and material world: it is properly concerned with how we treat each other, ie with our actions and omissions; it has no such proper direct concern with the character traits, with the virtues or vices, that lie behind our behaviour.

I will not defend that liberal thought here. The point to note is that it need not preclude positing vice or defect of character as a condition of criminal responsibility, especially if that condition operates as a defeasible

[71] For different versions see eg. Bayles, 1982; Brandt, 1985; Lacey, 1988: ch 3; Huigens, 1995, 1998, 2002; Gardner 1998b; Tadros 2005a. For detailed criticism see Moore, 1997: ch 13; Duff, 1993.

presumption. Proof of a criminal action or omission, that is, would create a presumption that the action or omission flowed from a relevant vice or defect of character (it would not now be important for offence definitions to specify the vice); but it would be open to the defendant to adduce a defence which would defeat that presumption. As we will see in Chapter 11, this is a plausible way to understand some excuses (though we will also see that it makes only a very aetiolated notion of character relevant to criminal law); my concern here is with its more general plausibility as a condition of criminal responsibility.[72]

To understand and assess any 'character' theory, however, we must grasp what is meant by 'character' in this context, and in particular what the relation between character and action is taken to be.[73] The simplest character theory is Humean.[74] Character traits are psychological conditions which cause actions, and which can therefore be inferred from actions in the way that causes can often be inferred from their effects; the various kinds of criminal defence, and perhaps denials of mens rea, aim to secure the defendant's acquittal by blocking the inference from action to defective character trait. A Humean theory raises very forcefully the question of why criminal action should be necessary for criminal responsibility, since we could on this view have other kinds of good evidence for the existence of the relevant character trait;[75] but it is for that same reason defective, since character of the kind that could interest criminal law is logically rather than contingently or causally related to action that manifests it. Cowardice and courage, for instance, can be displayed in many different ways and contexts—in how a person faces or fails to face up to different kinds of danger for the sake of different goods; but if we could imagine someone who has never faced a situation that calls for courage, and who has therefore never displayed either courage or cowardice, that would be to imagine someone who *is* (as yet) neither courageous nor cowardly.[76] The point is not just that we would not yet be able to know whether she is courageous: it is that there would be nothing yet to be known, since virtues and vices such as courage are part *constituted* by the actions that manifest them.

In sharp contrast to Humean theories stand those that identify character with dispositions to action: a person 'is dishonest if and only if she tends to

[72] See Tadros, 2005a (especially chs 1–3) for the most plausible version of this kind of view. What we will see in Ch 11 is, more precisely, that vice or defect of character can sometimes be understood as a condition not of responsibility, but of liability: see at n 81 below.

[73] See generally Hudson, 1986; Kupperman, 1991.

[74] See eg Bayles, 1982; Brandt, 1985.

[75] It also raises the question why one action suffices for criminal responsibility: see Moore, 1997: 577–84.

[76] See Dummett, 1978: 14–16; contrast Brandt, 1970: 26; Moore, 1997: 563–5.

act dishonestly'; so, apart from the 'diachronic aspect' of judging persons, 'the standard by which we judge a person dishonest is exactly the same standard as that by which we judge an action dishonest'.[77] On this view, talk of vices or character traits is still talk of actions—although of aspects of actions deeper than the action's impact on the world, the agent's 'choice' to do it, and other familiar elements of orthodox mens rea, since it includes 'the spirit in which and the reason for which' the action is done;[78] to say that the criminal law is properly concerned with character traits or vices is then not to deny that its proper focus is on actions. But this view of character is also untenable: character, especially in the aspects that constitute virtues and vices, includes more than dispositions to action. An Aristotelian conception is more plausible: character includes our conceptions of the good (the ends to which we commit ourselves); dispositions of desire and feeling as well as action; habits of attention and perception (what we notice or attend to), and of deliberation and decision (what kinds of reason we attend to and how we weigh them).[79]

On an Aristotelian conception of character and virtue, the fact that someone committed a crime certainly entitles us to infer, in the absence of any defence, that his character is morally defective: assuming that what the law defines as crimes are indeed wrongs, a person of true virtue, or even one with proper self-control who resists the kinds of temptation to do wrong that the truly virtuous person does not even feel, would not normally commit a crime.[80] However, the crime by itself does not entitle us to infer any specific defect of character: in particular, we do not yet know whether it manifested true vice—a commitment to evil ends; or only weakness of will—a failure to resist temptation, or to bring my actions into conformity with my proper ends and values. Nor, if it did display vice, might we know which of several possible vices it displayed. We know that the offender failed to show a proper respect or concern for the rights or interests on which her action impinged, or for the values that it flouted; but that is simply an inference from her action as a criminal wrong, which tells us nothing specific about what defect of character it manifested. We could of course inquire further, to find out what specific vice or weakness the action embodied, and such further dimensions to the crime might figure at the sentencing stage (an issue that we cannot explore here); but such further inquiries are no part of the initial determination (the determination expressed in the verdict) of whether the defendant is guilty

[77] Gardner, 1998b: 575.

[78] *Ibid.*

[79] See Aristotle, *Nicomachean Ethics*, especially Bks II–IV, VI–VII; Hursthouse, 2003.

[80] For the crucial distinction between virtue and self-control see Aristotle, *Nicomachean Ethics*: I.13, VII.1, VII.9; see also Urmson, 1988: ch 2.

of the offence—which is to say that they do not bear either on whether, or on for what, the defendant is criminally responsible.

To say that we are criminally responsible for our criminal actions, on condition that they flow from or manifest a suitable vice or defect of character, is thus usually not so much false as empty. It is true that if we are criminally responsible for an action, that action presumptively manifests a vice or defect of character; but that it manifests this is an inference from, not an independent condition of, our criminal responsibility for it.[81] Furthermore, whilst we will see in Chapter 11 that we can understand some excuses as defeating that presumptive inference from criminal action to defective character, we will also see that this is a matter not of responsibility, but of liability: for excuses are defences, which admit responsibility but block the normal transition from responsibility to liability.

Finally, however, we should note here one way in which the claim that criminal responsibility should be for, and focused on, action rather than character is less determinate, and less strict, than might at first appear. It would be both determinate and strict if we could draw a sharp distinction between 'the action' ('the action itself') and the character traits or vices or virtues that lie behind the action and are manifest in it; but no such sharp distinction can be drawn.

Action descriptions are famously open to the 'accordion effect':[82] we can include more or less about the circumstances and consequences in our description of 'the action'—as a trigger pulling, a shooting, a killing, a killing of a soldier. We can also include more or less about the agent's intentions, reasons and motives: he was running, running for the train, escaping from prison; he was taking revenge, asserting his superiority, showing off. This is especially true of rich moral descriptions: what makes an action honest or dishonest, generous or mean, is 'the spirit in which and the reason for which it is done'.[83] In thus enriching our descriptions of the agent's action, we bring in aspects that could equally be classed as aspects of character: although someone's action can be vengeful, arrogant, dishonest or mean without it being true that he has the vice of vengefulness, arrogance, dishonesty or meanness as a lasting character trait, such action descriptions begin to delve into the realm of character.

Such attitudinal and motivational factors sometimes figure in offence definitions. If, for instance, an assault is motivated by or 'demonstrates' hostility towards the victim's racial or religious group, the assailant is guilty

[81] Compare the sense in which it is true that we want or desire any result that we intend: in that sense, wants or desires are implications, rather than independent grounds or criteria, of intention: see Nagel, 1970: chs 2–3; McDowell, 1978: 14–15.

[82] See Austin, 1961: 148–9; Feinberg, 1970b.

[83] Gardner, 1998b: 575.

of 'racially or religiously aggravated assault'.[84] To hold that criminal responsibility must be grounded in action, rather than character, need not lead us to reject all offences of this kind: what we should rather say is that such motivational factors should be included only if they make some significant difference to the meaning of the action and to the nature of the wrong that it constitutes. One can see grounds for arguing that this is indeed so in the case of racially or religiously motivated assaults, at least when the hostility is 'demonstrated' in the assault: the motivation aggravates the attack as an attack on a particular (and typically vulnerable) racial or religious group.[85] This seems to be inconsistent with the familiar and often criticised slogan that motives are irrelevant to criminal liability:[86] but insofar as that slogan means anything more substantial than that in deciding guilt or innocence courts should not attend to any motives beyond those specified in the offence definition,[87] it cannot express anything stronger than a presumption that offence definitions should not delve too far into the motivational and attitudinal depths of citizens' actions.

Such depths are of course often crucial to the character and significance of moral wrongs. But the familiar liberal concern to limit the extent to which the criminal law can intrude into our souls underpins the presumption that criminal wrongs must generally be defined in more limited terms that lack the rich motivational and attitudinal depth of many moral descriptions. Within our extra-legal moral relationships, especially our close or intimate relationships, such depths and nuances are crucial: they determine the meaning and worth of our actions, and so determine what we must answer to each other for. The criminal law, however, is concerned with our relationships simply as citizens, who may have no closer connection to each other than that: it should aim to define the kinds of wrong that violate that civic relationship, for which we must answer to our fellow citizens. Its offence definitions should still specify what citizens can recognise as genuine moral wrongs,[88] and it might sometimes be concerned with, for instance, the expressive meanings of our actions; but it should not try to capture all the depths and nuances of our moral descriptions of actions.

The issues at stake here are neatly illustrated by the question of whether theft should be defined in terms of dishonesty, as in section 1 of the Theft

[84] Crime and Disorder Act 1998, ss 28–29: see Ch 3 n 16 above.

[85] We need not pursue the question whether these grounds are adequate (and whether they would justify identifying other motivational aggravations) here; my point is only that some such grounds are *necessary*.

[86] On which see Sistare, 1987; Husak, 1989a; Horder, 2000; Norrie, 2001: 36–46; Ormerod, 2005: 118–9.

[87] See Duff, 1998a: 173–5.

[88] See Gardner, 1994; Horder, 1994a; Duff, 2001: 188–93; Tadros, 2005a: 103–15.

Act 1968, or simply in terms of an unlawful taking with intent to deprive, as in section 223.2 of the Model Penal Code. Whilst the English definition does not require the prosecution to prove dishonesty as a character trait (a usually honest person could give in to temptation and commit a dishonest action), it brings a moral depth to the law that the Model Penal Code does not: if we are to justify that feature of English law, however, we must be able to show not merely that it brings such moral depth, but that such depth is in this context crucial to the identification of the kind of wrong which the law should define and condemn.

The conclusion of this section is very similar to those of the previous sections. An action presumption has a significant role to play in constraining the scope of the criminal law and the objects of criminal responsibility. It tells us that criminal responsibility should, normally, be for actions—rather than for mere thoughts or mere omissions, and rather than for or on the basis of deeper aspects of the agent's character. However, first, given the porous character of the distinction between 'action' and 'character', such a presumption cannot draw a clear line between that which is and that which is not presumptively relevant to criminal responsibility; it serves rather to urge restraint in how far we deepen the law's offence definitions. Secondly, it is still a presumption rather than a requirement: it leaves room for arguments to the effect that some aspect of the agent's character, as manifested in the action that constitutes the crime, makes such a significant difference to the character of that action as a public wrong that the criminal law should take formal note of it. Such a presumption, as thus understood, might set fewer and looser (or vaguer) limits on the criminal law than the act requirement purports to set; but it has the signal advantage of philosophical viability and normative plausibility.

It does not, however, take us very much further towards an account of the kinds of wrong that can properly concern the criminal law, given the vast range and diversity of wrongs that we can commit by our actions. It is time to try a further approach to that task.

6

Criminally Responsible For What? (3) Harms, Wrongs and Crimes

We should, I have argued so far, be held criminally responsible for wrongdoings which are 'public' in the sense that they properly concern all members of the polity, and merit a formal, public response of censure or condemnation.[1] However, although this helps to clarify the formal character of criminal law, it does not take us far towards a substantive account of its proper scope, since it does not help us determine which kinds of wrongdoing should count as 'public'. For a pure legal moralist, all wrongdoings in principle concern the criminal law; but we have seen that this is not a plausible view.[2] There are too many kinds of wrongdoing, even serious wrongdoing —hurtfully breaking off an affair, betraying a friend's confidence—that are not even in principle the business of the criminal law: I must answer for such wrongs to those directly involved, but need not answer for them to my fellow citizens as such. So which kinds of wrong are the criminal law's business?

A familiar answer to this question appeals to the Harm Principle: we have, in principle, good reason to criminalise conduct (only) if it is suitably related to an identifiable harm. This chapter will clarify that principle, and identify the proper, limited role that it can play.

1. Clarifying the Harm Principle

Some versions of the Harm Principle, notably Mill's, are exclusionary: '*the only* purpose for which power can be rightfully exercised over any member of a civilized community, against his will, is to prevent harm to others'.[3] Other versions, notably Feinberg's, are permissive. 'It is always a good reason in support of penal legislation that it would probably be effective in

[1] See Chs 2.3 and 4 above.
[2] See Ch 2.2(b) above.
[3] Mill, 1859: ch 1, para 9 (emphasis added).

preventing' harm to others:[4] but this leaves open the possibility that there are also other good reasons—such as the prevention of serious offence that does not amount to harm,[5] or of paternalistically motivated coercive infringements of others' freedom that invade autonomy even if they are not on balance harmful,[6] or even of 'free floating evils' that neither harm nor offend.[7] We must therefore ask two questions. First, is harm prevention always a good reason for criminalisation? Secondly, is harm prevention the only good reason for criminalisation?

To answer either question, we will need to clarify the relevant notion of harm; this will be the task of section 2, but a few further preliminaries are necessary.

One concerns 'to others'. Although discussions of the Harm Principle typically assume that 'others' means other people, it should also cover other non-human beings with interests that merit the law's protection: in particular, criminal laws protecting animals against abuse or maltreatment should be understood as protecting, not human interests, but the interests of those animals themselves.[8] The inclusion of 'to others' also, of course, rules out paternalist criminal laws that aim to protect people against harms they might do to themselves. This is another topic that I cannot pursue here, save to note that the account of criminal responsibility offered here highlights the two crucial questions about the justification of paternalist criminal laws—as distinct from other kinds of paternalist intervention by the state.[9] First, can conduct be morally wrong if it is harmful only to its agent? Some would count as morally wrong only conduct that injures others, while others would argue that self-harms can be morally wrong regardless of their impact on others;[10] the latter is more plausible (think of the person who wastes his talents, or corrupts his sensibilities by a diet of sadistic pornography), but does not by itself give us reason to criminalise self-harming conduct. We must ask, secondly, whether this is a kind of wrong that properly concerns our fellow citizens, as one that demands public condemnation: or should we rather say, as liberals traditionally

[4] Feinberg, 1984: 26.
[5] Feinberg, 1985.
[6] Feinberg, 1984: 78; 1986: especially chs 18–19.
[7] Feinberg, 1988: especially xix–xx, 318–38.
[8] See eg Protection of Animals Act 1911; Abandonment of Animals Act 1960; Wild Mammals (Protection) Act 1996; Fur Farming (Prohibition) Act 2000; Hunting Act 2004. I leave aside the question whether we (and the criminal law) should also recognise other aspects of the natural world as having intrinsic interests that we must protect: see eg Stone, 1974; Taylor, 1986 (on which see Brennan and Lo, 2002).
[9] Though Mill's Harm Principle, unlike Feinberg's, was concerned with the exercise of any kind of state power, not merely with criminal law. See generally G Dworkin, 1972; Husak, 1981; Shiner, 2003: 239–48.
[10] See Falk, 1968, for a useful discussion.

argue, that wrongful conduct becomes the business of our fellow citizens only when and insofar as it impinges on others?

Another preliminary concerns prevention. As both Mill and Feinberg formulate the Harm Principle, what justifies criminalising conduct is that doing so will prevent harm. The obvious way in which criminalisation prevents harm is by preventing harmful conduct: but this leaves open the possibility of criminalising conduct that is not itself harmful, if doing so could prevent conduct that was harmful. That possibility might not seem real, especially given that conduct must be wrongful before it can legitimately be criminalised: what makes conduct relevantly wrongful, from the perspective of the Harm Principle, must surely be that it is itself harmful. As we will see when we discuss *mala prohibita* again, that possibility is in fact sometimes actualised; for the moment, however, we need only consider conduct that is itself harmful.[11]

Finally, even if we attend only to harmful conduct, the Harm Principle must permit the criminalisation of conduct that either causes *or creates a risk of* harm.[12] We can, for instance, properly criminalise dangerous or drunken driving as such, not merely those instances that actually cause material harm:[13] such conduct is wrongful, and criminalisable, in virtue of its dangerousness even when it does not actually cause material harm. One could argue that dangerous conduct always causes harm—the harm of being exposed to a risk of substantive harm.[14] But, first, this would be only a 'secondary' harm, the harmful character of which derives from that of the primary harm which is risked.[15] Secondly, not every kind of dangerous conduct that we have good reason to criminalise actually exposes others to a risk of harm: someone who drives recklessly round a blind corner is guilty of dangerous driving even if the road is in fact clear and no one is actually exposed to a risk.[16] Rather than bringing dangerous conduct within the reach of the Harm Principle by portraying risk as a harm, we

[11] See Ch 7.3 below. The preventive formulation of the Principle also allows us to criminalise failures to prevent harm, even if we deny that they can be said to cause the harm; see above, Ch 5 at nn 56–59.

[12] See Feinberg, 1984: 11: 'conduct that causes serious private harm, or the unreasonable risk of such harm'.

[13] See Road Traffic Act 1988, ss 2, 4; Ch 7.2 below. It is a further question whether the law should distinguish between the dangerous or drunken driver who (luckily) causes no material harm and the one who causes harm—as it does when death is caused (Road Traffic Act 1988, ss 1, 3A): see Cunningham, 2002: 955–7.

[14] See eg Finkelstein, 2003: but she relies too heavily on the argument that we must count risk itself as a harm if the criminalisation of dangerous conduct is to be consistent with the Harm Principle (at 987–9).

[15] See Gross, 1979: 124–5.

[16] Which is why (*pace* Lanham, 1999: 962) the Model Penal Code is right to define reckless endangerment as 'conduct which places or may place another person in danger' (s 211.2).

should more simply say that the Principle permits the criminalisation of conduct that causes or creates a risk of harm.

Can the Harm Principle, as thus understood, help us determine which kinds of wrongful conduct can properly be criminalised? If it is to do so, we must make sure that 'harm' is not so defined that every kind of conduct that we have good reason to criminalise, or every kind of wrongful conduct, counts for that very reason as 'harmful':[17] but how should it be defined?

2. Harms and Wrongs

Feinberg's still influential account can be used to illustrate the problems that face an attempt to specify a conception of harm that will enable the Harm Principle to set substantive, and plausible, constraints on the scope of criminal responsibility.[18]

Feinberg begins with the conceptually 'fundamental' idea of a 'harmed condition', which is understood as a setback to interests. We 'can hope to analyze th[is] idea of harm ... without mentioning causally contributory actions'; a sub-class of harmed conditions consists of those that are caused (or preventable) by human action; and the criminal law's proper interest is in the sub-class of that sub-class that consists in harmed conditions that are caused by wrongful human action—'setbacks to interests that are wrongs'.[19] More precisely yet, the criminal law should focus on wrongful setbacks, not to any interest, but to 'welfare interests': our interests in those basic goods that are necessary for our pursuit of almost any of our varied 'ulterior' goals or interests.[20] We might add that if we attend to the ordinary concept of harm, the Harm Principle should cover only setbacks that are non-trivial and non-momentary: a very minor, or merely momentary, setback even to a welfare interest does not really count as harm.

That account of harm seems especially apt for harms to individuals, but we must also be able to talk of public interests and public goods (which may not be reducible to individuals' goods), and of harm to them.[21] Indeed, if crimes are 'public' wrongs, wrongful violations of public goods seem to be strong candidates for criminalisation—though we will need to look more carefully at the idea of public wrongs in section 5; this is

[17] Compare the way in which the 'act requirement' can be emptied of substantive content by stretching the definition of 'act' to cover whatever we can be held responsible for: above, Ch 5 at n 4.

[18] See generally Feinberg, 1984; Kleinig, 1978; Raz, 1986: ch 15, 1987; Holtug, 2002; Stanton-Ife, 2006.

[19] Feinberg, 1984: 31–6; the quoted phrases are from pp 31 and 36.

[20] *Ibid*, 37–8, 61–4.

[21] See Feinberg, 1984: 63–4, 222–5. On public goods see Raz, 1986; Taylor, 1989.

particularly true of our shared or public interest in the maintenance and efficient functioning of such institutions as taxation, the health and welfare systems, and the criminal justice system itself. For present purposes, however, we can focus on wrongful setbacks to individual interests.

There is of course ample room for controversy about 'interests'—for instance about the connections between interests, wants and needs, and about the extent to which my informed judgements of my own interests are authoritative.[22] For present purposes, however, the crucial point is that for Feinberg we must be able to identify the harms or setbacks to interests that are to concern the criminal law in a way that is (initially) independent of their wrongful character: we must first identify 'harmed conditions', and then see which such conditions are produced by wrongful human actions. Now one can see why such a non-moralised conception of harm would be attractive to a traditional liberal like Feinberg: for it seems to give the criminal law a grounding that is independent of, and thus neutral as between, different moral perspectives; although moral considerations, and disagreements, will arise when we ask which setbacks to interests are wrongful, we can at least begin from a non-moral account of our interests and of what can set them back with which members of a morally pluralist society should all be able to agree. However, this aspect of Feinberg's account opens the way to an objection that also illustrates a more general problem for the Harm Principle: that it can avoid being seriously under-inclusive only by becoming something close to vacuous.

We must examine two kinds of case: those that involve Feinbergian harm, but where the distinctive harm that properly concerns the criminal law cannot be captured by a Feinbergian account; and those that do not essentially involve any Feinbergian harm.

Burglary is an example of the first type. Consider a burglary committed whilst the victim is out, involving the theft of property and relatively minor damage. Feinbergian harms are certainly caused: the victim suffers property loss or damage, and setbacks to his interests in privacy and autonomy—to his private enjoyment of his home without intrusions by others, to his control over the contents and arrangement of his home.[23] These are harms that could have equally resulted from non-human causes (a hurricane blows off his roof, or blows a stranger into his house). But the victim might not see the harm he suffers in this light. His response to the loss and damage will probably be structured by the fact that they resulted from burglary, not from natural causes. His sofa has been not just damaged, but *vandalised*; the watch that his grandfather left him was not just lost, which would be painful enough, but *stolen*—which generates a

[22] See Barry, 1965: ch X; G Thomson, 1987; Weale, 1998.
[23] See von Hirsch and Jareborg, 1991: 26–7.

distinctive distress at the idea that someone has taken it for his own use, to sell for profit. The violation of privacy that burglary victims often highlight is a matter not merely of a stranger being in his home without his consent, but of the burglar's *invasion* of his home. The vandalism, theft and invasion are, surely, harms—significant setbacks to interests that are important to him: but they cannot be identified without reference to the wrongful actions that generate them. They are not separately identifiable consequences of the burglar's actions that could have been caused by non-human factors; they reflect the meaning of those actions as an attack on *V* and his home. Nor are they separable from the Feinbergian harms that *V* suffers: he does not suffer the loss of or damage to his property, plus the separate harms of vandalism and theft—of being wronged in these ways; rather, this is how he understands the loss and the damage as crimes. Nor can we identify the distinctive harm of burglary with *V*'s feelings, or with the effects they might have on his future life (his future anxieties and their impact on how he lives): for those feelings reflect his recognition of the wrongful harm that he has suffered—a harm that he would still have suffered even had he not realised that he had been burgled. He does not count as suffering the harm because he feels as he does; rather, he feels as he does because he has suffered this wrongful harm.

Similar points can be made about other 'result crimes', including murder: rather than saying, with Feinberg, that a murder victim suffers the same harmed condition as one who dies from natural causes, we should recognise the distinctive harm of being wrongfully killed, of having one's life attacked (successfully) by another.[24] On a Feinbergian account of harms as 'harmed conditions', the difference between the victim of a murder, or a burglary, and the victim of a natural disaster lies in the causation of the essentially identical harm that each suffers; but this fails to capture the distinctive features of what the victim of crime suffers, in virtue of which what is done to him is properly criminalised. We therefore cannot appeal to a non-moralised or pre-moral notion of harm to pick out the kinds of wrong that properly concern the criminal law: at least in these contexts the harm is partly constituted by the wrong.

The second kind of case—conduct that clearly constitutes a criminal wrong, but that does not essentially involve Feinbergian harm—is even more problematic. Consider what Gardner and Shute call the '*pure* case' of rape, in which the victim is raped whilst unconscious, never comes to know of the rape, and suffers no adverse physical or psychological effects.[25] This is an unusual case of rape, but not a dubious or borderline

[24] See Duff, 1990a: 105–15; 1996: 132–3, 366–9.

[25] Gardner and Shute, 2000: 197; I leave aside here their claim that this is the central case of rape, 'entirely stripped of distracting epiphenomena'. See also Ripstein, 2006, on 'harmless trespass'.

case: it is just as much and obviously a criminal rape as are those in which the victim knows what is being done and suffers the familiar consequential physical and psychological harms. So we must say either that this victim is still harmed, or that this constitutes an exception to the Harm Principle. The former move would preserve the Harm Principle by rejecting Feinberg's account of harm as grounded in harmed conditions that we can identify 'without mentioning causally contributory actions'; but this would threaten the substantive significance of the Principle as an independent principle by which we can determine which kinds of wrong can properly be criminalised. The latter move would save Feinberg's account of harm, but mark a further dent in the Harm Principle: since we have the same good reason to criminalise this unusual type of rape as we do to criminalise all other types of rape, the Harm Principle could not now explain why we should criminalise rape.[26]

Coercive paternalism presents a similar problem. If I interfere to prevent you carrying out a self-harming action, I set back your interest in liberty, but might on balance advance rather than set back your interests—in which case my action is not criminalisable under the Harm Principle, since it does not harm you. But liberals will want to criminalise such actions (if their victims are rationally competent): Feinberg therefore makes a 'liberal departure (though a small one) from the wholly unsupplemented harm principle', to permit the criminalisation of such 'infringements of an actor's *autonomy*'.[27] We may wonder why he does not count such infringements of autonomy as harms, since the exercise of our autonomy is surely a key welfare interest. But infringements of autonomy do not fit the Feinbergian model of harm: they are not independently identifiable effects of autonomy-infringing actions; nor is their wrongful impact on the victim a matter of their long term effects on her life. Rather than portraying them as harms to be weighed against the benefits that the infringement brings in a unitary harm-benefit calculus (as Feinberg weighs the invasion of the interest in liberty), we should portray them as infringements of a right, which belong to a different normative logic that cannot be captured by the Harm Principle. Nor is this simply a 'small' departure from the Harm

[26] Feinberg takes the former route: rape is 'a violent imposition of one person's will on another's, which is not just an alternative means to the same harm as [other serious sexual offences that the Model Penal Code distinguishes from rape], but *an important part of the harm itself*' (1986: 298). Gardner and Shute opt for a third possibility: rape is a 'non-instrumental wrong' that is not identifiable in terms of harm as a separable consequence of human action; but its criminalisation respects the Harm Principle, since we criminalise it in order to prevent the harms that would flow from 'the wider occurrence' of such wrongs (2000: 216–7). But this distorts the reasons for criminalising rape in the same way as attempts to portray it as a wrong against or harm to 'the public' (see at nn 66–68 below). Rape is indeed a kind of wrong that people should not have to fear and the fear of which is destructive of various goods: but what makes it worth criminalising is its wrongfulness.

[27] Feinberg, 1984: 78.

Principle. There might be relatively few criminalisable actions that infringe autonomy without also causing harm, but actions that are covered by the Harm Principle will also often, perhaps typically, infringe autonomy: murderers, rapists, thieves, defrauders, all infringe their victims' autonomy. If the infringement of autonomy gives us reason to criminalise action that is not otherwise harmful, it gives us reason to criminalise action that is otherwise harmful; in which case what we can call the 'Autonomy Principle' becomes relevant to decisions about criminalisation across a very wide range of cases.[28]

This illustrates the first general problem faced by a Feinbergian Harm Principle: there are cases in which the features that make conduct apt for criminalisation do not consist in 'harm' as he understands it. One way to deal with such cases is to revise the meaning of harm so that such cases can be said to involve harm: we recognise the distinctive harm of having property or privacy violated by a burglar, or autonomy infringed by a coercive paternalist. However, that threatens to render the Harm Principle vacuous: if we begin to count as 'harmful' every kind of wrongful conduct that we see good reason to criminalise, the Harm Principle will do little to constrain legal moralism. The other way to deal with such cases is to admit that they mark departures from the Harm Principle, and allow that we have reason to criminalise some kinds of wrong that are not necessarily harmful. This, however, threatens to reduce the Harm Principle from being the core principle of criminalisation to being one among other principles each of which specifies a good reason for criminalisation.

Two further examples should indicate the scope of this problem. The first is *R v Brown*.[29] The defendants, members of a sado-masochist group, engaged in various kinds of mutually consensual violence, involving the infliction of significant pain and of non-trivial physical injury; the House of Lords upheld their convictions for wounding and causing actual bodily harm, on the ground that consent neither negated the crime nor provided a defence. Now a standard liberal response would be to argue that whether or not the physical injuries that were inflicted constituted harm, the 'victims' were not wronged. '*Volenti non fit iniuria*': consent might not negate harm, but it negates the wrongfulness that criminalisation requires. A 'bold' liberal would stick to this principle, however serious the physical harm involved: if someone who is rationally competent truly gives informed consent to what another does to him, he is not wronged, and the

[28] And see Ripstein, 2006, on the 'Sovereignty Principle'; see text following n 60 below.

[29] [1994] 1 AC 212 (three of the defendants later applied, unsuccessfully, to the European Court of Human Rights: *Laskey et al v UK* (1997) 24 EHRR 39); see Giles, 1994; Kell, 1994; Allen, 1994; Bamforth, 1994; Roberts, 2001; Ashworth, 2006: 318–25; Bergelson, 2007. Feinberg discusses a fictional example of gladiatorial combat (1988: 128–33, 328–31; see Kristol, 1971).

conduct therefore cannot legitimately be criminalised.[30] However, as one imagines cases involving progressively more serious physical (or psychological) harms, even quite bold liberals tend to become uneasy, and find it harder to insist that consent should always preclude criminalisation.[31]

What grounds such unease is not, I suspect, just the degree of seriousness of the physical injuries caused, but a conception of the meaning of the actions that deliberately inflict them: if the point of the action is to inflict extreme pain or serious injury, or to degrade and humiliate others in a ritual of torture, consent surely cannot legitimate it.[32] I might consent to be treated in ways that degrade or deny my humanity; but that does not render the treatment other than wrongful. That is why a more plausible argument for acquitting the *Brown* defendants would appeal not simply to consent (whilst implicitly admitting that the 'victims' were harmed), but to the meaning of the actions in their context: although to the ignorant outsider their activities look like exercises in degradation and humiliation, we should realise that this way of finding sexual gratification is, within that sub-culture, a way in which the participants express their love and respect for each other.[33] But such an argument abandons the Harm Principle, and moves onto the Legal Moralist's ground.[34] For the argument is that the *Brown* defendants' conduct is worthy at least of our moral respect: it is oriented towards morally legitimate ends (mutual sexual pleasure); it is informed by morally admirable values (love and respect); even if the means by which those ends are pursued and those values are expressed are unusual, and to others' eyes shocking, when understood in their particular context they lose their *morally* shocking character. The argument is thus also that their conduct is not harmful: for it fulfils, rather than setting back, the interests of those involved. We need not accept it for ourselves, or approve of it; we may still think it wrong. But we should not see it as meriting public condemnation, since it does not

[30] For 'bold' as against 'cautious' liberalism see Feinberg, 1988: 324; on '*volenti non fit iniuria*' and 'the absolute priority of personal autonomy' see Feinberg, 1984: 115–17; 1986: ch 19; 1988: 130. A bold liberal view would cover even the case of consensual cannibalism, *if* one could be sure of the 'victim's' rational competence; but a German court decided that this constituted murder (see *The Guardian,* 10 May 2006, available at www.guardian.co.uk/germany/article/0,,1771382,00.html).

[31] And the two Law Lords who held that the *Brown* defendants should not have been convicted (Lords Mustill and Slynn) thought that consent would not bar conviction if *grievous* bodily harm was caused.

[32] Hence, perhaps, the importance attached in *R v Brown* to 'hostility' as an essential element of the offence.

[33] Thanks to Ryan Windeknecht for pressing this argument. Of particular importance for this argument is the role played by a system of agreed signals by which the 'victims' could stop things going too far, and the mutual trust on which those signals depended.

[34] For Legal Moralist arguments that bear on *R v Brown* see eg Finnis, 1987b (on which see Richards, 1987), 1994; George, 1993, 1999.

violate the values of mutual respect and concern by which our collective life as a polity is supposedly structured.

A liberal might be tempted to argue that the morality or otherwise of such conduct should not be what is at issue: as consensual sexual activity, it is a matter of 'private' morality which is, 'in brief and crude terms, not the law's business'.[35] The argument just offered was meant to show that this quick liberal response is inadequate. To show that we have no good reason to criminalise such conduct, according to the Harm Principle, we must show either that it is not harmful or that, though harmful, it is not wrongful. To show that it was not harmful we must attend, I have suggested, to its moral significance as an aspect of mutually respectful sexual relationships—which brings to bear a moralised conception of harm. To show that it was not wrongful we cannot, I have suggested, simply appeal to consent, but must look at the substantive character of the conduct, and in particular at whether it must count as degrading or dehumanising.

Consent would be a decisive consideration only if autonomy, understood procedurally as the unconstrained exercise of the will by a rationally competent agent, was always a decisive factor—decisive either as negating harm (that to which I autonomously consent cannot truly harm me); or as negating wrongfulness (*volenti non fit iniuria*); or as rendering the conduct in question a private matter that is not the law's business. But that is not a plausible conception of autonomy as the core value of a liberal polity: if autonomy is to be of such value, we must rather understand it in more perfectionist terms of a capacity to choose between and to pursue *valuable* ends.[36] The example of gladiatorial combat brings this out clearly.[37] What makes the commercial combats that Kristol and Feinberg imagine morally so outrageous is not simply the fact that the participants are trying to kill each other: it is at least arguable that some kinds of deliberate killing (in just wars; in duels governed by a strict code of honour) are consistent with respect for the other's humanity. What matters is that they are commercial events, aimed at paying customers who want, not a display of martial virtues that might be admired for their nobility, but 'brutal bloodshed' that they encourage by 'their bloodthirsty screams'.[38] But the 'brutality' that the spectators are paying to see, and that the gladiators must provide, denies (by definition) the humanity of those involved: they are reduced, they reduce themselves, to 'brutes' who try to maim and kill each other for

[35] Wolfenden, 1957: para 61; see Ch 2 at n 32 above.

[36] See especially Raz, 1986: 369–429; also Sher, 1997: chs 2–3; and for a useful overview Christman, 2003.

[37] See n 29 above.

[38] Feinberg, 1988: 129–30.

the amusement of a paying—and baying—crowd.[39] The gladiators might all consent, as do the spectators: but the perfectionist liberal will rightly argue that consent does not negate the harm that is done (the harm not merely of death, but of mutual dehumanisation); it does not negate the wrongs that they do to each other (and to themselves). Nor does it render such wrongs and harms purely private matters: since they constitute serious violations of the most basic values, of mutual concern and respect, by which the polity's members' dealings with each other are supposed to be structured, they are wrongs in which the whole polity has a proper interest.

This is not to claim that the activities of the *Brown* defendants are comparable to those of the gladiators, or that they should be criminalised; it is to claim that the fact of consent is not dispositive. Before we can say that an activity which aims to cause physical or psychological injury to others falls, in principle, outside the reach of the criminal law, we must ask not just about the consent of those involved, but—as I asked above in relation to *Brown*—about the moral meaning of that to which they consent: does the activity pursue ends, and express values, which we should respect?[40]

The second example concerns offensive behaviour. Some such behaviour is wrong (if it is wrong) because it is offensive: continuous loud noise is an example. Other such behaviour is offensive because it is wrongful: racist abuse is an example.[41] I will not discuss the former kind of conduct, which covers many kinds of 'anti-social behaviour', in detail here, but it is hard to deny that, whilst we must resist the rush to criminalise whatever we find offensive, such conduct can cause such persistent disruption and annoyance that we have reason—as a last resort—to criminalise it.[42] Advocates of the Harm Principle might argue that we reach that point only when the conduct begins to cause harm, but it is not clear that appeals to harm play a substantive role in the argument: it is simpler and more straightforward to ask whether the conduct in question has enough impact on rights or interests that the law should protect.[43] So too with 'public nuisance'—conduct the effect of which 'is to endanger the life, health,

[39] Does this imply that boxing (at least commercial boxing before paying spectators) is also a dehumanising, degrading enterprise (see Feinberg, 1988: 128)? I suspect that it is a borderline case (and the *Brown* court found it hard to explain why boxing should not be criminalised): the formal constraints on what the boxers may do to each other might still leave logical space for non-ironic talk of boxing as a 'noble art', but the actualities of commercial boxing leave little space in practice for any such idea.

[40] See also *Wilson* [1996] 2 Cr App R 241.

[41] For this distinction, and further discussion see Duff and Marshall, 2005.

[42] See eg Noise Act 1996, s 4.

[43] Compare Hörnle, 2001: 268–70. Feinberg deals with offensive conduct by adding an independent 'Offense Principle' (Feinberg, 1985). The range of conduct that is, at least arguably, criminalised as being offensive rather than harmful is illustrated by the 49 pages,

property, morals or comfort of the public, or to obstruct the public in the exercise or enjoyment of rights common to all Her Majesty's subjects'.[44] This common law offence is, of course, too broad and vague to be acceptable; but the fact that a kind of conduct causes inconvenience or discomfort rather than harm is not a conclusive reason against its criminalisation, as a minor offence subject to appropriately mild censure and punishment. Conduct that is offensive because it is wrongful, however, raises more complicated issues.

To say that a racist insult is offensive is not (just) to say that people are in fact offended by it; I could indeed call it offensive even if it actually offended no one. It is rather to say that it would be reasonable to be offended by it, or even that people *should* be offended by it. We should be offended by it because it intentionally denigrates or demeans those against whom it is directed; because it denies its victims' membership of the community to which the racist belongs and casts doubt on their legitimate membership of the polity. It attacks their civic standing in the community—an attack that is particularly disturbing when, as is typically the case, the insulted group also suffers other kinds of systemic disadvantage in that society. Our existing criminal laws tend to criminalise such insults only if they are also intended or likely to 'stir up racial hatred', or to cause 'harassment, alarm or distress' to those who might hear them,[45] which suggests an attempt to bring them within the scope of the Harm Principle: racial hatred is liable to lead to violence; alarm and distress are liable to be psychologically harmful. But we have reason to criminalise such insults independently of such consequential harms. Such insults are admittedly disturbing in ways that make them apt for criminalisation only in a context in which those at whom they are directed are liable to find them threatening —perhaps not physically threatening, but threatening to a secure sense of their membership of the polity; we would not have such reason to criminalise racial insults against confident members of a secure and privileged majority. What makes them public wrongs, however, is their blatant and derogatory denial of their victims' status as members of the polity.[46]

The previous paragraph was not meant to show that we should, on balance and all things considered, criminalise racial or any other kinds of insult: there may be very good reasons not to do so, including problems of

covering 9 categories of offence, devoted to 'Offensive Conduct' in Glazebrook, 2006 (though one could quarrel with some of his classifications).

[44] *Goldstein* [2004] 2 All ER 589; Spencer, 1989; Rees and Ashworth, 2004; Ormerod, 2005: 991–6.

[45] See eg Public Order Act 1986, ss 4A–5, 17–19.

[46] Similar points apply to debates about pornography: a focus on the consequential harms that are caused by its production or consumption should not distract us from key questions about its intrinsic character.

enforcement and the difficulty of distinguishing criminal insults from robust free speech.[47] My concern throughout this chapter is with the question of what can count in principle as a good reason for criminalising a certain kind of conduct, and whether the Harm Principle can help us to identify or set the limits of such reasons; and my argument has been that in this context, as in the other cases discussed in this section, it cannot play the role that its advocates want it to play. If we stick to a Feinbergian notion of harm, we cannot capture the grounds that we surely have for criminalising several kinds of wrongful conduct; if, in order to bring such conduct within the scope of the Harm Principle, we revise the notion of harm, we risk depriving the Principle of the kind of substantive content that it needs if it is to set stricter constraints on the scope of the criminal law than legal moralism already sets.

There are of course other versions of the Harm Principle, structured by other accounts of harm, than Feinberg's, which I have not discussed and will not discuss here.[48] I would simply suggest that all face the same problem—the problem, to put it crudely, that they can avoid the defect of under-inclusiveness only by so stretching the notion of harm that the Harm Principle ceases to set substantial independent constraints on the scope of the criminal law.

The Harm Principle also faces another kind of objection: that once we allow, as we must, that we have reason to criminalise harm-threatening as well as harm-causing conduct, we will again find it hard to use the Harm Principle to constrain the scope, and the expansion, of the criminal law.

3. Harms, Risks and Remote Harms

The previous section focused on the objection that the Harm Principle, if it is substantive, is also under-inclusive; this section focuses on the objection that it is over-inclusive.[49]

One such objection is that it captures conduct that causes what we should count as private rather than public harm. If I break off an affair in a callously unfeeling way, this wrongs the other person and might well

[47] See Ormerod, 2005: 990; *Jersild v Denmark* (1995) 19 EHRR 1.

[48] See eg Raz, 1986: ch 15, 1987, on which see Stanton-Ife, 2006. A problem for Raz's account is that he takes criminalisation to involve coercion which infringes autonomy; criminalisation can thus be justified only if on balance it fosters autonomy by preventing conduct that itself infringes autonomy. But we do not violate a person's autonomy merely by defining conduct as criminal, requiring him to answer for it in court, and requiring him to undertake or undergo an appropriate punishment if he is convicted (see Duff, 2001).

[49] See also Harcourt, 1999, on the way in which, in recent American political debate, '[c]laims of harm have become so pervasive that the harm principle has become meaningless' (at 113).

harm her—it sets back her significant interest, not in a continued relationship with me, but in relationships structured by the respect and concern that I notably fail to show her. There are no doubt even better reasons not to criminalise such conduct; but the Harm Principle itself does not provide them. Similarly, Feinberg thinks that:

> repeated rude and disrespectful remarks to parents, spouses, teachers, and others who have a right to better treatment ... not only 'wound feelings', but indirectly harm the interest in personal efficiency by causing depression and anger sufficiently great to distract and debilitate.

Such harms are excluded from criminalisation, he argues, because they are too trivial, so that it would cause more harm to criminalise them.[50] The harm to my (ex-)lover cannot be said to be trivial, however; and what should preclude criminalisation either of my treatment of her or of my rudeness to my partner or parents is not that the harm is too trivial, or that it would be too harmful to try to prevent it, but that it is the wrong kind of harm: such harms, we would naturally say, are a private matter between the parties directly affected and those close to them; they are not the criminal law's business. If that is right, the Harm Principle needs to be turned into a Public Harm Principle, but it is not clear how we are to establish an appropriate meaning or criterion for 'public harm'. I will return to the issue of public harms and wrongs in section 5, but we must turn now to the other over-inclusiveness objection.

I noted earlier that the Harm Principle must permit the criminalisation of conduct that creates a risk of harm, as well as of conduct that actually causes harm.[51] But once we start down this road, it is not clear where we can set the limits of the criminal law.

It is easy to bring conduct that is intended, or that threatens, directly to cause harm within the scope of the Harm Principle. We can differ about just how far the law of attempts should reach;[52] about whether our laws should contain general offences of 'reckless endangerment', or only more specific offences covering particular kinds of endangerment;[53] about when and how far merely negligent conduct should be criminalised; and so on. But whether our concern is to prevent harm or to criminalise harmful conduct, we clearly have reason to criminalise such directly dangerous conduct.[54] However, our existing laws reach far wider than this. They

[50] Feinberg, 1984: 188–9.

[51] See at nn 12–16 above.

[52] Contrast eg Criminal Attempts Act 1981, s 1, with Model Penal Code, s 5.01(1). I leave aside here the issue of 'impossible attempts', at least some of which do not actually threaten to cause harm: see Duff, 1996: chs 2, 3.

[53] See eg Model Penal Code, s 211.2 ('reckless endangerment'); KJM Smith, 1983.

[54] See at nn 11–16 above; also Gross, 1979: 427–30 on 'dangerous' and 'harmful' conduct.

capture conduct that is no more than preparatory to the intended commission of a crime,[55] or that simply makes it more possible that a crime will be committed, by oneself or by others, as with many possession offences.[56] They cover conduct whose connection to harm of any kind is even more remote than that, such as failing to display a car's excise licence or to produce driving documents when required to do so by a police officer.[57] One could no doubt make a case for most, if not all, such offences by arguing that they contribute ultimately or indirectly to the prevention of harm, but that is just the problem: if the Harm Principle extends to cover conduct that is not itself directly harmful or dangerous, it is hard to see how it can set tight or determinate limits on the scope of the criminal law.[58]

Various replies are available to advocates of the Harm Principle; none are persuasive. It might be argued, first, that the Principle should be read as permitting the criminalisation only of conduct that itself threatens directly to cause harm, but that would be too quick; as we will see in Chapter 7, we can have good harm-preventive reasons to create *mala prohibita* that are only indirectly related to the actual causing of harm. It might be argued that conduct must be wrongful before it can be criminalised, and that conduct that is not directly related to harm is not wrongful in the appropriate way; but we will see in Chapter 7 that if we are justified for harm-preventive reasons in creating rules prohibiting conduct that might not itself be harmful or dangerous, breaches of those rules can be wrongful in a way that merits criminalisation. It might be argued that in its full version the Feinbergian Harm Principle gives us good reason to criminalise conduct only if doing so would effectively prevent harm '*and* there is probably no other means that is equally effective at no greater cost to other values',[59] and that the more remote from the relevant harm the conduct lies, the more likely it is that other and less costly ways of preventing the harm will be available; but that still leaves the proposed legislation's harm-preventive efficacy as *a* good reason in support of it, even if that reason is outweighed by the moral and other costs of the legislation and the availability of less costly alternatives.

I am not suggesting that advocates of the Harm Principle are committed to supporting all the kinds of expansive criminal legislation with which we are depressingly familiar; they will certainly often be able to argue that, even when what is to be prevented is some harm that it is the proper

[55] See eg Prevention of Crime Act 1953, s 1; Criminal Law Act 1967, s 4; Criminal Damage Act 1971, s 3(a).

[56] See eg Misuse of Drugs Act 1971, s 5; Firearms Act 1968, s 5; Terrorism Act 2000, ss 57–58. See generally Dubber, 2005.

[57] Vehicle Excise and Registration Act 1994, s 33; Road Traffic Act 1988, ss 164–165.

[58] See von Hirsch, 1996; Harcourt, 1999.

[59] Feinberg, 1984: 26 (emphasis in original).

business of the state to try to prevent, the proposed legislation will make too small a contribution to that prevention, or will violate other important rights and values. The point is, however, that the Harm Principle itself, as the principle that the harm-preventive efficacy of criminalising a certain type of conduct gives us good reason to do so, can do little work in limiting the expansion of the criminal law.

4. Giving Harm its Due

If the Harm Principle cannot play the role, in setting the proper focus and limits of criminal law, that its advocates claim for it, should we seek to replace it by another master principle? Some argue that we should, but I think that such arguments are doomed to failure for reasons like some of those that undermine the Harm Principle; in particular, that so long as the master principle appeals to some normative concept with a tolerably determinate meaning, it will be under-inclusive (even if it is not also, as I have argued that the Harm Principle is liable to be, over-inclusive). Ripstein's suggestion that we should replace the Harm Principle by what he calls the 'sovereignty principle' illustrates the problem faced by any such master principle.[60]

What 'provide[s] the legitimate basis for criminalization', Ripstein argues, is not harm, but the 'violation[] of equal freedom' or of sovereignty;[61] and he shows that this can capture kinds of in principle criminalisable wrongdoing that the Harm Principle cannot capture. But criminalisable violations of sovereignty involve 'usurping' or 'destroying' another's 'powers'—which must be intentional: bodily injury, for instance, 'only violates your sovereignty if I deliberately inflict it on you', since only then is it 'a manifestation of despotism'; sovereignty 'can only be violated by the intentional deeds [the 'intentional wrongdoing'] of others'.[62] The sovereignty principle can thus cover crimes that consist in attacks (I leave aside here the issue of whether we can best capture the wrongfulness of attacks by appeal to the single notion of sovereignty, rather than to the more varied range of more specific rights and interests that are attacked). As we will see in detail in Chapter 7, however, another broad category of criminal conduct involves endangerment rather than attack: there is no intention to harm, dominate or destroy; the wrong rather consists in the

[60] Ripstein, 2006; see also Dan-Cohen, 2002, on the 'dignity principle'; Dubber, 2002b, on autonomy.

[61] Ripstein, 2006: 216.

[62] Ripstein, 2006: 234, 235, 239.

culpable doing of what endangers others' interests or safety. The sovereignty principle cannot show why endangerment is properly criminalisable; but it is hard to see how it could be plausibly argued either that one who recklessly endangers others commits no wrong, or that such wrongs cannot in principle be matters of such public concern that they merit the condemnation of the criminal law.

The desire to find some single concept or value that will capture *the* essence of crime, or *the* essential characteristic in virtue of which crimes are properly punished, runs deep in some theorists.[63] I will suggest in the following section that we should resist this desire in favour of a pluralism that recognises a diversity of reasons for criminalisation, matching the diversity of kinds of wrong which can legitimately be the criminal law's business; but we should first note that, despite the criticisms offered in the previous section, the Harm Principle captures something important about the focus of a liberal criminal law. More precisely, its Feinbergian version picks out what is distinctive about one large category of crimes, whilst its moralised version expresses a significant, if vague and indeterminate, constraint on liberal criminal law.

As we saw in section 2, the Harm Principle cannot deal with crimes the 'harmfulness' of which is essentially tied to their wrongfulness. This is typically true of crimes that consist in attacks on protected rights or interests. But many crimes are matters of endangerment rather than of attack, and such crimes are more straightforwardly covered by a Feinbergian Harm Principle; what makes them criminalisable is their culpable relationship to harms that can be identified independently of the conduct's wrongfulness. This point will be clarified in Chapter 7.

A moralised version of the Harm Principle does not aim to identify harms independently of the wrongs that generate them; it counts the violation of the victim's sexual integrity in a 'pure rape' as a serious harm even if (since she never discovers that she was raped) it has no consequential impact on her interests, and even though the harm consists solely in the wrong that is done to her. To hold that crimes must involve harm in this extended sense does not, I argued in section 2, help us to determine which kinds of wrong are criminalisable; but it does express the liberal idea that only conduct that has some wrongful impact on the world can be the business of the criminal law. Mere thought or feeling is not the criminal law's business, nor are mere conditions or states of affairs that do not express agency, whilst omissions can only be its business if they involve the failure to discharge a specific duty—a failure that then counts as having an

[63] For just a few instances see Murphy, 1973 (crime as taking an unfair advantage over the law-abiding; later criticised in Murphy, 1985); Becker, 1974 (crime as causing 'social volatility'); Hampton, 1992 (crime as 'demeaning' the victim); Dimock, 1997 (crime as undermining trust).

impact on the world; but conduct that has a wrongful impact on the world can for that very reason count as harmful, and is captured by a Harm Principle that applies a suitably extensive conception of harm. That is indeed true, but I think unhelpful. In one way, it says no more than is said by the action presumption explained and defended in Chapter 5—that we are properly held criminally responsible for wrongful actions which make an impact on the world that we share with our fellow citizens, and on our dealings with them. We have seen that that presumption does not help us to determine the proper limits of criminal law or of criminal responsibility; for it does not help us to determine which kinds of wrongdoing can be the criminal law's business, once we reject the simple Legal Moralist view that every kind of moral wrongdoing is in principle apt for criminalisation. The Harm Principle was supposed to assist that further determination, by marking out as apt for criminalisation those kinds of wrongdoing that cause or threaten harm; but we have found that it cannot help us.[64]

5. Crimes as Public Wrongs

In seeking for ideas or principles that could help us to determine which kinds of wrongdoing are in principle apt for criminalisation, we might now turn back to the classical idea of crimes as essentially 'public' wrongs;[65] but how can this help us?

Some criminal offences count as 'public', of course, simply because they wrong or harm the public collectively or the polity as a whole, rather than any distinct identifiable individual. These include such serious crimes against collective, shared goods as treason and attempting to pervert the course of justice; tax evasion (one of the crimes that does fit the idea of taking an unfair advantage over the law-abiding); but also the kind of 'public nuisance':

> which is so widespread in its range or so indiscriminate in its effect that it would not be reasonable to expect one person to take proceedings on his own responsibility to put a stop to it, but that it should be taken on the responsibility of the community at large.[66]

[64] Compare the discussion in German criminal law theory of whether '*Rechtsgutstheorie*' can help determine the proper scope of criminal law by identifying the individual and collective *Rechtsgüter* that the criminal law should protect (Roxin, 2006: 8–47; von Hirsch, 2002; Wohlers *et al*, 2003).

[65] See Blackstone 1765–9: Bk IV, ch 1, at 5, on 'breach and violation of the public rights and duties, due to the whole community, considered as community, in its social aggregate capacity': see above, Ch 2 at nn 38–40.

[66] *A-G v PYA Quarries Ltd* [1957] 1 All ER 894, 908 (Denning LJ); see Ormerod, 2005: 994.

Given the wide range of criminal offences that do not directly wrong individuals, but consist rather in breaches of rules laid down for the sake either of preventing harm or of the efficient administration of state and social institutions, this notion of a 'public wrong' in fact covers quite a lot of the criminal law. The trouble is, however, that there is a lot that it seems not to cover, including most traditional *mala in se*. If we then argue that such *mala in se* as murder and rape count as public wrongs only because they too have a harmful or wrongful impact on 'the public', as well as on their individual victims, we are likely to distort the wrongfulness that makes them criminalisable. Even if a rapist takes unfair advantage over the law-abiding (which is at best arguable), or creates 'social volatility' or undermines trust, that is not what is central to the criminal wrongfulness of his action; what he is properly convicted and punished for is the wrong done to his victim.[67] One could of course say that if we did not as a society condemn such wrongs, through our criminal law, the bonds of mutual trust and concern that unite us as a polity would be undermined; but that would be an implication of our failure to condemn what we should condemn—it does not give us reason to condemn rape and murder.

We should interpret a 'public' wrong, not as a wrong that injures the public, but as one that properly concerns the public, ie the polity as a whole. Some wrongs, even if committed in public, remain private matters: unless my unkind taunting of my friend in the street is so loud or violent that it intrudes on others' peaceful enjoyment, it remains a matter between me and him—it is not the passing strangers' business. Some wrongs, even if committed in private and with no material impact on the wider world, remain public; violent domestic abuse is no less properly criminal for being committed in the privacy of the home. What makes domestic abuse a public wrong is that, as we now recognise, it concerns us all, as a wrong in which we share: we must not leave the victim to pursue her own grievance, but must collectively pursue it with her and for her; her assailant should answer not merely to her, but to us as her, and his, fellow citizens for his attack on her and his violation of the core values by which we define ourselves as a polity.[68] A public wrong is thus a wrong against the polity as a whole, not just against the individual victim: given our identification with the victim as a fellow citizen, and our shared commitment to the values that the rapist violates, we must see the victim's wrong as also being our

[67] See above, Ch 2 at nn 39–40; also Dubber, 2002b.

[68] See further Marshall and Duff, 1998. Note that in not leaving the victim to pursue her grievance by herself, we also do not leave her so free not to have it pursued: the prosecution can in principle proceed without her assent and even against her wishes (although for pragmatic or moral reasons the prosecutor might in fact drop the case if the victim did not want it to go ahead).

wrong. But this does not replace the idea that the wrong is directly done to the individual victim: it is a way of understanding that wrong, as one that concerns all of us.

That crimes are in this sense public wrongs follows from the argument of Chapter 2, that we are criminally responsible as citizens to our fellow citizens: we must answer to them for wrongs that are their business as citizens. But the 'public' character of crime is therefore an implication, rather than a ground, of its criminalisable character: the reasons that justify its criminalisation are the very reasons why it is 'public'. An appeal to the 'public' character of crime thus cannot directly help us determine the legitimate grounds for criminalisation: but it can point us in the right direction by focusing attention on the idea of the 'public'. That idea is, in this context, both normative and context-relative: what is 'public' is what is properly the business of some specifiable group of others, what they have a legitimate interest in; but what that is will depend on the character of the practice in question. In the context of my academic life, what is public is what properly concerns my colleagues, other philosophers, my students, my employer; what is private is what is not their business. What is public depends on how we understand the academic enterprise and the values that structure it: but among the wrongs that should presumably count as public will be plagiarism (as a betrayal or violation of one of that community's essential values) and other types of intellectual dishonesty, as well as failures in my teaching and displayed disrespect for my colleagues; wrongs that are private arguably include my conduct towards my partner (that might concern colleagues who are also our friends, but not *as* colleagues), my financial affairs, my religious or political views and activities—though there are familiar controversies about the last of these. In other contexts—families, religious communities, political parties, sports clubs—the group in relation to which items are public is different (though its membership may overlap), and what counts as public will be different, given the different aims and values of the relevant community.[69]

An account of what should count as public wrongs in a liberal polity thus depends on an account of the defining aims and values of such a polity—an account of the civic enterprise in which members of such a polity are participants. I will not offer such an account here (since my interest is in the structure of the criminal law rather than in its precise content), nor need we think that the criminal law lacks the rational foundation it requires until we can provide such a determinate account of the civic enterprise: for if we abandon, as I have suggested we should, attempts to derive the content of the criminal law from a single master principle, we can accept that debates about its scope will be more

[69] See further Duff, 2001: ch 2.

piecemeal, gradual affairs, more focused on particular offences (actual or suggested), and informed by a range of values, presumptions and considerations that are defined and fleshed out in being applied to such particular cases.[70]

Some wrongs it would be hard to imagine not being criminal in any legal system (though their precise contours will vary in different systems): such wrongs as murder and other kinds of serious physical assault, rape, attacks on property (other than in imaginable property-less societies) constitute serious violations of any polity's core values, whether they are expressed in terms of well-being, rights, autonomy, or any of the other ways in which human societies define themselves.[71] They are wrongs against which any polity must protect its members, and from which its citizens should be able to expect to be safe as they go about their ordinary lives; wrongs which can be called categorical in the sense that, even if the victim was imprudent in exposing himself to the risk of suffering the wrong, his imprudence does not mitigate the wrongfulness of the action or the culpability of the wrongdoer.[72] They are wrongs that must be publicly identified and condemned, in that for a polity not to condemn them, or not to make efforts to identify and condemn their perpetrators, would be to fail to take seriously both the wrongs as they impact on their victims, and the values to which the polity is supposedly committed.[73]

We certainly cannot say that of everything that is criminal in our existing systems, or of everything that we can claim to have good reason to criminalise: once we move beyond the minimum core, there is progressively more room for argument both about which wrongs are or are not the business of the polity as a whole, and about which are such that our response should focus on their wrongfulness, ie treat them as crimes. A justification of criminalisation will need to begin by specifying some value(s) that can be claimed to be public, as part of the polity's self-definition; show how the conduct in question violates that value or threatens the goods that it protects; and argue that that violation or threat is such as to require or demand a public condemnation. Often the question will revolve around the importance of the value or the goods in question and the seriousness of the violation or threat: but the seriousness of a wrong is not itself a reason for criminalisation, unless we have first

[70] Compare Ashworth, 2006: chs 2–3, on the range of different (sometimes conflicting) principles and policies that should bear on issues of criminalisation and offence definition; and see Gardner, 1998a, Duff, 1998a, on why this does not detract from the law's rationality. For an original and promising approach see Husak, 2007.

[71] Compare Hart's account of 'the minimum content of natural law': Hart, 1994: ch IX; see Epstein, 2005.

[72] Hence the justified outrage provoked by judges who suggest that a rapist's culpability is mitigated by what they clearly see as the victim's contributory negligence.

[73] For a similar suggestion about a core class of wrongs see Jareborg, 2005.

shown the wrong to be a public one; nor is seriousness always necessary, since we have reason to criminalise conduct that causes inconvenience, and that is wrong but not seriously wrong. Of course, insofar as the criminal justice system is expensive (materially and morally) and oppressive, we have very good reason to try to limit its grasp: but just as morality covers both serious and minor offences, so should a rational legal system be able to, providing modest and non-oppressive trials and punishments for relatively minor wrongs.

The only way to make progress is to discuss particular cases. One example will help to illustrate the points made above. Adultery is still criminal, and occasionally prosecuted, in some American states;[74] but to liberals it is *clearly* a private matter.[75] One question is whether marriage is or should still be part of our polity's self-definition, as an institution that should be promoted and protected by the law:[76] not merely as one kind of voluntary arrangement among others that the law should facilitate, but as *the* publicly validated mode of private and sexual partnership. Even the answer to that question is becoming less certain (which implies that bigamy should not be criminal, except when it involves deceit): although the rhetoric of government (and of churches) still preaches this, the social reality is that it is coming to be seen as one among other possible ways of sharing one's life. Another question is whether the normative definition of marriage is becoming more fluid, so that sexual fidelity is no longer seen as absolutely crucial—so that the idea of an 'open' marriage is familiar rather than self-contradictory. But even if (a very large 'if') it was still and rightly a core aspect of our public conceptions of the right and the good that marriage is *the* form that long-term sexual relations and child-rearing should take, and that sexual fidelity is crucial to marriage, to argue that we should criminalise adultery would also require arguing that it is a wrong that cannot be left to the individuals concerned to deal with (or to ignore), but that *must* be publicly condemned and sanctioned. That is what we do now say about domestic violence, for instance, and about intra-marital rape:[77] these are not 'problems' that should be resolved by the people concerned (with help being offered but not imposed by the state), or private wrongs that it should be left to the victim to pursue or not as she sees fit; they are public wrongs that we should collectively condemn. We

[74] See *Washington Post*, 26 Feb 2004, B.02, B.08: the convicted defendant began (but then dropped) an appeal on the grounds that the criminalisation of adultery must be as unconstitutional as that of sodomy between adults in private (see *Lawrence v Texas* 123 S 2472 (2003)).

[75] Thus Turkey dropped a proposal to criminalise adultery, which EU states made clear would have caused problems for its attempt to join the EU (see www.guardian.co.uk/international/story/0,,1311428,00.html).

[76] See Devlin, 1965: ch 4.

[77] Though in England only since 1991 (*R* [1992] 1 AC 599).

do not take this view of adultery—nor do I suggest that we should. My point is only that by asking *why* it should seem so obvious that it should not be criminal, we may become clearer about what can constitute a proper ground for criminalisation.

We could also look at relatively new offences such as incitement to racial and religious hatred, and ask what in principle could justify such extensions of the criminal law (leaving aside here the further question of whether this is likely to be practically advisable). I take it that, apart from concerns about consequential harm (the dangers of religiously or racially motivated violence, and of defensive pre-emptive violence by those who feel threatened), what could properly ground such laws is a recognition of the symbolic importance of assured citizenship for groups which are in various ways vulnerable,[78] of the way in which such assured citizenship is denied and thereby also threatened by racial or religious abuse, and of the way in which public condemnation of those who perpetrate such abuse can protect such groups.

I will not try to go further than these two illustrations in discussing the grounds that we can properly cite for criminalising conduct; all I have tried to do in this chapter is to show how we can go about determining what we should be criminally responsible for: for what should we have to answer to our fellow citizens, on pain of condemnation and punishment if we have no satisfactory answer? The only even moderately determinate answer suggested is that we should be criminally responsible for wrongs (presumptively for wrongful actions) that can properly count as 'public' wrongs—with the further, negative suggestion that we cannot identify any simple principle or set of principles for identifying such wrongs, and particularly that the Harm Principle can play only a modest, limited role in this context.[79]

Readers might well, and reasonably, think that this is hardly a satisfactory conclusion to this chapter: especially at a time when governments are prone to mobilise an ever-expanding criminal law as a first rather than as the last resort in addressing a range of actual or perceived social ills, we surely need to identify some more robust constraints on the proper scope of the criminal law than I have offered here. That is indeed a major, if not the most important, task facing liberal theorists of the criminal law,[80] but it is not one that I can undertake here (though I aim to do so in a

[78] Compare Braithwaite and Pettit, 1990: 63–8, on the importance not just of freedom, but of assured freedom —the assurance that one is and will remain free.

[79] Another significant limiting principle that I have not discussed, and cannot discuss here, is that the criminal law should be used only as a 'last resort' (see Husak, 2004, 2005c; Jareborg, 2005; also Roxin, 2006: 45–7, on the '*Subsidiaritätsprinzip*'): that implies at least that, even if we have good in principle reasons to criminalise a type of conduct, we should normally still hesitate before doing so.

[80] For an important contribution see Husak, 2007.

subsequent book): my concern here is with the structure more than with the content of the criminal law, and there is more that we need to say about its structure, in particular about the structural differences between different types of criminal wrongdoing. That will be the topic of the following chapter.

7

Structures of Crime: Attacks and Endangerments

Criminal responsibility should be, paradigmatically, for kinds of wrongdoing that have some adverse impact on our fellow citizens and on the world we share with them, and that merit or demand a formal public response of censure and punishment. As I argued in Chapter 6, we cannot identify any master principle, or set of definitive criteria, by which to determine which kinds of wrong these are; that can only be worked out in a piecemeal way, paying attention both to the character of different types of wrong and to the nature and self-understanding of the polity within which they are committed.[1] The central question will always be: which wrongs are the business of my fellow citizens simply in virtue of our shared membership of the polity? For which kinds of wrong should I have to answer publicly to them, on pain of formal condemnation and punishment if I cannot offer an exculpatory answer?

In this chapter we turn away from the inconclusive discussion about the proper content of the criminal law that occupied Chapter 6 to further issues about its structure, in particular to a distinction between two types of criminal wrong that runs throughout the law—attacks and endangerments. This distinction helps to explain the limitations of the Harm Principle, which can deal with endangerments but not with attacks. The discussion of endangerment offences will also bring us back to the problem of *mala prohibita*:[2] we will be able to see more clearly how at least some such offences can be justified in a criminal law which aims to identify and censure public wrongdoing; but we will also have to tackle the question of how far beyond the categories of directly hostile or dangerous

[1] As I noted earlier (above, Ch 2 at n 42), to argue that what wrongs count as 'public' in this way is, to at least some degree, relative to the particular character of the polity is not to espouse moral relativism.

[2] See above, Ch 4.4.

action the criminal law can properly extend, to capture kinds of conduct that are wrongful only as breaches of a regulation that serves some aspect of the common good.

1. Attacks and Endangerments

Some crime types or tokens consist in attacks on legally protected interests. If I shoot at you, intending to injure you;[3] or start a fire, intending to damage your property;[4] or lie to you, intending to obtain money from you,[5] I attack your interests in physical integrity, in property, in not being harmfully deceived—interests that the criminal law protects against such attacks; I directly violate your rights—rights that the criminal law protects against such violations. If my attack is successfully consummated, I am (absent a further defence) guilty of wounding with intent, of arson, or of obtaining by deception. If my attack is unconsummated, I am guilty of attempting to commit one of those crimes; attempts are attacks that fail.[6]

Other crime types or tokens consist in endangering rather than attacking legally protected interests. If, without intending harm, I act in a way that I realise might injure you or damage your property, I endanger your physical security or property; if, without intending to deceive, I am careless about the truth of my descriptions of the goods I am selling you, I endanger your interest in having accurate information about what you are buying. The criminal law protects these interests against such endangerments. If the endangerment is consummated—you are injured, your property is damaged, or my description is false—I am probably guilty of wounding, of criminal damage, or of applying a false trade description.[7] If the endangerment is unconsummated, I might or might not be guilty of an offence; English and American law have no general offence of unconsummated endangerment analogous to the law of attempts. The Model Penal Code could convict me of 'reckless endangerment' if I risked causing you serious physical injury, but English law could convict me only if I endangered you

[3] Offences Against the Person Act 1861, s 18: since wounding with intent requires an intention to injure, this crime type consists in an attack.

[4] Criminal Damage Act 1971, s 1: since arson does not require an intention to damage, this crime type does not consist in an attack; but some tokens—those involving such an intention—are attacks.

[5] Theft Act 1968, s 15: obtaining by deception requires an 'intention of permanently depriving' the victim; but given the extended definition of that 'intention' in s 6 and the fact that the deception need only be 'reckless', the crime type does not consist in an attack, though most tokens do.

[6] See Criminal Attempts Act 1981, s 1(1); Duff, 1996: 221–8, 363–74.

[7] Offences Against the Person Act 1861, s 20; Criminal Damage Act 1971, s 1; Trade Descriptions Act 1968.

in one of the specific ways that are criminalised.[8] Neither system criminalises endangering property as such, although I could be guilty if I endangered it by, for instance, causing an explosion or a fire.[9] In neither system is it normally criminal to make a statement that I realise might be false unless it actually is false or misleading.[10]

The distinction between attacks and endangerments should be intuitively obvious, but needs some explication.

(a) Distinguishing Attacks from Endangerments

An attack is an action or omission that is intended to injure some value or interest. I can attack your body by trying to injure you; your tangible property by trying to steal or damage it; your reputation by slandering you; your intellectual property by plagiarising your work. Attacks need not, however, be directed against particular people: they can be indiscriminate, aimed at whoever happens to be in their way; they can be aimed at institutions or practices, or even at more abstract values, as when we call propaganda an attack on truth.

Both injury-intending mens and injury-threatening actus are necessary for attacks. By firing a gun I might endanger *V*, but I attack *V* only if I intend to injure him. To form an intention to injure *V*, however, or to prepare to carry the intention out, is not yet to attack *V*: an attacker must progress beyond the 'merely preparatory' to be 'in the process of committing' the attack;[11] and his actions must engage appropriately with the world.[12]

A certain hostility towards its object is intrinsic to an attack—a practical hostility towards the interests or people it attacks, in that it is aimed against those people or their interests;[13] its intentional structure is determined by the injury that it is to do. This hostility is not an attitude lying behind and motivating the action that constitutes the attack: a contract killer or fraudster might feel no animus towards his victims. It is a practical attitude intrinsic to, and constituted by, the action as an attack: to attack

[8] See Model Penal Code, s 211.2; in England, see eg Road Traffic Act 1988, s 2; and at nn 53–7 below.

[9] Explosive Substances Act 1883, s 2; Model Penal Code, s 220.1(2).

[10] But a sworn witness who makes a true material statement that she does not believe to be true commits perjury under English law: Perjury Act 1911, s 1. On American law, see Model Penal Code, s 241.1(1); 18 USC 1621; Green, 2001.

[11] Criminal Attempts Act 1981, s 1(1); *Gullefer* [1990] 1 WLR 1063.

[12] See Uniacke, 1994: 162; Duff, 1996: 53–61, 219–33, 380–97.

[13] Compare *DPP v Smith* [1961] AC 290, at 327 (Lord Kilmuir); *Hyam* [1975] AC 55, at 79 (Lord Hailsham): murder requires an action that is 'aimed at someone'.

another person *is* to display hostility towards them.[14] It might be objected that talk of 'hostility' then adds nothing (except possible confusion) to an account of attacks set simply in terms of an intention to injure; but it helps to make clearer the kind of wrong that attacks (by contrast with endangerments) involve.

Someone who intends what would normally count as injury might deny that her action is in this sense hostile: someone who commits voluntary euthanasia might argue that her action manifests the compassion that motivates it; someone engaging in consensual sado-masochism might claim that his actions display the mutual respect, and concern for the other's pleasure, that structure such sexual encounters.[15] What such people deny, however, is that their actions constitute attacks, since they deny that what they intend constitutes injury (just as a surgeon would deny that she attacks the patient whose leg she amputates, since she aims to benefit rather than injure the patient). We can disagree about such cases: some would insist that such actions are still wrongful attacks—in the case of euthanasia, on the person killed (and his inalienable right to life) or on the more abstract value of life; in the case of sado-masochism, on the person's 'real' interests or on some value that the person embodies. But this would be to argue that what these agents intend is an injury, and that their actions therefore do manifest practical hostility towards the interests or values against which they are now seen as directed. Such examples show, not that attacks are not by definition hostile actions that are intended to do harm, but that there can be normative disagreement about what counts as an attack, since there can be normative disagreement about what counts as injury or harm.

Attacks typically endanger their objects: in attacking *V*, I create a risk that she will suffer the injury I am trying to do her. But I can endanger *V* without attacking her, and my concern is with endangerments that do not constitute attacks. My concern is also with endangerment as something that human agents do. Many dangers, including some that arise from human beings, involve no human agency. There is a danger that visitors to my sickbed will catch my infectious disease, but I do not endanger them, unless I am failing to do what I should do to protect them. If I am a kind of person who is likely to commit crimes of violence, I might be called dangerous, and risk-fearing governments might look for ways of incapacitating me:[16] but I endanger others only if I begin to actualise my dangerous disposition in violent action.

[14] Compare Duff, 1990a: ch 7, on criminal recklessness as a matter of 'practical indifference'.

[15] See *Brown* [1993] 2 All ER 75, discussed above in Ch 6 at nn 29–40.

[16] On the 'risk society' and the threats it poses to justice see Hudson, 2003.

I endanger another if I create a significant risk that he will be harmed (a risk is significant if it constitutes a reason against acting as I do, or for taking precautions in acting thus). If the risk is not actualised, I merely endanger him; if it is actualised, I endanger him and harm him. I endanger him whether or not I realise, or could reasonably be expected to realise, the risk: whilst mens rea is necessary for attacks, endangerment need involve only the actual creation of risk; criminal liability for endangerment could thus be strict.[17] If criminal liability should require fault, however, and we ask what type of fault endangerment offences should require, we will naturally think not of an intention to injure, but of recklessness as the paradigm fault (with negligence as a lesser type of fault), and of practical indifference (rather than hostility) to the threatened interests as the attitude that such culpable endangerment displays. One who recklessly endangers others does not thereby display active hostility towards them; but in her willingness to take the risk of harming them, and in her failure to take adequate precautions against doing so, she shows that she does not care as she should for their interests.

Attacks and endangerments constitute two distinct types of wrong. An attack manifests a practical hostility towards the interest at which it is directed; the non-occurrence of the injury marks the failure of the enterprise. Endangerment rather involves a failure of proper practical concern: although I take the risk that I will cause harm to others, that harm is not the object of my action, but a side-effect; its non-occurrence would not mark the failure of my enterprise, and might be a source of relief to me (whereas one who intends injury cannot be relieved at his failure to cause it unless he has forsworn that intention).[18]

The difference between the kind of wrong I do to one whose interests I attack and the kind of wrong I do to one whose interests I culpably endanger lies in part in the difference between being guided by wrong reasons and not being guided by right reasons. If I attack you, the injury I intend figures in my reasons for acting as I do: I act thus because I believe that by doing so I will injure you—though that is not a reason by which I should be guided. If I culpably endanger you, by contrast, my reasons for acting as I do may be quite legitimate; what goes wrong is that I am not guided by the reason against acting thus that the risk of harm to you provides.

[17] See eg Water Resources Act 1991, s 85(1) (causing 'poisonous' matter' to enter any controlled water'); *R v Milford Haven Port Authority* [2000] 2 Cr App R (S) 423. But it be hard to determine causation without attending to fault: see *Alphacell Ltd v Woodward* [1972] AC 824. See further Ch 10.2 below.

[18] On the 'test of failure' see Duff, 1990a: 61–3. Compare Horder, 2005: 22; Simons, 1992 (see also his 2002; for critique, see Ferzan, 2002). Contrast Alexander, 2000, on which see Dressler, 2000b.

Two aspects of the distinction between attack and endangerment are worth noting here. The first concerns intended endangerment. An agent might intend, not to cause substantive harm, but to create or expose another to a risk of harm. I set fire to the house of my rival in love, intending to frighten him into leaving town by exposing him to a risk of serious harm: I attack his property, since I intend to damage it; but I also attack him, even if I do not intend to injure him and will be relieved if he escapes without injury.[19] So too if I try to see how close I can swing my golf club to your precious vase without hitting it, when the risk of hitting it is part of the point of the action, I attack your vase.[20] Such intended endangerments are attacks: even if we do not see the risk of harm as a harm,[21] the actions are aimed against those whose interests the agent intends to endanger; they manifest hostility rather than mere indifference. Endangerments, as distinct from attacks, consist in the creation of risk without any intention to cause either the relevant substantive harm or the risk of it. (Other offences involve acting in ways that might cause fear, but need create no actual risk. I commit an offence if I threaten to kill *V*, intending him to fear that I will do so, even if I do not intend to do so; or if I use 'threatening, abusive or insulting words' that might cause 'harassment, alarm or distress'.[22] Such offences amount to attacks if they are intended to cause fear, or to endangerments absent such an intention.)

The second aspect concerns 'oblique' intention. An attack requires 'direct' intention; so-called 'oblique' intention, the foresight that my action will cause harm as a side-effect, is not enough. One who acts with such foresight of harm does not manifest the hostility that attacks displays, but her utter indifference to the harm she expects to cause: she might wish that the harm would not ensue, but its prospect makes no difference to her action. Rather than treating foresight of harm as a type of intention, as the misleading terminology of 'oblique intention' suggests, we should treat it (absent a justification) as the limiting case of recklessness; one who acts with such foresight commits an extreme type of endangerment. I cannot defend the claim that there is a significant moral difference (not necessarily in degree of culpability, but in moral kind) between direct intention and

[19] Compare *Hyam* [1975] AC 55; Lord Hailsham held such an intention to be sufficient mens rea for murder.

[20] Compare *Chief Constable of Avon and Somerset v Shimmen* (1987) 84 Cr App R 7; see Horder, 1994b.

[21] See above, Ch 6 at nn 14–16.

[22] See Offences Against the Person Act 1861, s 16; Public Order Act 1986, s 5. See also Criminal Damage Act 1971, s 2; Ormerod, 2005: 517, on assault as intentionally or recklessly causing *V* to apprehend immediate personal violence.

confident foresight here, but the distinction drawn here between attacks and endangerments clearly depends on it.[23]

(b) The Significance of the Distinction

The difference in moral character between attacks and endangerments does not figure in a consequentialist perspective, since it depends on the significance (which consequentialists deny) of the distinction between intention and foresight. Nor can it figure in perspectives that, even if not purely consequentialist, give a consequentialist analysis of criminal wrongdoing. Feinberg's version of the Harm Principle does this: conduct is criminalisable in virtue of its causal relationship to an independently identifiable 'harmed condition'.[24] This exemplifies a familiar conception of criminal wrongdoing—the 'conduct-cause-harm' model: crimes are defined in terms of the causation (or creation of a risk) of independently identifiable harms that the criminal law seeks to prevent. Thus Robinson's Draft Code of Conduct—that part of the criminal code that is addressed to citizens rather than to courts—replaces all the complex, nuanced offences of violence against the person that current legal systems define by a single, simple clause: 'You may not cause bodily injury or death to another person'.[25] No distinction is drawn between attacks and endangerments: what makes both criminalisable is their causal relationship to harm; different offences can be distinguished in terms of the different types of harm that they cause or might cause.[26] Nor is the distinction drawn at the level of culpability requirements: either intention or recklessness will in most cases suffice.

A 'conduct-cause-harm' model of criminal wrongdoing fits very happily with a 'choice' conception of criminal responsibility. The causation of harm by one's conduct constitutes the actus reus of a crime; if we ask what mens rea or fault should be required to ground criminal responsibility for the harm our conduct causes, and especially if we find our intellectual home in a liberal neo-Kantianism, a natural answer will be that criminal responsibility depends on choice: I am responsible for the harms that I

[23] But see Nagel, 1980; Simester, 1996b; Duff, 1996: 363–74. For a survey of the debate in criminal law see Kugler, 2002. It should be noted that an attack does not require intention as to every aspect of the action that constitutes the wrong: rape and attempted rape are attacks upon the victim even if the attacker acts recklessly, rather than with intent or knowledge, as to the victim's lack of consent (see Duff, 1996: 5–29).

[24] Feinberg, 1984: 31–6; see Ch 6 at nn 18–20 above.

[25] Robinson, 1997: 213 (s 3 of the Code); compare Law Commission, 1989a: ss 70–72 on causing (serious) personal harm. See further Duff, 2002a: 56–61.

[26] Although Robinson does distinguish attempts from the general endangerment offence of creating a risk of a criminal result: 1997: 218, 225 (Draft Code of Conduct, ss 49, 51; Draft Code of Adjudication, s 200).

choose to cause. From this perspective, intention and recklessness (defined as conscious risk-taking) exemplify the same type of fault, since both consist in the choice to cause or to risk causing harm: the only difference is that intention is a more serious fault, since the merely reckless agent does not choose actually to cause harm.[27] Negligence is then either not a species of 'fault' at all, since it involves no culpable choice, or a lesser type of fault consisting in a failure to make choices (to pay attention, to take care) that one could and should have made.[28]

However, the difference between attacks and endangerments also seems less significant from perspectives that focus not on choice, but on character. Insofar as an attacker takes the intended injury to another as his end, he does reveal a different defect of character from one who endangers others in pursuit of ends that do not involve injuring others; but the difference vanishes when we turn from ends to means. One agent attacks another's property simply as a means to a further end (he cuts down his neighbour's tree because it blocks his view); another does what he realises will damage another's property in the course of his intended enterprise (he aims to burn his own tree, because it blocks his view, but realises that the fire will spread to his neighbour's tree). Each, we might think, displays the same vice or defect of character—a willingness to damage another's property in pursuit of his own ends, a serious indifference to others' rights and interests. If criminal responsibility is grounded in defects of character, we might then think that each commits the same kind of wrong, even though one attacks, whereas the other endangers, his neighbour's property.

The significance of the distinction between attack and endangerment appears clearly only when we shift our focus away from choice or character to action—to the intentional structure of the agent's actions (which helps to determine their meaning and moral character), and to the practical attitudes displayed in and part-constituted by those actions. One who intends to destroy another's tree might not be motivated by malice, but his action is still structured by and oriented towards that injury to another's rights and interests. One who unjustifiably does what he is sure will damage another's property as a side-effect still acts wrongly, displaying an unacceptable practical indifference to his neighbour's interests: but his action is not in the same way structured by wrongful injury to another. If criminal responsibility should focus on actions (as I argued in Chapter 5), the distinction between attacks and endangerments is then significant;

[27] Which is why such theorists typically argue that foresight of harm as virtually certain should be treated as a species of intention (see at n 23 above): one who acts with such foresight chooses to cause harm.

[28] See eg Hart, 1968a; Ashworth, 1987; Moore, 1997: ch 13; Ferzan, 2001. I have constructed a composite figure that each of these authors might reject; but that figure still reveals central strands in contemporary theorising.

likewise, if we see that distinction as significant, we see further reason to ground criminal responsibility in action.

We can now see more clearly both the force and the limited scope of a familiar criticism of the 'conduct-cause-harm' model of criminal responsibility. If we work with that model, it will be natural to classify criminal wrongs in terms of the type of harm caused, and perhaps of the agent's culpable responsibility for the harm (to distinguish intentional, reckless, and negligent offences). As I argued in Chapter 6.2, such a perspective cannot identify kinds of criminal harm (such as those suffered by victims of murder, or rape, or burglary) that are partly constituted by the actions that generate them; it cannot do justice to the intrinsic wrongfulness of certain kinds of crime. Critics of the conduct-cause-harm style of offence definition, which Robinson and the Law Commission favour,[29] argue that adequate definitions of the kinds of wrong that properly concern the criminal law cannot be so austere. If we are to label offences fairly, in ways that capture the wrongfulness in virtue of which they are criminalised,[30] we must eschew the aetiolated language of harm and its causation in favour of a richer, morally laden language of thick concepts that captures the moral contours of the actions in question, reflecting not merely the harm that is caused, but the wrongful injury that is done, and the way, context and spirit in which it is done.[31]

There are of course difficult questions to be tackled about just how fine-grained the law's offence definitions should be. Should it, for instance, distinguish attacks on the body from attacks on psychological well-being?[32] Should it formally mark the difference between trying to choke or suffocate, administering a stupefying or overpowering drug and using other kinds of force, with intent to commit an offence?[33] Like degree classifications, criminal verdicts are for good (partly practical) reasons fairly coarse-grained; but the offences of which defendants are convicted should nonetheless give a substantive idea of the wrongs they have committed.

[29] And proponents of the Model Penal Code, who want a code that will provide descriptive, rather than morally loaded, definitions of the elements of each offence: eg Robinson and Grall, 1983; Gainer, 1988.

[30] See G Williams, 1983b; Ashworth, 2006: 88–90.

[31] See, eg, Shute and Horder, 1993; Horder, 1994a; Gardner, 1994; Green, 2001; Simester and Sullivan, 2005; Tadros, 2005b. On 'thick' concepts in ethics see B Williams, 1985: ch 8. Contrast Michaels, 2000, arguing that we can do justice to such critics' concerns, whilst preserving a criminal law that defines offences in descriptive rather than normatively laden criteria.

[32] As English law does not: Offences Against the Person Act 1861, s 20, as applied in *Ireland* [1998] AC 147.

[33] See Offences Against the Person Act 1861, ss 21, 22; both Horder, 1994a and Gardner, 1994 seem to go too far down the particularising route. The issues can be usefully explored in relation to property offences: see Glazebrook, 1991; Clarkson, 1993; Shute and Horder, 1993; Simester and Sullivan, 2005.

The significant point here, however, is that such criticisms of the 'conduct-cause-harm' model apply only to attacks. The distinctive wrongfulness that makes an attack criminalisable cannot be identified by looking for the consequential harm that it wrongfully causes; nor can we distinguish the different wrongs of different kinds of attack by distinguishing the different interests that are set back: we need the thick ethico-legal concepts for which a conduct-cause-harm model has no room. What makes that model inappropriate for attacks is that it separates the criminal harm from the action that causes it—a separation that distorts the wrongful character of such crimes as murder, rape and burglary (all of which are attacks). That separation is not thus distorting, however, in endangerment offences, when the conduct is not structured by an intention to injure. What is wrong with action that endangers another's life or property is precisely that it is liable to cause a harm that we can identify independently of the action that causes it. If I am injured or my property is damaged, not by an attack, but by another's culpably dangerous conduct, I am wronged; but the harm I suffer does not differ in character from that suffered if I am injured or my property is damaged by natural causes. If I discover that some injury or damage that I had supposed to be the result of natural causes was actually the intended result of another's attack, that will radically change my conception of what I have suffered. If I instead discover that it was the result of another's recklessness, my attitude will of course alter—I will now blame that person for causing me harm; but my view of the harm itself need not alter. In criminalising attacks, we are criminalising harmful wrongs—wrongs that do a relevant kind of harm; endangerment offences instead criminalise wrongful harms —conduct that is wrongful because it is (potentially) harmful.

The task of offence definition may therefore be simpler for endangerment offences than for attacks. We must attend to the likelihood and seriousness of the harm caused or risked, to the value of the endangering conduct, to whether the agent was or should have been aware of the risk: but we need not attend to other factors, such as the context in which, or the intention with which, or the means by which the harm was done, that bear on the moral character of an attack; we can define and individuate offences more simply in terms of the kind of harm that is caused (or threatened).

There is a further way in which the structure of endangerment offences might be simpler than that of attacks, to do with the meaning of recklessness, and whether it should always be understood as requiring conscious risk-taking.[34] The cases in which it is plausible to argue that an

[34] See Duff, 1990a ch 7; Simester and Sullivan, 2007: 134–42; Ashworth, 2006: 181–6.

agent's unawareness of risk can itself constitute recklessness, as manifesting the kind of practical indifference in which recklessness consists, are cases in which the recklessness is integral to an attack: homicide, for instance, when an assailant displays 'extreme indifference to the value of human life' in his very failure to advert to the obvious risk that he will kill his victim;[35] or rape, when a man is convinced, without good reason, that a woman on whom he forces sexual penetration consents to it.[36] So perhaps recklessness in endangerment offences always requires conscious risk-taking; only in attacks, when the action is directed against a legally protected interest, can the failure to notice a risk display the kind of directed practical indifference to the very interests that are at risk that should constitute criminal recklessness.

(c) Legislating the Distinction?

The distinction between attacks and endangerments, as drawn here, is certainly exclusive: although I can attack someone by attempting to endanger him, such intended endangerments count as attacks. It is tempting to argue that the distinction is also exhaustive: that every kind of criminalisable conduct must either attack or endanger a legally protected interest or good. Now such a claim seems plausible for 'primary' offences—offences which involve the actual occurrence or commission of the mischief, injury or harm against which the law is aimed: for a mischief that is to justify criminalisation must surely consist in some injury to or violation of a value (an interest, a right, a good) that the criminal law properly aims to protect; and such injury or violation must flow either from an attack on that value or from conduct that endangers it.[37] It also seems plausible for the most immediate kinds of 'secondary' offence—those in which the injury or harm need not in fact ensue, but which involve a direct attempt to injure or an immediate risk of harm. But as we move further away from primary offences to criminalise remoter kinds of conduct (a movement to be discussed in section 2), it becomes less plausible to describe the criminalised conduct as an attack (as distinct from preparation for an attack) or as endangerment (as distinct from conduct that could lead to endangerment): we have reason to criminalise

[35] Model Penal Code, s 210.2(1)(b); see *Miller and Denovan* (1960; Gordon, 2000: 303–7); *Parr v HM Advocate* 1991 SLT 208.

[36] See *Morgan* [1976] AC 182. One can read the Sexual Offences Act 2003 as giving statutory form to the view that recklessness as to the victim's consent in rape does not require awareness of a risk that *V* does not consent; it is enough that *D* did not act with a reasonable belief that *V* consented (s 1(1)(c)).

[37] Though talk of attacks and endangerments might seem over-dramatic when what is at stake is annoyance or inconvenience rather than substantial harm: see Ch 6 at nn 42–44 above.

carrying a knife with intent to use it to wound,[38] but merely carrying a knife with such an intent is not an attack; we have reason to criminalise being in charge of a motor vehicle when unfit to drive through drink or drugs,[39] but merely being in charge of a vehicle does not yet endanger anyone. The most we can say is, therefore, that every justified criminal offence must either consist in an attack on or an endangerment of a legally protected value, or be suitably related to such an attack or endangerment.

Before turning to the question of what kinds of relationship can be thus 'suitable', there is a final question to notice in this section.

If, as I have argued, the distinction between attacks and endangerments distinguishes two quite different kinds of criminal wrong, it is surely a distinction that the law should mark: but our existing laws do not always mark it. Sometimes they do mark it: wounding with intent is distinguished from wounding (which can be committed recklessly) in English law;[40] murder requires an intention at least to cause serious bodily injury, and one who causes death through recklessness is guilty of manslaughter.[41] But often they do not: *D* commits the same offence of criminal damage whether he damages *V*'s property deliberately or recklessly;[42] the same offence of assault or wounding whether he injures *V* deliberately or recklessly.[43] Although there are limits to the extent to which the offence definitions should reflect even significant moral distinctions, they should in principle reflect a categorial difference like that between attacks and endangerments, both to advance 'fair labelling' and to ensure that matters that bear significantly on sentencing (as the difference between deliberate and reckless actions should bear) are properly proved in court. This could cause problems if the prosecution can prove that *D* recognised a risk of the relevant harm but is not sure that it can prove intention: but such problems could be remedied by counting the endangerment form of the offence as an 'included' offence in relation to the attack form.[44]

[38] See Prevention of Crime Act 1953, s 1(4); see P Smith, 2003: 457–64.

[39] See Road Traffic Act 1988, s 4; the defendant will be deemed not to have been in charge if he proves that there was no likelihood of his driving the vehicle whilst unfit.

[40] Offences Against the Person Act 1861, ss 18, 20.

[41] See Ormerod, 2005: 436–7. Even when the mens rea of murder is defined in terms of 'wicked recklessness' (see Gordon, 2000: 295–310) or 'extreme indifference' (see Model Penal Code, s 210.2(1)(b)), it is arguable that that recklessness or indifference must be displayed in the course of an attack on another person.

[42] See Criminal Damage Act 1971, s 1(1); Model Penal Code, s 220.3.

[43] Model Penal Code, s 211.1(1); Offences Against the Person Act 1861, s 20.

[44] See Criminal Law Act 1967, s 6(3); Model Penal Code, s 1.07(4).

2. Extending the Law?

We have good reason to criminalise both attacks on legally protected values and conduct that unjustifiably endangers legally protected interests. One who deliberately destroys another's property without good reason commits a wrong for which—given the role that property plays in the collective life of polities like our own—he should have to answer not just to the owner of the property, but to the polity as a whole. One who destroys another's property through his reckless risk-taking also commits a wrong for which he should have to answer publicly: for whatever disagreements there may be about the extent of our prospective responsibilities in relation to side-effects of our actions, we surely owe it to each other to take some care not to damage others' property. But how extensive a criminal law can this line of thought justify?

(a) Attacks and Preparations

Attacks may succeed or fail: if my attempt to defraud you fails, I have still attacked your property rights. If we have reason to criminalise attacks, as wrongful violations of protected values, we have reason to criminalise those that fail as well as those that succeed, since they too constitute public wrongdoings that merit condemnation; if an attempted fraud fails, we have reason to be relieved, and to qualify our condemnation of the would-be fraudster,[45] but not to refrain from condemnation altogether. We therefore have reason to maintain a general law of attempt: if Φ-ing is criminal as an attack on a legally protected value, attempting to Φ should also be criminal.[46] However, this justifies only a narrow law of attempts, narrower for instance than the Model Penal Code's: someone who has taken 'a substantial step in a course of conduct planned to culminate in his commission of the crime' might not yet be engaged in an attack as distinct from preparing for an attack;[47] a would-be attacker is attacking his target only once he is 'in the process of committing' the crime that would complete the attack.[48]

One question then is whether we should extend the general law of attempts—of inchoate attacks—more broadly than this, to capture at least

[45] I cannot here defend the view that the failure of an attempt should make a difference to the agent's criminal liability: see Duff, 1996: ch 12.

[46] See Criminal Attempts Act 1981, s 1; Model Penal Code, s 5.01 (though neither attempt provision is wholly general).

[47] Model Penal Code, s 5.01(1)(c), 5.01(2); see Commentary to s 5.01, 303–32.

[48] See *Gullefer* [1990] 1 WLR 1063, n 11 above.

some conduct that does not yet amount to an attack.[49] Another question is whether, even if we should maintain a narrow general law of attempts, we should add a number of more specific offences of preparation for particular substantive crimes. English law includes a wide range of such offences, typically defined in terms of the further criminal intention with which the preparatory conduct is done: it is, for instance, an offence to do 'any act with intent to impede [the] apprehension or prosecution' of an offender, to carry something that counts as an offensive weapon only because one intends to use it, or to have in one's possession something that one intends to use to damage another's property.[50] We have good reason to criminalise some kinds of 'merely preparatory' conduct, rather than waiting until the intending criminal actually embarks on the crime: someone who prepares a bomb for a terrorist attack, for instance, is doing wrong of a kind that concerns and should be condemned by the whole polity. Indeed, we have *some* reason to criminalise even very early steps in an intended criminal enterprise: if Φ-ing is a public wrong that merits the criminal law's formal condemnation, preparing to Φ is also wrong in a way that in principle concerns the polity as a whole; if a police officer or a fellow citizen happened to discover an intending criminal's intention, and warned him that he should not be preparing to commit the intended crime, he could hardly protest that it was none of their business. There are also, of course, good reasons against the creation of such preparatory offences: reasons to do with the difficulty of proving the requisite intention without opening the door to intrusive modes of surveillance and investigation, and with the importance of leaving citizens as wide as possible a *locus poenitentiae* in which to decide for themselves whether or not to persist in a planned criminal enterprise.[51]

I will not pursue the topic of preparatory crimes further here, but turn instead to the more complex issues raised by endangerment offences.

[49] Both English and American law also include general offences of incitement and conspiracy, which involve conduct falling well short of an attack: see Model Penal Code, s 5.02, 5.03; Ormerod, 2005: 349–400.

[50] See, respectively, Criminal Law Act 1967, s 4; Prevention of Crime Act 1953, s 1(4); Criminal Damage Act 1971, s 3(a); and generally Horder, 1996. Anti-terrorism statutes are full of such preparatory offences, but often define them in terms of endangerment as well as attack, to cover not just conduct that is intended to assist terrorist activities but also conduct that the agent has reason to suspect will assist terrorism: see eg Terrorism Act 2000, ss 15–18, 58; contrast ss 54, 57, under which it is a defence to prove that the conduct was not undertaken for terrorist purposes.

[51] See Ch 5 at nn 28–31 above; Duff, 1996: chs 5, 13.5.

(b) Endangerment and 'Remote' Harms

To say that *D* 'endangered *V*', or 'acted dangerously', formally leaves open the question of whether the harm the prospect of which constituted the danger materialised: I can truly say that D endangered *V* by administering a drug known often to have harmful side effects, without knowing whether those harmful side effects ensued. It would admittedly be misleading to say only that *D* endangered *V* if I knew that the relevant harm did materialise: I should say that *D* harmed *V*. However, for our present purposes it will be convenient to treat 'endanger' and its cognates as being analogous to 'attack' and its cognates: to cover all cases in which someone endangers others, whether or not the harm actually materialises. We can then distinguish 'consummate' from 'non-consummate' endangerments, as we can attacks.[52]

We have reason to criminalise consummate endangerments that harm legally protected interests—conduct that causes death or injury to others, for instance, or damage to others' property, or significant setbacks to other important interests, if that conduct is also wrongful in virtue of its harmfulness. We owe it to each other not only not to attack others, but to take reasonable care that our actions do not harm others: if I cause harm to others by conduct that displays a serious lack of that modest level of care that we can reasonably demand of each other, I should expect to be called to account not only by the people I actually harm, but by other members of my community. Indeed, since endangerers do not select their victims in the way that attackers often do, it could be said that their conduct is dangerous, not just to those who are actually harmed, but to others generally. We also have some reason to criminalise non-consummate endangerments, just as we have to criminalise non-consummate attacks: one who recklessly creates a risk of a kind of harm for which he would be criminally responsible if he actually caused it commits a wrong that also merits public condemnation; the fact that the harm did not ensue gives us reason to be relieved, and to qualify our condemnation, but not to refrain from condemnation altogether.

One question then is why the law should not include a general offence of endangerment analogous to the law of attempts: why should it not be an offence to 'act in a way that creates a substantial and unjustified risk of causing a result' the actual causation of which is criminal?[53] I will not

[52] For a useful general discussion of non-consummate offence and their criminalisation see Husak, 1995a.

[53] Robinson, 1997: 218 (Draft Code of Conduct, s 51): see K Smith, 1983; Clarkson, 2005. The question is particularly acute for those who think that outcome luck should not affect criminal liability. It is, in their eyes, bad enough that one who causes death by his dangerous driving is convicted of a more serious offence, attracting a heavier punishment, than is one whose equally dangerous driving luckily does not kill anyone (Road Traffic Act 1988, ss 1–2;

discuss that question here. We have reason in principle to create a general offence; but countervailing reasons to do with the costs of criminalisation, and with the difference that the non-occurrence of harm makes to the conduct's wrongfulness, might tip the scales against such a general offence, in favour of a series of more specific offences involving, for instance, particularly serious harms,[54] or especially dangerous activities,[55] or agents who can properly be assigned special responsibilities,[56] or especially vulnerable potential victims.[57]

A further issue, of course, is how the law should specify the kind and level of risk the creation of which is to be criminal. Although the fact that what I am intending to do would create some risk of harm usually constitutes a reason against acting thus, it would be absurd to require us to answer for all such risk-creation—however obviously reasonable—in a criminal court: the law will instead criminalise the creation of a 'substantial and unjustifiable' risk,[58] or conduct that falls 'far 'far below what would be expected of a competent and careful' agent, by whom the conduct would have been seen as obviously dangerous.[59] This will require courts to make some difficult determinations, requiring attention not just to the seriousness and likelihood of the threatened harm, and to the value of the activity that creates the risk, but to the context of that activity and to the responsibilities (to take care or precautions) that can plausibly be laid on the defendant and others.[60]

More relevant to present purposes, as we consider the ways in which we could properly criminalise types of non-consummate endangerment, is a

Road Traffic Offenders Act 1988, Sch 2 Part 1). It must be even worse that one whose reckless conduct damages another's property is guilty of criminal damage while one whose similar recklessness luckily causes no damage is guilty of no offence at all (see Duff, 1996: 138–40, 171–2.

[54] See eg Model Penal Code, s 211.2: 'conduct which places or may place another person in danger of death or serious bodily injury'; the Scottish offence of 'causing danger to the lieges by culpable recklessness' (Gordon, 2000: 427–30); Australian Model Criminal Code, s 5.1.25–6 (see Lanham, 1999: 965–7).

[55] Eg Road Traffic Act 1988, ss 2, 4, 12, 22, 40; Explosive Substances Act 1883, s 2; Dangerous Dogs Act 1991, s 3; Food Safety Act 1990, s 8.

[56] Eg Health and Safety at Work etc Act 1974 (employers); Merchant Shipping Act 1995, ss 58, 98, 100 (masters, seamen, ship-owners).

[57] Eg Children and Young Persons Act 1933, ss 1, 11; Mental Health Act 1983, s 127; for further examples of all these categories see Glazebrook, 2006: 85–145.

[58] Model Penal Code, s 2.02(02)(c), defining recklessness; see s 211.2 on reckless endangerment.

[59] Road Traffic Act 1988, s 2A, on 'dangerous driving'. See also Robinson, 1997: 224: 'creating a prohibited risk' es 'a gross deviation from the standard of conduct of a law-abiding person' (Draft Code of Adjudication, s 113).

[60] Cases involving the risk of HIV transmission through unprotected sexual intercourse exemplify the issues here (see Lanham, 1999; Chalmers, 2002; *Dica* [2004] 2 Cr App R 28; *Konzani* [2005] 2 Cr App R 14). The risk is statistically low, perhaps 1 in 2,000: so does criminalisation mark a moral panic, or a judgement based on the seriousness of the harm and the supposed breach of trust?

set of issues that arise once we move beyond cases of simple endangerment, in which the agent acts in ways that directly endanger other people or their interests.[61] We should note three such issues, all involving prospective harms that are in some way 'remote' from the agent's conduct.[62]

First, an agent can act dangerously without actually endangering anyone: someone who drives round a blind corner on the wrong side of the road acts dangerously whether there is anyone coming the other way or not; but if no one is in fact coming, he does not endanger anyone. We could say that the risk he takes is a secondary risk—a risk that his conduct will expose other people to a risk of serious harm; but his conduct still constitutes a serious breach of his responsibilities as a driver, for which he can properly be held criminally responsible. That is why the Model Penal Code defines 'recklessly endangering another person' in terms of 'conduct which places or may place another person in danger',[63] whilst German theorists distinguish between offences of 'concrete' endangerment that actually endanger someone and offences of 'abstract' endangerment involving conduct that typically endangers others but need not actually do so in every case.[64]

Secondly, dangerous conduct is often 'directly' dangerous, in that it is likely to cause harm without the mediation of further human action. Sometimes, however, endangerment is 'indirect', in that harm would ensue only in virtue of the intervening actions of others. If I sell a firearm to someone who, as I know, might misuse it, or keep my firearms somewhere from which they could easily be stolen, I act in a way that might lead to harm, but only in virtue of what others might do with the firearms that I supply or fail to keep securely. Such intervening human agency poses no problems of principle if it is genuinely innocent: if I give a gun to a child,[65] or wave a gun at someone who does not know it is unloaded,[66] harm might ensue because of what the child does with the gun, or what the other person reasonably does in trying to escape the

[61] For simplicity's sake I focus on dangerous actions rather than omissions. The latter are clearly in principle criminalisable if they involve a breach of an appropriate duty: see eg *Pittwood* [1902] TLR 37 (failing to close the gates of a level crossing when a train was due, thus endangering road users and train passengers: see Simester and Sullivan, 2007: 69); but they raise no special issues here. Sometimes, of course, what makes an action or course of action dangerous is an omission—the agent's failure to take the care or precautions that she should take; this is typically true of offences of negligence: but it is still the action, as done without taking the proper precautions, that endangers others (see above, Ch 5 n 63).

[62] For more detailed discussion see Duff, 2005; see also von Hirsch, 1996.

[63] Model Penal Code, s 211.2; see above, Ch 6 at n 16.

[64] See Roxin, 2006: 337–8, 423–32; compare ss 315c and 316 of the German Criminal Code.

[65] See Firearms Act 1968, ss 24–25.

[66] See eg *Thomas v Commonwealth* 567 SW 2d 299 (1978); *Commonwealth v Gouse* 429 A 2d 1129 (1981).

perceived threat; but my conduct can still count as directly dangerous if we can see that intervening agency as suitably innocent. Endangerment is properly indirect only if the occurrence of harm would depend on a non-innocent *novus actus interveniens*.[67] Whether and when we have good reason to criminalise such indirect endangerment depends on what view we should take of our responsibilities in relation to the conduct of others: whilst we cannot plausibly deny that we have some general responsibility to guard against the direct risks of harm that our conduct creates, there is more room for argument about whether, when or how far we should be expected to attend to the risk that our conduct will give others the means or opportunity to do harm. Our laws do in fact criminalise indirect endangerment both by criminalising particular types of indirectly dangerous conduct,[68] and through the general offence of aiding and abetting; we can see what is both plausible and problematic about such provisions by looking very briefly at aiding and abetting.[69]

Aiding and abetting requires an intention to facilitate the commission of the substantive crime. If that intention is direct, there is good reason to hold the agent criminally responsible, so long as his contribution is not too remote from the crime's commission (if I lend you a pen with which to forge a signature as part of a planned fraud, my contribution looks too remote); but since English law is prone to count confident foresight of a result as 'intention', it is also liable to convict a person who realises that what he does will facilitate the commission of an offence, even if it is not his purpose to facilitate it—which raises more problematic questions about the extent of our responsibilities in relation to the conduct of others.[70] If I sell someone a knife knowing that he intends to use it to commit robbery; or lend someone my car knowing that she intends to use it to make a drug deal: can I argue that I am merely plying my trade as a shopkeeper or doing a favour for an acquaintance, and that what they do with what I supply is not morally, and therefore should not be criminally, my business? Should a host who offers his driving guests more drinks be criminally responsible for aiding and abetting their drunken driving, since he knows that he is facilitating it? We should not expect to find simple answers to such questions, nor should we expect the criminal law simply to reflect the

67 On *novus actus interveniens* see Simester and Sullivan, 2007: 83–98. I leave aside here the problems that arise when we try to specify what should count as 'non-innocent'.

68 Hence the various provisions concerning the possession and supply of firearms in the Firearms Act 1968. See also *Khaliq v HM Advocate* 1984 JC 171, *Ulhaq v HM Advocate* 1991 SLT 614: Ch 3 at nn 24–26 above.

69 See Accessories and Abettors Act 1861, s 8; Ormerod, 2005: 169–90. Contrast Model Penal Code, s 2.06: the Code avoids the problems to be discussed here by requiring that the accomplice act 'with the purpose of promoting or facilitating the commission of the offense'.

70 See above, Ch 1 at nn 35–36, Ch 3 at nn 24–26; also Duff, 1990b.

moral answers that we would give: not all our moral or civic responsibilities in relation to others' conduct are so significant that a failure to discharge them should attract criminal liability.

Thirdly, in other cases of indirect endangerment, what would connect the initial conduct to the prospective harm is the conduct, not of others, but of the agent himself. This is often true of possession offences—for instance possessing what counts as an offensive weapon in virtue of its being 'made or adapted for use to cause injury to the person'.[71] Of course, if I act with the intention of causing that future harm (if, for instance, what I have counts as an offensive weapon in virtue of my intention to use it to injure), the issues are those already discussed in relation to offences of preparation: how far along the path that leads back from the completed crime to the formation of the criminal intention should criminal responsibility extend?[72] But if no such intention is involved, to criminalise my conduct is to criminalise me on the basis of what I might go on to do: what connects my present conduct to the prospective criminal harm is not my intention to do that harm (which would be a morally relevant connection), but an empirical prediction about what people might do—a prediction whose use in this way denies my responsible agency by treating me as someone who cannot be trusted to guide his actions by the appropriate reasons.[73] Such offences are no doubt a convenient way to prosecute those who are suspected of acting with a criminal intention without the need to prove that intention—offences related to terrorism are an obvious example:[74] but we should not quickly surrender principles of respect for responsible agency to police and prosecutorial convenience. Again, however, my purpose is not to argue for a particular account of when, if ever, we can have good reason to criminalise conduct that would lead to harm only in virtue of further, directly dangerous but not currently intended conduct by the agent herself: it is rather to reveal the structure of this kind of offence and the problems that it raises.

We have so far been discussing conduct that has some connection to a kind of harm that properly concerns the criminal law: conduct that is intended to lead to the commission of a crime, or that is connected to such

[71] Prevention of Crime Act 1953, s 1. On possession offences generally see Dubber, 2005.

[72] See at nn 49–51 above. For other examples of 'possession with intent' offences see eg Offences Against the Person Act 1861, s 64; Theft Act 1968, s 25; Firearms Act 1968, ss 16, 18; Criminal Damage Act 1971, s 3(a); Forgery and Counterfeiting Act 1981, s 17; Communications Act 2003, s 126.

[73] Unless the offence definition includes a condition that could properly ground mistrust, as with the offence of being in charge of a motor vehicle when under the influence of drink or drugs: Road Traffic Act 1988, s 4.

[74] See eg Terrorism Act 2000, ss 57, 58; see also Civic Government (Scotland) Act 1982, s 57, on being found in a building under circumstances such that 'it may reasonably be inferred that he intended to commit theft there' (on which see Tadros, 2007: 198–9; and below, Ch 10 at nn 70–72.

a crime either through a chain of potential natural causes or through the potential further conduct of others or of the agent herself. Further problems arise when we turn to other cases in which the conduct that is criminalised might not even have one of these kinds of connection to the harm the prospect of which grounds its criminalisation.

3. 'Implicit Endangerment' and *Mala Prohibita*

The two kinds of case that we must now consider both involve what could be classed as *mala prohibita* —although in the first case, as we will see, a *malum in se* underpins the offence.

(a) 'Implicit Endangerment' and Civic Responsibility

Offences of 'explicit' endangerment should be distinguished from offences of 'implicit' endangerment. Endangerment offences are *explicit* if their commission requires the creation of the risk that grounds their criminalisation—a risk specified in the offence definition; they are *implicit* if their definition does not specify that risk and they can be committed without creating it.[75] While dangerous driving and 'reckless endangerment' are explicit endangerment offences, driving with excess alcohol and speeding are implicit endangerment offences,[76] as is pretending to be a qualified doctor:[77] the conduct they criminalise is criminalised because it might lead to relevant kinds of harm, but no reference to such harms appears in the offence definitions. Conviction for an explicit endangerment offence requires proof that the defendant created a risk of the relevant harm, but no such proof is required for an implicit endangerment offence; nor would proof that the defendant did *not* create such a risk—for instance that this driver's competence was not impaired by consuming an amount of alcohol that put her over the limit—save her from conviction.[78]

Explicit endangerment offences typically declare 'standards', whereas implicit offences lay down 'rules'.[79] The merit of criminalising endangerment through explicit endangerment offences is that, if the law is properly

[75] See Husak, 1995a: 168–9, on 'complex' and 'simple' non-consummate offences; also Husak, 2005b.

[76] See respectively Road Traffic Act 1988, s 5; Road Traffic Regulation Act 1984, ss 81–89.

[77] See Medical Act 1983, s 49.

[78] The distinction between 'explicit' and 'implicit' endangerment offences depends on identifying the kind of harm with which each offence is concerned: if there is uncertainty about what that harm is, there may also be uncertainty about whether the offence is one of explicit or of implicit endangerment.

[79] On standards and rules see Schlag, 1985.

applied, we convict only those who actually endanger others in ways that deserve condemnation. The drawback is that they require courts to make judgements of what kinds of risk are 'substantial and unjustifiable', or are 'unreasonable' for the agent to take:[80] unless we can rely on some quite specific shared understandings of what counts as an 'unreasonable risk', and of what kinds of care people should take, in a range of contexts, courts will apply not the polity's shared standards, but the individual standards of each (set of) fact finder(s)—which generates the familiar defects of uncertainty in the law's content, and unpredictability and inconsistency in its application. This drawback grounds one reason in favour of offences of implicit endangerment.

For example, English law defines explicit endangerment offences of driving when unfit through drink or drugs and dangerous driving; and implicit endangerment offences of driving with more than a specified concentration of alcohol in one's blood and of exceeding specified speed limits.[81] The implicit offences lay down rules that aim to capture part of the content of the standards declared in the explicit offences. An obvious attraction of such implicit offences for prosecutors is that proof of legal guilt is easier; they are also likely to be more effective in dissuading dangerous types of driving, since drivers will know that they have less chance of avoiding conviction. These attractions, however, do not speak to their justice.[82] Such offences also promote certainty and consistency: citizens can know what they must or must not do;[83] courts can apply the law with greater consistency. It is also true that, if the rules are sensibly specified, most of those who break them will have violated the standard: most of those who speed, or drive when above the prescribed alcohol limit, will be driving dangerously;[84] most will thus have committed a genuine *malum in se*. But such offences will also capture some drivers whose conduct is not appropriately dangerous: one whose capacities and willingness to drive safely are not impaired by an amount of alcohol that puts him over the legal limit still commits an offence if he drives after drinking that much, although he does not thereby create the increased risk of harm that justifies this drink-driving law; so too for a driver whose skills and car are such that she can drive as safely at speeds well over the legal limit as others

[80] See Model Penal Code, ss 2.02(2)(c), 211.2; and at nn 58–60 above.

[81] Road Traffic Act 1988, ss 2–5; Road Traffic Regulation Act 1984, ss 81–89.

[82] See Ashworth, 2006: 84–5.

[83] It might be hard to identify the point at which one more drink would put me over the limit: but the law's message is that drinking *any* alcohol before driving is risky ('Don't drink and drive'), which opens the way to the 'thin ice' principle; once we start to drink we are on thin ice, and 'can hardly expect to find a sign which will denote the precise spot where [we] will fall in' (*Knuller* [1973] AC 435, at 463 (Lord Morris); see Ashworth, 2006: 73–4).

[84] See Husak, 2005b: 79–80 (and 74–82 generally on 'hybrid' offences).

can at speeds within the limit.[85] Can it be fair to demand that such people obey these laws, or just to convict them if they do not? They commit *mala prohibita*: their conduct is not wrongful prior to the creation of the legal regime of speed limits or alcohol limits. As we saw in Chapter 4.4, we can justify criminalising *mala prohibita* only by showing that even if the conduct was not wrongful prior to its legal proscription, it is wrongful once it is legally proscribed—and prior to its criminalisation: but how could we show this for such driving offences?

For another example, consider offences involving sexual activity with children. Even the underlying *mala in se* are controversial here, but two could be suggested: that of involving a young person who is not yet mature enough to make rational decisions about such matters in sexual activity which could have a serious impact on his or her life (a type of endangerment); and that of sexual exploitation, when an older person exploits a vulnerable young person for his or her own sexual gratification. However, our criminal law does not define the offences in *malum in se* terms of maturity or exploitation, as offences of explicit endangerment: instead, it criminalises sexual activity with anyone under a certain age—typically 16 or 13.[86] These offences are related to the relevant *mala in se*, in that they are aimed against the wrong (the mischief) that such *mala* involve, but, rather than defining the offending conduct in terms of the relevant *mala*, they involve definitions that—as we and the legislature know—do not precisely match those *mala*: there are individuals under the specified age who are capable of rational consent (more capable than some who are over that age), whilst sexual relationships between 'victims' below the specified age and 'offenders' of the specified age or position are not always exploitative (or as exploitative as many relationships that are not criminal). Whilst many who commit such offences will commit a relevant *malum in se*, we can therefore be confident that some will not: their offence will be a *malum prohibitum*, which again raises the question of whether and why it is a kind of *malum* that we have good reason to criminalise. Such laws are, it seems, both over- and under-inclusive: they criminalise some who do not commit a relevant *malum in se*, and fail to capture some who do commit one—some whose sexual partners are not mature enough, although they are over the legally specified age limit, or whose relationships are seriously exploitative. The under-inclusiveness might not be cause for complaint if it would not be practicable to try to formulate a standard that would capture

[85] Hence the common complaint that rules, if they are not under-inclusive, are over-inclusive: see eg Schauer, 1993: 31–4, 47–52; Husak, 1998b.

[86] Eg Sexual Offences Act 2003, ss 5–7, 9, 16; Model Penal Code, s 213.3(1). Offences that include conditions to do with the agent's age or position relative to the victim seem to concern the *malum in se* of exploitation; those without such conditions presumably concern the immaturity-focused *malum in se*.

all those who commit a relevant *malum in se*;[87] but the over-inclusiveness raises a question both about the justice of such laws (of convicting those whose partners are not too immature or being exploited) and about the viability of the version of legal moralism that I have been defending.[88] Unless I can show that such people do commit a genuine wrong for which they should have to answer to their fellow citizens, I must either argue that all criminal laws of this kind are illegitimate, or abandon even this qualified version of legal moralism.

We should not, of course, rule out the first alternative. That would involve rejecting large swathes of our criminal law, however; it is worth asking whether we could justify such hybrid offences—offences specifying rules that imperfectly capture standards which define genuine *mala in se*, the commission of which will therefore often, but not always, involve the commission of the relevant *malum in se*. If we cannot, there is a familiar question about what obligation, if any, citizens still have to obey them: but that question arises in the same way for unjustified laws that purport but fail to define *mala in se* (that do not define *mala* at all, or define *mala* that are not the criminal law's business, or radically misdefine *mala* that are its business), and is not what concerns us here. The question now is whether we can justify such laws: whether and how the regulations can be justified; and whether and how breaking them is a wrong for which we should be criminally responsible. Can we say to the driver who believes, truly and on the basis of good evidence, that her driving capacities are not impaired by an amount of alcohol that takes her above the limit; or to the adult who believes, truly and on the basis of good evidence, that his under-age sexual partner is mature: not just 'even if the law should not have been so formulated as to define your conduct as criminal, you still ought to obey it', but 'the law is rightly so formulated that it captures your conduct, which is why you ought to obey it and do wrong if you disobey it'?[89]

We should not expect to find a single argument that will apply to all such offences, nor to find arguments that will justify them all; all we can do is look in turn at a range of offences to see whether they can be justified—and be ready to reject or radically to revise those that cannot be

[87] In the case of dangerous driving there are offences of explicit endangerment (dangerous driving and driving when unfit) that can remedy the defect of under-inclusiveness: but how would one formulate a standard- rather than a rule-based offence of sexual exploitation?

[88] See Husak, 2005b.

[89] This problem about hybrid offences is a type of 'false positives' problem. In the context of incapacitative detention based on predicted dangerousness, false positives are those who are identified as future offenders, and subjected to extended detention for that reason, but who would not have offended had they been left free (see eg Walker, 1982; von Hirsch, 1985). In the present context, a false positive is one whose conduct satisfies a hybrid offence definition, but does not constitute the *malum* at which that definition is aimed.

justified in their present form. Here is one line of argument that can, I think, justify some hybrid offences of the kind illustrated above.

Consider the offences of speeding and driving with excess alcohol in the blood. Someone who exceeds the speed limit, or drives with what the law defines as excess alcohol, might still be driving safely, and be acting on the true belief that he can drive safely at that speed or that the amount of alcohol he has consumed does not impair his capacity or his attentiveness. But that does not yet show that he is not acting dangerously, if he cannot claim to *know* that he is driving safely: he might still be taking an unreasonable risk that his belief is false. The point is not just that human beings are fallible. There are particular reasons for mistrusting drivers' judgements on such matters: we are notoriously prone to exaggerate our driving skills, and someone who is in a hurry, or who has already had a drink, is ill placed to decide whether he can drive safely at that speed or after another drink. We can thus see some hybrid offences of implicit endangerment as specifying safety precautions that everyone should take, in contexts in which we should not trust our own judgement: given the risks involved in the activity and our proneness to misjudgement, we should follow simple rules ('Don't exceed speed limits'; 'Don't drink and drive'), rather than allowing ourselves to decide on each occasion how fast to drive or how much to drink before driving.[90] The law demands not only that we drive safely, but also that we *ensure* that we do so;[91] such requirements declare that part of what we must do to ensure safety is to obey these restrictions.

Surely, however, there are people who *know* that they can safely break such rules: who *know* that they can drive safely though over the legal limit as to their speed or alcohol intake. Can we argue that they ought still to obey such laws; or must we admit that justice demands their exemption, and that to convict them is to sacrifice their rights for the sake of the social good that flows from not allowing such public exceptions? We might appeal now to two considerations. First, we owe it to each other not merely to *ensure* that we act safely, but to *assure* each other that we are doing so, in a social world in which we lack the personal knowledge of others that could give us that assurance; we provide such assurance in part by publicly following public safety-protecting rules, such as the speed limit.[92] Secondly, a driver who claims to know that he can safely ignore

[90] This argument embodies a familiar type of rule-consequentialism: see Hare, 1981. See also Raz's account of legitimate authority: Raz, 1986: ch 3.

[91] Compare Health and Safety at Work etc. Act 1974, ss 2–3, on an employer's duties to 'ensure' the health and safety of her employees and others; see Ch 10 at nn 52–56 below.

[92] Similar considerations also apply to the requirements that drivers be licensed, after passing a test, and that they carry at least third party insurance: these are ways of ensuring and assuring that drivers are minimally competent and that damage they cause will be paid for. See further at nn 96–100 below.

such rules claims a certain superiority over his fellows: '*they* must obey the rules, because they cannot be trusted to decide for themselves, but *I* need not'. What is wrong with such a claim is not that it is false (although it often will be), but that it is a denial of civic fellowship: a recognition of fellow citizenship (and of the dangers of allowing exemptions to the law) should motivate me to accept such laws even if I know that they are unnecessary in my case; so long as the demands the law makes on me are not onerous, I ought to accept this modest burden as an implication and expression of citizenship.[93]

Similar arguments will apply to the age rules for sexual activity. This is also a context in which we have reason not to trust our own judgements (a man excited at the prospect of sex with a young woman is ill placed to judge her maturity), and in which we perhaps should, in view of the dangers involved, follow moderately strict rules rather than deciding for ourselves on each occasion. I suspect that this may be the only way to justify hybrid offences. If the law lays down a standard that citizens must apply for themselves, too many of us will misapply it too often, given not just our human fallibility but the particular reasons why judgement is likely to be misguided in the contexts in which the standard will typically have to be applied. But if the law instead lays down a rule, and citizens follow it, the mischief against which the law is aimed will be significantly reduced, at the cost of only a modest burden on those who must restrain themselves even though they know that they can trust their own judgement; they should then thus restrain themselves, rather than seeking exemptions from the rules that others must follow, for reasons of mutual civic assurance and recognition.[94]

It might be argued that the most that such arguments can justify are hybrid offences that define the relevant conduct (speeding, driving with alcohol above the prescribed limit, having sexual intercourse with an

[93] Suppose the driver argues that he is not seeking an exception just for himself—that the same leeway should be allowed to any driver who is thus competent (see Husak, 2005b: 81)? But how would this be done? Are we to imagine a special set of licences, obtainable by drivers who could prove the appropriate competence? But that would not meet the need for assurance noted in this paragraph; and one could also argue that there are symbolic merits in sharing such common, modest burdens as citizens.

[94] Husak (2005b: 74–82) criticises an earlier version of this argument. I think that the current version (revised in the light of his critique) meets his objections. In particular, first, it does not imply that all actual hybrid offences are justified: if the grounds sketched here do not obtain (as is probably true in Husak's example of the medical prescription of marijuana), the law is unjustified—and we face the familiar question of what good reason, if any, we have to obey misguided laws (see text before n 89 above). Secondly, some of those who break such laws commit the genuine *malum in se*, whilst others commit the type of wrong explained here. Husak worries that if they receive the same sentence, this is unjust. But they must be sentenced on the basis of what is proved against them: unless we create an aggravated form of the offence that requires proof of the genuine *malum in se* (which would undercut some of the point of creating the hybrid offence), they must be sentenced for the same wrong.

under-age person), but allow a defence if the defendant can prove that his particular conduct did not constitute the relevant *malum in se*. We will discuss such burden-shifting provisions in Chapter 10, and will see that they sometimes play a legitimate role. To allow proof that the conduct was not dangerous as a defence, however, would often undercut the point of the hybrid offence: it would invite agents to engage in just the kind of deliberation that they should not engage in, about whether on this occasion their breach of what would now be no more than a rule of thumb would be permissible.

This argument fleshes out that sketched in Chapter 4.4. It shows both why we have good reason to regulate certain types of conduct by rules rather than by standards; and how, once the regulations are in place, breaches of them are wrongs for which their perpetrators should answer to their fellow citizens. Driving along a particular road at 80 mph might well not be wrong, because it might not be unreasonably dangerous, prior to the legal specification of a 70 mph speed limit: but once that regulation is in place, breaking it does constitute a public wrong—if not because drivers should not trust their own judgement about safe speeds, then because it is a matter of civic duty to accept this modest burden. By thus distinguishing the question of whether and how we should regulate the conduct from that of how we should treat breaches of the regulation (in particular whether we should criminalise them), the legal moralist can maintain that conduct should be criminalised only if and because it involves wrongdoing, whilst recognising that some kinds of criminalisable conduct were not wrongful prior to their legal regulation. Any defence of *mala prohibita* must be of this kind.

(b) Pure(r) Mala Prohibita

Hybrid offences of implicit endangerment are impure *mala prohibita*; they are grounded in a genuine *malum in se*. Other *mala prohibita* also have clear connections to, or generate, genuine *mala*. Regulations that specify what counts as fair dealing, in contexts in which there is no pre-legal agreement on what is fair, do not define what was already indubitably *malum in se*:[95] but once they are in place, it is wrong, because unfair, to break them; if that wrong is committed in the course of a public activity to which all citizens have access, we can call it a public wrong. Regulations that solve coordination problems may also be such that breaches of them commit genuine *mala*: once it is specified that we should drive on a particular side of the road, breaking that rule normally constitutes dangerous driving.

[95] See eg Auctions (Bidding Agreements) Acts 1927, 1969; Criminal Justice Act 1993, Pt V.

However, there are other kinds of *malum prohibitum* offence that seem justifiable, but that cannot be straightforwardly connected to genuine *mala*. Examples of these include offences concerned with the licensing of various activities or with keeping or making available appropriate records. Many concern relatively specialised activities, especially those involving dangers to physical health (as with health and safety legislation) or financial security (as with offences concerning banking and investment activities); but they can be illustrated, and their possible rationale explored, by more familiar examples of offences connected to driving.

It is an offence to drive without a driving licence, which one can obtain only by taking an official driving test.[96] Someone who never took a test and drove while unlicensed might be a perfectly competent driver, but what justifies the regulation requiring a test-based licence is the need to regulate admission to this somewhat dangerous activity, by requiring proof of at least minimal competence before one engages in it. What justifies making it a criminal matter is that if we are to engage in this activity, we owe it to our fellow citizens to abide by rules that are designed to ensure its relative safety, and to be willing to prove our competence to engage in it in the prescribed way; again, this can be seen as a matter of both ensuring, and assuring others, that one's conduct is safe. This requirement brings others in its train—such as a requirement not to lie in order to obtain a licence, not to forge a licence, and to produce one's driving licence when properly required to do so by a police officer.[97] Such rules protect or assist the efficient working of this regulatory system, which serves an important aspect of the common good: to break the rules about lying and forgery is to attack the system; to refuse to obey a reasonable request endangers the workings of the system. A refusal to show one's licence is not as serious a wrong as lying or forgery: but the criminal law need not deal only with serious wrongs—it can also provide modest punishments for offences that are, while still genuine wrongs, relatively minor. Something similar can be said about other offences to do, for instance, with having and being able to prove that one has insurance, or having and being able to prove that one has had one's car tested for safety, or paying and being able to prove that one has paid excise duty on one's car.[98] Some of these matters could, of course, be dealt with by a non-criminal regulatory regime of penalties,[99] but we can see the shape that a rationale for criminalisation could take: these regulations serve the common good; breaches of them are therefore breaches (often minor breaches) of our civic responsibilities, which merit

[96] Road Traffic Act 1988, s 87.

[97] See respectively Road Traffic Act 1988, ss 174, 173, 164.

[98] See Road Traffic Act 1988, ss 45–48, 143–156, 165; Vehicle Excise and Registration Act 1994, esp ss 29–46.

[99] See Ch 4 at nn 6–7, 44 above.

(often mild) condemnation as wrongs.[100] Indeed, this provides a more transparent representation of the claims that such regulations have on our obedience than does their portrayal as merely administrative regulations: they are regulations that we ought to obey if they help to maintain the efficient workings of systems that serve the common good; we do wrong when we breach them. The claim that we should obey them is not just that we will make our lives easier or avoid penalties if we do; nor just that these are the conventional rules of this game: but that we have a duty as citizens to obey them.

I have tried in this section to show how the kind of qualified legal moralism defended in Chapters 4–6 can deal with *mala prohibita*. I do not suppose either that all the *mala prohibita* defined in our existing criminal laws can be justified (it would be surprising if they could be), or that those that can be justified will all be justified in the same way; no doubt very different arguments will be relevant to different kinds of offence.[101] Nor is it crucial to the argument of this book that the particular justifications offered in this section succeed, since my concern is with the structure of criminal law and the logic of arguments about its proper content, rather than with just what its substantive content or scope should be. The argument of this section has been that it can extend beyond the initial paradigms of attack and endangerment to cover offences that are to some degree *mala prohibita* rather than *mala in se*. We first ask whether the legislature has good reason, related to some aspect of the common good, to regulate the type of conduct in question. If such legal regulation can be justified, we can then ask whether breaches of the regulations constitute public wrongs that merit public censure and sanction—ie whether they should be criminalised: to criminalise them is then to create *mala prohibita*: offences consisting in conduct that might not be wrongful prior to its legal regulation.

[100] It is worth emphasising that a sane system of criminal law can include mild as well as harsh penalties, and appropriate procedures through which minor wrongdoers can be called to account as well as procedures suitable for more serious wrongdoers: see Duff *et al*, 2007: ch 6.3.

[101] See eg Green, 1997; for a critique see Husak, 2005b: 82–9.

8

Answering and Refusing to Answer

I have offered no determinate general account of the proper objects of criminal responsibility, of that for which we should be criminally responsible; no such determinate general account is possible. I have suggested that the criminal law should operate not with an act requirement, but with an action presumption, and that only conduct that properly counts as a public wrong should be criminalised; I have distinguished between attacks and endangerments as two types of criminal wrong, and discussed some of the ways in which the law can legitimately reach beyond direct attacks and direct endangerments to cover both further kinds of *mala in se* and at least some kinds of *mala prohibita*. Indeterminate though the results of those discussions are, they offer enough material for the next stage of the inquiry—the stage that takes us from criminal responsibility to criminal liability, by asking how defendants should or may respond when called upon to answer to a criminal charge.[1]

Before we discuss the ways in which the transition from responsibility to liability can be either made or blocked, we must address some preliminary issues about the determination or denial of criminal responsibility that the criminal trial brings into view.[2] Contested criminal trials, in which the defendant pleads 'Not Guilty',[3] are concerned with determinations both of criminal responsibility and of criminal liability: indeed, in contested trials most of the court's attention is typically on the issue of responsibility—on whether there is a criminal offence, as specified in the indictment, for which the defendant must answer; only once responsibility is established

[1] See Ch 1.1 above.

[2] I focus on the 'adversarial' trial that is characteristic of the English and American systems, rather than the 'inquisitorial' trials that characterise continental European systems (see Damaska, 1973). The sharpness of this distinction is controversial (see eg P Duff, 2004; McEwan, 2004); I hope that what I say here could be applied, with little revision, to a more inquisitorial process (see Duff *et al*, 2007).

[3] The majority of trials involve no contest about the defendant's guilt, since he pleads 'Guilty': see Ashworth and Redmayne, 2005: 266–8; Crown Prosecution Service, 2006: 81–3.

need the court ask whether the transition to liability can be blocked by a defence. We must therefore distinguish, which will be the task of section 1 of this chapter, the process of answering to a criminal charge, which is what any defendant is summoned to do, from that of answering for a criminal offence, which only a defendant who is proved to have committed the offence must do.

We must also attend in this chapter to the reasons (legal or moral) on the basis of which a defendant might refuse to answer to the charge, and might deny that he would be answerable for anything before this court even if the prosecution could prove all that it alleged; this will be the task of section 2.

1. Answering and Answering For

We are criminally responsible for that for which we can be called to answer to our fellow citizens in a criminal court. I answer for something, in this context, either by admitting liability or by offering a defence, a justification or excuse, that will show conviction and punishment to be unwarranted.

A criminal trial calls on a defendant to answer a criminal charge. If the offence is to be tried on indictment, rather than summarily, the defendant must appear in court to answer in person to the charge, and may be arrested if she fails to appear.[4] The first way in which she answers the charge is by pleading 'Guilty' or 'Not Guilty' when the charge is put to her. Until 1772, defendants in English courts who did not plead and who were found 'mute of malice' rather than 'by visitation of God' were either (in non-capital cases) deemed to have pleaded 'Guilty', or (in capital cases) liable to be subjected to the '*peine forte et dure*'—being crushed by heavy weights—to extract a plea.[5] A 'Not Guilty' plea is now entered for a defendant who refuses to plead,[6] but these earlier provisions show how important a plea was thought to be: by pleading, the defendant recognises the authority of the court and the law; she shows that she is willing to answer the charge of wrongdoing laid against her.

[4] See Bail Act 1976, s 7; Sprack, 2006: 344–6. For summary trials, the defendant can plead guilty by post, and the trial can proceed even in his absence (Magistrates' Courts Act 1980, ss 11–13; Sprack, 2006: 171–5).

[5] See Mckenzie, 2005; *Singer v US* 380 US 24 (1965); the *peine forte et dure* was abolished in 1772, but the rule that a refusal to plead was treated as a plea of 'Guilty' was not abolished until 1827. The *peine forte et dure* itself seems to have derived from a misreading of a 13th century provision for '*prison forte et dure*' (thanks to Lindsay Farmer for this point; Duff *et al*, 2007: ch 2 at n 44).

[6] Sprack, 2006: 287. I deal shortly with the case of defendants who are not fit to plead.

There is plenty to be said about the meaning and significance of either plea.[7] On its face a guilty plea looks like a public, formal confession of criminal wrongdoing—though in practice it is likely to be uttered simply as a formal move in a game of plea-bargaining the rules of which the defendant might not understand,[8] or as a tactical concession by a defendant who hopes to gain some mitigation of sentence. On its face, a plea of 'Not Guilty' looks like a denial of guilt: but in the context of the trial, given the burden of proof borne by the prosecution, it could instead be read either as a claim of 'Not provably Guilty', or simply as a non-assertoric challenge to the prosecution to prove guilt if it can.

The proper meaning of a plea of 'Guilty' is indeed the meaning that it has at face value. The criminal law's offence definitions purport to define 'public' wrongs, for which their perpetrators must answer to the polity. The criminal trial calls a defendant to answer a charge of committing such a wrong: it is the forum through which she must answer for her crime if it is proved against her. Given the meaning of the charge, a guilty plea is a confession of public wrongdoing: the defendant admits both responsibility and liability. There are of course good reasons why a liberal system of law should not enquire too closely into the sincerity of such pleas (as distinct from trying to ensure that they are voluntary). It must leave defendants free to enter such pleas for tactical reasons, rather than trying to establish whether the defendant is sincerely confessing her wrong: not because a sincere confession by the guilty defendant is not an ideal to which we can aspire, but because such attempts to determine sincerity would be oppressively intrusive.[9] Nonetheless, the meaning of the plea is a confession of criminal wrongdoing—even if such confessions are known not to be always sincere confessions.

As for pleas of 'Not Guilty', there is much to be said for the performative, non-assertoric, interpretation. First, it would be odd to say that the guilty defendant who pleads 'Not Guilty' *lies* to the court.[10] Secondly, the defendant is entitled to a verdict of 'Not Guilty' just so long as the prosecution fails to prove his guilt beyond reasonable doubt: his plea of 'Not Guilty', as a claim that he is entitled to an acquittal, need therefore claim only that the prosecution cannot prove his guilt; but since he has not

[7] See further Duff *et al*, 2007: chs 4.2, 5.3, 6.2.

[8] See eg Baldwin and McConville, 1977.

[9] Compare the reasons why, even if a defendant could properly be required to make a public apology, there should be no attempt to establish whether the apology is sincere (see Duff, 2001: 95–6, 109–11; Bennett, 2006). Of course, in some jurisdictions there is no formal provision for pleas of 'Guilty'—though there is often still room for something very like plea bargaining (see Ashworth and Redmayne, 2005: 265); but my interest here is in the meaning of such pleas where they are available.

[10] He is certainly not guilty of perjury—but that is because he is not speaking under oath: Perjury Act 1911.

yet heard the prosecution's case, it seems more plausible to interpret the plea as a challenge, rather than as a prediction that the prosecution will fail in its probative task. When the plea rests on something more than the hope that the prosecution will fail to prove guilt, it might rest on a denial of responsibility—a denial that the defendant did what the prosecution alleges (a denial that he committed the specified actus reus with the requisite mens rea), and thus that he was responsible for the specified wrong. Or it might rest on an admission of responsibility, but a denial of criminal responsibility—a denial that what he admits to having done constituted the alleged criminal wrong.[11] Or it might rest on an admission of criminal responsibility, but a denial of liability: the defendant admits that he committed the offence charged, but offers a defence that he claims blocks the transition from criminal responsibility to criminal liability.

Although pleas of 'Not Guilty' do not admit criminal responsibility for the commission of the crime charged, the charge and the plea are nonetheless exercises in the ascription and acceptance of responsibility. In summoning a defendant to trial, the polity (acting through its criminal justice system) addresses her as a responsible agent: as someone who can be called to answer to the charge, and to answer for the wrongdoing if she is proved to have committed it; as someone who is capable of thus answering and who is answerable to the polity before this court. Indeed, in providing for a system of criminal trials the criminal law also imposes new prospective responsibilities on the citizens—to appear for trial if summoned (or to turn up if summoned as a juror or witness), to play their assigned role in the trial, to refrain from perjury, and so on. I suggested in Chapter 4 that the law's definitions of central *mala in se* as crimes amount not to prohibitions that offer citizens new reasons to avoid such conduct, but to declarations that they are public wrongs for which we will be called to public account: the criminal law is thus creating a prospective responsibility to answer for such wrongs, and to answer charges of committing one.[12] These prospective responsibilities generate retrospective responsibilities for our conduct in relation to them: for failing to appear when summoned to trial, for instance, or for misconduct during one's trial.

In entering a plea, the defendant thus implicitly accepts responsibility: even if he does not admit responsibility for a criminal wrong, he accepts that he must answer before this court to the charge that he committed such a wrong. A defendant might, however, refuse to enter a plea either of

[11] See eg *Anderton v Ryan* [1985] 1 AC 560 (successful argument that handling what I mistakenly believe to be stolen goods does not amount to a criminal attempt to handle stolen goods; overruled in *Shivpuri* [1987] AC 1); *Hinks* [2001] 2 AC 241 (unsuccessful argument that appropriation consisting in acquisition of title by a valid gift cannot constitute theft).

[12] Or, we might say, it is formalising and institutionalising the prospective responsibilities we already have, pre-legally, to answer for such wrongs to our fellow citizens.

'Guilty' or of 'Not Guilty', just because he might deny this responsibility: he might deny that he should have to answer to this charge in this court.

2. Refusing to Answer

A defendant who pleads 'Not Guilty' might deny that she was responsible for the crime with which she is charged. By entering a plea, however, she accepts a responsibility to answer to this charge in this court, and to answer for the crime if it is proved that she committed it. That is why it is thought important for the defendant to enter a plea: for in doing so she accepts her own responsibility before this court.[13]

This aspect of the defendant's plea highlights a dimension of the trial that has received insufficient attention from theorists—perhaps because they focus too much on the question of liability, of 'who is liable for what?',[14] and too little on the question of responsibility, of who must answer for what to whom; perhaps too because, given that focus on criminal liability, issues about criminal procedure are separated too sharply from issues about the substantive criminal law. The criminal trial formally begins with the charge and the plea: that interchange presupposes that the defendant is responsible—that he must answer to this charge before this court; but what if he denies that he is thus responsible? Such a denial is not made by a plea of 'Not Guilty', which accepts this responsibility: rather, it is made by a claim that he should not be tried at all. Such claims, if made on legally recognised grounds, are pleas in bar of trial; as we will see, legally recognised bars to trial also have their moral analogues.

Legal bars to trial figure among what Robinson classes as 'non-exculpatory defenses',[15] but this label is misleading: defences are answers to a criminal charge that seek to block the transition from responsibility to liability; pleas in bar of trial are denials that the defendant should have to answer to the charge.[16] Two examples will illustrate this general point.

First, a successful insanity defence, which is focused on the defendant's condition at the time of the killing, justifies his acquittal: he answers this charge of culpable wrongdoing by denying culpability.[17] By contrast, a successful plea of unfitness to plead, which focuses on the defendant's condition at the time of the trial, does not answer the charge of wrongdoing, but shows that this defendant cannot be properly called to answer that charge, since he lacks the capacities necessary to understand or to answer

[13] Many defendants will plead from fear of power rather than respect for authority; but my claim concerns the meaning of a plea.

[14] Dubber, 2002a: 5: see Introduction at n 50 above.

[15] Robinson, 1984: i, 55–7, 102–14, 179–87; ii, 460–543.

[16] Robinson himself (1984: i, 1) admits that the label is misleading.

[17] See Simester and Sullivan, 2007: 643–56; LaFave, 2003: ch 7; and below, Ch 11.5.

it: the claim is not that he did not culpably commit the crime charged or that the prosecution cannot prove it, but that he cannot be tried for it.[18] If a defendant is unfit to plead, the trial cannot proceed, but an 'inquiry' is held, and the jury must determine whether it is 'satisfied ... that he did the act or made the omission charged against him as the offence'. If it is not thus satisfied, the defendant is acquitted 'as if the trial had proceeded to a conclusion', but if it is thus satisfied he is not convicted. Instead, the jury 'make[s] a finding that the accused did the act or made the omission charged against him as the offence'; the court can then make a hospital order, or a guardianship order, or a supervision and treatment order, or discharge the defendant.[19] If we ask why the trial cannot proceed, although such an inquiry can be held, the answer is that a trial requires a responsible defendant who can answer to the charge; an unfit defendant might have been responsible for committing a crime, but cannot now be called to answer for it.

Secondly, someone might answer a charge by arguing that she was authorised to engage in the conduct in question, conduct that would otherwise have been criminal; for instance, under English law a parent can answer a charge of assault on her child by arguing that her conduct constituted 'lawful chastisement'.[20] By contrast, someone who claims diplomatic immunity is not claiming that she was authorised to engage in the conduct that allegedly constituted the crime—indeed, she might admit that what she did was culpably criminal: but she is denying that this court has the authority to call her to account for her conduct—that she must answer to or before this court for that conduct.[21] She need not deny that she is morally responsible—to the victim, to her own polity; she might well be legally responsible to or before some other body, such as her own employers or courts: but she is not in law answerable before this court.

In neither of these cases does the defendant answer the accusation by arguing that she is not guilty of the offence (or that the prosecution cannot prove her guilt); she argues that it is not an accusation that she should have to answer in this court. We must therefore distinguish answers to the charge—pleas of 'Not Guilty', denials of an element of the offence, defences—from pleas in bar of trial: the former admit that the charge is one that the defendant can be required to answer by and in this court; the latter deny precisely that.

[18] See Sprack, 2006: 287–8; Robinson, 1984: ii, 501–8.

[19] Criminal Procedure (Insanity) Act 1964, ss 4A–5 (inserted by Criminal Procedure (Insanity and Unfitness to Plead) Act 1991, ss 2–3).

[20] See Ormerod, 2005: 538–9; the European Convention on Human Rights has led to the curtailment, but not to the abolition, of this parental right.

[21] See Diplomatic Privileges Act 1964, s 2(1); Consular Relations Act 1968.

The trial is concerned, ultimately, with whether the defendant satisfies the conditions of criminal responsibility and liability for the alleged offence. But the possibility of bars to trial focuses our attention on conditions that must be satisfied if the trial itself is to be legitimate: these are in one sense conditions of criminal responsibility, since they determine whether this defendant must answer for this alleged conduct before this court.

(a) Bars to Trial: An Initial Typology

We can distinguish four main types of bar to trial. The first concerns the defendant's own condition or status: *he* should not have to answer. The second concerns the conduct alleged to constitute the crime: he should not have to answer *for that*. The third concerns the evidence against him: he should not have to answer *that case*. The fourth concerns the state's conduct towards him: he should not now have to answer this charge, *given officials' prior conduct*.[22] We will pay most attention to the fourth type, which raises fundamental questions about the conditions of legitimacy for a criminal process.

The Defendant's Condition: A defendant who is called to answer a charge of wrongdoing must be *capable* of answering it, else his trial becomes a travesty. If his condition at the time of his trial is such that he is incompetent or unfit to plead, if he is incapable of understanding and responding to the charge against him, he should not be tried: not because his guilt could not be proved (an inquiry might still establish his guilt), but because his trial could not then be what it is supposed to be—a process through which he answers a charge of wrongdoing.[23] The defendant must also be answerable to this polity: even if the prosecution could offer admissible evidence sufficient to prove that a competent defendant committed the crime, she can avoid trial by claiming diplomatic immunity;[24] she is not answerable before this court.

The Alleged Conduct: A defendant who is fit to be tried can bar her trial by showing that the prosecution has not alleged anything for which she must answer. She might show that the alleged offence was committed

[22] I will not consider the various rules about excluding evidence: such exclusions can de facto bar trial if the evidence is vital to the prosecution's case, and the grounds of exclusion overlap with bars to trial when they involve police or prosecutorial misconduct, but they are not formally bars to trial. See Dennis, 2007: chs 3, 6, 8; Roberts and Zuckerman, 2004: chs 4–5; Duff *et al*, 2007: chs 4.3, 8.3.

[23] See at nn 17–19 above (also Ch 2 at nn 5–6); Duff, 1986: 29–35, 119–23. The provisions for exempting or (excluding) children from trial are also relevant here: see Sprack, 2006: ch 11; Maher, 2005; Nuotio, 2005.

[24] See at n 21 above; Sprack, 2006: 85–6.

outside the jurisdiction of this legal system,[25] or so long ago that its prosecution is barred by a statute of limitations;[26] or that she has already been tried, has already answered, for this conduct, so that to try her now on this charge would constitute double jeopardy;[27] or that the conduct in which she allegedly engaged does not constitute an offence, so that even if the prosecution proved every fact it alleged, it would not prove her to be guilty of an offence.[28]

The Prosecution's Case: A defendant needs to answer a charge, beyond entering a formal plea, only when there is sufficient evidence to constitute a case to answer: citizens should not be required to subject themselves to the burden of a trial unless and until the prosecution can adduce credible evidence of their guilt. This is one function of various pre-trial hearings—for instance grand jury proceedings under American law, which must determine whether there is 'probable cause to believe' that the defendant committed the offence charged; and committal proceedings under English law, which must decide whether the prosecution has made out at least a prima facie case for the defendant to answer.[29]

Prior Official Conduct: Conduct (or misconduct) by state officials towards the defendant in advance of the trial can also constitute a bar to trial. Perhaps he was promised immunity in relation to this charge—as part of a plea bargain, or to avoid Fifth Amendment obstacles to his testifying against others.[30] Or he might argue that some misconduct by police, prosecutor or other officials was so outrageous that it undermines the trial's legitimacy. If, for instance, he appears in court only because he was kidnapped abroad by agents of the state or with the state's connivance, the court might agree that such gross misconduct in getting him to trial undermines the 'integrity' of the trial, and renders it an 'abuse of process'.[31]

[25] See eg Model Penal Code, s 1.03(1)(f); German Criminal Code, ss 5, 7 (and above, Ch 2 at nn 17–20). One could instead see this plea as denying the authority of this court, ie as falling into the fourth category.

[26] See eg Model Penal Code, s 1.06.

[27] See Ashworth and Redmayne, 2005: 364–8 on the double jeopardy rule and the exceptions now created to it in English law (Criminal Procedure and Investigations Act 1996, s 54; Criminal Justice Act 2003, Pt 10); on American law see LaFave *et al*, 2004: ch 25.

[28] This is the (infrequently used) plea of 'demurrer' in English law: see Hampton, 1982: 188. On repelling the relevancy of a charge in Scots law, see Gordon, 2000: 15–40.

[29] See LaFave *et al*, 2004: chs 14.3, 15.2; see Sprack, 2006: 213–14. The defendant can also claim that there is no case to answer after the prosecution has presented its case at the trial (and cannot do so before then if there is no pre-trial hearing): see Sprack, 2006: 337–40; LaFave *et al*, 2004: ch 24.6(a).

[30] See LaFave et al, 2004: chs 8.11, 21.2.

[31] Contrast *R v Horseferry Road Magistrates' Court, ex p Bennett* (1994) 98 Cr App Rep 114 with *US v Alvarez-Machain* 504 US 655 (1992). See Ashworth, 2002a; Dennis, 2007: ch 2(E) on 'legitimacy'; Roberts and Zuckerman, 2004: 157–60. On the issues in this section see also Duff *et al*, 2007: ch 8.

There is of course much more to be said about the details of such bars to trial, about how and by whom they should be decided, and about what their effects should be; but we cannot pursue these questions here.[32] Instead, I want to focus on some bars to trial of the fourth kind, since they will bring out some important features and implications of seeing responsibility as a matter of answerability, and of taking seriously the question 'To whom must I answer?'—implications that raise disturbing questions about the legitimacy of our criminal process.[33]

(b) Estoppel

Prior official conduct can sometimes be said to 'estop' the prosecution. Estoppel is most familiar in civil law, where it fills some of the gaps left by the law of contracts. It is:

> a mechanism for enforcing consistency; when I have said or done something that leads you to believe in a particular state of affairs, I may be obliged to stand by what I have said or done, even though I am not contractually bound to do so.[34]

Someone who induces or allows another to rely, to her potential detriment, on some explicit or implicit assurance or commitment may not be allowed to go back on that assurance to the other's detriment: if I promise my tenant that I will accept just part of the rent she owes me this year, rather than demanding the full rent, and she relies on that promise, the doctrine of promissory estoppel precludes me from going back on my promise and suing for the full rent, even if the promise was not legally binding as a matter of contract.[35] The tenant still owes the rent, since a promise not to enforce a debt does not cancel the debt; but I am estopped from demanding it.[36]

Several bars to trial involve estoppel. If the prosecutor promises the defendant immunity on a specific charge in return for a guilty plea to a lesser charge or for testimony against other defendants, she is then bound

[32] Robinson suggests that, when a 'non-exculpatory defense' succeeds, courts should still be able to impose some of the 'collateral consequences' of conviction upon the defendant—if necessary after a process of 'culpability determination' that results in a special verdict of 'guilty but not punishable': the court could order preventive or protective detention for someone unfit to plead, or order that this offence should figure in the defendant's criminal record, even though he could not be formally convicted for it (1984: i, 179–87). But if the defendant cannot be tried, he cannot be justifiably punished; and we must ask more carefully than Robinson does what could justify imposing the measures he envisages on responsible agents who have not been duly convicted of an offence (or on non-responsible agents who are unfit to plead).

[33] On the issues in the following two sub-sections see Duff *et al*, 2007: ch 8.2–3.

[34] Cooke, 2000: 1.

[35] See *Central London Property Trust Ltd v High Trees House Ltd* [1947] KB 130.

[36] On the complications that I have ignored here see Richards, 2002: 65–70.

by that promise—especially if the defendant relied on it to his potential detriment and kept his side of the bargain; she is estopped from breaking it.[37] The defendant might be guilty; it might be possible to prove his guilt by admissible evidence: but the prosecutor, and the polity in whose name she acts, must keep her and its word. There are pragmatic reasons for holding prosecutors to such promises: if defendants could not rely on them, they would cease to be effective. However, the basic reason is one of justice: a polity should not break its word to its citizens.

The idea of estoppel is also applied to cases in which the defendant acted in reasonable reliance on mistaken official advice that his contemplated course of action was not criminal: such reliance is sometimes said to ground a plea of 'entrapment by estoppel'[38] and, given the unwarranted persistence of the doctrine that even reasonable mistake of law is not a defence, one can see why some such provision is necessary. If, however, we abandon that doctrine, as we should, we can distinguish two kinds of reasonable reliance. In one, the official acts in good faith; in the other she acts in bad faith, intending to induce the commission of the crime. In the latter case, we can talk of entrapment, to be discussed in the following sub-section. In the former case, it could be argued that reasonable reliance should constitute a defence rather than a bar to trial: the defendant's culpability is negated by the fact that he made reasonable efforts to conform his conduct to the law's demands, which gives him an exculpatory answer for the crime for which he must admit responsibility. But one could instead argue that this too should be an estoppel-based bar to trial: if the state, in the person of the official, tells me that my proposed conduct is non-criminal, it should not then turn round and prosecute me for it. If it is ever reasonable to rely on advice about the law from someone other than an official, that would be grounds for a defence of 'reasonable mistake of law'; but one who relies on official advice should not face prosecution, since the official advice constitutes a kind of promise or guarantee that he will not face prosecution if he follows it.[39]

[37] See eg *R v Croydon Justices ex p Dean* [1993] CLR 758 (Simester and Sullivan, 2007: 627).

[38] See Connelly, 1994; *US v Levin* 973 F 2d 463 (1992); *US v Sousa* 468 F.3d 42 (2006). See generally Ashworth, 1974, 2002a; A Smith, 1984; Husak and von Hirsch, 1993; Parry, 1997.

[39] This is not to say that citizens can legitimately thus rely on *any* advice that an official gives: if the advice is obviously unreasonable or absurd, we might say that the official can no longer be regarded as acting in an official capacity, and that the advice-seeker, as a responsible citizen, should realise that he cannot rely on the advice.

(c) Prior Official Misconduct

The example of malicious official misinformation takes us away from cases in which the prosecution is estopped by some prior official action that might have been quite legitimate, and in which it is only the subsequent prosecution that is illegitimate, to cases in which what bars the prosecution is some prior official misconduct which, we can say, taints the criminal process. I have already mentioned one such case, in which a defendant is present for trial only because he was illegally kidnapped abroad: in England the House of Lords held that his trial would be an abuse of process; in America the Supreme Court refused to bar trial, and seemed interested only in whether the kidnapping violated the extradition treaty between the USA and the country from which the defendant was kidnapped.[40]

It might be argued that the (mere) fact that the defendant's availability for trial is due to serious misconduct by officials or others should not bar his trial. The court must condemn that misconduct, and demand that its perpetrators, if available, be prosecuted themselves; it should formally disown the wrong that brought the defendant here. But if it does thus disown the misconduct, trying the defendant does not undermine the integrity of the criminal process. For what undermines that integrity is official misconduct by the polity that claims through that process to be upholding the rules of law; but by thus disowning the misconduct, the polity turns it from *official* misconduct to *officials'* misconduct—misconduct which does not infect the criminal process of which it is, once it is disowned, no longer properly a part.

This argument is unpersuasive. Even if we could not then accuse the polity of profiting from its own wrong,[41] since the wrong is no longer its own, it is still taking advantage of another's wrong; and whilst there is room for argument about when and how it is or is not legitimate to make use of the fruits of another's wrongdoing, it seems clearly wrong to do so when the wrongdoing was committed against the person against whom its

[40] See at n 31 above. The best known such case was that of Adolf Eichman, kidnapped from Brazil by members of the Israeli Mossad to be taken to Israel for trial for war crimes. The only way to justify this would be to argue that his were crimes against humanity, falling under international rather than national jurisdiction, so that the agents were acting as agents of humanity (see above, Ch 2 at nn 44–49).

[41] See famously *Riggs v Palmer* 115 NY 506 (1889)—a case and principle made much of by Dworkin (1978; 1986: 15–20). Victor Tadros also pointed out to me that it is not clear who 'profits' in such a case.

fruits are now to be used. Making such use of the fruits of wrongdoing also undermines our disowning of it: if we are to disown it, we should have nothing to do with it or its fruits.[42]

Another case in which prior official misconduct undermines the legitimacy of the trial is that in which the defendant can show that, even if she was provably guilty as charged, the decision to prosecute her was grounded in a vindictive motive,[43] or that her selection for prosecution, from among many others who could have been prosecuted successfully, was 'deliberately based upon an unjustifiable standard such as race, religion, or other arbitrary classification'.[44] Here again the point is not that the defendant is not provably guilty, or that she cannot be called to account for her wrongdoing by someone, but that the manner or motivation of her prosecution renders it illegitimate. She is not being prosecuted to serve the proper aims of justice; the injustice of the prosecutor's treatment of her undermines the right of the polity (for whom the prosecutor acts) to call her to account—at least on this occasion. 'You're picking on me unfairly' does not exculpate me, but it does (if true) undermine your standing to demand that I answer to you.

Not any kind of official misconduct towards the defendant undermines the legitimacy of his trial: it must be misconduct that bears directly on the trial or the criminal process that led to it. Similarly, in our extra-legal moral lives prior misconduct towards another can undercut one's right to call them to account for what might be genuine wrongdoing. If, for instance, I set out to provoke you into attacking me, your attack might be neither justified nor excused, but my deliberate provocation undercuts my right to protest about it.

The ways in which prosecution can be rendered illegitimate, as an 'abuse of process', by prior official misconduct towards the defendant will also help us to understand why official entrapment should preclude the defendant's conviction.

[42] Compare the American doctrine of the 'fruit of the poisonous tree', in the context of excluding improperly obtained evidence: *Nardone v US* 308 US 338, 341 (1937); see LaFave *et al*, 2004: ch 9.3.

[43] See eg *Dixon v District of Columbia* 394 F2d 966 (1968); LaFave *et al*, 2004: ch 13.5(a).

[44] *Oyler v Boles* 368 US 448, 456 (1962); see generally LaFave *et al*, 2004: ch 13.4. Such claims are of course notoriously hard to prove; sometimes the alleged discrimination infects not decisions to prosecute, but prior decisions—for instance about which cars to stop for traffic violations, with a view to searching them for drugs (*New Jersey v Soto et al* 734 A 2d 350 (1996); see also *Yick Wo v Hopkins* 118 US 356 (1886)); sometimes the remedy sought is not a bar to trial, but the exclusion of the evidence improperly obtained (see *New Jersey v Soto et al*). But my interest here is in the point of principle that is raised most directly by the simple case of discriminatory decisions to prosecute.

(d) Entrapment

American law recognises entrapment as a defence: the defendant admits committing the offence, but pleads that he should be acquitted because he was entrapped into committing it by someone whom he now knows to have been a police officer or other official, who induced him to commit the offence only in order to secure his prosecution. English law recognises no such defence, though evidence obtained by entrapment can be excluded on 'abuse of process' grounds; this suggests that any expanded recognition of entrapment as a bar to conviction in England would treat it as a bar to trial rather than as a defence.[45]

The American approach is problematic. The entrapped defendant committed the crime; unless the entrapper used such pressure as to constitute duress (which would be a defence), the fact that he committed it because he was encouraged by someone who was (unknown to him) a state official does not reduce his culpability—as is evidenced by the fact that purely private 'entrapment' is no defence. Allowing entrapment as a defence might discourage or deter such police misconduct: but, apart from the fact that there are better ways of achieving this, such as the direct prosecution of the entrappers, this can hardly ground a *defence*—an exculpatory answer for the defendant's commission of the crime; nor does it show why we should find the trial and conviction of an entrapped defendant *inherently* worrying. We can more plausibly see entrapment as a bar to trial grounded in the entrapper's official misconduct. If I encourage you to commit a wrong (especially if I do so in order to be able then to condemn you for it), I am ill-placed to condemn you for committing it: not because it was not a culpable wrong, but because my complicity in the wrong undercuts my standing to call you to account for it. You are answerable to others—to the victim, if there is one, to others with a proper interest in the matter; but you are not answerable to me. So too, if the polity's officials induce someone to commit a crime in order to prosecute him for it, this undercuts the polity's right to call him to account for that crime: there may be those to whom he should answer for it, but he is not now answerable to the polity as a whole.[46]

The previous paragraph admittedly played fast and loose with some complex and difficult issues about entrapment, including the questions of what should count as 'entrapment' and of what relevance, if any, the defendant's 'predisposition' to commit such crimes should have to his plea

[45] On American law see Robinson, 1984: ii, ch 6 s 209; LaFave *et al*, 2004: ch 5. On English law see Choo, 1993: ch 6; Ashworth, 2002a, 2002b; Simester and Sullivan, 2007: 680–2; *Loosely* [2001] UKHL 53.

[46] See Robinson, 1984: i, 112; Ashworth, 2002a: 310–22.

of entrapment (though my remarks imply that it should have no relevance). It adopts the 'objective' approach favoured by the minority on the Supreme Court in *Sorrels*, *Sherman* and *Russell*,[47] focusing on the conduct of the entrappers, rather than the 'subjective' approach focused on the conduct, intentions and predisposition of the person entrapped: but much more argument is needed to show whether that is the right approach. All I have tried to do here is to suggest that, if someone who induces another to do wrong thereby loses her moral standing to call the other to account for that (admittedly culpable) wrongdoing, we can see entrapment as a bar to trial that is based on the same moral idea. The entrapped defendant admittedly did not rely, as someone who acts on official misinformation relies, on a supposed official guarantee that he will not face a criminal charge.[48] His culpability is therefore not reduced, nor is the wrongfulness of his conduct: but he is not now responsible, ie he cannot now be called to answer, to or before this court.

I am not, I admit, confident that this is the right account of entrapment. Two other views should at least be noted. On the first, entrapment should not bar either trial or conviction: the polity should instead prosecute the entrappers for their wrongdoing, thus formally disowning it, whilst still prosecuting the entrapped defendant for his wrongdoing; by thus transforming the entrapment from official misconduct to officials' misconduct, the polity and its courts can retain the right to call the defendant, as well as the entrappers, to account.[49] This view would be especially attractive if (which for obvious reasons is not the usual case) the defendant was entrapped into committing a victimising crime—burglary, perhaps. The victim of a burglary can usually expect that (if the crime can be solved) the offender will be called to account for that public wrong by the polity: that is what we collectively owe him as our fellow citizen. If the burglar was entrapped, all citizens, in whose name the entrappers claimed to be acting but who should want to make clear that it was not in their name, should be able to expect that the entrappers will be called to answer for their wrong; but should they not also be able to expect that the burglar will be called to account for the burglary? This would not be to profit from or to take advantage of the wrong committed by the entrappers, as trying a kidnapped defendant would be:[50] for the polity's aim is not to 'out' and then

[47] *Sorrels v US* 287 US 435 (1932); *Sherman v US* 356 US 369 (1958); *US v Russell* 411 US 423 (1973).

[48] See at nn 38–39 above.

[49] But it would be crucial, and might be difficult, to show that the officials were not implicitly encouraged to such misconduct by the attitudes, policies or habits of thought that structured their official activities.

[50] See at nn 31, 40–42 above.

prosecute those who are predisposed to burglary (which was the entrappers' aim); it is rather to respond appropriately to burglary as a public wrong, and prosecuting the entrapped burglar still legitimately serves that end.

Of course, entrapped crimes do not usually have a direct victim: a more familiar example is that in which a drug dealer is induced to supply drugs to undercover police officers. In such cases we could also say—*if* we agree that drug dealing is properly criminalised—that not one but two criminal wrongs have been committed for which their perpetrators should be called to answer: the entrapment and the supply. But we might now see another reason for not convicting the entrapped defendant, and another alternative view of entrapment: not that the polity lacks the standing to call him to answer, but that there was no offence of a kind that should concern the criminal law. If drug dealing is properly criminalised, it is because of the dangers that drugs create for their users, or the way in which dealers exploit their customers;[51] but if the dealer is entrapped, the police will ensure that no such danger or harm is actualised. Seen objectively, therefore, no criminal wrong is committed: the dealer has the requisite mens rea, an intention to supply, but a genuine actus reus is lacking. This line of argument leads us into the murky realms of 'impossible attempts': the case is comparable to that of someone who buys what she mistakenly believes to be stolen goods in what turns out to be a police sting. We cannot explore those realms here.[52]

We need not decide between these different accounts here; nor should we assume that the same account will be appropriate for every kind of case. The point of this discussion has been simply to show that once we ask not only what agents should be criminally responsible for, but to whom they should be responsible or by whom they can be called to answer, we can see more clearly the way in which official misconduct (perhaps including some entrapments) can undermine the legitimacy of the criminal trial by undermining the polity's right to call this defendant to answer, through its criminal courts, for what might well have been a genuine, and provable, criminal wrong.

It is worth highlighting two aspects of the argument that serious prior official misconduct can constitute a bar to trial. First, the argument depends on a conception of what a polity owes its citizens, what counts as fair dealing between polity and citizens, in the investigation and prosecution of crimes. Aspects of that conception are of course controversial:

51 See Alldridge, 1996.

52 See eg *People v Jaffe* 185 NY 497 (NY 1906); *Haughton v Smith* [1975] AC 476: for discussion see Duff, 1996: 98–106, 206–19. Compare *Sorrels v US* 287 US 435 (1932), 448, 451: conduct that is 'induced' in a way that constitutes entrapment 'lies outside the purview' of the relevant criminal statute.

which kinds of inducement of crime, for instance, count as legitimate police tactics and which as illegitimate entrapment; which other kinds of police deception are legitimate, which illegitimate;[53] what constitutes improperly discriminatory prosecution, given that prosecutors must retain a wide discretion about whom they prosecute? However, it is not controversial that there are moral limits, which should also be legal limits, on police and prosecutorial tactics; that if those limits are flouted the legitimacy of the trial is undermined; and that those limits apply to the treatment of the innocent and the guilty alike. Promises to guilty defendants are binding; their discriminatory or vindictive prosecution is still improper—which is to say that they are still citizens to whom the polity owes respect and justice.[54] This point might seem too obvious to be worth stating, but it is obvious only on the assumption that offenders are still citizens to whom fair dealing is owed; although that assumption should be uncontroversial, it is implicitly denied by much of the rhetoric of the 'war on crime'—by the ways in which criminals (or those who commit the kinds of crime that 'we' do not commit) are portrayed as the enemy against whom 'we' must protect ourselves. To call someone to answer for her wrongdoing is to address her as a member of the polity whose essential values (as expressed in the criminal law) she is accused of violating; it is to treat her as a fellow citizen. But we must then ask what else is demanded by such a recognition of citizenship: what tactics may the state or its officials use in detecting and prosecuting crime; what kinds of misconduct by the state or its officials would undermine its standing to prosecute, judge, condemn and punish an offender? I will discuss a disturbing expansion of this question in the following section.

Secondly, the strongest ground for barring trial is that the defendant suffered misconduct at the hands of the polity itself: she can say to the court (and to the polity in whose name it calls her to answer) 'How can *you* call me to account for this alleged crime given the way in which *you* have behaved towards me in the events that led to my trial?'. Now if the misconduct that led to the defendant's appearance in court can be effectively disowned, and transformed from *official* misconduct into *officials'* misconduct,[55] there is room to argue that the defendant's trial can proceed, so long as the officials are also called to account for their misconduct. But that separation of the officials and their misconduct from the polity that now seeks to try the defendant presupposes that the polity's

[53] See Ashworth, 1998.

[54] The doctrine that someone who is 'predisposed' to commit the kind of crime that he is induced to commit cannot plead entrapment is inconsistent with this view: in dealing with a dispositionally 'guilty' citizen, the police may use tactics that they should not use on dispositionally 'innocent' defendants. But that is what is objectionable about that doctrine: see *US v Russell* 411 US 423, at 443–4 (Justice Stewart, dissenting).

[55] See at nn 40–42, 49–50 above.

hands (its citizens' collective hands) are appropriately clean in its dealings with the defendant; and that, we will now see, might be doubted.

3. Criminal Responsibility and Citizenship

Criminal defendants are called to answer by their fellow citizens collectively for wrongs that they allegedly committed against the defining values of their polity: to summon a defendant to trial is to address and treat him as a fellow citizen. But being treated as a citizen is not just a matter of being held criminally responsible: it involves being included, allowed to share, in both the burdens and the benefits of citizenship; being allowed—indeed encouraged—to take part in the political life of the community, to share in its material and social goods, to benefit from its welfare, educational and medical provisions, and so on.[56] Suppose that a defendant belongs to a group whose members have not been treated with the respect and concern due to them as citizens: they have been (if not by design, certainly in effect) systematically excluded from full participation in the polity. Could he not with justice argue that, whatever wrongs he has committed, the polity lacks the standing to call him to account for them?

A simple example of this kind is that of a black South African brought to trial in the apartheid era. Suppose he is charged with committing what any legal system would define as a crime—burglary, or a serious assault against a neighbour; he does not deny committing it. He need not claim that what he did was not a wrong, or that it was justified or excused. He need not claim that he has no obligation to obey the law: that might be argued, but, as we have seen, the criminal wrongfulness of such *mala in se* does not consist in disobedience to a law that prohibits them.[57] He need not deny that he must answer to others—most obviously to his neighbours—for his actions. All he need claim is that, given his systematic exclusion from citizenship in the polity in whose name the courts act, he is not responsible for his conduct before this court, or to this polity.

One question we must then ask ourselves is this: how confident are we that all those who appear as defendants in our courts are properly answerable to us for their crimes? Of course they are not excluded from citizenship in the way that black South Africans were: but can we be confident that we have collectively treated them with the respect and concern that are due to them as citizens? We know that too many people and groups in our societies suffer various kinds of serious and systematic disadvantage that should be seen as matters of social injustice rather than

[56] See Duff, 2001: ch 3.1, and ch 5.2 for fuller discussion of some of the issues raised in this section.

[57] See above, Ch 4 at nn 22–27.

of bad luck; we know that they have been in significant ways excluded from, or not offered decent opportunities to achieve, adequate participation in the rights and benefits of citizenship. We know that this is particularly true of many who appear as defendants in our criminal courts—which is to say that we know that we have, collectively, seriously failed to treat them as fellow citizens. So how can we now claim (as the courts claim in our name and on our behalf) the right to call them to account for their wrongs, with suitably clean collective hands and with clear consciences?[58] Imagine that we are jurors: could we honestly look this person, a member of this disadvantaged group, in the eye and condemn him for his crime?[59] What we must first ask ourselves is not whether the evidence we have heard suffices to prove his guilt, but whether we, as the jurors who are supposed to judge this defendant as our fellow citizen, have the right or the moral standing to do so; and the answer to that question depends partly on whether we, as members of the polity of which we and he are supposedly fellow citizens, have collectively treated him as a citizen.

This casts light on the question of whether penal justice is possible in contexts of serious political and social injustice. We rightly feel uneasy when we realise how many of those who are convicted in our courts, receiving what are supposed to be their just deserts, have been the victims of systemic injustice at the hands of the polity of which they are supposedly citizens (and thus at our hands as their fellow citizens). That unease sometimes motivates suggestions that serious (unjust) social disadvantage should be recognised as providing either a partial or complete defence: perhaps an excuse of 'duress of circumstances', or lack of fair opportunity to gain ordinarily available goods by non-criminal means; or even a (partial) justification, if the crime can be seen as a response to, or as an attempt to remedy, the injustice.[60] But we can more plausibly see the serious, systemic injustice that the defendant has suffered at the hands of the polity, not as a defence that (partially) justifies or excuses his crime, but as a moral bar to trial. If we fail to treat a person or group with the respect or concern due to them as fellow citizens, we may lose the moral standing to call them to account, to judge them or condemn them, for the wrongs that they commit as citizens.

If this is indeed our position, we face the acute question of what we can properly do; that question become more acute when we recognise that

[58] What dirties our hands in this context is not just the fact that we are ourselves wrongdoers: it is our prior and continuing treatment of the defendant, or of the group to which he belongs, that undercuts our right to call him to account.

[59] Compare Clark, 1999, 2006, on the significance of jury service and the 'confrontation' rule in American trials.

[60] See, eg, Bazelon, 1976; Delgado, 1985; Hudson, 1995. For a useful general, and critical, set of discussions see Heffernan and Kleining, 2000.

those whom we may lack the proper standing to call to account have often committed wrongs against victims who should be able to look to the criminal law for a suitable response to the public wrongs they have suffered. We must ask how we can begin to remedy the injustices that these offenders have suffered (a question that is pressing independently of the criminal law): but what can we do meanwhile in response to their crimes? Part of an answer is that we must ourselves be collectively ready to be called to account, and indeed show that we hold ourselves to account, for the injustices such defendants have suffered at our collective—and typically passive—hands: my standing to call you to account for the wrongs that you commit against me is at least strengthened if I am ready to be called and to hold myself to account for the wrongs I have committed against you. Another part of an answer might be to develop more nuanced legal procedures, or post-conviction processes, that would have room for genuine recognition and discussion of such injustices: we could look for inspiration here to 'restorative justice' procedures, which seek to restore, or to (re)create, the social relationships that are damaged by both crime and social injustice—although we should resist the idea, which is too prevalent among both advocates and critics of restorative justice, that restorative justice cannot include punishment.[61]

We cannot pursue these questions further here. The point of this section has been to show how, by focusing on the idea of responsibility as answerability and on the consequent question 'To whom must I answer?', our attention is drawn to significant issues about the conditions that must (legally and morally) be satisfied if a defendant is to be legitimately tried—if she is to be legitimately called to account, by a criminal court, for her alleged criminal wrongdoing. These issues have not received the theoretical attention they deserve—perhaps partly because theorists have paid insufficient attention to this relational dimension of responsibility; it is a merit of a relational account of criminal responsibility that it highlights such issues about the conditions of criminal responsibility, and helps us to see why the possibility of doing justice in an unjust society is so morally problematic.

It is time now to move on, however, from questions about when a defendant must answer to the charge that she faces, and about the conditions under which she could properly refuse to answer, to questions about how she can answer.

[61] See further Duff, 2001: 197–201; for useful discussions of restorative justice see von Hirsch *et al*, 2003.

9

Offences, Defences and the Presumption of Innocence

The previous chapter discussed some of the grounds, legal and moral, on which defendants might argue that they should not be required to answer to the criminal charges that they face at their trials. Suppose, however, that no such argument is offered or succeeds; the trial proceeds. We need now to examine how the analytical structure of responsibility and liability and the relational dimensions of responsibility are displayed in the structure of the criminal trial.

1. The Presumption of Innocence and Proof Beyond Reasonable Doubt

The defendant must answer to the charge, unless he can persuade the court that there exists a valid bar to trial. But if his initial answer is 'Not Guilty', there is nothing more that he need do to rebut the charge until the prosecution has introduced evidence sufficient, if not rebutted, to prove his guilt beyond reasonable doubt. This is the familiar meaning of the Presumption of Innocence, which is now enshrined in the European Convention on Human Rights (Article 6(2)): anyone 'charged with a criminal offence shall be presumed innocent until proved guilty according to the law'. It also constitutes the 'golden thread' running 'throughout the web of the English Criminal Law'—'it is the duty of the prosecution to prove the prisoner's guilt'.[1] In its bare form the Presumption is silent on the standard of proof: it does not preclude taking proof on the balance of probabilities to be sufficient. However, it is typically interpreted to require proof 'beyond reasonable doubt'. 'If, at the end of and on the whole of the case, there is a reasonable doubt' about the defendant's guilt, 'the

[1] *Woolmington v DPP* [1935] AC 462, 481 (Viscount Sankey): he added 'subject to what I have already said as to the defence of insanity and subject also to any statutory exception'. See Model Penal Code, s 1.12.

prosecution has not made out the case and the prisoner is entitled to an acquittal'.[2] The European Court of Human Rights has also taken Article 6(2) to require that 'any doubt should benefit the accused'.[3] Although this might look like an extension rather than an implication of the Presumption of Innocence, we can see why it should be interpreted thus by looking at the values underpinning it.[4]

A detached observer, who is wondering whether this person committed this crime, need not operate with such a presumption: she can start with an open mind about the person's guilt or innocence, and see where the reasons lead her; and she can end by believing it probable, on balance, that he did commit the crime. But a court whose task it is to acquit or convict the defendant should not start with such an open mind, since it is not involved in such a detached, theoretical inquiry. The obvious reason for this concerns the implications and consequences of each verdict. If a guilty defendant is acquitted, justice is not done: he is not condemned as he should in justice be. Nor are the further ends of criminal justice—the reduction of crime, the proper satisfaction of victims —served: he gets away with his crime (except to the extent that others may still, informally, see him as guilty). However, so long as 'Not Guilty' does not mean 'Proved Innocent', the acquittal of a guilty person does not *perpetrate* injustice, in the way that the conviction of an innocent does; indeed, if the prosecution fails to discharge its probative burden, an acquittal does justice by declaring, rightly, that the Presumption of Innocence has not been defeated. By contrast, in convicting and punishing an innocent, even in good faith, the court perpetrates a serious injustice. Given the consequences of a mistaken conviction (the penal hard treatment the defendant might suffer, the further effects on his life of being known as an offender, the symbolism of his condemnation), we should be cautious before subjecting anyone to them; given the injustice involved in their misapplication, we should be even more cautious. Hence the rhetorical force of the slogan that it is better for 10 guilty people to be acquitted than for one innocent to be convicted.

There is another dimension to the Presumption of Innocence in a liberal polity. It requires courts to see the defendant as a citizen who has committed no criminal wrong unless and until it is proved that she is guilty of a particular wrong. This does not reflect an empirically naïve belief that people do not commit crimes. It requires us to treat our fellow citizens,

[2] *Woolmington v DPP* [1935] AC 462, 481.

[3] *Barberà, Messegué and Jabardo v Spain* (1989) 11 EHRR 360. But contrast *Austria v Italy* (1963) 6 YB 740, 784: the evidence need only be 'sufficiently strong in the eyes of the law to establish his guilt' (see Simester and Sullivan, 2007: 53–5).

[4] On the meaning and implication of the Presumption of Innocence: see especially Roberts, 1995, 2005; Roberts and Zuckerman, 2004: 327–91; Tadros and Tierney, 2004; Sullivan, 2005: 210–14; Tadros, 2007.

especially when we are called to judge them in a criminal court, as if they are people who can be trusted to refrain from crime: for they are citizens, and that is what is expected of citizens. We must also treat them as responsible agents: only if they are thus responsible can they be tried for the crimes they are accused of committing. Now a responsible agent is one who is responsable to reasons—one who can recognise reasons for action, deliberate about them and from them, and guide her actions by them;[5] to treat someone as a responsible agent is therefore to treat her as someone who can respond appropriately to relevant reasons for action, including the reasons provided by or expressed in the criminal law. But that is to say that we should treat our fellow citizens as citizens who are responsive to, ie guided by, such reasons—as citizens who will refrain from what the law defines as criminal wrongs.

This attitude, which we could call civic trust, is manifest in our dealings with each other outside the criminal court and the police station. Of course we take precautions against crime: we lock our houses and cars, we fit burglar alarms; we design housing and public spaces in ways that do not encourage crime; we install CCTV; and so on. Such measures raise their own ethical issues;[6] but whilst we might, in nostalgic mood, regret the need to lock our doors, or think that some measures reflect a paranoid rather than a rational mistrust, we do not doubt the need for and legitimacy of some such protective and preventive measures. But matters are different when such measures are directed against particular people. If I lock my car or cross to the other side of the road because I see this person (or a member of this identifiable ethnic group) approaching, and he knows this, he will have reason to feel insulted, just because my conduct shows that I am presuming him to be guilty, a likely criminal, rather than innocent.[7] The same is true with even more force of the polity's formal treatment of citizens in criminal courts: to treat the defendant as a citizen, we must treat him as one who has not committed a public wrong—until it is proved that he did. He is suspected—that is why he is in court as a defendant, and we cannot brush off the suspicion simply by presuming him to be innocent; but suspicion does not warrant treating him as guilty.[8]

[5] See above, Ch 2.1.

[6] See von Hirsch *et al*, 2000.

[7] But suppose I know that he has committed frequent assaults or car thefts before? Perhaps his known prior record gives me legitimate reason to take special precautions, whereas the defendant's prior record is still—subject to a worryingly growing number of exceptions—presumptively excluded from his criminal trial (see Criminal Justice Act 2003, ss 98–113; Roberts and Zuckerman, 2004: 500–79; Duff *et al*, 2007: ch 4.4).

[8] Pre-trial detention marks a glaring exception to this claim, and raises serious problems about the pre-emptive detention of those who have not been proved guilty: see Ashworth and Redmayne, 2005: ch 8.

We should note two further aspects of the Presumption of Innocence and the requirement of proof beyond reasonable doubt, as they (supposedly) operate in our own legal systems, and one general question about the significance of the Presumption.

First, the 'golden thread' requires the prosecution to prove both actus reus and mens rea: proof that the defendant caused the victim's death, for instance, does not shift the onus onto the defendant to prove the absence of the 'malice' required for murder; the prosecution must prove the malice too.[9] Proof of the actus reus in fact often gives the court sufficient reason to convict, since it also proves mens rea beyond reasonable doubt, unless the defence offers an explanation of how mens rea was lacking: if it is proved that *D* threw a stone in the direction of *V*'s nearby window,[10] a court could reasonably conclude that *D* was at least reckless as to the risk of damaging another's property, unless *D* offers evidence that he did not realise that risk. But there can be no *legal* presumption here: the court is not entitled to presume mens rea given proof only of the actus reus; there can be no formal shift of burden from prosecution to defendant. As we will see later, that aspect of the golden thread has become frayed over the years: but we must first attend to its significance.

Secondly, the prosecution bears both the evidential and the persuasive burden in relation to the commission of the crime: it must introduce all the necessary evidence, and prove beyond reasonable doubt that the defendant committed the crime. But if it discharges that persuasive burden, the defendant bears an evidential burden in relation to any defence on which he wants to rely: the prosecution need not prove the absence of a defence (duress, for instance, or self-defence) until the defendant adduces evidence which raises the possibility that he satisfied its conditions; if such evidence is adduced (or the prosecution's evidence includes it), then the prosecution bears the persuasive burden of disproving the defence.[11] The defendant, we can say, is to be presumed innocent until it is proved that he committed the offence; once that is proved, he is presumed to be guilty, ie to have acted without exculpatory defence, until he adduces evidence that he had such a defence—evidence that would, if not rebutted, create a reasonable doubt about his guilt.

One striking feature of contemporary English criminal law is the way that the legislature regularly imposes further evidential or persuasive burdens on the defendant, either by creating what is formally classed as a

[9] *Woolmington v DPP* [1935] AC 462, 481–2.

[10] Though proof of 'throwing' is proof of more than a bare actus reus; it includes an intention to throw.

[11] For a summary see Simester and Sullivan, 2007: 54–5. The defence bears a persuasive burden for insanity, but the standard of proof is now 'on the balance of probabilities' rather than 'beyond reasonable doubt'.

defence or by creating a legal presumption that the defendant has the onus of defeating.[12] A shopkeeper who sells 'food which fails to comply with food safety requirements' commits an offence, but has a defence if she can prove that she 'took all reasonable precautions and exercised all due diligence' to avoid committing it.[13] If a civil servant receives a gift from a contractor, the gift 'shall be deemed to have been ... given and received corruptly ... unless the contrary is proved'.[14] The logic and the legitimacy of such burden-shifting provisions will be discussed in Chapter 10; our concern in this chapter is with the more traditional common law allocation of burdens in relation to offences and defences.

The question about the significance of the Presumption is whether or how far we should read it in formal or in substantive terms. A purely formal reading would take it to require that the defendant be presumed innocent until it is proved that he committed what the law defines as an offence. Consider again section 57 of the Civic Government (Scotland) Act 1982:

> Any person who, without lawful authority to be there, is found in or on a building or other premises ... so that, in all the circumstances, it may reasonably be inferred that he intended to commit theft there shall be guilty of an offence.[15]

Although the mischief at which this section is aimed, as declared in its heading, is '[b]eing in or on building etc. with intent to commit theft', taken at face value it mandates the conviction of defendants who are not proved beyond reasonable doubt to have been acting with any such intent: 'may reasonably be inferred' is weaker than 'is proved beyond reasonable doubt'. On the formal reading of the Presumption of Innocence, this provision respects it: for the 'guilty' in law are not only those who intend to steal, but those of whom it can reasonably be inferred that they intend to steal; and guilt as thus defined must be proved beyond reasonable doubt.

Similarly, section 57 of the Terrorism Act 2000 is consistent with the Presumption if it is read in formal terms:

> A person commits an offence if he possesses an article in circumstances which give rise to a reasonable suspicion that his possession is for a purpose connected with the commission, preparation or instigation of an act of terrorism,

It is, however, a defence to prove that my possession was not for any such purpose. Now this section is aimed at the mischief of '[p]ossession for terrorist purposes'. If that is what 'guilt' involves, it violates the Presumption: it requires the defendant to prove his innocence rather than the

[12] See Simester and Sullivan, 2007: 55–61.

[13] Food Safety Act 1990, ss 8(1), 21(1).

[14] Prevention of Corruption Act 1916, s 2.

[15] See *Fulton v Normand* 1995 SCCR 629; above, Introduction at n 42; Tadros, 2007: 198–9.

prosecution to prove his guilt. But if the Presumption is read in formal terms, this section is consistent with it: the offence is possessing an article in circumstances that give rise to such a reasonable suspicion, but the law allows one who is proved to have committed that offence to mount a defence (for which the onus can, consistently with the Presumption, be laid on him) that his possession of the article was not for terrorist purposes.[16]

We might certainly object to such provisions, on the ground that they permit (or indeed mandate) the conviction of defendants who are not proved guilty of what could plausibly be regarded as public wrongdoing of a kind that merits condemnation or punishment—that they create a radical gulf between 'guilty in law' and the kind of substantive guilt that could justify conviction and punishment. However, as Tadros and Tierney point out, that does not capture the precise defect in such provisions.[17] If a legislature criminalises consensual homosexual activity between adults, on the ground that it is a punishment-worthy public wrong, we can equally object that such a law mandates the conviction of those who are not proved guilty of what can properly count as a public wrong. The problem with the provisions discussed above, however, is that (as is clear from the sections' headings) the legislature itself does not think that all those whose conviction these provisions sanction are guilty of any punishable wrong. The sections are aimed at those who intend to steal or who have items in their possession for terrorist purposes: but they permit, or mandate, the conviction of people who are not proved beyond reasonable doubt to have any such intent or any such purpose.[18] We could distinguish (as Tadros and Tierney do) these two kinds of case by saying that the statute criminalising consensual homosexual acts respects the Presumption of Innocence if conviction requires proof beyond reasonable doubt that the defendant engaged in such supposedly wrongful conduct; but that these provisions violate the Presumption by mandating conviction without proof of the commission of what the legislature takes to be a public wrong. That would give the Presumption of Innocence a substantive rather than a purely formal reading, as requiring conviction to be based on proof of what the legislature takes to be a public wrong.

What is true is that legislation can display three kinds of defect connected to permitting the conviction of those who are not proved 'guilty'. It can, first, unequivocally define as a public wrong conduct that cannot be plausibly thus defined, but respect the Presumption of Innocence by requiring proof beyond reasonable doubt that the defendant

[16] Which is how Ormerod interprets the provision (Ormerod, 2000, commenting on *Kebilene* [2000] 2 AC 326, and the precursor to this section).

[17] Tadros and Tierney, 2004; Tadros 2007.

[18] See further below, Ch 10.3(c).

engaged in conduct of the specified kind (that he engaged in homosexual sex, for instance). It can, secondly, define an offence in terms that are, in the light of its own conception of the wrong or mischief at which the legislation is aimed, too broad, so that—at face value—it requires the conviction of some who are not guilty of that underlying wrong (some who do not in fact intend to steal or to support terrorism); it could still respect a formal Presumption of Innocence, so long as it required proof beyond reasonable doubt that the defendant satisfied the offence definition, but would be inconsistent with the more substantive version of the Presumption. Thirdly, it can violate even the formal Presumption of Innocence, by not requiring proof beyond reasonable doubt that the defendant satisfies the formal offence definition. Although these are different defects, we could in each case express our objection by saying that the legislation sanctions the conviction of the 'innocent', or sanctions convictions without proof of 'guilt'. Although it would not be helpful to say that the first kind of defect violates the Presumption of Innocence (by permitting the conviction of those who are not proved guilty of what can plausibly be declared to be a public wrong),[19] we could say that of each of the other defects: the third violates the Presumption of Innocence, understood formally, whilst the second violates it if we understand it in more substantive terms.

The question does have some practical significance, since the Presumption is enshrined in the European Convention on Human Rights (ECHR), and the Human Rights Act 1998 requires courts to interpret legislation, as far as is possible, 'in a way which is compatible with the Convention Rights', and allows them to declare legislation which cannot be thus interpreted to be 'incompatible with a Convention right'.[20] To argue that either of the first two defects violates the Presumption of Innocence would thus be to argue that it should be the courts' responsibility to remedy, if that can be done by suitably creative interpretations, or failing that to declare, such legislative defects.[21] But such arguments are not my present concern. All we need note here is that legislatures should aim to define as criminal only conduct that constitutes a genuine public wrong, ie to define as 'guilty' in law only those who are guilty of such a wrong; and that, in accordance with the Presumption of Innocence, the prosecution should bear the burden of proving that the defendant committed the wrong defined by the legislature.

[19] As I by implication suggested in Duff, 1986: 151–5; for apt criticism see Tadros, 2007: 198–200.

[20] Human Rights Act 1988, ss 3–4. See Roberts, 2002, 2005; Sullivan, 2005.

[21] This is one of the main concerns in Tadros and Tierney, 2004, and Tadros, 2007: just what power should the courts have to reinterpret legislation or declare it to violate human rights? In that context, we can see good reason for democrats not to count the first kind of defect as a violation of the Presumption.

In the remainder of this chapter, we will begin to look in more detail at the ways in which criminal responsibility and criminal liability are structured by the Presumption of Innocence, and by the distinctions between actus reus and mens rea and between offences and defences. For any criminal offence, it would be in principle possible simply to list the conditions that must obtain if a person is to be guilty of it. A defendant is guilty of false accounting under section 17(1) of the Theft Act 1968 if she destroys, defaces, conceals or falsifies any account or any record or document made or required for an accounting purpose; she does it dishonestly, with a view to gain for herself or another, or with intent to cause loss to another; she is not *doli incapax*, or insane in a way that negated criminal responsibility, or acting under exculpatory duress or necessity—and similarly for other offences. Such lists are cumbersome; but, more importantly, they fail to distinguish different kinds of factor that bear in different ways on the defendant's criminal responsibility or liability.

Two distinctions that theorists standardly draw are between actus reus and mens rea, and between offences and defences: I will say something about the former in section 2, and rather more about the latter in sections 3–4.

2. Actus Reus and Mens Rea[22]

If we needed to draw a clear general distinction between 'actus reus' and 'mens rea' as the two elements of a criminal offence, or between 'conduct elements' and 'fault elements', we would face some serious problems. One familiar problem is that it is quite often impossible to specify the actus reus without incorporating an aspect of the mens rea, since what makes the relevant act 'reus' is the intention with which it is done: what constitutes lighting a match as the actus reus of attempted arson is the intention to start a fire with which the agent lights the match.[23] The larger problem is that if we seriously try to identify an 'actus' distinct from any 'mental element', we will end up, first, by failing, since we will be able to identify only something like 'bodily movements' plus their circumstances and consequences, which loses any idea of agency as distinct from mere happening altogether. Secondly, to remedy that defect we will be tempted to introduce a minimal 'mental element' of 'volition' or 'will', so that the actus reus consists essentially in 'willed' movement:[24] but this drives us

[22] See generally A Smith, 1978; Robinson, 1993.
[23] See further Lynch, 1982.
[24] See eg G Williams, 1961: 11–12; compare Ormerod, 2005: 45–8.

towards an account of action as willed bodily movement which is normatively unhelpful—and philosophically at best highly problematic.[25]

However, it is now generally recognised that the distinction between actus reus and mens rea is at best 'a helpful expository device but not an analytical necessity'; 'an analytical tool, and at that a rather "rough and ready" one'; a matter of 'convenient exposition'.[26] If we ask why it is even helpful as an 'expository device', the answer might run roughly as follows.

Offence definitions can typically be seen as complex action-descriptions (or, sometimes, omission-descriptions)—descriptions of something done that include a number of the relevant circumstantial and consequential aspects of that doing.[27] Such descriptions of what was done (or omitted) posit or assume an agent as the doer (or omitter): someone who was exercising (or failing to exercise) her capacities for action. That assumption is challenged when there is room for doubt about whether the putative offender was involved as an agent at all: perhaps he was unconscious, in a state of automatism, or in some other way not merely not exercising, but unable to exercise, his capacities for action.[28] But when agency is not negated, the putative offender will have been doing something—typically intentionally.[29]

However, it is a familiar fact that in or by doing *X* intentionally I can also do many other things as to which I do not act intentionally, or even in the knowledge that I am or might be doing them. I press a switch intentionally; by doing so I cause the bomb to which the switch is connected to explode, thereby causing damage to your property; but I might neither intend to explode the bomb, nor realise that pressing this switch might have that effect (perhaps I mistakenly believe it to be a light switch); or I might not intend to damage your property, or realise that I might do so (perhaps I mistakenly believe it to be my property). Whilst some aspects of an offence can be identified only as something done intentionally, others can thus be identified, and their occurrence can be proved, independently of the putative offender's intentions or beliefs. Appropriation as an aspect of theft, for instance, can only be identified as something done intentionally,[30] as can making a statement, as an element

[25] See above, Ch 5.1–3; Hornsby, 1993, 1999; Duff, 1996: chs 9–11.

[26] Simester and Sullivan, 2007: 63; Ashworth, 2006: 95; Ormerod, 2005: 35.

[27] Compare Moore, 1993: 169–70. On the meaning of 'action' in this context see Ch 5.3 above; on some apparent exceptions, see Ch 3 at nn 4–11 above.

[28] See eg *Hill v Baxter* [1958] 1 QB 277 (if a driver has been rendered unconscious, can he still be said to be 'driving'?). On automatism, see Ashworth, 2006: 98–105.

[29] For the claim that, if a person is acting, there is something she is doing intentionally see Davidson, 1980; Hornsby, 1993: I say 'typically' to leave open the possibility, unimportant here, that there are exceptions.

[30] See Theft Act 1968, s 3 on appropriation as an 'assumption … of the rights of an owner'.

of perjury.[31] But the appropriator might not intend that what he appropriates be another's property, or realise that what he appropriates is or might be another's property; someone who makes a statement need not intend it to be false, or realise that it is or might be false. Indeed, what an agent does intentionally might not fit any part of the offence definition, though what she does in doing it fits central aspects of an offence definition: I intentionally make a vigorous gesture, and in doing so hit and injure *V*, but do not intend to hit him, or even realise that I might do so.

We think that the commission of an offence, as a public wrong, normally requires not just agency, but intentional, knowing, or reckless (or negligent) agency as to its central aspects.[32] Offence definitions that simply specified what must be done would often not capture this requirement: we therefore need either to include a reference to intention, knowledge, recklessness or negligence in the offence definition itself, or lay down a general principle that some such reference must be read into every offence definition.[33] We may also want to specify different such agential relationships to different aspects of what is done—perhaps intention as to some aspect, but only recklessness (or negligence) as to others;[34] or specify further prospective consequences as to which the agent must act intentionally or recklessly if he is to commit the offence.[35] Furthermore, the difference between acting intentionally and acting recklessly as to some central aspect of the doing that constitutes the offence can make a difference to the nature and proper categorisation of the wrong that is committed.[36] For all these reasons, we will need to include specifications of such 'subjective' aspects of the agent's doing, as well as the 'objective' aspects of what is actually done, in our offence definitions; and so long as we do not take this very rough distinction between the 'subjective' and the 'objective' dimensions of the offence to mark some sharp ontological distinction between different parts of elements of the offence, we can talk of 'actus reus' and 'mens rea': a doing does not make a person guilty, does not constitute the commission of an offence, unless the doer acts with whatever is properly required in the way of intention, knowledge, recklessness or negligence as to the various aspects of the doing.

However, given the way in which talk of 'actus reus' and 'mens rea' can mislead us into thinking that the distinction is sharper or deeper than it really is, we might do better to follow the German analytical structure,

[31] Perjury Act 1911, s 1.

[32] Only normally, since we have not yet shown that responsibility or liability can never justifiably be strict: see further Ch 10 below.

[33] See eg Model Penal Code, s 2.20(1); Law Commission, 1989a, s 20.

[34] As in Sexual Offences Act 2003, ss 1–3.

[35] As in, eg, Criminal Attempts Act 1981, s 1; Theft Act 1968, s 1; Criminal Damage Act 1971, ss 1–3.

[36] See Ch 7.1 above, on the difference between attacks and endangerments.

which begins not with an actus reus but with a *Tatbestand*. German criminal law theory operates with a tripartite schema of *Tatbestand*, *Rechtswidrigkeit* and *Schuld*—although, of course, the precise content of each and the proper categorisation of various elements is controversial.[37] A *Tatbestand* specifies a criminal wrong—an *Unrecht* that is *strafbar*, worthy of punishment: there has been controversy about whether *Vorsatz* (usually translated as 'intention', but capturing a broader concept of fault) belongs in the *Tatbestand* or as an aspect of *Schuld*, but the more plausible view, grounded in the so-called teleological theory of action,[38] is that its place is as an aspect of the *Tatbestand*. The *Tatbestand*, we can say, constitutes the 'offence', including (what Anglo-American theorists would distinguish as) both actus reus and mens rea; whilst German textbooks distinguish the 'objective' from the 'subjective' aspects of a *Tatbestand*, that distinction does not have the prominence or the apparent significance that the distinction between actus reus and mens rea has.

A *Tatbestand* involves the violation of (or an attack on or threat to) a *Rechtsgut*, a legally protected good or interest;[39] such a violation, attack or threat is presumptively wrongful—it presumptively constitutes *Rechtswidrigkeit*, criminal wrongfulness all things considered. But that presumption can be defeated by a justification (*Rechtfertigung*). A justification appeals to a permissive norm specifying an exception to the proscriptive norms found in the special part: for instance that the action protected a *Rechtsgut* more important than the *Rechtsgut* that it violated; or that the person whose *Rechtsgut* was violated consented to the violation. This structure makes clear why (absence of) justification does not belong within the definition of the offence: for if an action is justified a *Rechtsgut* has still been wilfully violated, whereas when an element of the offence is missing no *Rechtsgut* has been wilfully violated.

The combination of *Tatbestand* and *Rechtswidrigkeit* is not dispositive of criminal guilt: a defendant can avoid conviction by claiming lack of *Schuld* (of culpability or accountability) for the wrong that he committed.[40] *Schuld* is negated by *Schuldunfähigkeit*, a lack of capacity to grasp and be guided by the wrongness of the action (insanity or infancy); by unavoidable ignorance of law—of the criminality of the action; and by factors that make it unreasonable to expect a citizen to act in accordance with the law's proscriptions—in particular in cases of 'necessity' or self-defence in which the defendant's action was not justified but, given the immediate pressure,

[37] Fletcher has done most to familiarise Anglo-American theorists with the structure of German criminal law theory (Fletcher, 1978). See, exhaustively, Roxin, 2006; for a useful introduction see Ebert, 2001.

[38] See Fletcher, 1978: 434–9.

[39] There is controversy about the substantial utility of the idea of a *Rechtsgut*: see Wohlers *et al*, 2003.

[40] On accountability see especially Fletcher, 1978: 454–9, 491–504, 577–9.

should be excused. There is an extensive literature on the (exculpatory or inculpatory) role of mistakes: all we need note here is that mistakes concern either an element of the *Tatbestand*, in which case they bear on whether the *Tatbestand* is committed at all, or a fact that bears on a justification, in which case they can ground an excuse but (normally) only if they are reasonable.[41]

It is not my purpose to embark on a detailed discussion of the German model of criminal wrongdoing here, although I will draw on aspects of it (in particular the distinctions between offences, justifications and excuses) in what follows. The main point to note here is that the concept of the *Tatbestand* (with its not always clearly separable subjective and objective aspects) might be a better way of capturing the idea of a criminal offence than the analytic or expository device of actus reus and mens rea.

The more substantial point to note is that, insofar as the principle so ringingly declared in *Woolmington* applies,[42] criminal responsibility is for the commission of an offence as thus understood, as including both actus reus and mens rea, both objective and subjective aspects. We will attend in Chapter 10 to the ways in which the scope and impact of the principle have been statutorily limited or qualified, but should focus here on those offences, which include most of the familiar *mala in se*, to which it does still apply, for which the prosecution must prove both actus reus and mens rea—the commission of a complete *Tatbestand*.

The defendant, we have seen,[43] is expected to make an answer to the charge. That answer can initially consist in nothing more than a formal plea of 'Not Guilty'. It might in practice have to involve more than that if the prosecution leads evidence that would suffice, if it is not rebutted, to prove that the defendant committed the offence; but even then the defendant does not have to answer *for* anything. He is still answering *to* the charge, and his answer can still be that he is not criminally responsible for the commission of the offence charged—that, for instance, he was not the agent of the doing that constituted the offence (he offers an alibi); or that he lacked the intention, knowledge or recklessness required as to an aspect of that doing. We can see the force of this point by seeing how things change once the prosecution proves that the defendant committed the offence: for instance that he intentionally wounded a human being, or intentionally damaged another's property, or intentionally lied in court.

Even given such proof, the defendant can avoid conviction by offering a defence: she can plead that, for instance, she acted in self-defence or under exculpatory duress. The prosecutor need not, however, disprove all such defences in advance, or as soon as the defendant claims to have a defence:

41 See Fletcher, 1978: ch 9.

42 *Woolmington v DPP* [1935] AC 462, 481; see at nn 1, 9–10 above.

43 See Ch 8.1 above.

only if the defendant supports that claim with evidence that would, if not rebutted, be sufficient to create a reasonable doubt about her guilt does the prosecutor need to disprove the defence that is claimed.[44] This procedural distinction between 'offences', as to which the prosecution bears the full burden of proof, and 'defences', as to which the defence bears at least an evidential burden, marks the substantial distinction between responsibility and liability in criminal law. To prove that the defendant committed the offence charged is to prove that she is criminally responsible for its commission—that she must answer for it. She may still be able to avert criminal liability by offering (and providing evidential support for) an exculpatory answer—a justification or excuse; but it is now up to her to provide such an answer, and in providing it she is answering for the commission of the offence. To place this evidential burden on the defendant is to claim that she owes it to the court (and to the polity in whose name the court acts) either to admit her guilt, or to offer an explanation of why she committed the offence which will exculpate her; but to admit guilt or to offer an exculpatory explanation of why she committed the offence is to answer for the offence. That is why the Presumption of Innocence requires only that citizens be presumed innocent until it is proved that they committed an offence, ie until it is proved that there is an offence for which they are criminally responsible: once criminal responsibility is proved, it is up to them to rebut the presumption that they are guilty by providing a suitably exculpatory answer that will block the transition—the presumptive inference—from responsibility to liability.[45]

We will look in a little more detail at the logic of defences in Chapter 11. My task in the remainder of this chapter is to explain the distinction between offences and defences in more adequate detail, as a distinction which maps that between responsibility and liability. We will also attend, in Chapter 10, to the very different way in which we draw the distinction between responsibility and liability in our extra-legal moral dealings with each other, and the different scope that ideas of justification and excuse have in those dealings. For the moment, however, we can focus on criminal law: I begin by showing in more detail why the distinction between offences and defences is important—and problematic.

3. Offences and Defences: Why the Distinction Matters

To some theorists, the distinction between offences and defences is, like that between actus reus and mens rea, no more than an 'expository device'

44 See at n 11 above.
45 See above, Ch 1.1.

to assist 'convenient exposition'.[46] It is convenient to separate 'defences' out if they are of general application: rather than listing the absence of each defence in the definition of each offence, we can define 'offences' without reference to any such general conditions of non-liability, and then list those conditions in the general part. But whether the law formally defines such conditions as duress as 'defences' in the general part, or their absence as elements of particular offences in the special part, makes no difference to their substantive character as conditions that can negate liability: the fact that *D* intentionally caused the death of a human being and the fact that *D* was not acting in self-defence are both equally elements of the crime of murder, even if only the former appears in the special part's formal definition of murder.[47] The distinction does seem to have significant practical implications, since the defendant bears an evidential burden in relation to defences, but no such formal burden in relation to elements of the offence: but if we are to justify that shift of burden from prosecution to defence, we must first show that the distinction between offences and defences is substantially significant in a way that can reconcile that shift with the Presumption of Innocence.

I will argue that the distinction marks a significant distinction between different aspects of criminal liability and different logical stages in the construction of criminal liability.[48] Two initial examples should help us to see why it matters.

(a) Rape and Consent

Fletcher argues that we should not see the victim's lack of consent as an element of rape; we should rather count consent as a defence (he argues this because he thinks that a mistake as to the other's consent should be 'reasonable' if it is to justify acquitting the agent, but that even unreasonable mistakes as to elements of the offence exculpate).[49] This seems bizarre: but why?

How could we define rape itself if consent is to be a defence? Fletcher argues that for any offence, the offence definition must specify a 'prohibitory norm' which is 'morally coherent', in that it can make plausible moral

[46] See at n 26 above.

[47] For classic examples of scepticism about the significance of the distinction see G Williams, 1982, 1988.

[48] See generally Fletcher, 1978: 552–79, 683–758; Campbell, 1987; Gardner, 2004; Tadros, 2005a: ch 4.

[49] Fletcher, 1978: 699–707, discussing *Morgan* [1976] AC 182; contrast Sexual Offences Act 2003, s 1, defining rape in terms of non-consensual sexual penetration and the lack of a reasonable belief in consent.

sense to members of the society whose law it is.[50] To put the same point in rather different terms, the offence definition must specify a type of conduct that constitutes what is at least presumptively a wrong for which the perpetrator can be called to answer to his fellow citizens—a presumptive wrong for which he can be held responsible by and to the polity. Fletcher argues (with some hesitation) that the prohibitory norm for rape prohibits sexual penetration: consent renders the violation of that norm permissible. But this is quite implausible. First, although a general prohibition on sexual penetration is coherent, it makes no moral sense to citizens of contemporary liberal democracies: we should not have to answer, to our fellow citizens through the criminal courts, for every act of sexual penetration. Secondly, many people do regard some acts of sexual penetration other than those that would ground a rape conviction as wrongs—for instance, sexual penetration outside marriage. But, apart from the fact that to take a norm against extra-marital sexual penetration as the basis of rape would preclude convicting a husband of raping his wife, which even English law now recognises as a crime,[51] that norm identifies a purported wrong of a different kind from rape: those who accept that norm do not think that consent justifies its breach (consensual extra-marital sex is indeed the paradigm of the wrong); they may well believe that extra-marital sex is not the kind of wrong that should concern the criminal law; and within the general category of extra-marital sexual penetrations they distinguish those that constitute consensual adultery or fornication from those that constitute rape, as a distinct wrong. What is supposedly wrong with extra-marital sex has to do with the proper role of sex in (paradigmatically consensual) human relationships, its connection to procreation, and so on; what is wrong with rape is that it exercises brutal power over the victim, whose sexual integrity it denies.

Perhaps we could instead define rape in terms of force or violence: the basic wrong now would be violent or forcible penetration; the putative victim's consent would be a defence to a charge of culpably committing that wrong.[52] Some theorists do indeed seek to *replace* 'lack of consent' by 'violence' as the defining mark of rape,[53] and we saw in discussing *R v Brown* that it is at least arguable that certain kinds of physical violence should be criminalised even when they are consensual:[54] so why should we

[50] Fletcher, 1978: 567. For apt criticism see Campbell, 1987: 81–2; Tadros, 2005a: 105–6.

[51] *R* [1992] 1 AC 599.

[52] Fletcher talks at one point of 'forcible sexual penetration' as the wrong (1978: 705–7), but his final view is that it consists merely in sexual penetration. Until recently, Scots law defined rape in terms of force, so that there was no rape if the victim was asleep or unconscious (Gordon, 2000: 509–13; see Tadros, 1999); that error was rectified in *Lord Advocate's Reference (No. 1 of 2001)* 2002 SLT 466.

[53] See eg Burgess-Jackson, 1999; P Smith, 1999.

[54] *R v Brown* [1994] 1 AC 212; see above, Ch 6.2.

not suggest, as a more liberal version of such views, that rape should be defined simply as forcible sexual penetration, but consent should be allowed as a defence? Such a suggestion would be unlikely to satisfy many self-declared liberals, who would argue that if we take '*volenti non fit iniuria*' seriously, we must recognise that consent negates rather than justifying the wrong:[55] lack of consent should be an element of the offence; we should not have to answer to the criminal law for what we do to each other with mutual consent. But it is also inadequate as an account of rape: rape under existing law can be committed without the use of violence—by threats, by deception, on a victim who is unconscious; in classing such wrongs as rape, along with sexual penetration that is achieved by force, the law seems rightly to recognise that they share a common moral core, as ways in which the sexual autonomy and integrity of the victim can be attacked and violated.[56]

A definition of rape, as a distinctive kind of criminal wrong, therefore cannot so define it that consent is a defence: for we would then be unable to specify the presumptive wrong, for which consent is to be a defence, in a way that captures the distinctive wrong of rape. But the main point of this example does not depend on agreement with that conclusion: its main point is to show why it matters whether we class a factor that bears on liability as an element of the offence or as a matter of defence. Anyone who wants to argue that we should count consent as a defence must offer an account of the offence in terms that do not include lack of consent, and show that the offence as thus defined constitutes a distinctive presumptive wrong, which can be plausibly argued to capture what we should understand by 'rape', for which we should have to answer in a criminal court. It is not enough to argue that such a definition would have procedural advantages in relation to the burden of proof (even if it would be an advantage to require the defendant to offer evidence of consent, rather than requiring the prosecution to prove lack of consent); for we need to ask whether it would be just to lay such an evidential burden on the defendant before it is proved that he has committed a presumptive wrong of the appropriate kind. Nor is it enough to argue that classing consent as a defence allows us to hold that a mistaken belief in consent must be reasonable if it is to exculpate:[57] we can argue that only a reasonable mistake should exculpate, or that the prosecution should have to prove only the lack of a reasonable belief in consent,[58] on quite other grounds—

[55] See above, Ch 6 at n 30.

[56] See Tadros, 2006a. Tadros argues that we should define rape in a way that makes lack of consent less prominent, focusing instead on ways in which the victim's sexual autonomy can be undermined. I am not concerned with the merits of that argument here; my point is only that we cannot plausibly define rape in a way that makes consent a defence.

[57] See at n 49 above.

[58] See Sexual Offences Act 2003, s 1(1)(b).

for instance that in this context a person who acts on the basis of an unreasonable belief in consent is reckless as to the victim's consent.[59] The argument must be that the proposed definition captures a kind of conduct for which a defence is needed—a kind of conduct for which a person can properly be called to answer in a criminal court, on pain of being condemned as a public wrongdoer if he cannot provide a suitably exculpatory answer.

The difference between specifying lack of consent as an element of the offence of rape and specifying consent as a defence to rape will often not make any practical difference to the course of the trial, so long as the defendant bears only an evidential burden in relation to a defence:[60] if the complainant alleges that the penetration was non-consensual, the defendant must usually offer evidence that it was consensual if he is to avoid conviction, even if lack of consent is an element of the offence. But it marks a substantial difference in our conception of the wrong that constitutes rape, and of what we must answer to each other for in a criminal court. A further example should make this point clearer.

(b) Murder, Consent and Self-defence

How should we define murder as a criminal wrong? To avoid controversy about the mens rea of murder,[61] which is irrelevant here, we can limit our attention to intentional killing, and focus on three conditions given which someone who intentionally kills another human being is not (or on some views should not be) guilty of murder. If I kill an attacker in defence of my life or of others' lives, I can avoid conviction for murder; if a soldier kills an enemy soldier in warfare, he is not liable to be convicted of murder; and, many would argue, the law should be so reformed that a doctor who kills a terminally ill patient at the patient's own competent and earnest request would not be convicted of murder. Of each of these conditions we must ask whether its absence should figure as an element in the definition of the offence of murder; or should it figure as a defence that can be offered by one who has committed that offence?

Under existing law, self-defence or defence of others constitutes a defence as to which the defendant bears at least an evidential burden: given proof of an intentional killing, it will thus be presumed that the killer is guilty of murder unless he adduces evidence that it was an action of

[59] See Duff, 1990a: 167–73; for a different argument to a similar conclusion see Archard, 1999. See further below, at nn 108–109, and Ch 10 at nn 62–67.

[60] See at n 11 above.

[61] See most recently Law Commission, 2006; see Tadros, 2006b; Wilson, 2007.

necessary defence.[62] By contrast, a soldier who kills an enemy soldier 'in the heat of war'[63] needs no defence under English law, since murder requires the killing of a 'reasonable creature *in rerum natura* under the king's peace', whereas enemy soldiers in wartime are not under the sovereign's peace;[64] the actus reus of murder is not committed. The soldier is still, of course, bound by the rules and laws of war, but a more extreme example is provided by the idea of an outlaw, or a '*hostis humani generis*'—an enemy of mankind:

> As [a pirate] has renounced all the benefits of society and government, and has reduced himself afresh to the savage state of nature, by declaring war against all mankind, all mankind must declare war against him.[65]

Taken at face value, this suggests that the outlaw is unprotected by any law: killing an outlaw would require no justification; it would not be a kind of killing that concerned the criminal law. As for voluntary euthanasia, we must ask whether, if it is to be legalised, this should be done by redefining murder as killing without the (free and informed) consent of the person killed, or by defining such consent as a defence.[66]

Why should it matter (other than perhaps as a matter of procedural convenience) whether we take such conditions to ground defences, or their absence to be ingredients of the offence? It matters because how we classify such conditions will reflect our conception of the wrong of murder, and of the moral standing of the person who is killed.

This is shown most clearly in the extreme case of 'outlaws' who are excluded (or who are taken to have excluded themselves) not just from 'the king's peace', but from the protection of the rules of war. The outlaw has no claim on our respect or concern: no legal claim, in that the criminal law takes no interest in what we do to him; perhaps no moral claim either, if we see his legal exclusion as a formal institutionalisation of his (self-)exclusion from the moral community.[67] We do not need to justify what we do to him, to him or to others, since he and his interests have no

[62] See Simester and Sullivan, 2007: 703–13; Model Penal Code, s 3.01, 3.04–5; German Criminal Code, s 32.

[63] Coke, 1628: iii, 47 (quoted in Ormerod, 2005: 429).

[64] See J Smith, 1989: 30–1; Ormerod, 2005: 433–4.

[65] Blackstone, 1765–9: iv, ch 5.iii, at 71. This is, of course, how many people now portray terrorists.

[66] The recent, and unsuccessful, bill to legalise voluntary euthanasia in England and Wales (Assisted Dying for the Terminally Ill Bill (HL) 2004) is not explicit on this point, providing simply that physicians who act in accordance with the Act's provisions will not be guilty of an offence (s 8); but the requirement that the physician send all the appropriate documentation to the regional 'monitoring commission' (s 11) suggests that it functions as a defence.

[67] Compare C Morris, 1991: 72: 'contract killers, war criminals, tyrants and certain terrorists' forfeit all moral standing; neither justice nor benevolence need constrain our treatment of them. See Campbell, 1987: 83.

claim on us. We do no wrong in killing him: it is not something that requires justification; we need not show that killing him is necessary to protect ourselves or to avert some evil, since that would imply that there are reasons against killing him which must be outweighed or defeated—but if he is an outlaw, there are no such reasons. However, if this is what it is to be an outlaw, we must question whether there are any moral outlaws, or should be any legal outlaws. For we could insist that every human being has a moral claim on us, whatever he has done: he is still a fellow human being who is a 'limit to our will'.[68] This is not to deny that we may be justified in killing him or coercing him; it is rather to say that we must justify our treatment of him. We must be ready to justify it to him, since part of what we owe each other as fellow human beings is to attempt to explain ourselves to those whom we treat in ways that are at least presumptively wrong.[69] We must also be ready to justify it to others, since the fellow members of the moral community to which—on this view—he still belongs have a proper interest in the commission of such presumptive wrongs.[70]

Similar points apply to the use of fatal defensive force. We could so formulate the law of murder that (self-)defence is not a defence: we could specify, for instance, that murder must involve the killing of an *innocent* person, and define 'innocent' as 'not currently engaged in attacking another's life or person'.[71] Some of the rhetoric of the right to use defensive force does suggest such a view: when someone says, for instance, 'if you go onto someone else's property you waive your right to civil liberties',[72] they are not far from saying that the burglar has no rights against the householder—he is not protected by the criminal law. In response to such comments, it becomes necessary, rather than the platitude that it should be, to say that whilst we 'must protect victims and law-abiding citizens, ... we have to recognise that others have some rights as well. They don't lose all rights because they're engaged in criminal

[68] Gaita, 1991: ch 1 (see also ch 3). Gaita emphasises how hard it is to sustain this view of those who commit the most terrible wrongs—how hard it is, we can say, not to see and to treat them as outlaws.

[69] Compare Nagel, 1972: 136–7.

[70] This also implies that there are limits on what could count as a justification for killing him. Note, however, that to say that he has a claim on us is not to say that it is a claim that he is well placed to make for himself: the arrogantly unrepentant tyrant is ill-placed to claim respect or concern from his victims, but that does not make it permissible for them to deny him that respect or concern; see Ch 8.2(c) above.

[71] On 'innocence' in the context of defensive violence see eg Norman, 1995: ch 5; McMahan, 1994.

[72] A neighbour of a householder who had shot and killed one burglar and injured another, reacting angrily to his imprisonment: *The Observer*, 13 July 2003, available at www.guardian.co.uk/crime/article/0,,997269,00.html.

conduct'.[73] That is why defence of life (or property) is rightly classed as a defence. If I use serious violence against a person, I commit what is at least presumptively a serious wrong, of a kind that properly concerns the criminal law: I must be ready to answer for my actions, in a criminal court, on pain of conviction for a crime of violence if I cannot offer an exculpatory answer. If I can claim that my violence was necessary and proportionate, I have a defence: but it is rightly up to me to adduce evidence of that proportionate necessity.[74] The attacker still has a claim on me: even if I am justified in using fatal violence against him, I show my recognition of that claim in recognising the need to justify myself—and the polity shows its recognition of that claim by requiring that I offer a defence if I am to avoid conviction.

What then of euthanasia, when what supposedly justifies the killing is not that the person killed is attacking others, but that she has earnestly requested it? Classical liberals who assert 'the absolute priority of personal autonomy',[75] and a strict version of *volenti non fit iniuria*, should in principle regard such a request (if it is free, informed and autonomous) as negating an element of the offence, rather than as a defence—though they may see good pragmatic reason to require the defendant to provide evidence of a request to defeat the natural (if not legal) presumption of no request. If personal autonomy has 'absolute priority', what is done to me at my autonomous request cannot wrong me; nor can it be the business of the polity. Indeed, it cannot constitute a wrong at all, unless it has further implications for other people given which it becomes wrongful: but the 'absolute priority of personal autonomy' would, I take it, preclude judging genuinely voluntary euthanasia to be an in principle criminalisable wrong on the grounds of its effects on or implications for other people. On this view the basic wrong in murder would not be killing a human being, but killing a human being without his (free, informed) request: only those who killed without request would be formally required to offer a defence to avoid conviction. Proof that *D* intentionally killed *V* would no doubt often suffice in practice to prove that *D* killed *V* without *V*'s request, which would place a de facto evidential burden on *D* to offer evidence that *V* had

[73] Lord Goldsmith, the then Attorney-General, responding to some of the wilder claims about the scope of the right to use defensive force, including the rights of householders to shoot burglars: *The Observer,* 12 Dec 2004 available at http://observer.guardian.co.uk/uk_news/story/0,6903,1371941,00.html.

[74] On the need for proportionality see Simester and Sullivan, 2007: 707–8; Criminal Law Act 1967, s 3 ('such force as is reasonable in the circumstances'). Contrast German Criminal Code, s 32; Schopp, 1998: ch 3.

[75] Feinberg, 1988: 130; see above, Ch 6 at n 30.

requested it; but *D* would formally have to answer for the killing only once it had been proved to be without *V*'s request.[76]

This suggestion will strike many as counter-intuitive: the prosecution should not, surely, have to prove that the killing was not at *V*'s request unless and until there is at least evidence that *V* had requested it; perhaps, indeed, *D* should bear a persuasive, not merely an evidential, burden in this context, so that if intentional killing is proved he must be convicted of murder unless he can prove, on the balance of probabilities, that it was done at *V*'s free and informed request. What lies behind such intuitions might in part be a practical concern to avoid making it too easy for real murderers to avoid conviction; but they might also reflect the thought that, if voluntary euthanasia is to be legitimated, *V*'s request should function as a defence—rather than its absence functioning as an element of the offence. But why should we think this? One implication of my right to dispose of my own property is that, if I consent to another taking it or ask her to take it, no wrong is done that requires a defence: it would be a distortion to say that the wrong in theft is taking another's property, and that the owner's request or consent constitutes a defence. Why then should we not say the same about my body and my life?

That we would not want to say the same is indicated by the way in which legislation to legalise some forms of euthanasia does not typically make a (free, informed) request by the person who is killed the only necessary condition of permissibility: conditions to do with the person's medical state and prospects must also be satisfied. The Assisted Dying for the Terminally Ill Bill 2004 (sections 2–5) required that the person requesting assistance be terminally ill and undergoing unbearable suffering; and, whilst some would argue that there should be a broader range of legitimating conditions than that, they do not typically argue that only a free and informed request should be required. What lies behind such arguments is not the single value of autonomy, understood in classical liberal terms: either other values, to do with the person's good and the value of human life, are implicated, or autonomy is understood in more perfectionist terms as being of value only insofar as it is a matter of being able to choose between genuinely valuable options.[77] If we see euthanasia in these terms, and if we see human life as having value independently of the person's own will, we can think that euthanasia involves a presumptive wrong for which the agent must answer, even when it is carried out at the

[76] I have talked of *V*'s request rather than of *V*'s consent because consent can be somewhat passive: I consent to what someone else proposes. The 'absolute priority of personal autonomy' has a stronger appeal in the context of active requests than in that of possibly passive consent; the Assisted Dying for the Terminally Ill Bill 2004 is set in terms of the patient's request to be helped to die.

[77] See eg Raz, 1986: 369–429; Sher, 1997: chs 2–3.

free and informed request of the person killed. We might agree that 'I killed *V* at *V*'s free and informed request and to spare him the intolerable suffering of his terminal illness' is an exculpatory answer; but it is an answer that *D* should have to offer the polity if she is to avoid conviction for committing that wrong.

My concern here is not with whether or when euthanasia is morally, or should be legally, justifiable, or with the precise conditions that must be satisfied if it is to be justified. Nor is it to reject the view that the wrong underpinning murder is not killing, but killing other than at the (free and informed) request of the person killed. It is simply to show why the distinction between offences and defences matters: why, that is, it matters whether we count the absence of such a request as an element of the offence of murder, or its existence as a defence against a charge of murder. Quite apart from the procedural implications of this question, different answers to it will reflect substantively different understandings of the wrong that is basic to murder, and thus also of what we should have to answer for in a criminal court.

I will say more about the implications of the distinction between offences and defences in the following two chapters. We must first, however, get clearer about the distinction itself and how it can be drawn.

4. Distinguishing Offences and Defences[78]

Proof of an offence, I have suggested, is proof of criminal responsibility: it constitutes proof, that is, that there is something for which the defendant must answer in court, on pain of being held criminally liable if she fails to offer an adequately exculpatory answer. Given the Presumption of Innocence and the persuasive burden that in its orthodox interpretation it places on the prosecution, proof of the offence must also constitute what would amount, if not rebutted by a defence, to proof beyond reasonable doubt that the defendant is guilty—that she merits conviction and condemnation for committing that offence. Proof of responsibility creates a presumption of liability—of guilt; it is then for the defendant to block that normal, presumptive transition from responsibility to liability.[79] I am held responsible for that which I had reason not to do (reason of a kind that properly concerns those who hold me responsible). If proof of the offence is to constitute proof of responsibility, it must therefore be proof that the

[78] Two of the best recent discussions, on which I gratefully draw, are Gardner, 2004; Tadros, 2005a: ch 4.

[79] See Ch 1.1 above.

defendant did what she had reason not to do,[80] reason of a kind that properly concerns the polity which calls her to answer for her conduct in a criminal court.[81]

Since the criminal law is concerned with wrongs that are public in the sense that they are of proper interest to the whole polity, and merit the polity's public condemnation,[82] we can therefore say that proof of the offence should be proof of a presumptive public wrong, which the defendant had relevant reason not to commit in virtue of its presumptive wrongfulness: to discharge its initial persuasive burden the prosecution must prove, beyond reasonable doubt, that the defendant committed a presumptive public wrong (as specified in the charge); the burden of rebutting that presumption, by offering a defence, then falls on the defendant.[83] Offence definitions should therefore define presumptive public wrongs. To say this is not yet, however, to say anything very helpful, since the idea of a 'presumptive wrong' has yet to be explained. In particular, we must ask whether a presumptive wrong is really a wrong.

(a) Prima Facie Wrongs and Reasons

This is a version of a question that notoriously arises about ideas of 'prima facie' wrongs or duties: is a prima facie wrong or duty something that we have reason to believe is a wrong or a duty, but that could turn out on further inquiry not to be a wrong or a duty at all; or is it something that really is a wrong or a duty, but that could turn out on further inquiry not to be an all-things-considered wrong or duty—not to be something that, all things considered, we should not do, or must do? In other words, is a prima facie wrong or duty only prima facie a wrong or duty; or is it a genuine, albeit only prima facie, wrong or duty?[84]

We can start to answer this question by looking at reasons. To say that *X* is prima facie a wrong is to say that there is reason to believe that we have good moral reason not to do it, but to allow that further inquiry might reveal that it is not a wrong—might reveal, indeed, that we have no reason not to do *X*: we have reason to believe that we have reason to act, but might not really have reason to act. On the other reading, to say that *X* is a prima facie wrong is to say that we have reason not to do *X*, whilst

[80] Or that she did not do what she had reason to do (see Ch 5.6 above); I will hereafter omit this qualification.

[81] Compare Campbell, 1987.

[82] See Ch 6.5 above.

[83] I leave aside here the question of whether that burden should be only evidential or persuasive: see at nn 11–14 above, and Ch 10.3 below.

[84] The problem is most familiar in the context of Ross's talk of 'prima facie duties': see Ross, 1930 (esp 18–36); Searle, 1978; Dancy, 1991, 1993: ch 6.

allowing that further inquiry might reveal there to be stronger reasons on the other side such that on balance, all things considered, we should or may do *X*: the reasons that we think we have not to do *X* are real (not merely apparent) reasons, but not necessarily conclusive.[85] As several theorists have pointed out, it is the second reading that is appropriate here:[86] offences must consist in conduct that we have, in the law's eyes, reason not to engage in. Proof that the defendant committed the offence charged is therefore, if the offence was properly defined, proof that he acted as he had in the law's eyes reason not to act; the onus is then on him to argue, and to offer evidence, that he nonetheless should not be condemned for acting thus, by offering a justification or excuse.[87]

Some might still find the idea of a prima facie wrong, as distinct from what is prima facie a wrong, unhelpful. Surely, they might say, if an action turns out, all things considered, to be something that I should or may do, it is not a wrong: there may have been reasons against it, such that it would have been wrong if they were conclusive; but if there are better reasons for it, it is not—though it looked as if it might be—a wrong. We have real reasons not to act in a certain way (not merely reason to believe that we have such reasons for action), given which the action is prima facie wrong; but there is no such thing as a prima facie wrong as distinct from what is prima facie a wrong. Or, as a revised version of this view, we might suggest that there are some contexts in which we can talk of wrongs that we must or may commit: those in which we face genuine moral dilemmas, such that no available action is unequivocally right, and we will be properly remorseful whatever we do.[88] In most cases, however, even when we act as we have moral reason not to act, if the reasons in favour of acting thus unequivocally defeat those against acting thus, it is at best misleading to say that we commit a wrong but are justified in doing so. If I miss my child's birthday party because I stopped to help the victims of a road accident, I had a reason not to stop to help—that I would miss the party; I also owe my child an apologetic explanation for my failure to turn up: but it would be an exaggeration to say that I committed a wrong, or wronged

[85] An analogous analysis can be provided for prima facie duties. Campbell talks of 'prima facie reasons', by which he means genuine (not merely apparent) reasons, which could be outweighed (1987: 79). This is, I think, less helpful: we do better to talk of the real reasons given which an action is a prima facie wrong.

[86] See eg Campbell, 1987: 79–80; Gardner, 1996: 107–8; Tadros, 2005a: 106.

[87] I have explained the idea of a prima facie wrong in terms that fit most happily with justificatory defences: the offence definition specifies something that we have reason not to do; we have a justification if we have other and better reason to do it on a particular occasion. But it can be adapted to excuses: one who offers an excuse admits that she acted as she had conclusive reason not to act, but offers an explanation of that action that shows her not to have been at fault in acting thus. See Tadros, 2005a: 107, and below, Ch 11.5.

[88] We need not decide here whether there really are such dilemmas (for a useful collection of views on this, see Gowans, 1987)—though my own view is that there are.

my child.[89] I have sympathy with this view, but in the end nothing hangs on whether we should say, or deny, that I commit a wrong when I miss the party. What matters is that the reason I have not to stop to help is a genuine reason, which is defeated by the reasons I have to stop, but which is still relevant to an understanding and assessment of my action: I stopped despite the fact that I would then miss the party.[90]

We can now see even more clearly why consent should not count as a defence in the context of rape, and why it should be a defence, rather than a negation of an offence element, that I used fatal force in defence of myself or others.[91] In the case of rape, if consent were a defence, the offence would need to be defined simply as 'sexual penetration'—which would be to say that we have good reason, endorsed by the criminal law, not to engage in such conduct, although that reason can be defeated by the other person's consent: but, as we saw, the law of rape does not rest on a claim that we have reason not to engage in sexual penetration. As for defensive violence, to treat it as negating an offence element would be to imply that we have no legally sanctioned reason not to kill the attacker—which would be to portray him as strictly an outlaw: but we do still have very good reason not to kill him, even if that reason is defeated by the need to save his intended victims; that is why we should use such force only if it is necessary, and should still regret the need to kill him.

We do not yet, however, have an adequate account of the distinction between offences and defences. First, to talk merely of what we have, in the law's eyes, reason not to do does not do justice to the idea of crimes as public wrongs: a public wrong surely amounts to more than something we have reason not to do. Secondly, if offence definitions should specify what we have reason not to do, why should they include mens rea as well as actus reus? We have reason not to harm others; but it seems odd to say that we have distinctive reason not to harm others intentionally or recklessly, or that only the latter kind of reason concerns the criminal law.[92] These concerns can be met by filling out the idea of a presumptive wrong in two ways.

[89] Contrast Gardner and Macklem, 2002: 467, rejecting talk of 'prima facie' wrongs, but insisting that in such a case I 'did something wrong'.

[90] On the significance of 'despite' see Duff, 1990a: 78–80. Gardner and Jung (1991: 571–2) point out that I fail to distinguish 'explanatory' from 'prescriptive' reasons in this passage; the charge is well-founded, but it does not undermine the point made in the text here.

[91] See at nn 49–59, 70–74 above; Campbell, 1987: 81–3; Tadros, 2005a: 105–6.

[92] See Tadros, 2005a: 107–8; and see further sect 4(c) below.

(b) Presumptive Wrongs

First, although wrongdoing involves doing what I have good reason not to do, it does not consist *merely* in that: if, in the honest belief that this is the £10 note I had lost, I take it and spend it, I act as I had good reason not to act (since the note is actually yours); but I have not committed the wrong of theft. It might be tempting to say that wrongdoing consists in doing, culpably, what I have good reason not to do: I do no wrong in taking the £10 note if my belief that it is mine is itself free from fault. But that would be too quick: the distinction between offences and defences in criminal law, and the analogous distinction in our moral thinking, highlight the fact that one can do wrong without being culpable or blameworthy. What is true is that wrongdoing involves a 'subjective' dimension,[93] which typically includes (or consists in, for criminal law) intention, knowledge, recklessness or negligence in relation to the key aspects of the conduct that is to be judged wrong: if I flick the light switch, not realising that due to an unpredictable fault in the wiring this will cause an explosion that will injure you, I act as I had (unknown to me) reason not to act, and cause your injury; but I do not commit a wrong, unless I could and should have realised that there was a risk of this happening.

Gardner denies this: some wrongs (such as theft) are 'constitutively sensitive to what the wrongdoer was trying to do or trying not to do'; but 'primary', 'basic' wrongdoing is 'strict', consisting simply in such actions as hurting or killing someone, or damaging property.[94] Now outside the criminal law, if I act in a way that in fact causes harm to you or your property, I must indeed answer to you (and perhaps to others) for doing so: moral responsibility is in that way typically strict; what counts in criminal law as lack of mens rea, negating an element of the offence, counts in extra-legal moral contexts as an excuse, ie a defence.[95] Lack of mens rea is not, however, typically an excuse in the criminal law: it normally negates an element of the offence; no excuse is needed. The kinds of wrong that concern the criminal law, and that its offence definitions should aim to specify, are thus not 'strict' wrongs: what I must answer for criminally is not merely causing harm, but doing so intentionally, knowingly, recklessly or (sometimes) negligently.[96] Nor, I think, does our extra-legal moral thought deal in strict wrongs. That I have caused

[93] See at nn 37–39 above. We can talk of a 'fault' element (Law Commission, 1989a: s 6; Ormerod, 2005: 90; Ashworth, 2006: ch 5), if we remember that 'fault' does not entail culpability: compare Gardner, 2004: 824–5.

[94] Gardner, 2004: 824–5, and 2005: 67–9; for a developed argument see Gardner, 2001.

[95] See above, Ch 3.3; and below, Ch 10 at n 3.

[96] But we will look in Ch 10 at some of the ways in which this claim about what is 'typical' or 'normal' in criminal law needs to be qualified.

harm to another, however accidentally or inadvertently (and non-culpably), certainly makes various differences to my responses and later actions—hence the importance of 'agent-regret';[97] but wrongdoing brings the prospect of remorse, and remorse is not in prospect if the harm was purely accidental.[98] For present purposes, however, the important point is that the wrongs that the criminal law's offence definitions specify are not normally (or should not be) Gardnerian 'strict' wrongs.

We could say, as Tadros suggests, that offence definitions should specify the wrongs for which the defendant will be convicted if he cannot offer a defence:[99] whilst there will still be room for argument about just how those wrongs should be specified and individuated, they must consist in more than acting as there was reason not to act. I am condemned, not simply for harming another person or her property, but for harming her or her property intentionally or recklessly: that is what I must answer for in a criminal court; that is the presumptive wrong which the offence definition should specify. We might understand a presumptive wrong as a wrong that justifies the presumption that the defendant is guilty—a presumption that she can defeat by offering a defence; or as conduct that a court can presume to be a wrong unless the defendant rebuts that presumption by offering a defence.[100] I suspect that we will find each of these understandings of a presumptive wrong appropriate in relation to different offences, but the point here is that this is one way in which a presumptive wrong, as that which the offence definition must specify, includes more than that one acts as one had reason not to act.

The second way in which the idea of a presumptive wrong is richer than that of acting as one had reason not to act concerns the character of the reasons against which one acts. They must of course be moral reasons, if we are to identify a kind of wrongdoing that can properly concern the criminal law.[101] As moral reasons they are therefore categorical reasons: what the law declares is not that if we wish to avoid punishment, or in other ways serve our interests, we should avoid doing what it defines as criminal; it declares that we must refrain from such conduct.[102] They are

[97] See B Williams, 1981a: 27–31.

[98] To which some might reply that Oedipus came to realise not just that he had caused harm, but that he had done wrong, although he could not have been expected to know that the person he killed was his father, or that the person he married was his mother (see eg B Williams, 1993: 69; Winch, 1972: 184–5; Phillips, 1982). However, it is crucial that Oedipus intentionally killed the man who was in fact his father, and intentionally married the woman who was in fact his mother.

[99] Tadros, 2005a: 108–15.

[100] See at nn 88–91 above.

[101] See Ch 4 above.

[102] See Gardner and Macklem, 2002: 465–6. One can of course represent some offences in hypothetical terms: if you are going to drive a car, you must get a licence—but you could avoid that requirement by giving up the end of driving a car. But such requirements are

also 'exclusionary' reasons, in slightly different ways, depending on whether the offence is *malum in se* or (to some degree) *malum prohibitum*.[103]

In the case of *mala in se*, what the law defining them as offences declares or reminds us of is not just that we have categorical reason to refrain from the specified conduct, but that that reason serves to exclude the conduct from normal consideration as an option—which is to say that it excludes from normal consideration what might otherwise constitute reasons in favour of acting thus. If I need money, I will consider various ways of obtaining it, weighing the reasons for and against each money-making option: but, as the law reminds us in defining murder and theft as crimes, the options that I consider should not normally include killing my wealthy uncle or stealing from another person. The fact that a course of action would enable me to acquire money that I need would usually be a reason in favour of pursuing it, but when the course of action constitutes murder or theft, its profitability is not a reason in favour of it: it is not even a weak reason that is obviously outweighed by the reasons against such actions —there is nothing to be weighed. In defining such crimes, the law reminds us that nothing normally counts as a reason for engaging in the specified conduct: it is simply ruled out of consideration (not by the law, but by the moral values that the law expresses).[104]

In the case of *mala prohibita*, the legal regulation which the criminal law enforces is part of the good citizen's reason for acting in conformity with it: I drive on this road at less than 30 mph because that is the posted speed limit. Such regulations typically require citizens not to think for themselves about how best to conduct certain aspects of their activities. I should not normally try to decide for myself whether I can safely drive at more than 30 mph on this road; or how much money I should contribute to the polity; or how I should ensure that I am competent to drive a car, or to practise as a doctor; or what counts as fair practice in various commercial activities: there are legal regulations that specify at least minimum requirements, which I should normally simply follow.

In both cases, of *mala in se* and of *mala prohibita*, the qualification 'normally' is crucial, since it is what opens the door to justificatory defences. If other and possibly countervailing reasons for action were always and absolutely excluded from consideration, we might still be able

conditional rather than hypothetical: they do not specify necessary means to your end, but what you must do given that you are pursuing that end.

[103] I am using the idea of exclusionary reasons somewhat loosely here: for its precise analysis see Raz, 1990: 35–84; Gardner and Macklem, 2002: 459–68.

[104] See Ch 4 at nn 23–27 above. What I say here applies to intentional wrongs: nothing can normally count as a reason for trying to kill or steal. Matters are more complicated when the wrong is one of endangerment rather than attack: see sect 4(c) below.

to offer an excuse for committing the offence,[105] but there would be in law no possibility of justifying the commission of the offence: it would be a categorical and absolute wrong. If, however, such other reasons are only 'normally' ruled out, this leaves open the possibility of claiming, and of the law recognising, that in certain exceptional circumstances other reasons can come into play, and can even defeat the reasons that are normally conclusive. Normally, nothing counts as a reason for killing another person; killing does not figure as an option, not even one that there is overwhelmingly good reason to reject: but in the abnormal situation in which someone is attacking me or others, killing him to save his intended victims becomes a legitimate option. That is not to say that it is therefore justified: we must still ask whether the use of fatal force is necessary and proportionate. But it is now an option, whereas normally it is ruled out of consideration. (In such contexts, 'normally' has both normative and statistical dimensions: situations in which killing is a legitimate option are normatively abnormal, in that there is a strong normative presumption not just against killing, but against considering it as an option; but they also need to be statistically unusual, if killing is to be ruled out from our everyday repertoire of available actions.)

We can now see more clearly what it means to say that offence definitions should define presumptive wrongs: they should define types of conduct that we normally have categorical and conclusive reason not just to avoid, but not even to consider as options, and define them in a way that identifies the wrong for which the defendant will be convicted if he cannot offer an exculpatory defence. Offence definitions should be such that, if the prosecution discharges its initial persuasive burden by proving that the defendant committed the offence, the court can legitimately presume that he committed it culpably unless he offers a defence that rebuts that presumption. Proof that he committed the offence should be such as to justify replacing the Presumption of Innocence by a Presumption of Guilt which it is for the defendant to defeat; it is proof of a presumptive wrong for which he must answer, and of which he is guilty unless he can offer an exculpatory answer to block the presumptive transition from responsibility to liability.[106]

Although this clarifies the distinction between offences and defences, and why it matters, it does not tell us which conditions that bear on the

[105] Unless some offences are so terrible as to be inexcusable: Aristotle, *Nicomachean Ethics* Bk III.1 1110a26–28; see Ch 11 n 95 below.

[106] A further issue is whether, if he offers a justificatory defence, he should have to provide evidence that he acted for the reasons that constituted the justification, or merely that the facts that grounded those reasons existed. I discuss this issue in Ch 11.4 below; but we can note here that if the defendant must answer for his commission of the offence, it seems plausible that a justificatory answer will need to explain that he acted as he did because the relevant facts obtained—not merely that they in fact obtained.

defendant's guilt should figure in the offence definition, and which in the specification of possible defences: it shows us only how we should go about deciding that question. Sometimes the answer is quite obvious: it would be hard to argue plausibly that consent should be a defence on a charge of rape, or that the fact that the violence used was defensive should negate an element of the offence.[107] Often, however, the answer is neither obvious nor incontrovertible; there is room for disagreement about just how we should conceptualise the presumptive wrong for which the defendant can be expected to answer in a criminal court. Consider just two examples.

First, under our current law, both lack of consent and lack of reasonable belief in consent are elements of the offence of rape:[108] this implies that the presumptive wrong is not just the intentional sexual penetration of a person who in fact does not consent, but non-consensual penetration in the absence of a reasonable belief in consent. It could be argued, however, that the presumptive wrong should simply be non-consensual sexual penetration; a mistaken (but reasonable) belief in consent would then constitute a defence.[109]

Secondly, a shopkeeper who sells food that 'fails to comply with food safety requirements' commits an offence; to avoid conviction he must prove, as a defence, that he 'exercised all due diligence to avoid the commission of the offence'.[110] This implies that we should see the presumptive wrong as selling food that is in fact unsafe—rather than as negligently selling such food:[111] but is this a reasonable view to take? We will attend to such issues as these in Chapter 10.3, but must briefly consider one more issue in this chapter, concerning the way in which the difference between attacks and endangerments bears on the distinction between offences and justificatory defences.

[107] See at nn 49–59, 71–74 above.

[108] Sexual Offences Act 2003, s 1(1).

[109] Part of what drove the arguments of the majority in *Morgan* [1976] AC 182 was the view that intention or recklessness as to consent must be part of the offence of rape: but one could argue (*pace* Lord Cross, at 203) that the victim has been raped, ie that the wrong has been committed, even if the agent acted non-culpably on the basis of a reasonable belief that she consented.

[110] Food Safety Act 1990, ss 8(1), 21(1); see at n 13 above.

[111] The argument about rape would be that non-consensual sexual penetration is the wrong which justifies the defeasible presumption of guilt; for the food safety offence, the argument would be that selling food which is actually unsafe is conduct that can be defeasibly presumed to be a wrong: see at n 101 above.

(c) Attacks, Endangerments and Justifications

When an offence consists in an attack, ie in conduct that is intended to injure a protected interest,[112] the distinction between offences and defences is in principle straightforward. It is for the prosecution to prove that the defendant committed the intended injury: it is then for the defendant to offer evidence either that, in that abnormal situation, it was permissible for her to recognise and be guided by reasons in favour of her action; or that, although her action was not justified, it was excusable. Matters are less straightforward, however, with offences of endangerment, involving the reckless rather than the intended causing of harm.[113]

If the prosecution proves that the defendant recklessly harmed another person, it is still of course open to her to offer an excusatory defence: insofar as duress constitutes an excuse, for instance, she could admit that she injured the victim recklessly, by taking a risk of causing injury that it was unreasonable to take, but argue that she should be acquitted because she acted under a kind of duress that, whilst it could not justify her action, should be taken to excuse it.[114] There is, however, no room for a justificatory defence: if the defendant's conduct was justified, it follows that it was not unreasonable for her to take the risk that she took; thus for the prosecution to prove recklessness, as an aspect of the offence, is also for it to disprove justification. The formal distinction between offences and justificatory defences thus seems to collapse in offences of endangerment (although in practice the defendant will still no doubt usually have to offer evidence of any unusual justificatory factor).

To see why that distinction does indeed collapse in this context we must look again at the kinds of reason against which one who commits an offence acts.[115] In the case of attacks, the law can speak of categorical and exclusionary reasons: 'You must not kill [or steal]' makes sense as a categorical requirement not to act with the intention of killing or of depriving another of her property, nor even to consider such intended actions as options. But it cannot sensibly speak in such terms of endangerment. We have reason not to cause death or other harms to others: the fact that a contemplated action would cause such harm is normally a reason

[112] On the distinction between attacks and endangerments see Ch 7.1(a) above.

[113] The points to be made here about offences of recklessness will also apply to offences of negligence; but for simplicity's sake I will focus on recklessness.

[114] It might seem that proof that the defendant took a risk that it was unreasonable to take requires proof that a 'reasonable person' would not have taken it: but since an excusatory plea of duress can succeed only if a person 'of reasonable firmness' would have acted as the defendant did (see Ormerod, 2005: 305; Model Penal Code, s 2.09(1)), proof of the offence would also be disproof of excusatory duress. The solution to this puzzle is to recognise that what underpins the excusatory force of duress is the way in which serious threats can drive even reasonable people to act unreasonably: see Ch 11 at nn 89–95 below.

[115] See at nn 104–105 above.

against it.[116] We also, therefore, have reason to take precautions against causing harm, to pay reasonable attention so that we notice risks that we might create, and not to act in ways that we realise might cause harm: if I do what I realise might cause harm, I act as I have reason not to act. Such reasons cannot, however, be either categorical or exclusionary. 'You must not do what will cause harm', and 'You must not do what you realise might cause harm', cannot be read as 'You must not kill' can be read as applying to attacks. The reason is simple: very many of our ordinary activities create *some* risk of harm (including harms that concern the criminal law) to others; a serious attempt to conform my conduct to either of those commandments, interpreted as categorical and exclusionary, would be a recipe for paralysis.

That is why Robinson is wrong to exclude 'culpability requirements' from his Code of Conduct (he locates them in the Code of Adjudication to guide courts in deciding liability).[117] Consider section 3:'You may not cause bodily injury or death to another person' (this aims to capture within one simplified conduct rule the range of existing offences involving physical harm to others).[118] Now the Code of Conduct is to 'provide *ex ante* direction to the members of the community as to the conduct that must be avoided';[119] but how could we be guided by this section? We can be guided by a rule forbidding attacks, but the only way to be sure of not violating this section would be to do nothing at all. We could of course draw from this section a slightly more practicable rule of conduct: 'Take care not to cause bodily injury or death to another person'; but even that is unhelpful, since it gives us no idea of what kind or degree of care to take. Any plausible conduct rule must talk of taking reasonable care (or specify what would count as reasonable care in particular contexts), or of not taking unreasonable risks:[120] but that is precisely to accept that the fact that my action might cause harm cannot constitute a categorical or exclusionary reason against it.

When an agent contemplates an action that she knows involves a risk of harm, she cannot treat that fact as a categorical, exclusionary reason against acting thus. She must recognise it as a reason against that action—perhaps a powerful reason, depending on the seriousness of the

[116] Unless I can argue that that prospective harm is not my responsibility: see above, Ch 1.3.

[117] Robinson, 1997: 129–37; see 133–6 for the 'few instances', concerning inchoate crimes, in which the conduct rules must include a 'culpability requirement'.

[118] Robinson, 1997: 213 (s 4 allows an exception to this rule covering 'minor bodily injury' to which the other person consents); see ss 24, 32, 37(c) for similarly strict prohibitions (and at 185–8 on simplification).

[119] Robinson, 1997: 125.

[120] As s 51 of Robinson's Code of Conduct does: 'You may not act in a way that creates a substantial and unjustified risk of causing a result made criminal by this Code', subject to an exception that need not concern us here (1997: 218).

harm and the likelihood of its occurrence; but it is a reason that must be weighed against the countervailing reasons in favour of the action—reasons that flow from its intended result. It might be entirely obvious which way the balance tips: either that it is a risk that she should not take, or that it is one that it is reasonable to take. But if there are factors that could justify taking that risk, they must figure in the balance of reasons for and against the contemplated action. The fact that if I kill my uncle I will acquire the money he has left me in his will is not a reason in favour of killing him that is outweighed by the reasons against—it does not figure as a reason at all. By contrast, the fact that introducing a new chemical process will improve the efficiency of my factory is a reason in favour of introducing it, and remains a reason even if it is obviously outweighed, indeed overwhelmed, by the countervailing reason that the new process would seriously endanger the lives of my employees.

We therefore cannot say that causing harm, or creating a risk of harm, is a presumptive wrong in the way that we can identify an attack as a presumptive wrong. One who creates a risk of a kind of harm the culpable causation of which would make him criminally liable does not act against a categorical exclusionary reason; if the law is to specify what could plausibly be seen as a presumptive wrong, it must build the lack of any adequate reason (any justification) for taking the risk of causing that harm into its definition of the offence. We can still maintain a distinction between offence and defence: but the defences will not include justifications.

Or, more precisely, we cannot plausibly count the mere causation of harm or creation of risk as a wrong that creates a defeasible presumption of guilt: it is not yet clear that we cannot count it as conduct that a court can properly presume to be a wrong unless the defendant can rebut that presumption by offering a defence. That is indeed what the Food Safety Act 1990 does: one who sells unsafe food creates a risk of harm, and is presumed guilty of a wrong of endangerment unless she can prove that she took all due care. We will attend to such cases in Chapter 10: all we need note here is that insofar as offences are defined in ways that include such subjective aspects as recklessness, they leave no room for separate justificatory defences (we will also see in Chapter 10 why offences, especially paradigm *mala in se*, *should* usually be defined in ways that include such subjective dimensions).[121]

[121] I have talked about offences of intention and of recklessness—but what of what theorists (misleadingly) call 'oblique intention', constituted by the realisation that my action is (virtually) certain to cause harm (see Ch 7 at n 23 above)? I am inclined to think that this should still be classed with recklessness: the certainty of harm might make the reason against the contemplated action even more overwhelmingly conclusive; but its logic is still that of a very weighty reason, not of a categorical or exclusionary reason.

I have argued in this chapter that the distinction between offences and defences is indeed substantially significant (and not just a matter of expository convenience), and shown how it can be understood. The orthodox view, reflected in the 'golden thread' that *Woolmington* celebrated,[122] is that offences should normally be so defined that they include the subjective dimension of intention or recklessness (or occasionally negligence); it should not be for the defendant to prove, or even to have to produce evidence, that he did not intend the harm that he caused or that he did not act recklessly in causing it. That orthodox view has, however, come under increasing pressure in recent years as legislatures create more offences in which that golden thread seems to be frayed, if not completely broken: we must therefore turn now to look at such developments, to see how far the account of criminal responsibility that I offer can help us to understand, to criticise, or perhaps sometimes to justify them.

[122] See at nn 1, 9–10 above.

10

Strict Liability and Strict Responsibility

The distinction between offences and defences, I have argued, fits that between responsibility and liability. Offences should be so defined that they identify presumptive wrongs. Proof that the defendant committed the offence charged is then proof that she is criminally responsible for committing a presumptive wrong for which she can be called to answer in the criminal court. Such proof creates a presumption of guilt or liability: the court is entitled to presume that she committed the offence culpably, and is thus liable to conviction and punishment for it. That presumption, however, is defeasible: the defendant can block the transition from responsibility to liability by offering a defence. The prosecution must first prove beyond reasonable doubt that the defendant committed the offence; if it discharges that persuasive burden, the defendant acquires an evidential burden of introducing evidence of a defence.

On a familiar, almost orthodox, normative understanding of criminal liability, the offence must include not just an actus reus, but mens rea as to all the essential elements of that actus; only once that is proved is it just to place the burden of introducing evidence of a defence on the defendant. This chapter discusses some ways in which our law does not fit that orthodox model—ways in which it imposes strict liability or strict responsibility. I begin, in section 1, by clarifying the orthodox view and its attractions. Section 2 discusses the varieties of strict liability and strict responsibility, and the roles of different kinds of presumption. Sections 3 and 4 then move on to the normative task of determining whether any forms of strict criminal responsibility or liability can be justified; we will see that strict criminal responsibility can be justified in some contexts, and that a very limited form of strict criminal liability could be in principle justifiable. As in earlier chapters, however, my concern is with structure more than with substantive content: with the logic of responsibility and liability in the criminal law, and the kinds of argument that would be needed to justify the statutory provisions and doctrines that I discuss, rather than in which of those arguments will ultimately prove to be sound.

1. Criminal Responsibility and Criminal Liability: The Simple Picture

Offence definitions, we noted in Chapter 9, are generally expected to include the subjective dimension of mens rea: the *Woolmington* 'golden thread' required the prosecution to prove both actus reus and mens rea.[1] Those who accept the 'correspondence principle' would insist that the offence definition should include mens rea as to every essential element of the actus reus: a complete fit between the objective and the subjective dimensions of the offence.[2] This gives us a simple account of the distinction between responsibility and liability, and of offences and defences. Responsibility is for the commission of an offence consisting in actus reus plus mens rea: only once that is proved does the defendant have anything to answer for; only then can any formal burden of proof be laid on the defendant. Liability then depends on whether the defendant can offer evidence in support of a defence that is sufficient at least to create a reasonable doubt about her guilt, all things considered.

There is then a striking contrast between criminal responsibility, as thus understood, and moral responsibility, since we have seen that moral responsibility for harms that we cause is typically strict, in the sense that it does not depend on anything analogous to mens rea. If I act in a way that in fact damages your property, I am morally answerable for that action and that harm, even if I caused it through wholly non-culpable accident or inadvertence: my denial of intention, recklessness or negligence blocks (if it is believable) liability to blame, but does not negate responsibility—whereas the absence of any such 'fault element' negates an essential element of the offence of criminal damage.[3] That is why in moral discourse inadvertence and accident count as 'excuses', whereas in criminal law they typically do not (and so why moral philosophers sometimes find legal theorists' use of 'excuse' puzzling): for, as we will see in more detail in Chapter 11, excuses admit responsibility but deny liability—which is how inadvertence and accident function in moral discourse, but not typically in the criminal law.

This contrast between moral and criminal responsibility raises one immediate question. Why should criminal responsibility not be strict in the way that moral responsibility is: why should the initial probative

[1] *Woolmington v DPP* [1935] AC 462, 481; see Ch 9 at nn 1, 9–10 above.

[2] For the correspondence principle see Ashworth, 2006: 87, 158–64; also Mitchell, 1999; for critique see Horder, 1995, 1999b.

[3] See Criminal Damage Act 1971, s 1(1): criminal damage must be intentional or reckless. On strict moral responsibility see Ch 3.3 above. Is this to agree with Gardner that 'basic' moral wrongs are 'strict' (see Ch 9 at nn 94–8 above)? No: the point is that moral responsibility can be for harm-causings that are not even presumptive wrongs (though it still for doing something, causing harm, that I had moral reason not to do).

burden on the prosecution not just be to prove that the defendant committed the actus reus—which would then place on the defendant at least the evidential burden of offering evidence that mens rea was lacking? A further question is this: if criminal responsibility is rightly less strict than moral responsibility, why should the conditions of criminal responsibility not be expanded even further, to include all the conditions of liability: why should the prosecution not have to prove the absence of any plausible defence, as well as the commission of the offence? An answer to the second question was effectively provided in Chapter 9: if offences are presumptive public wrongs, it is not unreasonable to expect citizens to answer to their fellows for committing an offence, ie for doing something that is certainly their business as a presumptive wrong—especially if answering need involve no more than producing evidence of a defence that suffices to create a reasonable doubt about guilt.[4] But what of the first question? Proof of an actus reus often of course creates such a strong factual presumption of intention, or at least recklessness, that a defendant who is to avoid conviction will in practice have to offer evidence of lack of mens rea; but the question here concerns the formal allocation of responsibilities and burdens between defence and prosecution.

An adequate explanation of why criminal responsibility should not generally be strict will involve an account of what it is reasonable for citizens to demand of each other, simply *qua* citizens, through the coercive apparatus of the criminal law. There are some obvious practical reasons for making criminal responsibility less strict than moral responsibility: the risk that innocents will be mistakenly convicted if they cannot discharge the evidential burden that strict responsibility would place on them; the costs (in time, money, emotional strain) that mounting a defence involves. Such reasons may not be quite as strong as they at first seem: innocents will often in fact have to give evidence of lack of mens rea to rebut the prosecution case; an adequate system of legal aid could ameliorate the burden of doing so. But there is a stronger reason of principle: that since the criminal law is concerned only with public wrongs that merit public condemnation, we should have to answer in a criminal court only for what is at least a presumptive wrong of the appropriate kind. Outside the law, I must answer for the harms that I cause, as a matter of moral responsibility. When what is at stake within the law is the question of who should pay for harm that was caused, as a civil law matter, it might also be reasonable to expect me to answer, in a civil court, for harm that I actually cause: to give an explanation, and if necessary evidence to support that explanation, if I am to avoid liability to pay for the harm. Within the criminal law, however,

[4] See at nn 26–27, 49, 57 below on whether it could ever be legitimate to lay a persuasive burden on the defendant.

what is at stake is not liability to pay the costs of repairing harm, but liability to condemnation for wrongdoing:[5] it would not be reasonable to expect citizens to answer (on pain of criminal conviction if they cannot offer an exculpatory answer) for anything less than a proved presumptive wrong. A presumptive wrong can, we have seen, be either a wrong that creates a defeasible presumption of guilt; or conduct that creates a presumption of wrongfulness:[6] but the mere commission of an actus reus is not sufficient to constitute either kind of presumptive wrong. The fact that I caused harm to another's person or property, for instance, might create a suspicion of wrongdoing; it might justify a police investigation, which could lead to a criminal charge which I am summoned to answer: but it cannot by itself justify a presumption of wrongdoing on my part that warrants requiring me to answer in a criminal court for that conduct.

This explanation seems to support the simple view of offences and defences, and of the relationship between criminal responsibility and criminal liability. But it raises a more serious question about the ways in which our criminal law is starkly at odds with that simple view.

2. Strict Liability and Strict Responsibility

Our existing laws conflict with the simple view of responsibility and liability when they make responsibility or liability strict. I begin with strict liability: given the variety of meanings that have been attached to 'strict liability', I should clarify my use of the phrase.

(a) Varieties of Strict Liability[7]

First, my concern is with liability that is 'strict' rather than 'absolute', in one sense of the latter term.[8] Liability would be absolute if it required no proof of mens rea as to *any* aspect of the offence: thus the offence of being found drunk on a highway would be an absolute offence if conviction required no proof of any mens rea either as to getting drunk or as to being in a highway.[9] Liability is strict if it requires no proof of mens rea as to *an* aspect of the offence: while mens rea must be proved as to some elements in the offence definition, it need not be proved as to every essential

[5] Which is precisely why many abolitionists object to criminal law as such: see above Ch 4 at n 9.

[6] See Ch 9 at nn 88–91, 100 above.

[7] See Husak, 1995b; Simons, 1997: 1075–93; Green, 2005.

[8] See Ormerod 2005: 117.

[9] See Licensing Act 1872, s 12; *Winzar v Chief Constable of Kent, The Times,* 28 Mar 1983: on *Winzar*, and *Larsonneur* (1933) 24 Cr App R 74, see Ch 1 at n 2, Ch 3 at nn 5–11 above.

element. I could be guilty of possessing an uncertificated firearm even I am sure that it is an antique (which would not require a certificate), and perhaps even if I do not realise that it is a firearm: but while liability is strict as to the fact that the item is a 'firearm', I must have at least known that I had that item in my possession.[10]

Secondly, some call liability 'strict' when, though it requires no positive proof of mens rea as to some aspect of the offence, it can be averted by proof or evidence of lack of mens rea; if it cannot be thus averted, they call it 'absolute'.[11] Liability for the unauthorised possession of a scheduled drug under section 1(1) of the Drugs (Prevention of Misuse) Act 1964 was in this sense 'absolute' as to the fact that the substance in my possession was a scheduled drug,[12] but liability for the matching offence under the Misuse of Drugs Act 1971 is 'strict': one who had possession of a controlled drug can now secure an acquittal by proving 'that he neither knew nor suspected nor had reason to suspect' that it was such a drug.[13] I will use 'strict liability' to refer to liability that cannot be averted even by evidence or proof of lack of mens rea; when liability requires no positive proof of mens rea, but can be averted by evidence or proof of its lack, I will talk of strict criminal responsibility.

Thirdly, we can distinguish formally strict from substantively strict liability.[14] Liability is formally strict if it does not require explicit proof of a legally recognised species of mens rea —such as intention, recklessness, or negligence—as to an aspect of the offence.[15] Liability is substantively strict if it does not require proof of appropriate moral culpability as to an aspect of the offence—proof of fault that would justify condemning the defendant for committing the offence. This distinction gives us four possible patterns of strict and non-strict liability.

(a) Liability can be formally and substantively non-strict. Conviction for criminal damage requires proof of intention or recklessness as to the damage to another's property that I cause; absent a 'lawful excuse', this constitutes proof of legal and moral fault—of mens rea and of a moral culpability that justifies condemning me for damaging the property.[16]

[10] Firearms Act 1968, ss 1(1), 58; see *Howells* [1977] QB 614 (on antiques); *Hussain* (1981) 72 Cr App R 143 (on not knowing it to be a firearm).

[11] See Simester and Sullivan, 2007: 185–6.

[12] See *Warner v Metropolitan Police Commissioner* [1969] 2 AC 256.

[13] Misuse of Drugs Act 1971, ss 5(1)–(2), 28: see *Ashton-Rickhardt* (1977) 65 Cr App R 67.

[14] Compare Simons, 1997: 1087–93; Green, 2005: 10–11; Husak, 2005d: 86–93; Simester, 2005: 22–3.

[15] I assume here that negligence-based liability need not be 'strict': see Simester, 2000.

[16] See Criminal Damage Act 1971, s. 1(1).

(b) Liability can be both formally and substantively strict. If I caused a 'poisonous, noxious or polluting matter ... to enter any controlled water', I am guilty of an offence even if I can prove that I took all reasonable care, in pursuing my legitimate activity, to prevent such pollution.[17] Such formally strict liability is also substantively strict if a defendant who took such reasonable care should not be condemned for the pollution.[18]

(c) Liability can be formally non-strict but substantively strict, if the legally defined mens rea does not constitute an appropriate kind of moral fault. A girl was guilty of criminal damage under English law because the risk of damage created by her action would have been obvious to a 'reasonably prudent' person, even if she did not herself appreciate that risk and (given her age and intelligence) would not have appreciated it had she given the matter any thought, since she was in law 'reckless' as to that risk.[19] Her liability was not formally strict, but it was substantively strict: for she did not display any fault sufficient to justify holding her as culpably responsible for the damage as if she had foreseen it.[20]

(d) Liability can be formally strict but substantively non-strict, if conviction requires proof of no legally recognised mens rea as to an aspect of the offence, but proof of legal guilt also constitutes proof of an appropriate moral fault in relation to the complete offence. I cannot yet offer uncontroversial examples of this pattern, since I will need to argue that it is not an empty category, but it underpinned the argument that since 'a taking of a girl, in the possession of some one, against his wi[ll]...done without lawful excuse is wrong, ... it should be at the risk of the taker whether or no she was under sixteen'.[21] Liability for unlawfully taking an unmarried girl of under 16 from the possession and against the will of her parent was formally strict as to her age: but the argument was that anyone who acted with the mens rea that the law required as to her being unmarried and in the possession of a parent who did not consent to her departure thereby displayed a moral fault as to the risk that she was under 16 sufficient

[17] Water Resources Act 1991, s. 85(1); *R v Milford Haven Port Authority* (2000) 2 Cr App R (S) 423. See Ch 7 at n 17 above.

[18] He might properly be held strictly liable to pay the costs of the pollution, but strict civil liability is a quite different matter from strict criminal liability; see Cane, 2000: 105–10.

[19] *Elliott v C* [1983] 1 WLR 939, applying *Caldwell* [1982] AC 341; overruled by *G* [2004] 1 AC 1034.

[20] Simons (1997: 1085–8) notes another kind of formally non-strict but substantively strict liability, when the law requires full mens rea, but defines the offence so widely that it captures conduct that is not wrongful: see Ch 9 at nn 15–19 above on formal as against substantive readings of the Presumption of Innocence.

[21] *Prince* (1875) LR 2 CCR 154, at 174–5 (*per* Bramwell B); Offences Against the Person Act 1861, s 55.

to justify convicting him of the offence if that risk was actualised, even if he was sure that she was over 16.

I will say no more here about (a), which is unproblematic. The objections to (b)—and so also to (c)—are familiar, and need not be rehearsed here. Those who seek to justify substantively strict liability argue that it can be justified, as being necessary to make the law effective, at least for offences that regulate voluntary activities that create significant risks to public health or safety (especially those motivated by profit), conviction for which attracts neither serious stigma nor oppressive penalties. Any injustice done is 'comparatively minor' and with such 'quasi-criminal offences … it does not really offend the ordinary man's sense of justice that moral guilt is not of the essence of the offence'.[22] But the criminal law should be concerned with public wrongs; criminal convictions should condemn those whose commission of such wrongs merits such public condemnation. Substantively strict liability is therefore both unjust and dishonest: it portrays as proven culpable wrongdoers those who have not been proved to be that.[23] My main interest is in (d).

We can distinguish two more specific patterns within (d). One is that of 'constructive' liability, which involves formally strict liability as to a fact that transforms a less serious into a more serious offence. Under the doctrine of implied malice, wounding with intent (a crime for which liability is neither formally nor substantively strict) can become murder if it causes death; liability is then formally strict as to the victim's death.[24] The other pattern involves no lesser offence out of which liability for the more serious offence is constructed: if I drive at a speed that in fact exceeds the speed limit, I commit an offence that involves strict liability as to my actual speed, and there is no lesser offence for which liability is not strict and of which the prosecution must prove me guilty.[25] The justification of some kinds of constructive strict liability is, as we will see, relatively easy, and provides a model for the justification of at least some kinds of non-constructively strict liability.

[22] *Warner v Metropolitan Police Commissioner* [1969] 2 AC 256 at 272 (Lord Reid). See Sayre, 1933: 70–5; *Gammon v A-G of Hong Kong* [1985] AC 1, at 14 (*per* Lord Scarman). For a useful survey of the main arguments see Simester, 2005.

[23] It might then be suggested that we should create a distinct category of non-criminal 'regulatory' offences, which involve no condemnation of purported wrongdoing, and for which liability could therefore be strict (see Ch 4 at n 7 above): though our concern here is with the criminal law, we should note that this kind of strategy of 'decriminalisation' is far from unproblematic: see Duff *et al*, 2007: ch 6.5.

[24] See Ormerod, 2005: 436–9. See also the American doctrine of felony murder: Model Penal Code, s 210.2; LaFave, 2003: 737–66.

[25] Road Traffic Regulation Act 1984, s 89.

(b) Strict Responsibility and Defences

It is, we saw in Chapter 9, consistent with the Presumption of Innocence to place at least an evidential burden on the defendant in relation to defences: if it is proved that he committed the offence, that he has that prima facie public wrong to answer for, it does not undermine the Presumption to require him, if he wants to block the transition from responsibility to liability, to adduce evidence sufficient, if not rebutted, to create at least a reasonable doubt about the legitimacy of that transition. One question then is whether it could ever be consistent with the Presumption to lay a persuasive burden on the defendant in relation to defences. It seems not to be. If he is required to prove his defence, even only on the balance of probabilities, he must be convicted if the evidence he offers, while strong enough to create a reasonable doubt about whether he satisfied the conditions of the defence, is not strong enough to make it on balance probable that he did so; but since if he satisfied those conditions he is innocent, that is surely to say that he must be convicted even if he provides uncontroverted evidence that is sufficient to create a reasonable doubt about his guilt—which is inconsistent with the Presumption. This explains decisions by the European Court of Human Rights and by the House of Lords that it is (sometimes) inconsistent with Article 6(2) of the European Convention to impose such a persuasive burden on the defendant (but permissible to impose an evidential burden)—though the jurisprudence of Article 6(2) is far from unequivocal on this issue, since courts have also allowed that imposing such a persuasive burden is sometimes legitimate.[26] I will return to this issue later;[27] the point to notice here is the way in which existing laws not only impose on the defendant an apparently persuasive burden, but do so by counting as a defence what should on the simple view count as negating an element of the offence—as to which the prosecution should therefore bear the entire probative burden.[28]

We have already noted three examples of this kind. Someone who sells food that fails to comply with safety requirements commits an offence, but has a defence if he proves 'that he took all reasonable precautions and exercised all due diligence to avoid the commission of the offence';[29] but lack of due diligence should on the simple view be an element of the

[26] For the courts' shifting views see eg *Salabiaku v France* (1991) 13 EHRR 379; *Kebilene* [2000] 2 AC 326; *Lambert* [2001] 3 All ER 577; *Sheldrake v DPP* [2003] 2 All ER 497. See Ashworth, 1999; Roberts, 2002; Simester and Sullivan, 2007: 32–7, 55–9; Tadros and Tierney, 2004.

[27] See at nn 49, 57 below.

[28] See Ashworth and Blake, 1996.

[29] Food Safety Act 1990, ss 8, 21; see Ch 9 at nn 13, 110–11 above. See also Licensing Act 2003, s 139 (see Ch 1 at n 6 above).

offence for the prosecution to prove. Someone who has a controlled drug in her possession commits an offence, but has a defence if she can prove that she 'neither knew … nor suspected nor had reason to suspect' that what she had was a controlled drug;[30] but such knowledge or (reason for) suspicion should on the simple view be an element of the offence for the prosecution to prove. Someone who possesses 'an article in circumstances which give rise to a reasonable suspicion that [the] possession is for a purpose connected with' terrorism commits an offence, but has a defence if he can prove that his possession 'was not for a purpose connected with' terrorism;[31] but on the simple view such terrorism-connected purpose should be an element of the offence for the prosecution to prove.

These statutory provisions do not make criminal liability strictly strict: the defendant can avoid conviction by proving lack of the relevant fault.[32] But they make criminal responsibility strict: whereas on the simple picture what the defendant has to answer for is the commission of an offence that is defined to include both actus reus and mens rea, such provisions require her to answer for the commission of an offence the definition of which does not include mens rea as to all its essential elements. Criminal liability is strict when conviction does not require proof of mens rea as to some aspect of the offence; criminal responsibility is strict when proof of the commission of the offence for which the defendant must answer does not require proof of mens rea as to some aspect of that offence. Strict criminal responsibility seems objectionable because it seems to require defendants to answer, on pain of conviction if they cannot offer an exculpatory answer, for conduct that does not constitute, and that the legislature could not plausibly have believed to be, a presumptive public wrong:[33] surely the mere possession of something that an observer might reasonably suspect I have for terrorist purposes is not even a presumptive wrong. But if it is not a presumptive wrong, it should not be an offence; and on any but the most formalist reading, it is then inconsistent with the Presumption of Innocence to place even an evidential burden, let alone a persuasive burden, on the defendant in relation to a supposed terrorist purpose that should be an element of the offence itself.[34]

There are three possible responses to such impositions of strict criminal responsibility. We might, first, reject them all as inconsistent with a

[30] Misuse of Drugs Act 1971, ss 5, 28; see at nn 12–13 above. The Act also provides an orthodox defence: that the defendant took possession of the drug in order to prevent the commission of an offence or to deliver it into someone's lawful custody (s 5(4)).

[31] Terrorism Act 2000, s 57 (see too s 58 on collecting or possessing 'information of a kind likely to be useful' to terrorists); see above, Introduction at nn 5, 25, Ch 9 at n 16.

[32] That is the key difference between the Misuse of Drugs Act 1971 and the previous legislation: see at nn 12–13 above.

[33] See at nn 4–6 above.

[34] See Ch 9 at nn 15–19 above.

substantive Presumption of Innocence, and with a principled understanding of the idea of a criminal offence: a presumptive wrong must include mens rea as to its essential aspects; and we can never justifiably demand that citizens answer to the polity, on pain of conviction for a criminal offence if they cannot offer an adequately exculpatory answer, for conduct that does not constitute a presumptive wrong.

Secondly, we might admit that they are inconsistent with the Presumption of Innocence and with that principled idea of a criminal offence, but argue that at least some of them constitute justified infringements of the Presumption. We might talk of the need to 'balance the interests of the individual and society',[35] or appeal to what 'is necessary in a democratic society in the interests of national security, public safety ... or for the protection of the rights and freedoms of others'.[36] We might more modestly argue that the Presumption can be qualified in relation to matters as to which it would be much easier for the defendant to prove what is required for an acquittal than for the prosecution to prove what is required for a conviction.[37]

Thirdly, we might argue that strict criminal responsibility is sometimes consistent with the Presumption of Innocence (even when it is interpreted substantively), and with the idea that criminal offences should consist in presumptive wrongs: that proof of what the prosecution is required to prove, proof of the commission of what is formally defined as an offence, is proof of a presumptive wrong for which the defendant can be properly called to answer, on pain of conviction as being guilty of that offence if she cannot at least produce evidence sufficient to create a reasonable doubt. This is the possibility that I will explore in section 4; but we must first take note of another way in which the law imposes strict criminal responsibility—by the use of legal presumptions.

[35] *A-G for Hong-Kong v Lee Kwong-kut* [1993] AC 951, 973 (*per* Lord Woolf); see also *Salabiaku v France* (1991) 13 EHRR 379, 388.

[36] Considerations that the ECtHR allows to restrict the Convention rights specified in Arts 8–11 (although not explicitly those concerning a fair trial and the Presumption of Innocence in Art 6)—I have omitted some of the less plausible grounds for restriction, such as 'the protection of health or morals'. See also the Canadian Charter of Rights and Freedoms, ss 1, 11(d). For a very useful discussion of the implications of the ECHR on some of these issues see Sullivan, 2005.

[37] See eg *Nimmo v Alexander Cowan & Sons* [1968] AC 107, 122, 125–6, 132; *Hunt* [1987] AC 352; Tapper, 1999: 129–30. The favourite example here is that of offences of Φ-ing without a licence, but they are hardly persuasive: it might be easy for *D* to prove that he had a licence, but in any efficient system it would also be easy for the prosecutor to adduce strong evidence that he did not have one.

(c) Strict Responsibility and Legal Presumptions[38]

Common sense or so-called 'factual' presumptions express ordinary rules of extra-legal reasoning and inference:[39] if we see smoke, we can reasonably presume that there is a fire until we find evidence to the contrary; if we see someone pull the trigger of a loaded gun that is pointing towards another person, we can reasonably presume that he intended to shoot that person until we are given an alternative explanation. Legal presumptions go beyond what is sanctioned by extra-legal common sense: they mandate courts to presume or conclude that *q*, given proof that *p*, even though *p* would not, by the standards of ordinary reasoning, amount to proof of *q* beyond reasonable doubt. If, in a corruption trial, it is proved that a government contractor gave a civil servant a present, this could, as a matter of common sense (depending on the context), lead jurors to wonder if the gift was corrupt, but they might reasonably think that it does not by itself prove corruption beyond reasonable doubt. However, as a matter of law, given such proof they must presume that the present was 'given and received corruptly ... unless the contrary is proved'.[40] Such rebuttable legal presumptions place on the defendant the burden of disproving, or of offering evidence sufficient to put into reasonable doubt, that which the court is mandated to presume: if it is proved that the defendant sexually penetrated someone whom he knew to be unlawfully detained, the court must presume that that person did not consent to the penetration, and that the defendant did not believe that she consented, 'unless sufficient evidence is adduced to raise an issue as to' either of those facts.[41]

Sometimes a presumption is implicit rather than explicit. Employers have a statutory duty 'to ensure, so far as is reasonably practicable, the

[38] On presumptions see generally Morgan, 1937; Ullmann-Margalit, 1983; Dennis, 2007: ch 12(F); Roberts and Zuckerman, 2004: 336–44. My treatment of presumptions, as ways of imposing strict criminal responsibility, commits what Roberts calls the 'functionalist' error of conflating matters of procedure with matters of substance (Roberts, 2005; on his argument see Sullivan, 2005: 212–13; Tadros 2007): I hope that my account shows that charge to be ill-founded, by showing how what is at stake both in the kinds of case discussed above in sect 2(b), when the law defines as a 'defence' something the absence of which figures more usually as an offence element, and when legal presumptions are used to impose an evidential burden on the defendant, is what we can be expected to answer for in a criminal court.

[39] Though the law sometimes explicitly specifies and sanctions them: see Ashworth and Blake 1996: 312–13.

[40] Prevention of Corruption Act 1916, s 2. See also, eg, Sexual Offences Act 1956, s 30; Dangerous Dogs Act 1991, s 5; Proceeds of Crime Act 2002, s 10; Sexual Offences Act 2003, ss 16–19. Presumptions of this sort are 'derivative': the court can presume that *q* only given proof that *p*. Other so-called presumptions (such as the Presumption of Innocence) are non-derivative, requiring courts simply to presume that *q*: these are not my concern here: see n 50 below.

[41] Sexual Offences Act 2003, s 75.

health, safety and welfare at work' of their employees, including 'the provision and maintenance of plant and systems of work that are, so far as is reasonably practicable, safe and without risks to health'.[42] It is, formally, for the prosecution to prove the commission of the offence as thus defined; but if an employee is in fact injured by the machinery, the employer will be convicted unless she can show that she had taken all 'reasonably practicable' steps to ensure safety.[43] In effect, then, there is a legal presumption that if the machinery caused injury, ie was not 'safe and without risks to health', the employer had failed to do all that was reasonably practicable to ensure its safety; the onus was then on her to rebut that presumption.

(There are also so-called 'irrebuttable presumptions of law', requiring courts to presume that *q* given proof that *p*, and leaving no room for the presumption to be rebutted by adducing evidence or even proof that not-*q*. So, given proof that *D* 'intentionally deceived [*V*] as to the nature or purpose' of a sexual act that *D* committed on *V*, 'it is to be conclusively presumed' that *V* did not consent to that act and that *D* did not believe that *V* consented.[44] These are not, however, properly 'presumptions' that mandate an inference from a proven fact *p* to a further fact *q*; they are disguised substantive rules of law that help define the relevant offence, which should be honestly expressed as such.[45] The presumption that the deceived *V* did not consent does not mandate an inference from deception to some further fact about lack of consent, but partially defines 'consent' for the purposes of the Act: assent obtained by deception does not amount in law to consent of a kind that renders the act in question non-wrongful. Similarly, the English rule that a voluntarily intoxicated agent who fails to notice a risk that he would have noticed if sober is reckless as to that risk might be described as creating an irrebuttable legal presumption that he 'is to be treated as having been aware of' that risk,[46] which suggests that the court must treat as (if) true, to the defendant's detriment, something that the evidence suggests might well be false. We can, however, make better (if not morally adequate) sense of this rule by seeing it as declaring that recklessness can be constituted *either* by awareness of a relevant risk *or* by unawareness that is due to voluntary intoxication:[47] recklessness must be

[42] Health and Safety at Work etc Act 1974, s 2.

[43] See *Nimmo v Alexander Cowan & Sons* [1968] AC 107; *Hunt* [1987] AC 352, at 373–5 (*per* Lord Griffiths).

[44] Sexual Offences Act 2003, s 76; see Tadros, 2006a: 523–4.

[45] See, eg, Ashworth and Blake 1996: 311–12; Roberts and Zuckerman, 2004: 341; Roberts, 2005: 184–5.

[46] JC Smith, commenting on *Bennett* [1995] Crim L R 877, at 878.

[47] See Simester and Sullivan, 2007: 141; *Majewski* [1977] AC 443, at 474–5 (*per* Lord Elwyn-Jones), 479 (*per* Lord Simon), 496–7 (*per* Lord Edmund-Davies), 498 (*per* Lord Russell).

'presumed', not because it can be inferred from such drunken unawareness, but because it is constituted by such unawareness. Such 'presumptions' mandate conclusions that go beyond the evidence that grounds them, but that 'going beyond' is now normative rather than factual: the court must conclude that *V*'s 'consent' was not such as to legitimise *D*'s sexual act, or that *D* was as culpable in relation to that risk as he would have been had he taken it consciously. We should call such provisions constitutive or definitional rules rather than 'presumptions'.)

Such legal presumptions do not make criminal liability strict, since the defendant has the chance to rebut the presumption, but they make criminal responsibility strict: if the defendant is to avoid liability, she has to answer for conduct that has not yet been proved beyond what would normally count as reasonable doubt to constitute an offence that includes both actus reus and mens rea. The civil servant who accepts a gift from a government contractor might be foolish to do so, given the risk that the gift will be misinterpreted; his conduct might create a reasonable suspicion of corruption: but if the offence consists in corruptly receiving the gift (as it surely must, if it is to constitute a plausible presumptive wrong), proof that he accepted the gift falls well short of proof beyond what would normally count as reasonable doubt that he committed the offence. Nonetheless, he must now answer for accepting the gift, and show that it was not done corruptly if he is to avert liability—which is to say that he is held strictly responsible, without proof of corruption, for accepting the gift.

As with defences, so with presumptions, the law sometimes lays a persuasive burden on the defendant, and sometimes only an evidential burden:[48] so we must ask again whether it could ever be consistent with the Presumption of Innocence to lay such a persuasive burden on the defendant.[49] The prior question, however, is whether this kind of strict responsibility can be legitimate at all, even if it lays only an evidential burden on the defendant.[50] Whether we see it as implicitly transforming

[48] For the latter see eg Sexual Offences Act 2003, ss 16–19, 75.

[49] See at n 26 above. Presumptions that place a persuasive burden on the defence in relation to an element of the offence element are unconstitutional in the USA: the Fourteenth ('due process') Amendment requires the prosecution to prove all elements of the offence beyond reasonable doubt; such presumptions violate that requirement (see *In re Winship* 397 US 358 (1970); *Sandstrom v Montana* 442 US 510 (1979)). The substantive force of this doctrine is reduced by the fact that the state can simply remove an element from the definition of the offence, either by making liability strict in that respect or by making it a matter of defence, for which defendants can carry a persuasive burden. Thanks to Alan Michaels for this point.

[50] It is worth noting that non-derivative 'presumptions' (see n 40 above) that place an evidential or persuasive burden on the defendant are not best understood as imposing strict responsibility. A presumption of sanity requires the defendant to prove an insanity defence; a presumption of 'voluntariness' requires the defendant to offer evidence of automatism (see Simester and Sullivan, 2007: 118; *Bratty v A-G for Northern Ireland* [1963] AC 386; *Hill v*

what would normally be an element of the offence into a matter of defence, or as relieving the prosecution of the burden of proving an element of the offence, it raises the issue identified in section 2(b): does it undermine the principle that the defendant should only have to answer for conduct that has been proved to constitute what is at least (or at least in the legislature's eyes) a presumptive wrong? As we saw with defences, we could simply reject all such provisions as being inconsistent with a substantive reading of the Presumption of Innocence and with the idea of offences as presumptive wrongs; or we could try to justify some of them as practically necessary infringements of the Presumption; or we could argue that some of them can be shown to be consistent with the Presumption of Innocence (even when it is interpreted substantively), and with the idea that criminal offences should consist in presumptive wrongs: it is the third response that I will explore.

3. Justifying Strict Criminal Responsibility

Provisions that impose strict criminal responsibility seem to fray, if not to break, the 'golden thread' celebrated in *Woolmington*: they require the defendant to answer for conduct that has not been proved to be what we would normally recognise as a presumptive wrong (an offence defined to include both actus reus and mens rea); since the failure to provide an exculpatory answer, supported by evidence, entails conviction, they seem to sanction conviction without proof of guilt beyond reasonable doubt, provided by the prosecution. I will argue, however, that some such provisions can be justified as being consistent with a substantive Presumption of Innocence. Given the special prospective responsibilities that a polity could reasonably impose on citizens who engage in certain kinds of activity, we can show how such provisions can reflect a legitimate specification of what is to count, in relation to those activities, as a presumptive wrong, and of what should count as proof of guilt 'beyond reasonable doubt'.

The pattern of argument will be this. In relation to some kinds of activity we can properly impose on an agent not merely a prospective primary responsibility to Φ, or to take precautions against some risk, but a secondary prospective responsibility to make sure that he will be able to show that he has discharged that primary responsibility—to make sure, in other words, that he will be able to answer for his conduct in relation to

Baxter [1958] 1 QB 277); but these do not require the defendant to answer for his conduct, since proof of insanity or evidence of automatism would be proof or evidence that he could not be expected to answer for the conduct (on insanity see Ch 11.5 below).

the primary responsibility. A failure to discharge that secondary responsibility might itself be a wrong to which criminal liability can attach; but what is crucial here is that it can also help to prove that the agent has failed to discharge the primary responsibility.[51] When that is so, retrospective responsibility as to Φ-ing, or as to taking the required precautions, can legitimately be strict. This will be easiest to argue when the burden laid on the defendant (to provide a defence or to rebut a presumption) is evidential rather than persuasive; as we will see, it is less clear that this line of argument could justify imposing a persuasive burden on the defendant.

The kinds of activity in relation to which such additional responsibility could justifiably be imposed are those that involve special risks, more serious than the kinds of risk that should be accepted as part of ordinary life, and against which it is appropriate to demand that the agent take special precautions. Sometimes the risk is of material harm; sometimes it is of a wrong.

(a) Risks of Harm

Someone engages in an optional activity that is known to create risks of serious harm to others, beyond those accepted as unavoidable features of ordinary life: she owns a factory, for instance, in which her employees must use machinery that can cause serious injury.[52] She has a prospective responsibility to ensure the health and safety of her employees, and to maintain machinery that is 'safe and without risks to health'.[53] An employee is injured by a machine, and she faces a criminal charge under this statute. The prosecution proves that the machinery was not 'safe and without risks to health'—which is not hard, since it caused injury. Now the statute could have made liability for such an offence strict: proof that the machinery was not 'safe and without risks to health' would then have been sufficient to convict the employer. It does not do so, since the law requires employers to ensure safety only 'so far as is reasonably practicable'. But it does make criminal *responsibility* for lack of complete safety strict: once it is proved that the machinery was not in fact safe, the employer will be convicted unless she can show that she had taken all 'reasonably practicable steps' to ensure safety.[54]

How could this be justified? The law lays on the employer not only a primary prospective responsibility to take care for the safety of her employees, but a secondary responsibility to ensure that she will be able, if

[51] Thanks to Victor Tadros and Bob Sullivan for forcing me to get clearer about this point.

[52] For simplicity's sake I focus here only on individual, not corporate, liability.

[53] Health and Safety at Work etc Act 1974, s 2; see at nn 42–43 above.

[54] See *Nimmo v Alexander Cowan & Sons* [1968] AC 107.

necessary, to show that she took such care; she can discharge that secondary responsibility by instituting recorded procedures that will enable her to show that she had taken all practicable care—and the law could provide for authoritative regulation or guidance about what kinds of procedure are needed.[55] One question is whether a failure to discharge that secondary responsibility should itself constitute a criminalisable wrong. If it is reasonable to impose that responsibility on the employer (which depends on the seriousness of the risks involved, and on how burdensome it will be to discharge the responsibility), we can say that a failure to discharge it is in principle criminalisable. What the law requires of her, in requiring that she ensure safety, is that she make sure that she can *assure* herself and others with an interest in the matter (her employees, but also the polity as a whole) that she is doing all that is reasonably practicable, by showing what safety procedures she has in place. This is a reasonable requirement, when the activity involves special dangers, not just because it helps to ensure that her employees actually are safe, but also because what matters to us is not merely that we in fact be safe, but that we have the assurance of being safe.[56] We can say, then, that once such a regime of safety regulations and requirements is in place, the employer owes it to her employees, and to the polity at large, to provide such assurance—and that she commits what can properly count as a public wrong if she fails to do so.

This does not yet, of course, justify holding her strictly responsible for the injury suffered by her employee, or for the lack of complete safety that the injury revealed. However, we can justify that imposition of strict responsibility by showing that an employer who had properly discharged her prospective responsibility to assure safety would also thereby have equipped herself to answer for the accident to her employee by showing that she had done all that was 'reasonably practicable' to ensure safety. For the only way to ensure safety in a factory (as a matter both of common sense and of law, insofar as the law provides for codes of practice) is to operate verifiable procedures for using, checking and maintaining the machinery: without such procedures, the machinery might in fact be safe and be used safely, but its safety is not ensured. The employer's primary prospective responsibility to take care is thus not sharply separable from the secondary responsibility to make sure that she can show that she is taking and has taken care; a failure to discharge the latter proves a failure to discharge the former.

[55] See eg the provisions concerning written statements by employers in the Health and Safety at Work etc Act 1974, s 2(3), and those concerning health and safety regulations and codes of practice in ss 15–17.

[56] See Braithwaite and Pettit, 1990: 63 (liberty as the assured absence of constraint); Ch 7 at nn 90–92 above.

This seems true, at least, if the burden on the employer at trial is merely evidential:[57] if she had had proper safety procedures in place, she would now be able to provide evidence of this. In most cases she would also be able to discharge a persuasive burden: she would be able to produce the records of her safety procedures, to prove on the balance of probabilities that she had taken all reasonably practicable steps to ensure safety. But this might not always be so—perhaps a fire destroys all the records. We can therefore say that she should be able to avoid conviction by providing evidence that suffices to cast reasonable doubt on the charge that she failed to take reasonably practicable steps to ensure safety—with the rider that normally only proof on at least the balance of probabilities will suffice to create a reasonable doubt.

In imposing such a secondary prospective responsibility on the employer, and in holding her strictly retrospectively responsible for her machinery's lack of safety, we are imposing on her responsibilities more burdensome than is usual: but it is not unreasonable to impose such burdens, given the risks of harm created by her activity and the fact that the burden that the prospective responsibility imposes is not unduly heavy. If the imposition of such additional responsibilities is legitimate, we can also argue that what she is held criminally responsible for is a presumptive wrong; and that proof that the machinery was not in fact safe constitutes proof beyond reasonable doubt that she failed to take all 'reasonably practicable' steps to ensure safety, unless she can offer sufficient evidence that she took such steps.

In this context, 'a presumptive wrong' is something that can be legitimately presumed to be a wrong unless the defendant offers evidence to defeat that presumption.[58] As we saw in section 1, the causation of harm is not normally itself sufficient to constitute a presumptive wrong in this sense; but if the extra responsibilities that the law imposes on the factory owner are justified, the lack of safety (as proved by the accident) constitutes a presumptive wrong. Those responsibilities also make a difference to what counts as a 'reasonable doubt' of guilt. If the employer's only legal responsibility was to ensure safety, proof that her machinery was not wholly safe could not constitute proof beyond reasonable doubt that she had failed to take reasonably practicable steps to ensure its safety: the inferential gap between 'the machinery was unsafe' and 'it would have been reasonably practicable to make it safer' is too large for the former to constitute proof of the latter. But, given her secondary responsibility (and its relationship to that primary responsibility), we can say that, given evidence that the machinery was not in fact safe, the court would have

[57] See text preceding n 26 above.
[58] See Ch 9 at nn 100, 111 above.

good reason to doubt that she had failed to take all reasonably practicable steps only if she offered evidence that she had taken them.

Such an argument could also justify holding a shopkeeper strictly criminally responsible for selling food that actually failed to satisfy safety requirements,[59] but its limitations can be seen if we look at the case of driving. Driving creates risks of serious harm, and is an optional activity (though for many people not driving would constrain their lives quite seriously): why then should criminal responsibility not be strict in this context? Why should the law not be that, if a driver in fact causes harm to others, it is presumed that he was driving dangerously, unless he can adduce evidence to the contrary that suffices to create a reasonable doubt? Part of the answer is that even if driving is optional, it is ordinary rather than specialised, creating (when conducted with due care) risks that are acceptable as part of ordinary life.[60] Another part of the answer is that a driver who conscientiously discharges his responsibility to drive with due care does not thereby equip himself (as the factory owner does) to show that he has done so. Drivers do have duties of assurance towards others: obtaining licences and obeying the speed limit are two such duties,[61] and a failure to fulfil my duty not to speed is of course evidence of dangerous driving, whilst evidence that I was not speeding is evidence (albeit not persuasive) that I was not driving dangerously. We can also legitimately impose on citizens not merely a primary responsibility to make sure that they are competent to drive safely, but secondary responsibilities to do so by passing a driving test and to obtain and keep a licence that assures others one has done so: but failure to discharge those secondary responsibilities does not constitute good evidence, let alone presumptive proof, of dangerous driving on the particular occasion, in the way that the factory owner's inability to provide evidence of her safety procedures is good evidence that she failed to take reasonable steps to ensure safety.

(b) Risks of Wrong

The second kind of case in which strict criminal responsibility could be legitimate is that in which someone is engaged in conduct that is, on the basis of what he knows, legally risky: not because it creates a risk of physical harm, like the factory owner's activity, but because it raises a

[59] Food Safety Act 1990, ss 8, 21; see at n 29, and Ch 9 at nn 13, 110–11, above. Could a similar argument justify holding a licensee strictly responsible for her employee's actions in selling alcohol (see Ch 1 at nn 5–6 above)?

[60] But those who take a different, more hostile view of private driving might be more sympathetic to the suggestion that we should make responsibility for many driving offences strict.

[61] See Ch 7 at nn 90–93, 96–97 above.

serious doubt about whether it involves the commission of a criminal wrong. Suppose that *D* sexually penetrates *V* when *V* is, as *D* knows, unconscious or asleep. If *D* is on trial for rape, the court will presume that *V* did not consent, and that *D* did not reasonably believe that *V* consented, 'unless sufficient evidence is adduced to raise an issue' about whether *V* in fact consented, or about whether *D* reasonably believed that *V* consented.[62] *V*'s unconsciousness puts *D* on notice that what he is doing might well constitute the criminal wrong of rape; so the law can legitimately hold *D* responsible not only, as it holds all of us responsible, for refraining from rape, but also for ensuring that he has *V*'s consent, so that he will be able to offer both *V* and their fellow citizens a well-grounded assurance that he made every reasonable effort to avoid committing that wrong.

The sexual penetration of an unconscious person is not necessarily rape: it could be done with the person's consent, in a way that respects the person's autonomy. *V*'s unconsciousness does, however, create a strong presumption that the penetration is rape—the penetration is in that sense a presumptive wrong. Now we all have a responsibility to ensure that our sexual dealings with each other are consensual: that is why under English law rape now requires not an awareness that the victim might not be consenting, but simply the absence of a reasonable belief that the victim is consenting.[63] When the context, such as *V*'s unconsciousness, creates a presumption that the penetration is non-consensual, that responsibility is more stringent: someone acting with the minimal respect for others' sexual interests that we demand of each other would not proceed unless he had made sure that the penetration was consensual; and if he had made sure of that, he would both be acting on the reasonable belief that *V* consented, and be able to adduce evidence of that—evidence sufficient at least to 'raise an issue' about whether he had such a belief—by explaining his grounds for coming to that belief.

D has a primary responsibility to refrain from non-consensual sexual penetration, and to make sure (when there is any reason for doubt) that his sexual activity is consensual. He will usually have to answer for failing to discharge that primary responsibility only if it is proved that he failed to discharge it—only if the prosecution proves *ab initio* that the penetration was non-consensual and that he did not reasonably believe it to be

[62] Sexual Offences Act 2003, s 75; for apt criticism of this part of the Act (which does not affect the point to be made here), see Tadros, 2006a: 519–31. Compare also ss 16–19 of the Act, covering offences committed against someone who is under 18 by a person in a position of trust, and making responsibility strict as to the person's age: a similar argument would be relevant for those offences, though it would need adaptation in light of the fact that they are 'hybrid' offences (see Ch 7 at nn 86–89 above, and at nn 97–106 below).

[63] Sexual Offences Act 2003, s 1(1): contrast Sexual Offences (Amendment) Act 1976, s 1(1), as interpreted in the light of *Morgan* [1976] AC 182; see further at nn 65–67 below.

consensual: what he is called to answer for is sexually penetrating a non-consenting person without any reasonable belief that the person consented. However, when the context is such as to put him on notice that what he is doing might well constitute rape, he incurs the secondary responsibility to make sure that he will be able to answer for his conduct by doing all that he reasonably can to ensure that he is acting with *V*'s consent: he can then be called to answer for sexually penetrating someone who was, for instance, unconscious; and if he cannot offer an answer which explains why he had good reason to believe that *V* did consent, the court can properly conclude that he failed to discharge not only his secondary responsibility, but also his primary responsibility—that he is guilty of rape. Given the stringency of the responsibility to ensure that sexual activity is consensual, we can say, the only way to create a reasonable doubt about his guilt (to give the court what could count as good reason to doubt his guilt) is to provide evidence that he did have adequate grounds to believe that *V* consented.

The argument sketched above focused on *D*'s responsibility to provide evidence that he acted on the reasonable belief that *V* consented. The law also requires evidence to be adduced that *V* did consent, to rebut the presumption of non-consent: is this a responsibility that can legitimately be laid on *D* as the defendant? Of course, if *V* did consent, there would normally be no trial unless *V* was lying; and if *V* lies, the proved fact of her unconsciousness would as a matter of common sense give a court good enough reason to conclude that the penetration was non-consensual unless *D* can adduce evidence that it was consensual.[64] Evidence that *D* reasonably believed that *V* consented is also usually evidence that *V* consented: what gave *D* reason to believe that *V* consented also gives the court reason to believe that. As a matter of principle, however, we should not see it as being formally *D*'s responsibility to give evidence of *V*'s consent: it should still be the prosecution's responsibility to prove lack of consent (and of course *V*'s responsibility to declare consent); all that can be demanded of D is evidence of the steps taken to ensure consent, or of the grounds for believing in consent—evidence, that is, of a reasonable belief in consent.

This suggests a further, more radical, possibility: that the offence should be defined simply as non-consensual sexual penetration, proof of which would place on the defence the formal burden of adducing evidence that *D* acted on a reasonable belief that *V* consented. I suggested earlier that we could see the basic wrong in rape as non-consensual penetration,[65]

[64] This is not because unconsciousness is evidence from which the further fact of non-consent can be inferred, but because unconsciousness normally constitutes lack of consent. On the problems created by the 2003 Act's failure to distinguish evidential from constitutive issues see Tadros, 2006a: 525–31.

[65] See above, Ch 9 at n 109.

because we can properly say that the person who suffers that has been raped, and thus wronged, even if it was done in a non-culpably mistaken belief in consent: why should we not hold the person who commits (what is in fact) that wrong strictly responsible for its commission, so that the onus is on him to block the transition from responsibility to liability by giving an exculpatory answer; and hold that an exculpatory answer must provide evidence of a reasonable belief in consent?[66] This is of course what anyway happens de facto: if the prosecution proves lack of consent, the court will normally be entitled, as a matter of common sense, to conclude that *D* lacked a reasonable belief in consent. The reason for making it a formal matter of law would be primarily expressive: it would express our recognition of the fact that the non-consenting victim has been wronged, and of the stringency of the responsibility to ensure consent if there is any room for doubt about it—a responsibility such that a defendant who had discharged it would be able to offer appropriate evidence of having done so, by pointing to the very factors that gave reason to believe that *V* consented.[67]

In other cases, however, the arguments in favour of strict criminal responsibility are less persuasive. Consider again the presumption that a gift to a civil servant from someone who holds or seeks a government contract is 'given and received corruptly … unless the contrary is proved',[68] and suppose that the burden on the defendant is lightened from persuasive to evidential: is it reasonable to hold a civil servant strictly criminally responsible for accepting such gifts? Such gifts are of course liable to arouse reasonable suspicion of corruption, and it would normally be relatively easy for the non-corrupt civil servant to adduce the necessary evidence—most obviously by showing that she had no connection to or possible influence on the contract that the donor held or sought: but should the mere fact of the gift be sufficient to create a presumption of guilt in this way? I suspect not: we surely need stronger grounds than that before we can presume someone to be corrupt and demand—on pain of conviction for a serious wrong—that she provide evidence that she is not corrupt.

It might be argued that, given the danger of corruption, it would in principle be legitimate to make it a criminal offence for public officials

[66] For the reasons suggested earlier (text preceding n 26 above), the defendant's burden should be evidential, not persuasive.

[67] Only in very few imaginable kinds of case would proven lack of consent leave room for a reasonable belief in consent—a belief based on grounds adequate to justify acting on it: but we can imagine a case in which *V* mistakenly believes *D* to be a violent attacker (based not on *D*'s conduct, but *D*'s likeness to a picture on the news of a dangerous rapist), and *D* not unreasonably mistakes *V*'s submission for consent.

[68] See Prevention of Corruption Act 1916, s 2; see at n 40, and text preceding n 48, above.

simply to accept gifts from those holding or seeking public contracts; that the actual law is more lenient than that, in allowing a defendant to avert liability by adducing evidence that the gift was not received corruptly; and that it is therefore surely legitimate, as bearing less harshly on defendants than would that alternative, legitimate law.[69] But the criminal wrong under that alternative law would not be corruption: it would be conduct that created a reasonable suspicion of corruption. We might have reason to criminalise such conduct: for the sake of maintaining public trust, officials should accept the (minor) burden of refusing all gifts from actual or would-be contractors. We could criminalise such conduct, but allow a defence of non-corruption as to which the defendant would bear an evidential burden. But if the offence is corruption (as it is under our actual law), the prosecution should have to provide more by way of proof of that than the mere receipt of a gift from a contractor if it is to prove that the defendant committed a presumptive wrong of that kind.

(c) Abusing Strict Criminal Responsibility

I have sketched a pattern of argument that could, I suggested, justify some impositions of strict criminal responsibility. My aim has not been to show that that argument is persuasive in the examples I have discussed, but to show that this is the kind of argument, concerning the responsibilities that the polity can properly impose on its citizens, that must be mounted if the imposition of strict criminal responsibility is to be justified in a way that makes it consistent with the Presumption of Innocence and with the idea of offences as presumptive wrongs. I do not suppose that many of the existing provisions for strict responsibility will be justifiable in this way: more often, no doubt, strict responsibility is used as an unprincipled device to make the prosecution's task easier and thus, supposedly, to assist the 'war on crime'. The argument of this section, however, should help us not only to justify those impositions of strict criminal responsibility that are justifiable, but also to see more clearly just what is wrong with those that are not justifiable. This point can be illustrated by looking, once more, at the provisions of section 57 of the Terrorism Act 2000 to see how they constitute an abuse, rather than a legitimate application, of strict criminal responsibility.[70]

[69] Compare the American doctrine of 'the greater power includes the lesser': if the legislature could make it a criminal offence to Φ, it can legitimately criminalise instead that sub-category of Φ-ings that also involve Ψ-ing, and specify that proof of Φ-ing is rebuttable proof of Ψ-ing: see Jeffries and Stephan, 1979: 1345–7.

[70] See at n 31 above. See also Civic Government (Scotland) Act 1982, s 57: above Introduction at n 42, Ch 9 at n 15.

The wrong at which section 57 is, according to its title, aimed is 'possession for terrorist purposes'. If the supposed wrong was the mere possession of items that could assist terrorists (though such a wrong would be absurdly broad in its scope), we could envisage a law which made such possession an offence, whilst allowing proof or evidence of lack of any purpose to assist terrorism as a defence;[71] but if what the defendant faces conviction for is a wrong that ascribes a terrorist purpose to him, we must ask what the prosecution should have to prove if it is to prove at least the presumptive commission of such a wrong—which is to ask about the responsibilities that we can reasonably impose on each other. We could justify this section if we could claim that citizens have a responsibility, not merely not to acquire or keep items for terrorist purposes, but not to acquire or keep items in ways that could, given their particular circumstances, give rise to a reasonable suspicion that they were pursuing terrorist purposes; that someone whose possession does give rise to such a reasonable suspicion therefore has a responsibility to ensure that he can give evidence that his purposes were innocent; *and* that a failure to discharge that latter responsibility could be treated as conclusive evidence that he had failed to discharge the responsibility not to acquire or keep items for terrorist purposes—ie as conclusive evidence that he did have them for terrorist purposes. We have only to spell these claims out to see how absurd they would be. A civil servant who accepts a gift from a contractor acts in a way that could, depending on the circumstances, give rise to a reasonable suspicion of corruption, but we have seen that we cannot properly turn such a suspicion into proof by placing on the defendant the burden of rebutting it; the same is true when someone's possession of an item gives rise to a reasonable suspicion of terrorist purposes.[72]

I am not suggesting that those who drafted this section saw it in these terms, as imposing such stringent responsibilities on citizens: they no doubt saw it as a way of assisting the 'war on terror' by making the prosecution's task easier—and would no doubt argue that we must rely on police and prosecutorial good sense and discretion not to prosecute those who are not (probably) truly guilty. The point is, rather, that such claims

[71] Compare the provisions of s 58 of the Act, concerning the collection or recording of information likely to be of use to terrorists, but allowing a defence of 'reasonable excuse' for such collection or possession.

[72] Indeed, unless the grounds that make the suspicion 'reasonable' are firmly tied to the defendant's conduct (and not, for instance, to his ethnic origin or religion), the argument for imposing strict responsibility in the case of terrorists is even weaker than that for doing so in the case of corruption. Similar criticisms can be made of the provisions of s 57(3), allowing the court to 'assume' that the defendant possessed any article that was on premises in which he was or which he owned or habitually used, thus placing on him the burden of proving that he was unaware of the article or had no control of it.

about our responsibilities must be made by anyone who wants to claim that this section defines what can properly count as an offence (as a presumptive wrong), in a way that is consistent with a substantive reading of the Presumption of Innocence: the utter implausibility of such claims brings out very clearly the reason why it is impossible to provide a plausible principled defence of this section.

I have argued so far that we should attend not only to strict criminal liability, but also to strict criminal responsibility—provisions which, whether by the use of legal presumptions or by defining as defences what would normally count as negations of an element of the offence, seem to require defendants to answer for their conduct before it has been proved to constitute a presumptive criminal wrong. Instead of the prosecution having directly to prove all aspects of the offence, including mens rea (a failure to take all reasonably practicable steps to ensure safety in a factory; the lack of a reasonable belief in *V*'s consent), the defendant carries the burden of proving or adducing evidence that he was not at fault in the relevant way. Although such provisions are no doubt often used simply as an unprincipled device to make it easier to secure convictions, I have argued that some of them can in principle be justified, and shown to be consistent with the fundamental principle that it should be for the prosecution to prove beyond reasonable doubt that the defendant committed a presumptive criminal wrong before he can be required to answer for his conduct on pain of conviction if he cannot provide an exculpatory answer.

Such provisions do not impose either formally or substantively strict criminal liability;[73] it is to strict liability that we must now turn.

4. Justifying Formally Strict Criminal Liability

I will not try to justify substantively strict criminal liability, which mandates conviction without proof of fault that would justify condemning the defendant for committing a wrong; it is flatly inconsistent with the principle that criminal conviction should require proof of the commission of a presumptive wrong.[74] I will argue, however, that formally strict liability can sometimes be justified, so long as the strictness is *merely* formal. Strictness is merely formal if, although there is a formal gap between the p that the prosecution must prove and the q that would

[73] On formal and substantive strictness see at nn 14–23 above.

[74] Someone charged with a strict liability offence can plead a general defence such as duress or necessity (see *Martin* [1989] 1 All ER 652; Simester and Sullivan, 2007: 178): but liability is still strict as not requiring explicit proof of mens rea as to every aspect of the offence.

constitute true guilt, there is no substantive, normative gap: there is no genuine space for the defendant to admit that *p* and yet deny that *q*; proof that *p* constitutes proof, beyond what could count as reasonable doubt, that *q*.

The possible justifiability of formally strict liability can be initially illustrated by looking at doctrines of constructive liability: these will provide a basis on which we can make sense of doctrines of non-constructive strict liability, when there is no lesser offence out of which liability for the more serious offence can be constructed.[75]

(a) Constructive Liability

Consider a version of the English doctrine of 'implied malice'. If *D* attacks *V* intending to cause grievous bodily harm, and the attack kills the victim, that is murder.[76] This involves formally strict liability, since no mens rea need be explicitly proved as to the death that is an essential element of the offence: but liability is constructive, since the prosecution must prove both subjective and objective dimensions of the lesser offence of wounding with intent to do grievous bodily harm;[77] if the commission of that offence causes death, the objective aspect of murder, liability for murder is constructed out of liability for the lesser offence. Those who oppose such constructive liability will argue that murder should require at least recklessness as to the risk that one's attack will cause death, constituted by an awareness of that risk; they will appeal to the correspondence principle,[78] and to the orthodox subjectivist definition of recklessness as conscious risk-taking. A principled justification of such constructive liability would argue that there is no need for explicit proof of recklessness as to death, if the intention to cause serious injury is proved: to engage in such an attack *is* to be reckless of the victim's life.[79]

If *D* is proved to have attacked *V*, intending at least to cause serious injury, is there room for him still to argue that he was not reckless of *V*'s

[75] See at nn 24–25 above.

[76] See Ormerod, 2005: 437. On the need for an attack, for the action to be 'aimed at' someone, see *DPP v Smith* [1961] AC 290, at 327 (*per* Viscount Kilmuir); and *Hyam* [1975] AC 55, at 79 (*per* Lord Hailsham). The Law Commission (2006: paras 1.67, 2.70–2.94) proposed that this should constitute second degree murder.

[77] Offences Against the Person Act 1861, s 18. I ignore complications about the meaning of 'grievous bodily harm' (see Law Commission, 2006: paras 2.82–2.94 on its preferred notion of 'serious injury'): for present purposes, we need say only that, even if 'grievous' is not defined as 'life-threatening', we must understand grievous bodily harm as being serious enough to involve a not insignificant risk of death.

[78] See eg Criminal Law Revision Committee, 1980: para 31; Ashworth, 2006: 257–62. On the correspondence principle see at n 2 above.

[79] For an argument in support of this conception of recklessness see Duff, 1990a: ch 7; Ch 7 at nn 34–36 above.

life? He cannot argue that he exercised 'due diligence' to avoid killing *V*:[80] that would have involved refraining from the attack. This does not yet justify a conviction for anything more than manslaughter by gross negligence in an unlawful act.[81] But we can argue that he was reckless of V's life. For either he realised that his attack would inevitably endanger *V*'s life, or he did not. If he noticed it, even subjectivists would call him reckless. If he did not notice it, we must ask how he could not have attended to something so closely (morally) connected to his intended action. The only possible answer is that he did not care about his victim's life: he acted with the kind of 'practical indifference' as to whether his victim lived or died that properly counts as recklessness.[82] That is why the formally strict liability involved in the doctrine of implied malice is not substantively strict: what must be proved (an intended serious attack) also proves the necessary fault as to death.[83]

We could achieve the same result through an irrebuttable legal presumption: adapting the Model Penal Code, we could provide that, given proof of an attack intended to cause serious injury, it is to be irrebuttably or conclusively presumed that the defendant was reckless of his victim's life.[84] As we noted, however, such irrebuttable presumptions are better understood as definitional or constitutive specifications:[85] talk of 'presumptions' might misleadingly imply that the recklessness is a further fact to be inferred from the intended attack, rather than being constituted by the attack.[86] If we want to make explicit the mens rea required, and how it can be proved, we could simply specify a constitutive rule: the law's definition of constructive murder would then require recklessness as to the risk of death, and would explicitly provide that such recklessness is displayed by someone who attacks another intending to cause grievous bodily harm.

[80] On defences of 'due diligence' see at note 29 above; Ashworth, 2006: 165–6.

[81] See Simester and Sullivan, 2007: 372–83.

[82] This is not an (inadequately based) causal explanation of his failure to notice the risk, but an interpretation of what that failure means: the failure is related constitutively, not causally, to the lack of care.

[83] On constructive liability see also Simons, 1997: 1105–20; Horder, 1995; Michaels, 1999: 891–3; Simester, 2005: 44–6. Some who are sympathetic to the doctrine of implied malice would argue that whilst *D* need not notice any risk of death, the injury he intends must be such as to create an obvious and serious risk of death, whether as a matter of the definition of 'grievous bodily harm' or as an additional requirement (see Duff, 1990a: 173–9; Law Commission, 2006: paras 2.88–2.94): this would still involve constructive liability.

[84] See Model Penal Code, s 210.2(1)(b) on what grounds a presumption of 'extreme indifference to the value of human life'. See also the Scottish doctrine of 'wicked recklessness' (Gordon, 2000: 295–310), which is displayed if death is 'within the range of the natural and probable consequences' of the attack (at 304, quoting Lord Wheatley in *Miller and Denovan* (1960)).

[85] See at nn 44–47 above.

[86] Compare also the confusions caused in English law by judicial talk of 'inferring' an intention to bring *x* about from foresight of *x* as a virtually certain effect of my action (see Ormerod, 2005: 94–7).

Constructive liability is constructed out of an underlying crime, for which fault is proved in the usual way: constructive liability for murder depends on non-constructive liability for a violent attack, intrinsic to which is a risk of the more serious harm that turns wounding into murder.[87] But can we justify strict liability which is not constructed out of an existing crime? There is a pattern of argument that, if it can be plausibly instantiated, would achieve this: it would show how formally strict (non-constructive) liability could be substantively non-strict.

(b) Justifying Formally Strict Liability

Suppose that the legislature decriminalises the supply (as well as the possession) of drugs that are now 'controlled' under the Misuse of Drugs Act 1971—not because it is persuaded that drug dealing is not a 'public' wrong, but because it realises that attempts to enforce the existing law are ineffective, and probably do more harm than good. However, drug dealing is not put wholly beyond the reach of the criminal law: new offences are created concerning a list of dangerous drugs—an offence of supplying drugs the impurity of which makes them more dangerous to users, an offence of supplying drugs that cause death; liability for such offences is legally strict as to the impurity of the drug or as to the death that it causes. Conviction thus depends on proof of intentional supply of what the defendant knew to be one of the specified drugs, but no other mens rea need be proved. Could such provisions be justified?[88]

We have laws that criminalise recklessly dangerous conduct, but only if it actually causes the relevant harm: an agent who is reckless as to whether her conduct will damage another's property is guilty of criminal damage if it causes damage, but might be guilty of no offence if it does not.[89] This is not an offence of strict liability: but it exemplifies a pattern that will help to make sense of certain types of strict liability.

First, there is a type of conduct—recklessly endangering property—that we have reason to criminalise. Secondly, our reasons for not criminalising

[87] See Simester and Sullivan, 2007: 187–91 on 'intrinsic' as against 'extrinsic' luck. On how criminal liability can properly depend on such matters of moral luck see Duff, 1996: 327–47.

[88] Compare Husak, 2005d: ss 1, 4; Simester, 2005: 46–9. Such provisions cannot be simply justified by the 'greater-includes-the lesser' doctrine (see n 69 above)—that since the legislature could criminalise drug-dealing as such, it could legitimately criminalise those sub-categories of drug dealing that involve impure drugs or death: what we need to justify is convicting the dealers of supplying impure drugs or of causing death (compare Husak, 2005d: s 3, on proportionality).

[89] See Criminal Damage Act 1971, s. 1(1): only 'might' because she might be guilty of a specific offence of endangerment (see the examples collected in Glazebrook, 2006: Pt V); she would not be guilty of the general endangerment offences in the Model Penal Code (s 211.2) or in Scots law (Gordon, 2000: 427–30).

that type of conduct as such have to do not with its not being wrongful in a way that properly concerns the criminal law, but with more pragmatic concerns about the difficulties and costs of enforcement, and about whether the benefits of creating such an offence would outweigh its costs.[90] Thirdly, we do criminalise that type of behaviour under the further condition that it actually brings about some harm the prospect of which provided an important part of the reason for criminalising it (actual damage to another's property). What the criminal law now says to those who engage in such conduct is that they do so at their own (as well as at their prospective victims') risk: if they are lucky, and cause no damage, they escape liability; if they are unlucky, and cause damage, they are criminally as well as civilly liable. They are given fair warning of their potential liability, on what is surely an uncontroversial version of the 'thin ice' principle that 'those who skate on thin ice can hardly expect to find a sign which will denote the precise spot where [they] will fall in'.[91] Although the law does specify 'the precise spot where they will fall in', the spot at which damage is caused,[92] that specification does not enable agents to identify it precisely in advance: but they can avoid criminal liability by refraining—*as they anyway should refrain*—from their reckless conduct.

The drug dealer's position is analogous to this, *if* we can say that dealing in the specified drugs already involves an appropriate kind of fault in relation to the harm that this might cause, and the causation of which makes a dealer criminally liable. Whether we can say that depends, of course, on controversial claims about the dangers of using certain types of drug, and about whether or why drug-dealing can properly concern the criminal law, but we need not assess such claims here:[93] the point is that *if* they are true, if the use of the specified drugs is dangerous enough to ground an in principle case for criminalising their supply, we can say that drug-dealing in itself displays the appropriate kind of fault, so long as the dangers are well enough publicised so that anyone engaged in drug dealing could reasonably be expected to be aware of them. Anyone who then deals in such drugs thereby shows herself to be at least negligent as to the risk they create: for, whilst in other activities one can take 'due care' in carrying them out, in this case (the law tells us) one takes 'due care' only by abandoning the activity. *D* cannot admit that she was dealing in drugs and claim that she was taking due care not to endanger life: there is no such thing as 'duly diligent drug dealing'. Drug dealers are thus given fair

[90] It thus passes the first of Schonsheck's three 'filters' on the way to criminalisation, but not the second or third filter: Schonsheck, 1994: 63–83.

[91] *Knuller v DPP* [1973] AC 435, at 463 (*per* Lord Morris); see Ashworth, 2006: 73–4.

[92] Whereas the worry in *Knuller* was that it was not clear what kind of conduct would fall under the offence of 'conspiracy to corrupt public morals' (an offence that I am not seeking to justify).

[93] See Husak, 1992; also Alldridge, 1996.

warning that if they embark on this activity they do so at their own, as well as their customers', risk: if they are lucky, they will escape liability; but if they are unlucky, they will be criminally liable —and cannot complain that this is unfair.[94]

This hypothetical argument about drug-dealing exemplifies a pattern of argument that could justify imposing formally strict liability, by showing that the liability is substantively non-strict. We identify a type of conduct that we have good reason to criminalise, but that we do not criminalise in itself, for reasons unrelated to its wrongfulness. We show that anyone intentionally engaged in such conduct thereby displays a relevant kind of fault in relation to a harm that it is liable to cause, and that provides part of the reason for criminalising it. We can then define an offence of causing such harm by such conduct, and make liability for that offence formally strict as to the occurrence of the harm. This is a formal, not a substantive, strictness, since any intentional engagement in the conduct constitutes substantive fault as to that harm: those convicted of the strict liability offence have been proved, beyond reasonable doubt, to be substantively guilty.[95] By contrast, while we might legitimately hold a shopkeeper strictly responsible for selling unfit food,[96] it would be unjust to hold her strictly liable: she must be given a chance to offer evidence of due diligence, since we cannot say that we have reason to criminalise selling food, or that to engage in that activity is to display a lack of due diligence, or that she could avoid liability by refraining, as she anyway should, from selling food.

(c) Formally Strict Liability: Some Problems

Another example will illustrate some of the problems that formally strict liability, as thus rationalised, can create. Sections 5–12 of the Sexual Offences Act 2003 make liability as to the victim's age formally strict in offences involving children under 13. To justify these provisions, we should identify an underlying intentional activity that we have good reason to criminalise (one that can properly be condemned as a 'public' wrong), engagement in which displays an appropriate kind of fault in relation to the mischief at which the law is aimed (a mischief itself connected to the aspect of the offence as to which liability is strict). In the case of drug

[94] For an actual example, though I cannot discuss its complexities here, see the money laundering provisions in 18 USC s 1956 (thanks to Alan Michaels for pointing me towards this example).

[95] The argument has affinities with Michaels' (1999) argument about when strict liability is constitutionally permissible: his concern, however, is with constitutionality, whereas mine is with justice, and whether we have good reasons of principle to criminalise the relevant kind of conduct; and constitutionality does not guarantee justice.

[96] See Food Safety Act 1990, ss 8, 21; and at nn 29, 59 above.

dealing, the activity is dealing in one of the specified drugs, which displays at least negligence as to the risk of death, the mischief at which the law is supposedly aimed. In the case of sexual activity with under-age children, however, the initial task of identifying the mischief presents two problems.[97]

First, 'under 13' is an artificial stipulation of the aspect of the offence as to which liability is strict, which does not purport to define the mischief. That mischief is the danger of psychological or moral harm to those who are led into sexual activity before they have gained sufficient maturity to make rational decisions about it, but for good reasons the law does not define the offence in those terms. It stipulates a precise age, though we know that some below that age are precociously mature, while some over that age are still immature (although those between 13 and 16 are also protected).[98] Secondly, there are at least two different paradigms of sexual activity involving children.[99] One is of children of similar ages mutually engaged in sexual experimentation; the other is of an older person exploiting a much younger person. Since the cases for criminalisation, and for strict liability as to the victim's age, are stronger in relation to the second paradigm, I will focus on that.[100]

'The man who has connexion with a child, relying on her consent, does it at his peril, if she is below the statutable age'.[101] So is 'sexual activity with a child' the relevant underlying activity? This is too vague a specification to meet 'rule of law' demands for certainty, whilst more precise specifications—'fornication', for instance—will not pick out conduct that we have good reason to criminalise.[102] However, this is not a fatal problem: for the impossibility of precise specification of the conduct does not rebut the claim that we have in principle good reason to criminalise it.[103] Why then should we not say that any adult who engages in sexual activity with someone he knows to be a child can be held strictly liable if the child is under 13, since he thereby displays a negligent, even reckless, lack of care for the possibility that … but that what? That the

[97] See Horder, 2001.

[98] By ss 9–12 of the Act: if *V* is over 13 but under 16, conviction requires proof that *D* did not reasonably believe *V* to be 16 or over. See further Ch 7 at nn 86–87, 93–94 above.

[99] See the comments in *B v DPP* [2000] 2 AC 428 by Lord Nicholls (at 464), and Lord Steyn (at 472).

[100] This suggests that the law should specify not just the child's age, but also the defendant's age: see eg the Washington Criminal Code, 9A 44.073, 076, 079; and compare Sexual Offences Act 1956, s 6(3).

[101] *Prince* (1875) LR 2 CCR 154, at 172 (*per* Blackburn J); and see at n 21 above.

[102] Fletcher (see Ch 9.3(a) above) might argue this—but not plausibly.

[103] See at n 90 above.

child is under 13? But that is not the mischief.[104] That the child is not mature? But perhaps he has good reason to believe that she is mature enough.

This problem might be resolved by a suitable account of why citizens should respect laws that contain such artificial stipulations of criminal conduct:[105] if part of the rationale for such stipulations is that citizens should not trust themselves to make such substantive judgements as whether their intended sexual partner is mature enough, the child's age becomes a guiding reason to which the would-be sexual partner should pay careful attention. But can we really say that any adult who intentionally engages in sexual activity with a child thereby culpably fails to attend as he should to the possibility that the child is under 13, and so properly takes the risk of criminal liability if the child is actually under 13—a risk he could avoid by refraining, as he anyway should refrain, from that activity? Can the thin ice principle save us from the charge that such a specification of the activity from which people should anyway refrain is intolerably vague?

We could rely on that principle only if 'child', despite its vagueness, would be generally so understood that anyone who was actually under 13 would obviously count as a child: only then would the potential defendant be put on notice, by the character of his intentional activity, that he should attend carefully to the child's age. We must, however, doubt whether this condition is met: not just because 'child' is vague, but because the appearance, clothes and behaviour of children can be quite misleading as to their true age.

One solution, given that there are also offences of sexual conduct with children under 16, for which the prosecution must prove that the defendant did not reasonably believe the victim to be 16 or over,[106] would be to make liability as to the age of a child who is actually under 13 constructive rather than strict: that is, a defendant should be guilty of an offence involving a child under 13 only on proof that he engaged in the relevant sexual activity, and did not reasonably believe the child to be 16 or over. Assume, for the sake of the argument, that sexual activity between adults and children involves danger (of exploitation, of consequential harms) that make its criminalisation legitimate; that the lack of a reasonable belief that the other person is over 16 is an appropriate mens rea as to age; and that 'under 13' is a reasonable (albeit, like 'under 16', artificial) stipulation of the age that makes the offence more serious in a way that merits formal recognition. We then have an underlying offence, sexual activity with

[104] Compare Horder, 2001, on how a child's being under or over 13 is not a 'guiding reason'.

[105] See above, Ch 7.3.

[106] Sexual Offences Act 2003 ss 9–12; see n 98 above.

someone under 16, which we have good reason to criminalise, for which fault must be proved. One who commits that offence thereby displays an appropriate fault, not only in relation to the risk that the other person is under 16, but also in relation to the risk that the other person is under 13; he takes the risk of being liable not just for an offence involving a child under 16, but for a more serious offence involving a child under 13—a risk which he could have avoided by refraining, as he anyway should have refrained, from that activity. It is therefore legitimate to hold him constructively liable for the more serious offence.

Once again, my concern is not to show that such an offence would be justified: we might agree that the criminal law should condemn exploitative sexual relationships between adults and children, but also think that in this context chronological age is too unreliably correlated with sexual maturity to serve even as an artificial rule-based stipulation of the wrong. My aim has rather been to display the pattern of reasoning by which formally strict criminal liability could in principle sometimes be justified—whilst also indicating how rarely that justification is likely to be available in practice.

We have been concerned in this chapter with some of the ways in which the simple, orthodox distinction between offences and defences is blurred or undermined. Offences are, or should be, presumptive wrongs for which a defendant can properly be called to answer in a criminal court, on pain of conviction and condemnation if she cannot offer an exculpatory answer, if it is proved beyond reasonable doubt that she committed such a wrong. Defences are pleas by which she can then block the presumptive transition from responsibility to liability. Doctrines of strict responsibility and strict liability threaten to undermine that distinction by weakening the idea of an offence—in particular by not requiring the prosecution to prove mens rea as to all objective aspects of the offence (whereas on the simple reading offences, as presumptive wrongs, must include both actus reus and mens rea): doctrines of strict responsibility lay on the defendant the burden (whether evidentiary or persuasive) of showing the absence of what would normally count as *mens rea* (ie as an aspect of the offence itself); doctrines of strict liability make conviction formally independent of either proof or disproof of mens rea as to some aspect of the offence.

It has not been my aim to defend any particular doctrines either of strict responsibility or of strict liability. My aim has rather been to clarify their logic, as doctrines concerning what citizens can properly be called to answer for in criminal courts, and what kinds of exculpatory answer should be available to them; to show the importance of strict criminal responsibility as an increasingly prominent aspect of our criminal law; and to explicate the ways in which doctrines of strict responsibility and of formally strict liability could in principle be justified. As the discussion in this section should have made clear, I do not suppose that such doctrines (especially those of formally strict liability) will often be justified; nor do I suppose that they are in fact typically introduced because they are thought to be justified in the ways outlined here—they are more often introduced as pragmatic, unprincipled devices to make it easier for prosecutors to obtain convictions. It is nonetheless important to see how they could, at least in principle, be justified: partly to guard against the idea that they must, as a matter of principle, be rejected wholesale; partly to equip ourselves with an appropriate normative framework for the critique of such doctrines in our existing law.

It is time now, finally, to turn our attention to defences as normally understood: to the ways in which a defendant who is proved to have committed a presumptive wrong, with whatever intention, knowledge, recklessness or negligence is properly required for liability, can nonetheless avert conviction by admitting responsibility but denying liability.

11

Understanding Defences

The prosecution has discharged its initial probative burden: it has proved beyond reasonable doubt that the defendant committed the offence charged—that she intentionally wounded or killed another person, for instance, or intentionally damaged another's property. In proving that, it has proved her criminal responsibility: if she is to avoid conviction, she must block the presumptive transition from responsibility to liability by offering a defence.[1] The task of this chapter is to clarify the logical structure of defences, as exculpatory answers for the commission of the offence for which responsibility has been proved.

By 'defence' here, as in Chapter 9, I mean a plea that does not deny responsibility for the offence charged, but claims that further relevant factors should block liability. Some theorists use 'defence' in a wider sense, to include pleas that deny responsibility—'failure of proof' or 'offence modification' defences that deny an element of the offence;[2] and 'non-exculpatory' defences that bar trial.[3] I am using it in the narrower sense that Fletcher, drawing on German legal theory, helped to embed in Anglo-American theorising.[4] Defences in that narrower sense are usually divided into justifications and excuses, in line with the German framework:[5] justifications deny *Rechtswidrigkeit* or wrongfulness, excuses deny *Schuld* or culpability. The use of that distinction has been criticised, on the ground that it cannot be drawn clearly, and therefore can play no useful role in the deliberations of criminal courts.[6] I will argue that the problem is not that the distinction is not significant and important, but that we need more than one distinction: needless confusion has been bred by

[1] English law formally includes the absence of a defence in the definition of the offence of criminal damage: the offence is committed only if *D* damages another's property 'without lawful excuse' (Criminal Damage Act 1971, s 1), and 'lawful excuses' clearly include the general common law defences (see Ormerod, 2005: 900–11). My concern here is with underlying logic rather than with form; but see at nn 31, 69 below.

[2] Robinson, 1984: i, 72–82; see Simester and Sullivan, 2007: 606–7.

[3] Robinson, 1984: i, 102–4; see Ch 8.2 above.

[4] See especially Fletcher, 1978.

[5] See Ch 9 at nn 37–41 above; Fletcher, 1978: chs 7, 9–10; also Fletcher, 1975, 1985.

[6] See especially Greenawalt, 1984, 1986.

attempts to fit all defences into a simple two-part schema of 'justification' and 'excuse'. After an initial discussion of the orthodox distinction between justification and excuse, and of justification in the context of beliefs, I will argue in section 3 that we can resolve one persisting controversy about that distinction, that of 'putative justifications', by introducing the idea of 'warranted' action. Section 4 deals with another persisting controversy, about 'unknown justifications'; its resolution requires a clearer grasp of the distinction between elements of the offence and justifications.[7] Sections 5–6 then deal with excuses: section 5 with the distinction between excuses and exemptions, and section 6 with that between reasonable and unreasonable mistakes.

1. Distinguishing Justification from Excuse

JL Austin suggested that in justifying an action 'we accept responsibility but deny that it was bad'; in excusing 'we admit that it was bad but don't accept full, or even any responsibility'.[8] One could quarrel both with 'bad' (a justified action could still be regrettable, or the lesser of two clear evils) and with 'responsibility' (since, we will see, to offer an excuse is precisely to answer for my action, ie to admit responsibility). Others put the distinction differently:

> [T]o say that an action is justified is to say … that though the action is of a type that is usually wrong, in these circumstances it was not wrong. To say that an action is excused, by contrast, is to say that it was indeed wrong (and the agent did commit the act we are saying was wrong), but the agent is not blameworthy.[9]

There is also room for argument about this way of specifying the distinction. Justifications do claim, and if successful show,[10] that the action was all things considered at least permissible; but we saw earlier that justified actions can still be properly described as wrongs.[11] Complete excuses do show that the agent was not blameworthy, and admit (at least by implication) that the action was wrong—something that the agent

[7] This will allow me to correct some errors in Duff, 2004b; thanks to Victor Tadros for helping me see them.

[8] Austin, 1961: 125.

[9] Baron, 2005: 389–90; see also Fletcher, 1978: 759; Robinson, 1997: 82, 96; Dressler, 2006: 218–19.

[10] We can talk of justifications and excuses as pleas that may or may not succeed (I offer a justification or excuse, which might or might not be accepted or acceptable); or as pleas that actually succeed, whether or not they should; or as pleas that should succeed, whether or not they actually do. I will use 'justification' and 'excuse' in the rest of this chapter in the third of these ways.

[11] See Ch 9.4 above.

should not have done;[12] but they also affect our understanding of the character of the wrong as committed by that agent in that context. When we learn that *D* committed perjury under exculpatory duress,[13] we can still say that she committed the wrong of perjury and should ideally not have done so; but we understand her action of lying to the court, as a token of that type of wrong, as differing significantly in its moral character from other tokens of that type. Although we might say that excuses block the attribution of the wrong to the agent, we should not try to draw too sharp or firm a distinction between the wrong that is or is not attributed and the agent to whom it is or is not attributed.[14]

We could alternatively say that an action is justified if it is, on balance and all things (that is, all relevant things) considered, right or permissible; and that it is excused if, although it was one that the agent should not (on balance and all things considered) have done, and although she is answerable for it, there were features of the action's context or of the agent given which it would be unjust or unfair for those to whom she is answerable to blame or condemn her for it.[15] However, I will argue in what follows that if we are to understand the range of defences and their different logical structures, we need to draw more distinctions than this. This will enable us to resolve some persisting controversies about the distinction between justifications and excuses, by showing how those on both sides of the controversy are engaged in a futile, procrustean attempt to force all defences into one of these two categories. One might indeed suggest that the orthodox distinction between justifications and excuses is now so misleading, given the assumption that it provides an exhaustive classification of defences, that we should abandon the terms altogether, and find a new set of terms that will do more accurate, and less misleading, justice to the different types of defence.[16] That would be an unnecessarily drastic solution: we can retain the terms 'justification' and

[12] Although outside the criminal law, excuses can negate wrongdoing altogether: when responsibility is strict, the fact that I broke your vase through non-culpable inadvertence or accident constitutes an excuse; but if I have such an excuse I did no wrong in breaking the vase, though I did do what I had conclusive reason not to do. See Ch 9 at nn 93–98 above.

[13] See *Hudson and Taylor* [1971] 2 QB 202.

[14] See further Duff, 2002a: 61–8; also Dressler, 1988: n 37. On excuses as blocking attribution see Fletcher, 1978: chs 6.6–6.7, 10.3.

[15] Some would argue that this is also misleading since, whilst justifications attach to actions, excuses attach to agents: see eg Husak, 1989b: 496–7; by contrast, Baron (2005) argues that justifications attach to agents. I prefer at this stage to talk indiscriminately of actions being justified or excused, or of agents being justified in or excused for acting as they did; we will see in later sections how far the conditions for justification or excuse involve the action's context or the agent (which is the crucial issue).

[16] Compare Colvin 1990, suggesting 'contextual permission' and 'mental impairment'; but, for reasons that will emerge later, neither this two-part schema nor these labels are adequate.

'excuse'; but we should also recognise 'warrants' as close relatives of 'justifications', and classify some of what have traditionally been called 'excuses' as 'exemptions'.

Before embarking on that argument, I should note two preliminary points. First, I assume that the justified includes the permissible. Outside the law, this is clearly true: the category of justified conduct includes conduct that is permissible as well as conduct that is required of us. I cancel a class that I am due to teach because I am ill—not so ill that it would be impossible for me to teach the class, but ill enough for it to be reasonable to decide to stay in bed. Now in some cases it might be true, and others might agree, that I should stay in bed—it would be seriously imprudent to endanger my health further by dragging myself to a class that was not important enough to warrant such sacrifice; or I owe it to others not to risk infecting them. In other cases, however, when the illness is less serious, it might be that turning up to teach my class would have displayed admirable devotion to my teaching, 'far beyond the call of duty'; but I am not required or expected to turn up—staying in bed is a legitimate option. If staying in bed is a legitimate option, it is justified: we might call this a 'weak', rather than a 'strong', justification,[17] but it is still a justification; I do not need an excuse for doing something wrong. Given this feature of extra-legal justification, and given the plausible presumption that the concept of justification should function in legal thought in at least roughly the way that it functions in extra-legal moral thought,[18] theorists who argue that conduct counts as legally justified only if it is expected or required or at least approved, rather than merely permitted, face a difficult task:[19] why should the criminal law, which is normally taken to permit what it does not define as criminal, adopt a narrower conception of justification than that which figures in our extra-legal thought? I do not think that they provide any plausible answers to this question.[20]

Secondly, part of what motivates the claim that what is merely permitted should not count as being justified might be the assumption that if an action is justified others may legitimately assist the agent, and may not legitimately resist him, together with the recognition that this cannot plausibly be said of conduct that is merely permissible.[21] This illustrates a pervasive problem in many discussions of justification and excuse: that theorists assume certain supposed logical relationships which then make the classificatory task even harder; another such assumption is that excuses

[17] See Uniacke, 1994: 14–15.

[18] For a useful discussion of this point see Berman, 2003: 18–38.

[19] See e.g. Fletcher, 1979: 1358–60, and 1985: 977–99 (on the less determinate position expressed in Fletcher, 1978, see Dressler, 1984: 69–73); Finkelstein, 1996 and 2002.

[20] See Dressler, 1984: 70–87; Husak, 1989b: 491–504.

[21] See, eg, Eser, 1976: 622–3; Fletcher, 1978: 759–69; Finkelstein, 1996: 644; Robinson, 1997: 96, 105–6.

cannot figure in the 'rules of conduct' which give citizens ex ante guidance—that they cannot be action-guiding.[22] I will not discuss the first assumption here—the errors it involves have been thoroughly exposed by others:[23] there are of course important questions about the conditions under which others may assist or resist an agent's enterprise, but they are not to be answered simply by classifying the agent's defence as 'justification' or as 'excuse'; nor should our answers to those questions determine that classificatory issue. I will comment briefly on questions of resistance and assistance later, but my main concern is with the deeper assumption that 'justifications' and 'excuses' provide an adequate classificatory schema for defences that do not negate an element of the offence; such an austere schema is, I will argue, quite inadequate.[24]

As a prelude to that argument, it will be useful to look briefly at the roles played by ideas of truth and justification in the context of beliefs, rather than that of actions. This will suggest a diagnosis of the source of some of the problems in the debate about justification and excuse—and a way of resolving them.

2. Truth, Justification and Belief

Beliefs aim at truth: a rational believer seeks to acquire and maintain beliefs that are true, and to avoid or reject those that are false. However, apart from judging beliefs to be true or false, we also judge them to be justified or unjustified, and (if they are unjustified) to be excused or unexcused. Whereas legal theory, in its analysis of criminal defences, tries to operate with a simple two-part structure of 'justification' and 'excuse', epistemology operates with a richer structure of truth, justification and excuse. It is worth asking whether legal theory can learn from epistemology here.

A belief is true if, roughly, the world is as the belief portrays it as being, false if the world is not as the belief portrays it.[25] A belief is justified if

[22] See, eg, Fletcher, 1978: 810–13; Alldridge, 1990; Robinson, 1997, locating excuses firmly in the 'Code of Adjudication'; Gardner, 1998b: 597; Ripstein, 1999: 164–5. For criticism see Duff, 2002a: 65–8.

[23] See Greenawalt, 1984: 1918–27; Dressler, 1984: 87–98; Husak, 1989b, 1999; Berman, 2003: 62–4.

[24] Three very useful discussions, on which I draw in what follows, are Uniacke, 1994: 9–56; Baron, 2005; Tadros, 2005a: chs 10–12.

[25] This should not be read as assuming a 'correspondence' theory of truth, as against e.g. a 'coherence' theory that portrays truth as coherence with other beliefs rather than of correspondence to any mind-independent world (see David, 2005; Young, 2001). Any philosophical theory of truth must posit an account of 'the world' as that against which beliefs are to be measured for their truth or falsity; the question of what that account should be need not concern us here.

there are good reasons for accepting it, reasons at least as good as those for rejecting it; it is unjustified if there are no, or insufficient, reasons for accepting it. We can distinguish the question of whether there are good reasons for a belief from that of whether a particular believer holds that belief for those reasons. *A* is justified in believing that *p* (*A*'s believing that *p* is justified) if there is good reason to believe that *p* and *A* believes that *p* for that reason, but we should hesitate to say that *A* is justified in believing that *p* if, although there are good reasons to believe that *p*, A's own belief that *p* is not based on those reasons: we might more plausibly say that a belief that *p* is justifiable (a believer would be justified in believing that *p* for those good reasons), but that *A*'s believing that *p* was not justified, because it was not based on reasons that would have justified it. An unjustified belief, held for inadequate reasons or in the face of sufficient reasons for disbelief, might be excusable: I might jump too quickly to the conclusion that *p*, or fail to attend to the evidence that not-*p*; but such failures may be excusable if I am, for instance, distressed or tired. If an unjustified belief is inexcusable, however, the believer is liable to criticism for his culpable failure of rationality.

I will not say more about what can make beliefs excusable or inexcusable here (although I comment in section 6 on reasonable and unreasonable action-guiding beliefs); my interest is rather in the relations between truth and justification. It is clear that truth and justification can come apart; this generates four possible assessments of beliefs.

(a) *A*'s belief that *p* could be *true* and *justified*: she holds the belief for good or adequate reasons, and *p* is indeed the case.
(b) *A*'s belief that *p* could be *true* but *unjustified*: *p* is indeed the case, but *A* has no good reason to believe it.
(c) *A*'s belief that *p* could be *false* but *justified*: *A* has good reasons to believe that *p* (and believes it for those reasons), but *p* is not actually the case.
(d) *A*'s belief that *p* could be *false* and *unjustified*: *p* is not the case, and *A* has no good reason to believe that *p*.

Of these four possibilities, (a) is the condition to which rational believers aspire, and it is (a) alone that should count, according to a venerable philosophical analysis, as knowledge—an epistemic state that brings credit to its possessor.[26] In relation to (b) and (c) we might talk of luck: of the bad luck that *A* suffers in (c), or of her good luck in (b); but she is still vulnerable to criticism in (b), and cannot take credit for the truth of her

[26] That analysis, of knowledge as justified true belief, appeared vulnerable to counter-examples proposed in Gettier, 1963. On the post-Gettier debates see Audi, 1998: ch 8.

belief. As for (d), we might say that A gets what she deserves; she should not be surprised that her ill-grounded belief is false.

Although truth and justification can come apart, they cannot be separated as direct guides to belief formation. It would be senseless to ask whether in forming my beliefs I should aim for truth or for justification—for beliefs that are true or for beliefs that are justified. I cannot aim for truth as distinct from justification, or for justification as distinct from truth, since the only way of aiming to acquire true beliefs is to aim to acquire beliefs that there is good reason to think are true—ie beliefs that are justified; in aiming for justification I am also aiming for truth, and cannot rationally aim for truth in any other way. Others might be able to distinguish those of my beliefs that are true from those that are justified but false (and I might be able to do the same later, as an observer of my own past beliefs), but I cannot myself, as a believer, separate the true from the justified but false amongst my current actual or potential beliefs. The distinction between truth and justification nonetheless still matters to the believer: for a rational believer aspires to belief that is true, and she seeks to acquire beliefs that are justified because this gives her the best chance of acquiring beliefs that are true.[27] If her justified belief turns out to be false, she may take some solace or credit from the fact that it was justified—from the fact that she was unlucky, rather than stupid or careless; but she must still recognise that she failed to achieve her aim.

The fact that our aim or aspiration is truth, but that our guide must be justification, gives a certain ambiguity to the question 'Should I have believed that *p*?', when it turns out that *p* was false, although there was good reason to believe it. We might say that I should not have believed it, as it turns out, since one should believe only what is true; or we might say that I should have believed it, since I had good reason to believe it and it would have been irrational not to believe it. Similarly, I can in one way regret having believed it, especially if relying on it caused me significant harm; but in another way I cannot rationally regret having believed it, since I cannot rationally regret having formed my belief in the only rational way available to me. To say that I should not have believed it, or to regret having believed it, reflects the fact that false beliefs are failed beliefs; to say that I should have believed it, and that regret is not rationally appropriate, reflects the fact that we can pursue success in beliefs only by pursuing justification—only by believing what we have good reason to believe. Similarly, if someone whose unreasonable, ill-founded belief that *p* luckily turns out to have been true asks 'Should I not have believed that

[27] Sometimes what ultimately matters to a believer is simply to acquire true beliefs; she will be as happy with an unjustified but true belief as with a justified true belief; sometimes what matters is that her belief be true and justified—that she reaches the truth by rational inquiry. But in both cases truth is her central aim.

p?', we might reply either that, as it turns out, he should indeed have believed that *p*, since that was after all the truth; or that he should not have believed it, since he had no good reason to do so and displayed irrationality in doing so. Or, if there were good reasons for believing that *p*, reasons that were available to him, and he believed that *p* but not for those reasons, we might say, not that he should have believed that *p simpliciter*, but that he should have believed that *p* for those reasons: that is, he should have attended to the available reasons, rather than leaping unreasonably to a conclusion that was only fortuitously correct.

There is much more to be said about justification and truth in relation to beliefs, but what matters here is whether there are illuminating analogies between the case of belief and that of action. I will argue that there are (although there are also equally illuminating disanalogies), and that they can help us to resolve the notorious problems of 'putative justification' and of 'unknown justification'.

In judging beliefs we operate with three dimensions of assessment: true or false, justified or unjustified, and (if unjustified) excusable or inexcusable:[28] we can then distinguish beliefs that are true and justified from those that are justified but false, and from those that are true but unjustified. In judging actions, by contrast, legal theorists seem to want to operate with just two dimensions of assessment: justified or unjustified, and (if unjustified) excusable or inexcusable. Perhaps this is the source of some of the problems that then confront them: they try to shoehorn different distinctions into the distinction between 'justified' and 'unjustified', when what we need is a structure analogous to that which applies to beliefs. For instance, we might begin by dropping the term 'justification' (as being too infected by the controversies surrounding its use in criminal law), and talk instead of 'right' and 'wrong' as the dimension of action appraisal analogous to truth and falsity, and of 'warranted' and 'unwarranted' as the dimension analogous to justification or its lack, thus enabling ourselves to say that an agent's action was right and warranted; right, but unwarranted; warranted, but wrong; or unwarranted and wrong.[29]

As an initial approximation, we can say that an action is right if it is what the agent ought to do, or may do; it is warranted if the agent acts thus

[28] This way of putting the point assumes that justifications have priority over excuses—only if an action or belief is unjustified do we need to look for excuses: see eg Baron, 2005: 389–90; on the other side see Husak, 2005e.

[29] Greenawalt (1984: 91–3) uses 'warranted' as a synonym for 'justified'. Horowitz objects that 'warranted' is too close to 'justified', and suggests that : a 'good way to begin the discussion of exculpation … is to ban words like warranted, since their usual function is to pronounce, and always to pronounce ambiguously, on the ultimate question of justification or excuse' (1986: 110). I will argue that so long as we make clear how we are using the term, 'warranted' can play a useful role—partly in helping us to see that there is no *single* 'ultimate question of justification or excuse'.

because she reasonably believes that it is what she ought to do or may do. Rightness and wrongness thus have to do with the guiding reasons that there are for or against acting in a certain way,[30] while warrantedness and its lack have to do with the agent's reasons for believing that there is reason to act in a certain way.

As we will see in section 4, 'right but unwarranted' is very problematic in the context of criminal defences; we may have good reason to reintroduce 'justified' to deal with cases in which, as we can crudely put it, an agent's action is right only if and because it is warranted; but the category of 'warranted but wrong' is, as we will now see, just what we need to resolve the problem of 'putative justifications'.

3. The Problem of 'Putative Justification'

Diane goes by arrangement to call on Bill, an elderly relative who is visiting a friend nearby. The doorbell is not answered; when she looks through the window, she sees Bill lying face down on the floor; banging on the window does not attract his attention. Knowing Bill's history of heart problems, she thinks that he must have had a heart attack—but how can she help? The house is isolated; she has no mobile telephone; it would take too long to run to the nearest house for help (she came on foot). So she decides that she must break into the house in order to telephone for help and to give Bill emergency aid (as she is trained to do). She therefore reluctantly, but decisively, breaks in, knowing that she is causing expensive damage to the carefully restored window of the old house. The story develops in one of two ways—

(1) Bill has had a heart attack, and would have died had Diane not administered such timely first aid; she saves his life.
(2) Bill had fallen asleep, with his hearing aid turned off, whilst practising a new relaxation technique, and needed no medical attention.

Case (1) is unproblematic. There was good—indeed sufficient—reason for Diane to break the window; she realised and acted for that reason—to try to save Bill's life. She (and we) should regret the damage to the owner's property, but not her action: it is regrettable that she had to break the window to save Bill, but not that she broke it. She has a defence against a charge of criminal damage, since although she 'damage[d] tangible property of another purposely', she did so in order to prevent a clearly greater

[30] On 'guiding' reasons (those that should guide conduct, as distinct from 'explanatory' reasons that actually motivate it), see Raz, 1990: 16–20.

harm;[31] given the story so far, she deserves thanks and even admiration for her quick thinking and effective action—we should not condemn her action or suggest that she ought to have done anything other than she did.[32]

Case (2) leads us into a familiar controversy about the borders of justification and excuse; but even theorists who take different sides in that controversy ought to be able to agree on a number of substantive propositions about case (2).[33]

- Assuming that Diane acted on the basis of reasonable beliefs,[34] she should be acquitted of criminal damage and should not be subject to moral criticism for acting as she did.
- She should be acquitted because she acted in and on a reasonable belief that she had good reason to act thus.
- She might properly (perhaps even should) regret having damaged the house—whereas in case (1) the most that anyone could properly regret is that she had to do that damage.
- But she would presumably (and rightly) say that, faced by the same situation, she would do the same again—as would any reasonable person, given the available evidence.
- A third party who helped her break in should be free from both moral blame and criminal liability if he shared her beliefs, but not if he knew that she was mistaken.
- A third party who shared her beliefs would merit moral blame, if not criminal liability, if he resisted her attempt to break in. If he knew that she was mistaken, he should tell her—and if she refused to listen, her action would cease to be based on a reasonable belief.

But if they can agree on this much, why is there such persistent disagreement between those who argue that her defence constitutes a justification and those who argue that it constitutes an excuse?[35] The reason, we should suspect, is that the restrictive schema of 'justification'

[31] See Model Penal Code, ss 3.02(1), 220.3(1)(a). See also Criminal Damage Act 1971, s 1(1): she commits criminal damage, but with 'lawful excuse' (see n 1 above).

[32] A final moral appraisal of Diane's action would depend on her motives: if she saved Bill only because she anticipated a reward, her action would not reflect morally well on her. I assume, however, that even if the criminal law is properly interested in the reasons for which she damaged the property (see sect 4 below), its demands are satisfied if she damaged the property in order to save Bill, whatever her further motives.

[33] We might note that the Model Penal Code (s 3.02(1)) counts conduct as 'justifiable' so long as the agent believed it to be necessary to prevent greater harm, and would thus provide Diane with the same defence in case (2) as in case (1); see also the Criminal Damage Act's partial specification of 'lawful excuse' (s 5).

[34] I discuss cases in which the agent's beliefs are unreasonable later (sect 6 below).

[35] See eg Fletcher, 1978: 691–8 (excuse); Robinson, 1982: 239–40 (excuse); Byrd, 1987 (excuse); Gardner, 1996: 118–22 (excuse); Finkelstein, 1996 (excuse); Hurd, 1999: 1563–5 (excuse); Dressler, 1984: 92–5 (justification); Greenawalt, 1984: 1907–9 (justification);

and 'excuse' forces theorists to choose between just two alternative classifications, neither of which is satisfactory; the solution would then lie in adopting a richer classificatory schema.

(To complete the picture, we can imagine a version of the case in which Diane continues to act on the basis of a reasonable belief that her action is necessary to save Bill's life, despite the existence of a third party who knows her beliefs to be mistaken and can try to prevent her action, if she reasonably but mistakenly believed the third party to be unreliable. Such a case would instantiate theorists' worries about whether both the agent and one who resists her can be 'justified' in acting as they do.[36] I will not explore this problem here, but suspect that in many such cases each agent could be warranted in committing an offence against the other.[37])

Those who resist classing Diane's defence in case (2) as a justification have good reason to do so, since that conceals the significant difference between the two cases: that in case (2) she has reason to regret acting as she did, which she does not have in case (1). She did what was in fact the wrong thing: she damaged another's property when there was no good reason to do so. A good reason to damage that property would have been that this was necessary to bring Bill the medical help he urgently needed; but that reason did not obtain (although Diane believed that it did), since Bill was not ill. Diane therefore acted against the guiding reasons for action that applied to her: that what she damaged was the property of another person who did not consent to the damage constituted good reason not to damage it, and there was in fact no good countervailing reason to damage it.

It is important to be clear on this point, and to resist the temptation to say that Diane had, and acted for, good reasons to break the window, because she believed that by acting thus she would bring about a desirable result—saving Bill's life. Whatever we say about 'motivating' or 'explanatory' reasons, the reasons that actually motivate action and by reference to which actions are explained,[38] the 'guiding' reasons in virtue of which we have or lack good reason to act as we do are constituted not (simply) by our own desires and beliefs, but by features of the world. Had Bill been ill, Diane would have had good reason to break the window; since he was not

Tadros, 2005a: 280–90 (justification). For more nuanced discussions see Husak, 1989b: 506–9; Christopher, 1994; Uniacke, 1994: 15–25; Baron, 2005.

[36] For useful discussions see Fletcher, 1979; Dressler, 1984: 87–91; Husak, 1999; Christopher, 1994.

[37] Husak (1999) points up some of the difficulties involved in trying to explain what counts as a 'conflict of justifications'; the explanation of conflicts of warrant implied in the text, that such a conflict is found whenever each of two agents is warranted in committing an offence of which the other is the or a victim, should begin to address his worries.

[38] Many philosophers take motivating reasons to consist in the agent's beliefs and desires: for a persuasive argument against this orthodox view see Dancy, 2000 (and see Ch 3 at nn 47–48 above).

ill, she had no such reason to break it. Two more considerations should clarify this point. First, when Diane considers what she should do, she is wondering what reasons for action apply to her, which is to wonder not about her own internal states of belief, but about the world—is Bill ill; how can she help him? Secondly, suppose that just as Diane was about to break the window she saw Bill wake up and stand up: her new belief, that Bill is not ill, does not give her a new reason for action—a reason not to break the window; rather, it shows her that the reason she thought she had to break the window (Bill's need for help) did not exist. Diane did have good reason to believe that she had good reason to break the window, but that belief was false; to say simply that her defence constitutes a justification conceals this crucial difference from the case in which her belief is true.

On the other hand, those who resist classifying Diane's defence simply as an excuse also have reason to do so. That classification does take due notice of the fact that her belief was mistaken, and that she did not actually have good reason to break the window, but it conceals a crucial difference between her case and others in which we would naturally talk of excuses: excusing an agent reflects a judgement that it would be unfair to condemn him for not having acted differently and better on this occasion, and implies the judgement or hope that he would act differently and better if faced again by a similar situation; but that judgement and hope are inappropriate in Diane's case. We might, for instance, excuse an agent who acts under a kind of duress that is insufficient to make his action unqualifiedly right or permissible, in response to a threat that he should ideally have resisted, if to resist would have required a heroism that we cannot reasonably demand of citizens on pain of being punished if they do not display it; we recognise a 'reasonable' or 'human' weakness that does not deserve condemnation.[39] We might also excuse an agent who acted on an unreasonably mistaken belief if there is a suitably exculpating explanation for his irrationality. In both cases, however, in excusing the agent we express a belief that he should, and a hope that he would, act differently if faced in the future by a relevantly similar situation; but that is not what we hope or believe of Diane in case (2). As we saw, there is a sense in which Diane did the wrong thing, and now has reason to regret doing it: as it turns out, she should not have broken the window. But she also acted just as she should have: her practical reasoning was impeccable; she acted appropriately, in response to what reasonably appeared to be very good reasons for action. Had she asked for advice about what to do from others in the same epistemic position as her, they should have advised her to act just as she did;[40] if someone asks us what he should do in a situation like

[39] On duress see further at nn 90–95 below.

[40] This is true of others *in the same epistemic position as her*; if she asked someone who knew the truth, he would tell her not to break the window. Some theorists talk of what an

hers, we should advise him to act just as she did. What she sought, what anyone ought to seek, was the right thing to do; but, just as the only way to pursue truth in our beliefs is to pursue justification, ie to strive to ensure that we acquire and maintain only those beliefs that there is good reason to think are true, so the only way to pursue rightness in action is to strive to form reasonable, justified beliefs about what one should do (about what guiding reasons apply to one's situation), and to act in accordance with what thus reasonably appear to be good reasons.[41]

We should therefore be reluctant to classify Diane's (clearly legitimate) defence either as straightforwardly and unqualifiedly a 'justification' or as straightforwardly and unqualifiedly an 'excuse', because either classification ignores crucial differences between her defence and other defences that clearly fall into that category. We could still seek to preserve the structure of 'justification' and 'excuse', by distinguishing different ideas of justification. We could say that Diane had an 'agent-perspectival', but not an 'objective', justification (from the 'objective' perspective she had an excuse);[42] or that her action was 'formally', but not 'materially', right;[43] or that she was 'epistemically', but not 'morally', justified.[44] One danger with that approach is that we might be tempted to ask, unhelpfully, which is *the* appropriate idea in the context of the criminal law; another is that we will then feel impelled to say, misleadingly, that in terms of the idea of justification that does not apply to Diane, she has an excuse. An alternative strategy is to abandon the language of 'justification' in favour of two other terms that would perform in relation to actions the functions performed by 'true' and 'justified' in relation to beliefs.

We should, I suggested, talk of the 'right' and the 'warranted'. An action is right (only) if there actually are sufficient, undefeated reasons for the agent to do it;[45] it is 'warranted' if the agent acts on a reasonable belief

'objective observer', who knows all the relevant facts and norms, would judge to be right (eg Hruschka, 2005), but such a fictional observer could not *advise* Diane about what to do—whereas my concern is with what participants could do or say.

[41] See Husak, 1989b: 506–9, Baron, 2005: 395–8 (on 'formal rightness') on these points; see also Ripstein, 1999: 138–9.

[42] See Uniacke, 1994: 15–23. More precisely, since she acted on the basis of reasonable beliefs that anyone would have formed in her situation, her action was in one sense 'objectively' justified, ie reasonable; but, when judged against the actual facts, it was 'objectively' unjustified (*ibid* at 17, note 17).

[43] See Baron, 2005: 395–8. Baron notes the possibility of positing two distinct uses for 'justification': one tied to the 'material' rightness of the action, without reference to the agent's beliefs and motives; the other to the 'formal' rightness of the action as done by that particular agent, given her beliefs and motives. But she argues that we should tie justification to formal rightness.

[44] Hurd, 1999: 1564.

[45] I include, but bracket, the 'only' to avoid prejudging the question to be discussed in sect 4. On the idea of 'undefeated' reasons in this context see Gardner, 1996: 107–14.

that there are sufficient, undefeated reasons for her to do it.[46] Diane's action was therefore wrong, but warranted. Theorists who disagree about whether her defence should count as a justification or as an excuse, but agree that she should be acquitted, can therefore agree that it is sufficient that her action was warranted; and by calling her action warranted we can do justice both to the ways in which it is unlike straightforwardly 'justified' actions (because it is not right) and to the ways in which it is unlike excused actions (because it is warranted).

This solution can be applied across the whole range of 'putative justification' cases. It can apply to cases in which the wrong is far more serious, as when the agent kills another in the reasonable, but mistaken, belief that this is a necessary act of (self-)defence: his action is wrong, as a killing for which there is in fact no good reason; but he is warranted in acting as he does, given his reasonable belief. It applies to cases in which the agent acts to benefit or to protect herself rather than others: some argue that actions can be 'justified' (and thus 'right') only if they promote social welfare,[47] in which case self-regarding actions could at best be excused; but once we recognise that the right includes the permissible,[48] we can see that self-regarding (as distinct from selfish) actions can be both right and warranted—we might indeed criticise an agent on moral, not merely on prudential, grounds for failing to protect herself.

This does not, of course, help us to decide whether third parties may legitimately help, or resist, the warranted agent: but those questions cannot be resolved merely by deciding on the appropriate classification of the agent's defence as a 'justification', or as an 'excuse', or as a 'warrant'.[49] Such questions rapidly become complicated as we imagine ever more convoluted scenarios,[50] but we cannot pursue them here; all I would suggest is that they will be clarified, and perhaps made more tractable, if we distinguish the question of what it would be right or permissible for third parties to do from that of what they would be warranted in doing, given their reasonable beliefs about the situation.

We can, I have argued in this section, resolve at least some of the problems that cases of 'putative justification' seem to raise by abandoning the orthodox dichotomy of 'justification' and 'excuse' in favour of a modestly richer classificatory schema that distinguishes the 'right' from the

[46] Warranted action is thus analogous to justified believing (see text following n 24 above); we could also talk of an action being warranted (as distinct from the agent being warranted in doing it) if there is good reason to believe that it is right. On reasonableness in this context see sect 6 below.

[47] See eg Finkelstein, 1996, 2002.

[48] See at nn 16–19 above on justification as including the permissible.

[49] See at nn 20–23, 35–36 above.

[50] See especially Christopher, 1994.

'warranted'. We will now see whether this approach can help us with another long-running controversy—that concerning 'unknown justifications'.

4. The Problem of 'Unknown Justification'

Like Diane, Don goes to a friend's house and breaks a window. His intentions, however, are malicious rather than benevolent: he has fallen out with his (ex-)friend, and wants to hurt her by damaging the house that means so much to her. So far, it looks like a straightforward case of criminal damage. However, unknown to Don, there has been a gas leak in the house; Jane is having a sleep, and would have died from inhaling the gas, but the breaking of the window wakes her up and lets in sufficient fresh air to save her. Don's action has thus saved her life, at the cost of a broken window; had he done it in order to save her life, we would have said that he did 'the right thing', and praised him for his quick thinking.[51] But if he had no idea that she was in danger or that he was saving her life, what should we, or the law, say? Should he be acquitted of criminal damage because his action was (unknown to him) justified;[52] or should he be convicted because justification requires at least awareness of, if not motivation by, the facts that ground the justification?[53] Is justification a matter, as it is sometimes put, of 'deeds', or of 'reasons'?

Here again, as in the case of 'putative justification', there seem to be some propositions on which both sides to the dispute could and should agree:

— There is good reason for anyone who is in a position to do so (and thus for Don) to break the window—that although it will damage another's property (which constitutes a normally conclusive reason against an action) it is necessary to save Jane's life.
— Since Don acts not for that reason, but from malice, he deserves moral censure for his malicious action, and can claim no moral credit for saving Jane's life. He might be able to take a kind of 'agent pleasure' from the fact that he has saved Jane;[54] but 'saving Jane' is not something that redounds to his moral credit.

[51] Assuming again (see n 31 above), that his motives in saving her life were of a morally appropriate kind.

[52] See eg G Williams, 1961: 23–7; Moore, 1997: 65–6; Robinson, 1997: 95–124; Schopp, 1998: 29–38; Hurd, 1999: 1565–7.

[53] See eg Fletcher, 1975, and 1978: 555–66; Christopher, 1995; Gardner, 1996; Dillof, 2002; Baron, 2005; Tadros, 2005a: 273–80. See also Ripstein, 1999: 138–9, 191, 214–17; Berman, 2003: 48–62.

[54] Compare B Williams, 1981a: 27–31, on 'agent regret'.

— A third party who knows the facts should not try to prevent Don breaking the window, and should indeed encourage him to break it, if she cannot do it herself.[55]

Theorists also typically agree that Don merits criminal liability: those who would acquit him of criminal damage often argue that he should be convicted of attempted criminal damage.[56]

Why then should theorists disagree about how the law should judge Don, and especially about whether he or his action is justified? Is part of the reason again that they operate with too limited a classificatory schema? Could we at least clarify the issues by saying that Don's action was right, but not warranted—that his position is analogous to that of someone whose ill-founded, unjustified belief turns out fortuitously to be true? This would not of course settle the question of whether Don should be criminally liable, or for what: but it might clear away some irrelevant disputes, and clarify those substantive issues that remain.

To distinguish the 'right' from the 'warranted' might suggest that the issue here concerns agents who do 'the right deed for the wrong reason'.[57] But if we can properly say that Don, or any other 'unknowingly justified' agent, did 'the right deed for the wrong reason', this speaks in favour of the 'deeds' view—that he should not be convicted of criminal damage. Whilst what is expected of us morally is that we act not just in conformity with the right, but for the right reasons, the most that the criminal law can properly demand of us is that we do the right thing; if I refrain from theft or pay my taxes merely to avoid criminal punishment, my action might not be morally commendable, but it is legally innocent.

Of course, in typical cases of doing 'the right deed for the wrong reason', although the agent does not act for the reasons that make the action right, she does intend her action under the description under which it is 'the right deed': whatever my further reasons or motives for not stealing, or for paying my taxes, what I intend to do is 'not to steal' or 'to pay my taxes', which is precisely what the law requires me to do. This is not, however, true of Don. 'Saving Jane's life' does describe an action—an unintentional action—of his: whether 'breaking the window' and 'saving

[55] The position of a third party who shared Don's ignorance would be the same as his position (if she were to help him), or the same as that of the mistaken Diane in sect 3 if she were to try to prevent him.

[56] See the references in n 51 above; but see at nn 62–65 below.

[57] See the title of Fletcher's response to Robinson (Fletcher, 1975). Fletcher distinguishes 'justified acts' from 'just events': if a judge takes a bribe to decide against the claimant in a law suit, without knowing that the claimant had in fact perjured himself, the decision is 'just, without being justified' (1975: 320).

Jane's life' describe one act or two,[58] he saved Jane's life by breaking that window. But he did not intend his action under the description ('saving Jane'; 'breaking the window to save Jane') which showed it to be 'the right thing to do'. Should this matter to the criminal law, however? Suppose that I owe £1,000 in taxes, and post a money order for £1,000: I intend to post it to my sister, but by mistake put it in the envelope addressed to the Inland Revenue office (and put in my sister's envelope the letter designed to keep the Inland Revenue off my back for a bit longer). If the tax officer realises that the money comes from me, and keeps it as constituting full payment of the taxes I owed, surely I have—as far as the law is concerned—paid my taxes; I cannot be prosecuted for failing to pay them (although I can claim no moral credit for paying them).

What made breaking the window the right thing to do was simply that it was necessary to the saving of Jane's life: the good that was to be achieved was saving Jane's life—not saving it intentionally or for the right reason; someone who knew the facts would urge Don to break the window, whatever his reason for doing so; to urge him not to break it if he was not acting for the right reasons would be absurd. Breaking the window is, in that situation, what anyone ought to do, and what makes it what anyone ought to do has nothing to do with the agent's reasons for doing it. But how then can we say both that this is what anyone (including Don) ought to do, and that he should be convicted of criminal damage for doing it?

However, if this line of argument is right, what it shows is not that agents like Don, who act in ignorance of the facts that render their action right, should be able to plead a defence of justification; but rather that those facts should be treated as negating an essential element of the offence.[59] To offer a defence is to answer for my actions—in a way that I hope exculpates me; but on this account Don has nothing to answer for. To answer for my actions is to answer precisely for those actions as mine, as done with the intention with which and for the reasons for which I did them: I explain why I acted as I did; if I am claiming justification or warrant, I explain my action by reference to the reasons that I take, or that I reasonably took, to be good reasons for acting thus—reasons sufficient to defeat those against acting as I did. But for Don to point to the fact, which he discovered only after the event, that his action saved Jill's life is not to explain or answer for his action: that fact, being unknown to him, can play

[58] On 'coarse-grained' theories of action (see eg Davidson, 1980), if Don saved Jane's life by breaking the window, 'breaking the window' and 'saving Jane's life' are two descriptions of the same act; on 'fine- grained' views (eg Goldman, 1971), they describe two acts, one of which was done by doing the other.

[59] Compare the case discussed by Robinson, 1988: 664 (and Simester and Sullivan, 2007: 609–10) of a man who stole a bag that in fact (unknown to him) contained a bomb, thus saving many lives: the implication of this argument is not that he has a defence to a charge of theft, but that his action did not constitute theft.

no part in an explanation of why he acted as he did, or even of how he came to act thus.[60] If that mere fact warrants his acquittal, it must be because he in fact committed no criminal wrong in that actual situation, and therefore has nothing for which he must answer in a criminal court—not that he has a justificatory answer for his commission of a criminal wrong.

The 'deeds' theory is, therefore, not a theory of justification, as a criminal defence: it is a theory about where the distinction between offences and defences should be drawn, and holds that what 'reasons' theorists count as justificatory defences should rather be counted as factors that negate an element of the offence. In Don's case, we would redefine criminal damage as an offence, perhaps as causing 'unnecessary' damage to or destruction of another's property, with 'unnecessary' being explained in terms of the prevention of some greater harm.[61] This also makes it easier to see why 'deeds' theorists want to convict Don of attempted criminal damage:[62] his case would now be of just the same kind as notorious 'impossible attempts', in which what prevents the agent's conduct from constituting a complete offence is the absence of some circumstantial element of the offence, as when someone handles what she mistakenly believes to be stolen goods,[63] or illegal drugs;[64] and many think that in such cases the agent should be convicted of an attempt.[65]

This also shows that 'reasons' theorists are right about justificatory defences. If Don must offer a defence (if the necessity of breaking the window does not negate an offence element), it is not enough to adduce facts that would justify the breaking of the window—to show that there was a justification for such an action; he must show that *he* was justified in committing the action that he committed.[66] For if he must offer a defence, he must answer for his action —for his commission of a presumptive

[60] On the distinction between explaining why one Φ-ed and explaining how one came to Φ, see at nn 84–86 below.

[61] As noted above (n 1), the Criminal Damage Act 1971 formally includes the absence of 'lawful excuse' as an element of the offence; but its partial specifications of lawful excuses in s 5(2) are set in terms of what the agent intended or believed, and thus would not cover Don.

[62] See at n 56 above.

[63] See eg *People v Jaffe* 78 NE 169 (1906); *Anderton v Ryan* [1985] 1 AC 560.

[64] See eg *People v Siu* 271 P 2d 575 (1954); *Shivpuri* [1987]AC 1.

[65] See Duff, 1996: chs 3, 8. I will not repeat here my argument that, so long as the missing element does not frustrate the agent's purpose, these should not count as criminal attempts. That argument looks weaker in a case like Don's, since he did genuinely attack a legally protected interest: but since his attack succeeded, that suggests that he should be convicted of a complete offence of criminal damage—ie that the fact that his action saved Jill's life should not negate an element of the offence: see at nn 69–70 below.

[66] Compare the distinction drawn above (text following n 25) between showing that a belief that *p* is justifiable and showing that A's believing that *p* is justified. See also Baron, 2005, for the argument that justifications focus on agents rather than actions—although it is better to say that they attach to actions as done by their agents.

criminal wrong: but, we have seen, to answer for my action is to answer for my action as committed by me, which is to say that if my answer is to be a justificatory one, it must justify my commission of that action by reference to the good reasons for which I committed it. Indeed, it would not be enough for Don to point out that he was aware of the justificatory facts—that he realised that breaking the window was necessary to save Jane's life. If those facts are to justify his action, they must explain it; that is, he must have acted as he did because of those facts—for the reason that breaking the window would save Jane's life.[67] Of course, if he could claim knowledge of the relevant facts, and so long as the defendant bears only an evidential burden in relation to defences,[68] it will typically in fact be enough to adduce evidence that he was aware of the facts, since it would then be hard for the prosecution to prove that those facts did not constitute at least part of his reason for acting as he did; but what he must claim is precisely that he acted for the justificatory reason.

I suggested in the previous section that we can deal with cases of 'putative justification' by recognising that the action was wrong but warranted: the wrongfulness lies in its character as an offence; the agent's warrant for doing it constitutes a defence. What we can now see is that warrant is crucial to any justificatory defence: what matters is not just that the action was right, but precisely that its commission was warranted—that the agent acted as he did because he believed that he had good reason, of a kind recognised by the law, so to act. If that belief was true, we can say, the agent's action was unqualifiedly justified, in that he was justified in acting as he did; if it was false (but reasonable), his action was warranted. Justification, we might say, requires both rightness and warrant—in the same way that, on traditional views, knowledge requires both truth and justified (ie warranted) belief; but we will see shortly that the distinction between rightness and warrant is not as clear as this way of putting the matter assumes.

These points about the logic of justification do not really settle the 'deeds versus reasons' debate in favour of the 'reasons' theorist. Although they do show that the 'deeds' theorist is wrong about justifications, they effectively relocate the debate: it is, we now see, not really a debate about the logic of justificatory defences, but one about how and where to draw the line between offences and defences. This then takes us back to the discussion of Chapter 9, about how we should understand the idea of a presumptive criminal wrong. In particular, if what I said there was right, we must ask, in all cases of 'unknown justification', whether the reasons

[67] See Dressler, 1984: 78–81; Gardner, 1996; Tadros 2005a: 274–80.
[68] See above, Ch 9 at n 11, Ch 10 at nn 26–27, 57.

against acting as the agent did are the kinds of categorical and exclusionary reason that mark a presumptive criminal wrong.[69] I will not embark on that discussion here: but it does seem at least plausible to regard Don's action as constituting the offence of criminal damage, since it does constitute an attack on an interest that the criminal law protects, which is something that we normally have categorical reason not to do. Someone who breaks the window in order to save Jane also commits that offence, and acts as she had categorical and exclusionary reason not to act: the difference between her and Don is that she can justify acting thus. This point applies even more forcefully when the action is a killing or a wounding (the kind of context in which the 'deeds versus reasons' debate is often conducted): if I deliberately kill or wound someone, I should have to answer for that attack as a presumptive wrong; I might be able to avert liability by justifying my action, but I should be held criminally responsible for it.[70]

There is, however, a problem for this account of justification. To convict Don of criminal damage is to condemn him for what he did: this implies, surely, that we wish he had not done it, and that he should come to repent, and therefore regret, having done it. An offender who is brought, perhaps by his conviction and punishment, to repent his wrongdoing must look back with the thought, 'If only I hadn't done that': not because it brought about his punishment, but because he now recognises it as a wrong that he should not have committed. Surely, however, we should not wish that Don had not broken the window or want him to come to wish that he had not done it: we should—on balance, all things considered—be glad that he broke it; and unless he is to exhibit a distorted concern with his own moral condition, he too should be glad that he broke it, because he should be glad that he saved Jane's life.

We can resolve this problem by distinguishing more carefully between the right and the good. What Don did was in fact good, since it saved Jane's life; it was indeed the best thing to do, if there was in fact no other way to save her life. Now for consequentialists, rightness is derivable from goodness: an action is right, objectively or materially,[71] if its actual effects are at least as good as those of any available alternative. From this perspective Don did indeed do 'the right thing', albeit 'for the wrong reason'; it is therefore no coincidence that Robinson, a prominent 'deeds' theorist, understands justifications in broadly consequentialist terms.[72]

[69] See Ch 9 at nn 101–105 above.
[70] See Ch 9.3(b) above.
[71] See Baron, 2005: 395.
[72] See Tadros, 2005a: 276–80.

But even if that is *a* possible conception of rightness,[73] it is not the appropriate conception for the criminal law. Whilst the criminal law should indeed, as argued in Chapter 5, focus on actions, its focus must be on actions as performed by the actual agents who are then called to answer to criminal charges and for criminal actions: but that is to say that its focus must be on actions as including the intentions with which, the beliefs in which, the reasons for which they are done. Our gladness that Don broke the window is about goodness—the fortuitously good effects of his action: but the criminal law's judgment on his action must focus on whether it was right, as done by him in that situation; and rightness here cannot be reduced to goodness.[74]

What of the intuitively plausible suggestion that a third party who knew the facts should not only not prevent Don breaking the window, but encourage him to do so: how could it be right to encourage someone to commit an offence that he will not be justified in committing? The problem here is only apparent. The bystander should indeed encourage Don to break the window, as being the right thing to do: but the encouragement will properly involve pointing out that breaking the window is necessary to save Jill, and will therefore be encouragement to break the window *for that reason*. The bystander might of course realise that Don will act for his own malicious reasons: but that is not what she encourages him to do.[75]

It is therefore a mistake (one committed by some 'reasons' theorists as well as by some 'deeds' theorists) to talk in this context of 'the right deed for the wrong reason': at least in the context of justifications, the rightness of the deed must be in part a function of the reasons for which it is done. The right deed can still be done 'for the wrong reason' if the *further* reasons for which or the further intentions with which it is done are not as they should be—as when Don saves Jane's life only because he hopes for a reward; but the immediate reason for action is still the appropriate one,

[73] Which is a large 'if', given how radically it separates 'the action' from its agent's intentions, beliefs and reasons.

[74] The same point holds if the agent was aware of the relevant facts, but acted for quite other reasons. Tadros (2005a: 276–80) suggests that the consequentialist thought that the law should not aim to deter such an agent from doing what he knows will avert a greater evil has some force in this context, and that we could meet it by recognising such knowledge of justificatory facts as an excuse. This seems to me a misuse of the notion of excuse (see sect 5 below); the most we should allow is that such facts about the actual effects of the action could figure as mitigating factors in sentencing.

[75] Similarly, a passing police officer who knew the facts should not try to prevent Don breaking the window: but this is not because Don does the right thing, or will not be guilty of criminal damage if he breaks it; it is because in this context saving life is more important than preventing crime.

and the criminal law is not usually interested in the moral worth of the further reasons, any more than it is interested in the reason why I pay my taxes.[76]

We have dealt so far with two kinds of defence—two kinds of exculpatory answer that a defendant can offer to block the normal transition from criminal responsibility for committing an offence to criminal liability for that offence: she can claim to have been justified in acting as she did, or to have been warranted. Both kinds of defence involve claims of justification and of good reason: to be warranted in acting as I do is to act on the basis of my reasonable belief that there are sufficient reasons to act thus—my justified belief that the action is right; to be justified in acting as I do is to act on the basis of what really are sufficient reasons to act thus. Justification stands to warrant in the sphere of action as knowledge stands to justified belief in the sphere of belief.[77] One argument in this chapter has been that we should mark out 'warrant' as a kind of defence distinct both from 'justification' and from 'excuse'; another has been that the debate between 'deeds' theorists and 'reasons' theorists is best understood, not as a debate about the criteria for justificatory defences (on that issue, 'reasons' theorists are clearly right), but as a debate about where and how the line between offences and defences should be drawn. Both arguments flow from taking the distinction between responsibility and liability, and the conception of responsibility as answerability, seriously: what matters is not whether some justification or warrant was abstractly available for what the defendant did, but whether he can claim to have been justified or warranted in acting thus.

We turn now to exculpatory answers that make no such claim to justification for action or for belief: answers that admit that the defendant's action was neither justified nor warranted, but claim that he should nonetheless not be liable to conviction and punishment.

5. Excuses and Exemptions

In our extra-legal moral engagements, as we have seen, 'excuses' cover a very wide range of exculpatory factors, including non-culpable inadvertence and accident: that is because outside the law responsibility is typically strict, so that I must answer for the harm that I cause even if I caused it

[76] There are other contexts in which it is even less appropriate to talk of 'the right deed for the wrong reason', most obviously those in which what makes a deed right is precisely its expressive character, which it would lose if it were done for the wrong reasons; and cases of 'weak justification' in which an action is permissible without being 'the right' thing to do (see Duff, 2004b).

[77] See at nn 25–26 above.

through wholly non-culpable inadvertence or accident.[78] Within the criminal law, by contrast, the category of excuses is narrower, since some factors (such as inadvertence and accident) that count as excuses outside the law normally count in criminal law as negations of an offence element.[79] This does not show that 'excuse' is ambiguous as between its legal and its extra-legal uses: in both contexts, excuses admit responsibility, but avert liability by citing factors that show the agent not to have been culpable. The difference in the scope of 'excuse' within and outside the criminal law simply reflects differences in the scope of responsibility within and outside the criminal law.[80]

There is an apparently obvious counter-example to the claim that to offer an excuse is to admit responsibility for an action for which I then offer an exculpatory answer. Insanity is a defence in criminal law, and is surely an excuse: the defendant admits that he committed the offence, with the requisite mens rea, but claims that due to his mental disorder at the time he cannot be justly condemned for committing it. But what he claims is precisely that, given his mental disorder, he was not responsible for the actions that constituted the offence. This is, therefore, an excuse that denies responsibility.

We can deal with this problem, and clarify the structure of non-justificatory defences, by drawing on the distinction that some theorists draw between 'excuses' and 'exemptions'.[81] An exemption is an exemption from responsibility: the exempted person is not, or should not be, expected to answer for her actions. We discussed various exemptions under the heading of 'bars to trial' in Chapter 8.2: those that concern us now are based on the agent's condition, and in particular on his capacity for rational thought and action—on whether he is or was a responsible agent.[82] As we have seen, someone who is at the time of his trial so disordered that he cannot understand the charge that he faces or take part in the trial—so disordered that he cannot answer rationally for his past actions—is exempt from responsibility: he cannot be tried or called to answer for the offence that he might well have committed.[83] But someone

[78] See Chs 3.3, 10.1 above.

[79] This is true, at least, insofar as criminal responsibility is not made strict: see Ch 10.2–3 above.

[80] Philosophers often talk of excuses as denying or negating responsibility (see eg Austin, 1961: 125, quoted at n 8 above); this is because they either do not draw the distinction between responsibility and liability or use 'responsibility' to mean something more like 'liability'.

[81] See especially Horder, 1996b, 1999b, and 2004: 8–10, 103–6 ('denials of responsibility'); Gardner, 1998b, 2003; Tadros, 2005a: 124–9.

[82] See Ch 2.1 above: responsible agency can be understood in terms of reason-responsiveness—the agent's capacity to recognise, respond to, deliberate in terms of and be guided by reasons for belief and for action.

[83] See Ch 8 at nn 17–19, 23 above.

who was at the time of the alleged offence so disordered that he was not then a responsible agent is also exempt, even if he is rationally competent at the time of his trial; so too is one who was too young to be capable of responding to the appropriate kinds of reason. He might now be capable of answering *to* a charge—his trial is not barred by present incapacity; but his answer must be that he cannot, and should not be expected to, answer *for* the actions that he is accused of having committed.

The distinction between excuses and exemptions is clearest when the agent was suffering from some serious, all-embracing disorder or deficiency, such that he was in general, across all aspects of his life, incapable of functioning as a rational agent—of operating within the realm of reasons; such a person lacks 'capacity-responsibility' or 'status-responsibility'.[84] He might have acted in a way that matched the definition of an offence, including both actus reus and mens rea: perhaps he intentionally killed a human being. If he is now rationally competent (which is admittedly unlikely), he can explain, or call witnesses to explain, how he came to commit the offence, in a way that exculpates him. But that will not be an explanation of his reasons for acting as he did, as distinct from the reasons why he acted thus: it might include explanations of his deluded belief that he had good reason to act as he did, but they will appeal not to his grasp of reasons for belief or action, but to the disorder that made him incapable of grasping relevant reasons. That is why it is misleading to say, without qualification, that he committed the offence with the requisite mens rea: for the criminal law's specifications of mens rea rest on the assumption that the specified intentions and beliefs are those of a rationally competent agent; if the person was so radically disordered, that presumption of rationality is defeated.[85]

The exculpatory account that a defendant who was radically disordered gives of his past actions draws on psychiatric expertise, and might be better given by an expert psychiatrist; it is a third person account of what went wrong with his rational capacities, and of the effects of the disorder on his actions. To answer for one's actions, by contrast, is to answer in the first person: I explain my actions in terms of my reasons for belief and for action—reasons which I know because they were mine; I speak as an agent, not as an observer of my past agency. This is obviously true if my answer claims that I was justified or warranted in acting as I did, or admit

[84] See Hart, 1968a: 227–30; Tadros, 2005a: 55–7, 124–6. Mental disorder, I assume, is best analysed in terms of an impairment of the capacities for rational thought, emotion and action that constitute responsible agency.

[85] See Fingarette and Hasse, 1979.

my guilt as a culpable wrongdoer: I speak as an agent endorsing or confessing my own past action. But it is also true if I offer an excuse, as I am using the term here.[86]

To offer an excuse is to admit that I got it wrong: I acted as I should not have acted; my action was not guided by the reasons that should have guided it. Perhaps I failed at the time to give due weight to those reasons, or gave undue weight to countervailing reasons that should not have weighed with me so strongly (if at all); perhaps I simply failed to deliberate, rushing into action in the heat or panic of the moment; perhaps I failed to abide by the outcome of my deliberation.[87] I admit, that is, that my action was in one sense unreasonable: I did not have good enough reason to act as I did, or to believe that I had good enough reason to act as I did. This marks one difference between excuses and exemptions. To get it wrong, as the person offering an excuse admits to having got it wrong, is to fail in the exercise of one's capacities for rational deliberation and action; it is to operate within the realm of practical reason, but to do so deficiently. The seriously disordered agent does not 'get it wrong' in that sense, since he is not operating within the realm of reason: he is not insufficiently sensitive to the reasons that should guide him, since he is not within their reach. The difference between an excusable agent and a seriously disordered agent is analogous to that between someone who makes an understandable mistake in playing a game and someone who is not playing the game at all.[88]

The distinction between excuses and exemptions will become clearer as we see how one who offers an excuse can claim exculpation whilst admitting that she acted as she should not have acted. This is not the place for a discussion of the various kinds of excuse that the law recognises or should recognise:[89] one example, duress, should suffice to make the point.

Someone has deliberately wounded another person. One defence he might offer is duress: that he committed the attack only because another person had made a credible threat to cause much greater harm to him and his family if he refused to do so—a threat which he could not have averted

[86] What matters is not the terminology of 'excuse' and 'exemption', but the substantive distinction it is used to draw. We could use 'excuse' in its traditional broad sense, to cover insanity as well as what I will call 'excuses': but we would then need to find another way to distinguish 'excuses' that negate responsibility, as insanity does, from those that exculpate without negating responsibility.

[87] Compare Aristotle, *Nicomachean Ethics* Bk VII.7 on different types of weakness of will.

[88] That is why we should not say that someone suffering delusions holds mistaken beliefs: mistakes are made by those operating within the realm of reason, and are in principle correctable by rational argument, whilst delusions are beliefs that have no such relation to reason.

[89] See especially Dressler, 1988; Gardner, 1998b; Horder, 2004; Tadros, 2005a: chs 11–13.

or avoided in any other way. Now duress sometimes constitutes a justification,[90] but suppose that in this case the threat was not sufficient to justify committing that crime. He might still be able to plead duress as an excuse. This will involve arguing, first, that he was motivated by a reasonable fear: what he feared was indeed fearful, and the strength of his fear was not grossly disproportionate to the seriousness of the threat. Secondly, that reasonable fear would reasonably motivate anyone to do what he could to avert the threat; although it did not give him good (enough) reason to do what he actually did to avert the threat, a 'reasonable' person, one with an appropriate commitment to the values that the law protects, might have been tempted to act thus: to be so tempted displays a lack of 'superhuman excellence',[91] but not a lack of the more modest level of commitment that we can demand of each other as citizens. Thirdly, such reasonably strong fear is an emotion that is apt to destabilise—to disturb the rational deliberations even of a 'sober person of reasonable firmness':[92] its motivational power is liable to exceed its rational authority. These considerations show that in giving in to that threat and committing this crime, the defendant did not display a lack of those modest levels of courage, self-control and commitment to the values that the criminal law protects, that citizens can properly demand of each other on pain of public condemnation for failure.[93]

Duress, as thus understood, exemplifies one central pattern of excuse, which involves an essential appeal to the idea of reasonableness or the 'reasonable person'. I will not embark on a discussion of the problems and confusions created by the reasonable person in criminal law,[94] save only to note, first, that we should not let the idea of the reasonable person conceal the fact that the question that this mythical figure is used to answer is whether this particular defendant showed herself to be reasonable or unreasonable; and, secondly, that reasonableness in this context is a matter, not of intellectual skill or competence, but of normative attitude. A reasonable person, for these purposes, is a person who displays the kinds of practical attitude that citizens can properly demand of each other under the aegis of the criminal law: the kind of (quite modest) respect and concern for each other, and for the values expressed in the law, the lack or absence of which the commission of a crime normally displays.

[90] Some (eg Westen and Mangiafico, 2003) claim that it is always a justification, others (eg Alldridge, 1986; Fletcher, 1978: 829–35; Dressler 1989) that it is always an excuse: but see Duff, 2002a: 63–8.

[91] Aristotle, *Nicomachean Ethics* Bk VII.1, 1145a20–30.

[92] *Graham* (1982) 74 CR App R 235, at 241; see also *Hudson & Taylor* [1971] 2 QB 202.

[93] This account is roughly Aristotelian; see further Duff, 2006. For a similar account see Dressler, 1989.

[94] On which see Moran, 2003; Tadros, 2005a: ch 13.

A defendant who claims justification or warrant claims that her action was, in its context, reasonable: it was done for (what she had good reason to believe were) good and sufficient reasons; we need not go on to ask whether she acted as a reasonable person would have acted, since the reasonableness that exculpates her is manifest in her action itself, given the context in which and the reasons for which it was done. One who offers an excuse does not claim that her action was itself reasonable; she admits that it was unreasonable: but, she claims, this was a reasonable unreasonableness—a specific failure to act reasonably that did not show *her* to be unreasonable, because even a reasonable person (a 'sober person of reasonable firmness') might have acted in that unreasonable way in that situation. The reasonable person is not a saint or a hero, since that is not what we (normally) demand of each other as citizens:[95] even someone with a reasonable commitment to the values expressed in the criminal law could be driven by the pressure of particular, abnormal situations to act unreasonably. If that was the defendant's situation, she has an excuse; while her unreasonable action did not show her to be a reasonable person, it did not show her to be in the relevant sense an unreasonable person—which, given the Presumption of Innocence, is what matters in a criminal trial. If I commit an offence that a reasonable person would not commit, I show myself to be (I constitute myself as) unreasonable in a way that merits conviction and condemnation: I display a lack of those practical attitudes of modest respect and concern that we properly demand of each other. But if even a reasonable person might have committed such an offence in such a situation, my commission of it does not show me to be unreasonable.

By contrast, a person whose serious mental disorder at the time of the offence precludes liability cannot claim such a reasonable unreasonableness. This is not because his action, as one that a reasonable person would not have committed, showed him to be unreasonable; it is because he was not operating within the realm of reason at all, and was thus neither reasonable nor unreasonable. 'Reasonable' and 'unreasonable', like 'rational' and 'irrational', appraise the thoughts and actions of those who are operating within the realm of reason; but if a person is so disordered that he is not operating within that realm at all, he should be described as 'a-rational' or 'a-reasonable' rather than as irrational or unreasonable.

[95] We do not normally demand it, but if Aristotle was right that 'some acts, perhaps, we cannot be forced to do, but ought rather to face death after the most fearful sufferings' (*Nicomachean Ethics* Bk III.1, 1110a26–28; his example was matricide), some crimes cannot be excused, however terrible the threat, and the reasonable person will sometimes be expected to be a hero. This clearly bears on the issue of whether duress can be a defence to murder (see *Howe* [1987] AC 417, *Gotts* [1992] 2 AC 412; Simester and Sullivan, 2007: 669–70)—though it is not plausible to portray murder as such as a wrong of the kind Aristotle was talking about.

When I am called to answer in a criminal court for my commission of a criminal offence, I face a charge that I acted as I had conclusively good reasons not to act, and thus that I failed to be guided by those reasons as I should have been. If my answer claims a justification, my claim is that in that particular situation those normally conclusive reasons were outweighed by other reasons that the law, and this court, should recognise as sufficient. If I claim warrant rather than justification, I claim that I had sufficient reason to believe that I was justified. If I offer an excuse, I claim that, given the situation and the reasons for committing the offence that it generated (reasons which, even if they were not good reasons in that context, were at least not disreputable reasons), my admitted failure to be guided by the reasons that should have guided my actions did not display a kind of fault that merits a criminal conviction. But if my defence is that I was at the time so seriously disordered as to be non-responsible, I am not engaging in such discussion of the reasons by which I was or should have been guided; my defence is, rather, that I and my actions fell outside the reach of reasons, and thus beyond the reach of the criminal law's judgment.

The distinction between excuses and exemptions can be discerned clearly in the contrasting cases that I have discussed so far: in the contrast between the person who claims to have acted under a kind of duress which would have led anyone (other than a saint or hero) to commit the offence, and the person who was so radically disordered that he was not operating within the realm of reason at all. Matters become more complicated when we look at cases in which the defendant who pleads an excuse cites particular characteristics of his own as part of his account of why he was led to commit the offence, or in which the defendant's disorder at the time of the alleged offence was not so general and all-embracing; these complications combine when the defendant's explanation of why he gave in to a threat or was provoked to use fatal force cites a disorder from which he was suffering—for instance that he reacted as he did to provocation partly because he was suffering from depression.[96] I cannot pursue such complications here, important though they are for the development and application of the distinction between excuses and exemptions, and for a proper understanding of the scope of and conditions for excuses. We should simply note two points.

First, to determine whether the defendant should be exempt from responsibility we must ask whether his psychological condition at the time of the offence was such that, in relation to the course of conduct that included the commission of the offence, he was not functioning as a

[96] See eg *Smith (Morgan)* [2001] 1 AC 146: see Gardner and Macklem, 2001a, 2001b; Tadros, 2005a: 355–8.

responsible agent. Were the beliefs, attitudes and emotions that informed his deliberations and actions within the realm of reason; or were they so disordered, so detached from reason, that he was not operating within that realm at all?[97] We are of course dealing here, in all but the most extreme cases, with matters of degree: how seriously were the person's capacities for rational thought and action impaired? Given the radical implications, both practical and symbolic, of finding that a person was not a responsible agent, we should be slow to make such a finding, and should therefore set the bar of responsibility as low as we sensibly can.

Secondly, in asking whether a 'reasonable person' might have responded as this defendant did, we should ascribe to the reasonable person any of the actual defendant's characteristics that made a difference to his response to the situation, and that are not inconsistent with being a 'reasonable person' in the sense which that phrase should bear in this context. That is why we should ask how a reasonable person of this defendant's age,[98] or with a physical defect of the kind suffered by this defendant,[99] might have responded to the provocation offered to this defendant; but not how a 'reasonable person' who was as bad-tempered as this defendant, or who held such violently racist views as this defendant, might have responded. Neither youth nor physical defect renders a person unreasonable in the normative sense relevant here: both conditions are compatible with having the kinds of practical attitude that we expect of each other as citizens. Bad temper and racist attitudes, by contrast, if displayed in criminal action, do render the person unreasonable: he reacted to the situation as he did because he lacked the practical attitudes that we demand of each other. We can also ascribe to the reasonable person mental disorders that do not destroy the person's capacities for rational thought and action: if the defendant was still, in relation to the course of conduct that included the offence, capable of rational thought and action despite his disorder, we can ask how it would be reasonable for a person suffering such a disorder to respond and act in the defendant's situation.

We can clarify some of these points about reasonableness and unreasonableness, and the distinction between excuses and warrants, by looking at reasonable and unreasonable beliefs.

[97] For a very useful recent discussion of the insanity defence see Tadros, 2005a: ch 12.

[98] See *Camplin* [1978] AC 705. Of course, if the defendant was so young as not to be a responsible agent, we cannot ask how a reasonable person of that age might have responded; but that simply reinforces the point that such a defendant is exempt, not excused.

[99] Compare *Bedder* [1954] 2 All ER 801: the court held, absurdly, that in asking whether a reasonable person might have responded to taunts of impotence as the defendant (who was impotent) did, the jury must assume the 'reasonable person' not to be impotent.

6. Reasonable and Unreasonable Mistakes

I argued in section 3 that Diane could claim to have been warranted in breaking the window if she acted on the basis of a reasonable (albeit mistaken) belief that Bill was in urgent need of medical attention and that she had to break the window in order to help him: she then had good reason to believe that she had good reason to act as she did.[100] But not every agent who acts on a mistaken belief in the existence of facts that would render his action right or permissible acts on the basis of a reasonable belief: so we must ask what makes belief reasonable in such contexts, and how we should judge those who act on the basis of unreasonable mistaken beliefs.[101]

One way in which the belief that *p*, someone's believing that *p*,[102] can be unreasonable is that it is held on the basis of evidence that would not persuade a rationally competent and moderately careful observer to believe that *p*, and/or in the face of evidence that would have persuaded such an observer not to believe that *p*: a belief is in that sense unreasonable if it is not grounded on epistemically adequate reasons. One who holds such an unreasonable belief might do so because he is rationally incompetent: though he does his incompetent best, it is not good enough. Assuming that he is not so incompetent as to be non-responsible, and that we could not expect him to have realised his incompetence and therefore refrained from action, he is presumably excusable: although he falls short of the standard of care, in belief and action, that we normally expect of citizens, he is not at fault or negligent in doing so.[103]

A rationally incompetent (or less than wholly competent) agent can still answer for his actions, and his answer might exculpate him: he can explain, in the first person, his reasons for believing and acting as he did; we can judge that, had the situation been as he believed it to be, his actions would have been justified as being done for sufficient reason;[104] and we can accept that the deficiencies in his belief-formation and practical reasoning

[100] I assume that Diane also has a defence (that her action was right) if her belief was true, even if it was also unreasonable: she is then open to criticism for forming and acting on such a belief, but not to a conviction for criminal damage, since she has still done the right thing, for the right reason—although it was a matter of luck that her belief about that reason was true.

[101] On reasonable belief in these contexts see generally Moran, 2003, esp chs 7–8: Moran's concern is with the reasonable person; but a reasonable person is, inter alia, one who forms and acts on reasonable beliefs.

[102] See text following n 24 above.

[103] I assume that negligence, as a basis for criticism or conviction, must involve a failure to take care that one could and should have taken: see Simester, 2000; Simester and Sullivan, 2007: 147–51.

[104] Whereas it makes no sense to ask of a disordered agent whether, given his deluded beliefs, his action would have been justified (as the M'Naghten court thought we must ask of an agent suffering 'partial delusions': *M'Naghten* (1843) 10 Cl & Fin 200, at 210): that

were not such as to show him to be either unreasonable in the normative sense explained in the previous section, or so rationally incompetent as not to be responsible at all. This is then another sense or way in which a defendant can show that his actions displayed a reasonable unreasonableness: the beliefs on the basis of which he acted were epistemically unreasonable, but in forming and acting on those beliefs he did not show himself to be normatively unreasonable.

We might be tempted to relativise the standard of epistemic reasonableness to the agent's rational capacities, and ask whether it was reasonable *for him* to form that belief—suggesting that his action could have been warranted. We should resist that temptation. He achieved the standard of care that we could reasonably expect him to achieve (this distinguishes him from someone who was not even doing his incompetent best), but his belief was still epistemically unreasonable, and his action unwarranted. An action is warranted only if the agent had good reason to believe that there was good reason for her to act as she did; and 'good reason' must, in relation to both belief and action, be given an objectivist reading. Diane's reasoning was impeccable: she deliberated just as an agent should deliberate, and treated the evidence, the reasons for belief, just as it should be treated—which is why her action was warranted. We cannot say the same of a rationally incompetent person; that is why he is excused for, rather than warranted in, acting as he did.

One who forms and acts on a belief that is in this sense epistemically unreasonable might do so not because she is rationally incompetent, but because she is careless: she did not pay the attention to the reasons for or against the belief that she could and should have paid. She might still gain an acquittal under English law: an agent has a 'lawful excuse' for damaging another's property whether or not his belief that the relevant facts obtained was 'justified';[105] one who inflicts violence on another in the belief that this is necessary as defensive force is not guilty of assault or battery even if his belief is unreasonable, since he does not then intend *unlawful* force.[106] This is the result of turning what should be a matter of defence—whether the agent had good reason to commit the presumptive wrong of criminal damage or assault—into an offence element, which can be negated by a mistaken belief, however epistemically or normatively unreasonable that belief is:[107] we should rather recognise that one who acts on a carelessly formed, epistemically unreasonable and mistaken belief is neither warranted in nor excusable for acting as she does: the question is

would be to judge him as someone still operating within the realm of reason; but if he is genuinely deluded he is not operating within that realm.

[105] Criminal Damage Act 1971, s 5(3).

[106] See *Williams (Gladstone)* [1987] 3 All ER 411; *Beckford* [1988] AC 130.

[107] See generally Simester, 1992; Simester and Sullivan, 2007: 606–9.

whether she should be convicted of the same offence as one who acts without a belief in facts that would justify his action; or of a lesser offence to mark the distinctive, and less serious, character of the wrong she commits.[108]

Apart from this epistemic notion of reasonableness in belief, however, we must recognise a normative notion: beliefs, like actions, can be normatively reasonable or unreasonable. The issue now is not simply whether a rationally competent and careful observer would form the relevant belief, or whether the belief is based on epistemically adequate reasons. The question is whether it is a belief that it is reasonable for an *agent* to form and to act on in the particular situation, and what makes a belief unreasonable in this sense is that in holding and acting on it as he did in the particular situation the agent displayed an 'unreasonable' lack of the kind of respect and concern for others that the law demands. If a belief is in this sense unreasonable, neither it nor the action based on it can be excused. Two examples will bring this point out.

First, a defendant claims to have believed that the woman whom he sexually penetrated consented to it because her husband told him that she was willing.[109] What makes that belief, as held and acted on, unreasonable is not just that that reason is epistemically inadequate, but that it is the wrong kind of reason for such an action-guiding belief: to rely on it is to display the very kind of disregard or contempt for the woman's sexual autonomy and standing as a moral agent that rape itself displays.[110] Similarly, someone who is approached by a group of young black men asking him for money might, given what he thinks he knows about black youths, interpret their behaviour as an attack, and use what he therefore takes to be defensive violence against them:[111] what makes his belief that they are about to attack him unreasonable is not (merely) the epistemic inadequacy of its grounds, but the way in which basing a belief that is to warrant my use of violence against a person on my assumptions about the typical behaviour of a racial group to which he belongs constitutes an insulting failure to see or treat him as a moral agent and fellow citizen.[112] Agents whose beliefs are in this way unreasonable have neither warrant nor excuse for what they do.

Secondly, a rationally competent agent might be so fearful or anxious that in the heat of the moment he does not assess the evidence in the

[108] Compare the American doctrine of 'imperfect self-defense': LaFave, 2003: 550.

[109] *Morgan* [1976] AC 182; *Cogan and Leak* [1976] QB 217; similar points apply to beliefs based on the victim's sexual history or her manner of dress. See Sexual Offences Act 2003, s 1; Ch 10 at nn 63–67 above.

[110] See further Moran, 2003: 220–30, 248–66.

[111] Compare the issues raised in *People v Goetz* 497 NE 2d 41 (New York 1986); see Fletcher, 1988.

[112] See Ch 9 at n 7 above.

rational way that the detached observer would assess it (and that he himself would have assessed it were he not so disturbed). Police officers approach someone whom they believe to be armed and dangerous, misinterpret his behaviour as the start of an attack, and shoot him; in fact, he was not armed, or was not the person they thought him to be, or was not about to attack them.[113] A householder sees an intruder, panics and, mistakenly thinking that he is in danger, shoots the intruder (who was in fact turning to flee). We might think in some such cases that we should not condemn the agent for jumping to the wrong conclusion: there was *some* reason to believe what he believed; had his belief been true, his action would have been legitimate; the situation was a disturbing one.[114] If we think that his fear or panic was reasonable, in the sense sketched in the previous section, and that his reaction did not display an 'unreasonable' lack of firmness of character or regard for others, we could then say that there was 'reasonable explanation or excuse' for reacting as he did.[115] That is not to say that his belief was epistemically reasonable, or that his action was warranted: there was in fact no adequate reason to believe that he had good reason to act as he did; although his fear or panic could provide an exculpatory explanation of how he came to form that belief, they are not epistemically relevant grounds for his belief. The point is rather that there was an exculpatory explanation for his failure of practical rationality—an explanation of the same kind as that which can excuse a person who acts under duress: that a reasonable person, one with the firmness of character and regard for others that we demand, might have been driven to such unreasonable belief and action in such a situation. Both these agents acted in ways that were practically unreasonable: their practical reasoning, from belief formation through the recognition and consideration of reasons to action, was not as it should have been. Both can nonetheless be excused, if they did as well in belief-formation and action as could reasonably be expected in such a situation—as well as a normatively reasonable person would have done.

What constitutes a reasonable process of belief-formation in what is, or might well be, an emergency situation is of course often different from the process that would be reasonable for a detached observer—if only because of the need to act rather quickly. But we must take care to distinguish the factors that can go to the reasonableness of a belief (and thus to the warrant for the action that is based on that belief) from those that go to

[113] Compare *Beckford* [1988] AC 130.

[114] We might of course expect more in the way of calm practical reason from a trained police officer than from a civilian, and thus be readier to exculpate the latter: see Gardner, 1998b: 579–87.

[115] Compare Model Penal Code, s 210.3(1)(b) on when 'extreme mental or emotional disturbance' can reduce what would otherwise be murder to manslaughter: see further Duff, 2006.

exculpate the agent without warranting his action. The fact that the agent faced an (apparent) emergency can generate factors of either kind: it could give the agent good reason to act without further inquiry on the basis of a belief that would count as 'hasty' from a wholly detached observer's perspective; and it can ground an exculpatory explanation for the agent's failure to appraise the evidence as he should ideally have appraised it, or to make the kinds of checks that, even allowing for the emergency, he should ideally have made. The agent may be entitled to an acquittal in both kinds of case, but the grounds for acquittal are very different: in the former case they show his action to be warranted, whilst in the latter they show it to be excusable.

An agent whose beliefs and actions are both epistemically and normatively reasonable is at least warranted in what she does—as Diane was in breaking the window; if her beliefs are also true, she is indeed justified in acting as she does. Whether warranted or justified, she can answer for her actions with a clear conscience, even when they involved the commission of a crime: her practical reasoning was impeccable, and she acted reasonably in accordance with its conclusions; she acted either as she had sufficient reason to act, or at least as she had good reason to believe that she had sufficient reason to act. One whose beliefs are epistemically unreasonable lacks adequate warrant for what he does (although, if they are luckily true, the criminal law can count him as justified in acting as he does), but he can claim an excuse if he displayed no normative unreasonableness in forming and acting on those beliefs: his practical reasoning was far from impeccable, and his actions were therefore unreasonable in the sense that he had sufficient reason neither to act thus, nor to believe that he had sufficient reason to act thus; but that unreasonableness did not show him to be at fault in a way that would merit the criminal law's condemnation. One whose action is normatively unreasonable, in that it does not display (indeed, is inconsistent with) a proper regard for the values that the criminal law expresses and protects, can also be excused if this was a reasonable (or not unreasonable) unreasonableness: if, that is, even a normatively reasonable person might have been driven to such unreasonable action by the pressures under which she acted; she can now answer for her wrongdoing, not with a wholly clear conscience, but in a way that will properly avert liability to the public condemnation and punishment provided by the criminal law. One whose beliefs and actions are, by contrast, unreasonably unreasonable has no such excuse: if someone with the kind of respect and concern for others, and for the values expressed in the law, would not have formed the beliefs on which he acted, or given in to the temptation or pressure to which he gave in, he cannot answer for his actions in a way that shows a criminal conviction to be unjustified; nothing now blocks the presumptive transition from responsibility to liability.

7. Finally ...

Earlier chapters of this book were concerned with criminal responsibility: for what should we be held criminally responsible, as what, and to whom? I aimed to show that we can gain new insights into the structure and logic of criminal law, and thus eventually into the substantive principles by which it should be structured and its content determined, by taking seriously the distinction between responsibility and liability, and by focusing on the relational dimensions of responsibility as answerability—on the way in which to be responsible is to be responsible not merely for *X*, but to *S* and as Φ. The discussion has been focused on structure and logic rather than on substantive content (insofar as they can be separated). I have not offered any determinate criteria by which we could decide what should or should not be criminalised, or determinate views on when a trial should be barred, or when (if ever) criminal responsibility or liability could properly be strict: my aim has rather been to show that we can understand such substantive questions more clearly, and see more clearly how to work towards answers to them, if we distinguish more sharply between responsibility and liability, and understand responsibility as a matter of answerability.

This final chapter has been concerned with the exculpatory ways in which defendants can answer for the criminal wrongs that they commit. I have argued that, in place of the traditional two-part classificatory schema of justification and excuse, we should use a four-part schema of justification, warrant, excuse and exemption (although only the first three of these involve answering for one's actions); this makes clearer the different logical structure of each kind of answer, and saves us from fruitless controversies about how to fit particular kinds of defence into the two-part schema. I have offered no substantive account of the appropriate grounds for these kinds of defence—of what kinds of consideration could justify an action; of what kinds of situational pressure or personal limitation should ground an excuse. My concern has again been more with structure and logic than with substantive content; my claim is that we will be able to make progress in understanding defences, and in assessing different potential defences, if we see them in the light of the overall structure suggested in this book. To offer a criminal defence is to offer an exculpatory answer for the commission of a criminal wrong: I admit responsibility for that wrong, which is to admit that I must answer for it (an admission that might of course be only implicit or hypothetical in the context of the trial); and I answer for it in a way that will, I hope, block the presumptive transition from criminal responsibility to criminal liability.

If this book succeeds at all, its success will therefore lie not in providing direct answers to the substantive questions about the scope and content of the criminal law, about the criteria of criminal responsibility and liability, about the definitions of offences and the conditions of defences, that properly exercise both theorists and practitioners. Its success will rather lie in suggesting new ways of understanding and approaching such questions—ways which should then enable us to work towards better, and better grounded, answers to them.

References

Alexander, L (2000), 'Insufficient Concern: A Unified Conception of Criminal Culpability', 88 *California Law Review* 931

Alldridge, P (1986), 'Developing the Defence of Duress', *Criminal Law Review* 433

——(1990), 'Rules for Courts and Rules for Citizens', 10 *Oxford Journal of Legal Studies* 487

——(1996), 'Dealing with Drug Dealing', in AP Simester and ATH Smith (eds), *Harm and Culpability* (Oxford, Oxford University Press) 239

Allen, MJ (1994), 'Consent and Assault', *Journal of Criminal Law* 183

Altman, A and Wellman, CH (2004), 'A Defense of International Criminal Law', 115 *Ethics* 35

American Law Institute (1985), *Model Penal Code and Commentaries* (Philadelphia, Penn, American Law Institute)

Anscombe, GEM (1963), *Intention*, 2nd edn (Oxford, Blackwell)

Archard, D (1999), 'The Mens Rea of Rape: Reasonableness and Culpable Mistakes', in K Burgess-Jackson (ed), *A Most Detestable Crime* (New York, Oxford University Press) 213

——(2005), 'Political Reasonableness', 35 *Canadian Journal of Philosophy* 1

Ashworth, AJ (1974), 'Excusable Mistake of Law', *Criminal Law Review* 652

——(1987), 'Belief, Intent and Criminal Liability', in J Eekelaar and J Bell (eds), Oxford Essays in Jurisprudence, 3rd Series (Oxford, Oxford University Press) 1

——(1989), 'The Scope of Criminal Liability for Omissions', 105 *Law Quarterly Review* 386

——(1998), 'Should the Police be Allowed to Use Deceptive Practices?', 114 *Law Quarterly Review* 108

——(1999), 'Article 6 and the Fairness of Trials', *Criminal Law Review* 261

——(2002a), 'Testing Fidelity to Legal Values: Official Involvement and Criminal Justice', in S Shute and AP Simester (eds), *Criminal Law Theory: Doctrines of the General Part* (Oxford, Oxford University Press) 299

——(2002b), 'Redrawing the Boundaries of Entrapment', *Criminal Law Review* 159

——(2004), 'Social Control and "Anti-Social Behaviour": The Subversion of Human Rights?', 120 *Law Quarterly Review* 263

——(2006), *Principles of Criminal Law*, 5th edn (Oxford, Oxford University Press)

—— and Blake, M (1996), 'The Presumption of Innocence in English Criminal Law', *Criminal Law Review* 306

—— and Redmayne, M (2005), *The Criminal Process* (Oxford, Oxford University Press)

References

Audi, R (1998), *Epistemology: A Contemporary Introduction to the Theory of Knowledge* (London, Routledge)

Austin, JL (1961), 'A Plea for Excuses', in JL Austin, *Philosophical Papers* (Oxford, Oxford University Press) 123

Baldwin, J and McConville, M (1977), *Negotiated Justice* (London, Martin Robertson)

Bamforth, N (1994), 'Sado-Masochism and Consent', *Criminal Law Review* 661

Baron, MW (2005), 'Justifications and Excuses', 2 *Ohio State Journal of Criminal Law* 387

Barry, B (1965), *Political Argument* (London, Routledge)

Bayles, MD (1982), 'Character, Purpose, and Criminal Responsibility', 1 *Law and Philosophy* 5

Bazelon, DL (1976), 'The Morality of the Criminal Law', 49 *Southern California Law Review* 385

Becker, LC (1974), 'Criminal Attempts and the Theory of the Law of Crimes', 3 *Philosophy and Public Affairs* 262

Bennett, C (2006), 'Taking the Sincerity Out of Saying Sorry: Restorative Justice as Ritual', 23 *Journal of Applied Philosophy* 127

Bennett, J (1966), 'Whatever the Consequences', 26 *Analysis* 83

——(1995), *The Act Itself* (Oxford, Oxford University Press)

Bentham, J (1776/1977), *A Comment on the Commentaries*, in JH Burns and HLA Hart (eds), *Collected Works of Jeremy Bentham* (London, Athlone Press) iii.

Bergelson, V (2007), 'The Right to be Hurt: Testing the Boundaries of Consent', 75 *George Washington Law Review* 165

Berman, MN (2003), 'Justification and Excuse, Law and Morality', 53 *Duke Law Journal* 1

Bhaskar, R (1993), *Dialectic: The Pulse of Freedom* (London, Verso)

Bianchi, H (1994), *Justice as Sanctuary: Toward a New System of Crime Control* (Bloomington, Ind, Indiana University Press)

Blackstone, W (1765–9), *Commentaries on the Laws of England* (4 vols; Oxford, Clarendon Press, available at www.yale.edu/lawweb/avalon/blackstone/blacksto.htm)

Braithwaite, J and Pettit, P (1990), *Not Just Deserts: A Republican Theory of Criminal Justice* (Oxford, Oxford University Press)

Brandt, RB (1970), 'Traits of Character: A Conceptual Analysis', 7 *American Philosophical Quarterly* 23

——(1985), 'A Motivational Theory of Excuses in the Criminal Law', in J Pennock and J Chapman (eds), *Criminal Justice* (New York, New York University Press) 165

Brennan, A and Lo, Y-S (2002), 'Environmental Ethics', in EN Zalta (ed), *The Stanford Encyclopedia of Philosophy* (http://plato.stanford.edu/archives/sum2002/entries/ethics-environmental)

Burgess-Jackson, K (1999), 'A Theory of Rape', in K Burgess-Jackson (ed), *A Most Detestable Crime: New Philosophical Essays on Rape* (New York, Oxford University Press)

Burns, RP (1999), *A Theory of the Trial* (Princeton, NJ, Princeton University Press)

Byrd, BS (1987), 'Wrongdoing and Attribution: Implications Beyond the Justification-Excuse Distinction', 33 *Wayne Law Review* 1289

Campbell, K (1987), 'Offence and Defence', in IH Dennis (ed), *Criminal Law and Justice* (London, Sweet & Maxwell) 73
Cane, P (2000), *Responsibility in Law and Morality* (Oxford, Hart)
Casey, J (1971), 'Actions and Consequences', in J Casey (ed), *Morality and Moral Reasoning* (London, Methuen) 155
Cassese, A (2003), *International Criminal Law* (Oxford, Oxford University Press)
Chalmers, J (2002), 'The Criminalisation of HIV Transmission', 28 *Journal of Medical Ethics* 160
Choo, AL-T (1993), *Abuse of Process and Judicial Stay of Criminal Proceedings* (Oxford, Oxford University Press)
Christie, N (1977), 'Conflicts as Property', 17 *British Journal of Criminology* 1
Christman, J (2003), 'Autonomy in Moral and Political Philosophy', in EN Zalta (ed), *The Stanford Encyclopedia of Philosophy* (http://plato.stanford.edu/archives/fall2003/entries/autonomy-moral)
Christopher, RL (1994), 'Mistake of Fact in the Objective Theory of Justification: Do Two Rights Make Two Wrongs Make Two Rights ...?', 85 *Journal of Criminal Law and Criminology* 295
——(1995), 'Unknowing Justification and the Logical Necessity of the Dadson Principle in Self-Defense', 15 *Oxford Journal of Legal Studies* 229
Clark, SJ (1999), 'The Courage of Our Convictions', 97 *Michigan Law Review* 2381
——(2006), '"Who Do You Think You Are?": the Criminal Trial and Community Character', in RA Duff, *et al* (eds), *The Trial on Trial II: Judgement and Calling to Account* (Oxford, Hart) 83
Clarkson, CMV (1993), 'Theft and Fair Labelling', 56 *Modern Law Review* 554
——(2005), 'General Endangerment Offences: The Way Forward?', 32 *University of Western Australia Law Review* 1
Cleckley, H (1964), The Mask of Sanity, 4th edn (St Louis, Miss, CV Mosby)
Coke, Sir Edward (1628), *Institutes of the Laws of England* (3 vols; London, Society of Stationers)
Coleman, J (1998), 'Incorporationism, Conventionality and the Practical Difference Thesis', 4 *Legal Theory* 381
Colvin, E (1990), 'Exculpatory Defences in Criminal Law', 10 *Oxford Journal of Legal Studies* 381
Connelly, S (1994), 'Bad Advice: The Entrapment by Estoppel Doctrine in Criminal Law', 48 *University of Miami Law Review* 627
Cooke, E (2000), *The Modern Law of Estoppel* (Oxford, Oxford University Press)
Cotterrell, R (1995), *Law's Community* (Oxford, Oxford University Press)
Criminal Law Revision Committee, (1980), *Offences against the Person* (14th Report; London, HMSO)
Crown Prosecution Service (2006), *Annual Report 2005–2006* (London, Crown Prosecution Service, available at www.cps.gov.uk/publications/docs/annualreport06.pdf)
Cunningham, S (2002), 'Dangerous Driving a Decade On', *Criminal Law Review* 945
Dagger, R (1997), *Civic Virtues: Rights, Citizenship, and Republican Liberalism* (New York, Oxford University Press)

Damaška, M (1973), 'Evidentiary Barriers to Conviction and Two Models of Criminal Procedure', 21 *University of Pennsylvania Law Review* 506
Dan-Cohen, M (1984), 'Decision Rules and Conduct Rules: On Acoustic Separation in Criminal Law', 97 *Harvard Law Review* 625
——(2002), 'Defending Dignity', in M Dan-Cohen, *Harmful Thoughts: Essays on Law, Self and Morality* (Princeton, NJ, Princeton University Press) 150
Dancy, J (1991), 'An Ethic of Prima Facie Duties', in P Singer (ed), *A Companion to Ethics* (Oxford, Blackwell) 219
——(1993), *Moral Reasons* (Oxford, Blackwell)
——(2000), *Practical Reality* (Oxford, Oxford University Press)
——(2004), *Ethics Without Principles* (Oxford, Oxford University Press)
David, M (2005), 'The Correspondence Theory of Truth', in EN Zalta (ed), The Stanford Encyclopedia of Philosophy (http://plato.stanford.edu/archives/fall2005/entries/truth-correspondence)
Davidson, D (1980), 'Agency', in D Davidson, *Essays on Actions and Events* (Oxford, Oxford University Press) 43
Delgrado, R (1985), '"Rotten Social Background" Should the Criminal Law Recognize a Defense of Severe Environmental Deprivation?', 3 *Law & Inequality* 9
Dennis, IH (2007), *The Law of Evidence*, 3rd edn (London, Sweet and Maxwell)
Devlin, P (1965), *The Enforcement of Morals* (Oxford, Oxford University Press)
Dillof, AM (2002), 'Unravelling Unknown Justification', 77 *Notre Dame Law Review* 1547
Dimock, S (1997), 'Retributivism and Trust', 16 *Law and Philosophy* 37
Dolinko, D (1991), 'Some Thoughts about Retributivism', 101 *Ethics* 537
Dressler, J (1984), 'New Thoughts about the Concept of Justification in the Criminal Law: A Critique of Fletcher's Thinking and Rethinking', 32 UCLA *Law Review* 61
——(1988), 'Reflections on Excusing Wrongdoers: Moral Theory, New Excuses and the Model Penal Code', 19 *Rutgers Law Journal* 671
——(1989), 'Exegesis of the Law of Duress: Justifying the Excuse and Searching for its Proper Limits', 62 *Southern California Law Review* 1331
——(2000a), 'Some Thoughts (Mostly Negative) About "Bad Samaritan" Laws', 40 *Santa Clara Law Review* 971
——(2000b), 'Does One Mens Rea Fit All? Thoughts on Alexander's Unified Conception of Criminal Culpability', 88 *California Law Review* 955
——(2006), *Understanding Criminal Law*, 4th edn (New York, Lexis)
Dubber, MD (2001), 'Policing Possession: The War on Crime and the End of Criminal Law', 91 *Journal of Criminal Law and Criminology* 829
——(2002a), *Criminal Law: Model Penal Code* (New York, Foundation Press)
——(2002b), *Victims in the War on Crime* (New York, New York University Press)
——(2005), 'The Possession Paradigm: The Special Part and the Police Model of the Criminal Process', in RA Duff and SP Green (eds), *Defining Crimes: Essays on the Special Part of the Criminal Law* (Oxford, Oxford University Press), 91
—— and Kelman, MG (2005), *American Criminal Law: Cases, Statutes, and Comments* (New York, Foundation Press)

Duff, P (2004), 'Changing Conceptions of the Scottish Criminal Trial: The Duty to Agree Uncontroversial Evidence', in RA Duff *et al* (eds), *The Trial on Trial I: Truth and Due Process* (Oxford, Hart) 29

Duff, RA (1977), 'Psychopathy and Moral Understanding', 14 *American Philosophical Quarterly* 189

——(1986), *Trials and Punishments* (Cambridge, Cambridge University Press)

——(1990a), *Intention, Agency and Criminal Liability* (Oxford, Blackwell)

——(1990b), 'Can I Help You?: Accessorial Liability and the Intention to Assist', 10 *Legal Studies* 165

——(1993), 'Choice, Character and Criminal Liability', 12 *Law and Philosophy* 345

——(1996), *Criminal Attempts* (Oxford, Oxford University Press)

——(1998a), 'Principle and Contradiction in the Criminal Law: Motives and Criminal Liability', in RA Duff (ed), *Philosophy and the Criminal Law. Principle and Critique* (Cambridge, Cambridge University Press), 156

——(1998b), 'Dangerousness and Citizenship', in AJ Ashworth and M Wasik (eds), *Fundamentals of Sentencing Theory* (Oxford, Oxford University Press) 141

——(2001), *Punishment, Communication, and Community* (New York, Oxford University Press)

——(2002a), 'Rule-Violations and Wrongdoings', in S Shute and AP Simester (eds), *Criminal Law Theory: Doctrines of the General Part* (Oxford, Oxford University Press) 47

——(2002b), 'Virtue, Vice and Criminal Liability: Do We Want an Aristotelian Criminal Law?', 6 *Buffalo Criminal Law Review* 147

——(2004a), 'Action, the Act Requirement and Criminal Liability', in J Hyman and H Steward (eds), *Agency and Action* (Cambridge, Cambridge University Press) 69

——(2004b), 'Rethinking Justifications', 39 *Tulsa Law Review* 829

——(2005), 'Criminalizing Endangerment', in RA Duff and SP Green (eds), *Defining Crimes: Essays on the Special Part of the Criminal Law* (Oxford, Oxford University Press) 43

——(2006), 'The Virtues and Vices of Virtue Jurisprudence', in TDJ Chappell (ed), *Values and Virtues: Aristotelianism in Contemporary Ethics* (Oxford, Oxford University Press) 90

——, Farmer, L, Marshall, SE and Tadros, V (eds) (2004), *The Trial on Trial I: Truth and Due Process* (Oxford, Hart)

——, ——, —— and —— (eds) (2006), *The Trial on Trial II: Judgement and Calling to Account* (Oxford, Hart)

——, ——, —— and ——(2007), *The Trial on Trial III: Towards a Normative Theory of the Criminal Trial* (Oxford, Hart)

—— and Marshall, SE (2005), 'How Offensive Can You Get?', in AP Simester and A von Hirsch (eds), *Incivilities: Regulating Offensive Behaviour* (Oxford, Hart) 57.

Dummett, M (1978), *Truth and Other Enigmas* (London, Duckworth)

Dworkin, G (1972), 'Paternalism', 56 *The Monist* 64

——(1982), 'Is More Choice Better than Less?', in PA French *et al* (eds), *Midwest Studies in Philosophy* (Minneapolis, Minn, Minnesota University Press), vii, 47

Dworkin, RM (1978), 'The Model of Rules I' in Dworkin, *Taking Rights Seriously* (London, Duckworth) 17
——(1986), *Law's Empire* (London, Fontana)
Ebert, U (2001), *Strafrecht Allgemeiner Teil*, 2001 3rd edn (Heidelberg, CF Müller)
Epstein, RA (2005), 'The Not So Minimum Content of Natural Law', 25 *Oxford Journal of Legal Studies* 219
Eser, A (1976), 'Justification and Excuse', 24 *American Journal of Comparative Law* 621
Falk, WD (1968), 'Morality, Self, and Others', in JJ Thomson and G Dworkin (eds), *Ethics* (New York, Harper & Row) 349
Feinberg, J (1970a), 'The Expressive Function of Punishment', in J Feinberg, *Doing and Deserving* (Princeton, NJ, Princeton University Press) 95
——(1970b), 'Action and Responsibility', in J Feinberg, *Doing and Deserving* (Princeton, NJ, Princeton University Press) 119
——(1984), *Harm to Others* (New York, Oxford University Press)
——(1985), *Offense to Others* (New York, Oxford University Press)
——(1986), *Harm to Self* (New York, Oxford University Press)
——(1988), *Harmless Wrongdoing* (New York, Oxford University Press)
Ferzan, KK (2001), 'Opaque Recklessness', 91 *Journal of Criminal Law and Criminology* 597
——(2002), 'Don't Abandon the Model Penal Code Yet! Thinking Through Simons's *Rethinking*', 6 *Buffalo Criminal Law Review* 185
Fingarette, H and Hasse, AF (1979), *Mental Disabilities and Criminal Responsibility* (Berkeley, Cal, University of California Press)
Finkelstein, CO (1996), 'Self-Defense as a Rational Excuse', 57 *University of Pittsburgh Law Review* 621
——(2000), 'Positivism and the Notion of an Offense', 88 *California Law Review* 335
——(2002), 'Excuses and Dispositions in Criminal Law', 6 *Buffalo Criminal Law Review* 317
——(2003), 'Is Risk a Harm?', 151 *University of Pennsylvania Law Review* 963
Finnis, JM (1987a), 'On "The Critical Legal Studies Movement"', in J Eekelaar and J Bell (eds), *Oxford Essays in Jurisprudence*, 3rd Series (Oxford, Oxford University Press) 145
——(1987b), 'Legal Enforcement of "Duties to Oneself": Kant v Neo-Kantians', 87 *Columbia Law Review* 433
——(1994), 'Law, Morality, and "Sexual Orientation"', 69 *Notre Dame Law Review* 1049
Fischer, JM and Ravizza, M (1998), *Responsibility and Control* (Cambridge, Cambridge University Press)
Fletcher, GP (1975), 'The Right Deed for the Wrong Reason: A Reply to Mr Robinson', 23 *UCLA Law Review* 293
——(1978), *Rethinking Criminal Law* (Boston, Mass, Little, Brown)
——(1979), 'Should Intolerable Prison Conditions Generate a Justification or an Excuse for Escape?', 26 *UCLA Law Review* 1355
——(1985), 'The Right and the Reasonable', 98 *Harvard Law Review* 949
——(1988), *A Crime of Self-Defense* (New York, Macmillan)

——(1994), 'On the Moral Irrelevance of Bodily Movements', 142 *University of Pennsylvania Law Review* 1443

Frankfurt, H (1969), 'Alternate Possibilities and Moral Responsibility', 66 *Journal of Philosophy* 829

——(1978), 'The Problem of Action', 15 *American Philosophical Quarterly* 157

Fuller, LL (1964), *The Morality of Law,* rev edn (New Haven, Conn, Yale University Press)

Gainer, RL (1988), 'The Culpability Provisions of the Model Penal Code', 19 *Rutgers Law Journal* 575

Gaita, R (1991), *Good and Evil: An Absolute Conception* (London, Macmillan)

Gardner, J (1994), 'Rationality and the Rule of Law in Offences Against the Person', 53 *Cambridge Law Journal* 502

——(1996), 'Justifications and Reasons', in AP Simester and ATH Smith (eds), *Harm and Culpability* (Oxford, Oxford University Press) 103

——(1998a), 'On the General Part of the Criminal Law', in RA Duff (ed), *Philosophy and the Criminal Law. Principle and Critique* (Cambridge, Cambridge University Press), 205

——(1998b), 'The Gist of Excuses', 1 *Buffalo Criminal Law Review* 575

——(2001), 'Obligations and Outcomes in the Law of Torts', in P Cane and J Gardner (eds), *Relating to Responsibility: Essays for Tony Honoré on his 80th Birthday* (Oxford, Hart) 111

——(2003), 'The Mark of Responsibility', 23 *Oxford Journal of Legal Studies* 157

——(2004), 'Fletcher on Offences and Defences', 39 *Tulsa Law Review* 817

——(2005), 'Wrongs and Faults', in AP Simester (ed), *Appraising Strict Liability* (Oxford, Oxford University Press) 51

—— and Jung, H (1991), 'Making Sense of *Mens Rea*: Antony Duff's Account', 11 *Oxford Journal of Legal Studies* 559

——and Macklem, T (2001a), 'Compassion without Respect? Nine Fallacies in R v Smith' *Criminal Law Review* 623

——and—(2001b), 'Provocation and Pluralism', 64 *Modern Law Review* 815

——and—(2002), 'Reasons', in J Coleman and S Shapiro (eds), *The Oxford Handbook of Jurisprudence and Philosophy of Law* (Oxford, Oxford University Press) 440

—— and Shute, S (2000), 'The Wrongness of Rape', in J Horder (ed), *Oxford Essays in Jurisprudence*, 4th Series (Oxford, Oxford University Press) 193

George, RP (1993), *Making Men Moral* (Oxford, Oxford University Press)

——(1999), 'Marriage and the Liberal Imagination', in RP George (ed), *In Defense of Natural Law* (Oxford, Oxford University Press)

Gettier, EL (1963), 'Is Justified True Belief Knowledge?', 23 *Analysis* 231

Giles, M (1994), '*R v Brown*: Consensual Harm and the Public Interest', 11 Modern Law Review 121

Ginet, C (2000), 'The Epistemic Requirements for Moral Responsibility', in *Action and Freedom* (*Nous* Supplement vol 14) 267

Glannon, W (2002), *The Mental Basis of Responsibility* (Aldershot, Ashgate)

Glazebrook, PR (1978), 'Situational Liability' in PR Glazebrook (ed), *Reshaping the Criminal Law* (London, Stevens) 108

——(1991), 'Thief or Swindler: Who Cares?', 50 *Cambridge Law Journal* 389

——(2006), *Blackstone's Statutes on Criminal Law,* 15th edn (Oxford, Oxford University Press)

Goldman, AI (1971), 'The Individuation of Actions', 18 *Journal of Philosophy* 761

Gordon, GH (2000), *The Criminal Law of Scotland*, 3rd edn, by MGA Christie (W Green, Edinburgh) i.

Gowans, CW (ed) (1987), *Moral Dilemmas* (New York, Oxford University Press)

Gray, RL (1995), 'Eliminating the (Absurd) Distinction between Malum in Se and Malum Prohibitum Crimes', 73 *Washington University Law Quarterly* 1369

Green, SP (1997), 'Why it's a Crime to Tear the Tag off a Mattress: Over-Criminalization and the Moral Content of Regulatory Offenses', 46 *Emory Law Journal* 1533

——(2001), 'Lying, Misleading, and Falsely Denying: How Moral Concepts Inform the Law of Perjury, Fraud, and False Statements', 53 *Hastings Law Journal* 157

——(2005), 'Six Senses of Strict Liability: A Plea for Formalism', in AP Simester (ed), *Appraising Strict Liability* (Oxford, Oxford University Press) 1

——(2006), *Lying, Cheating, and Stealing: A Moral Theory of White-Collar Crime* (Oxford, Oxford University Press)

Greenawalt, K (1984), 'The Perplexing Borders of Justification and Excuse', 84 *Columbia Law Review* 1897

——(1986), 'Distinguishing Justifications from Excuses', 49 *Law and Contemporary Problems* 89

Gross, H (1979), *A Theory of Criminal Justice* (New York, Oxford University Press)

Gustafson, D (1986), *Intention and Agency* (Dordrecht, Reidel)

Hall, J (1963), 'Negligent Behavior should be Excluded from Penal Liability', 63 *Columbia Law Review* 632

Hampton, C (1982), *Criminal Procedure*, 3rd edn (London, Sweet & Maxwell)

Hampton, J (1984), 'The Moral Education Theory of Punishment', 13 *Philosophy & Public Affairs* 208

——(1992), 'Correcting Harms versus Righting Wrongs: The Goal of Retribution', 39 *UCLA Law Review* 201

Harcourt, BE (1999), 'The Collapse of the Harm Principle', 90 *Journal of Criminal Law and Criminology* 109

Hare, RM (1981), *Moral Thinking: Its Levels, Method and Point* (Oxford, Oxford University Press)

Harré, R (1983), *Personal Being* (Oxford, Blackwell)

Hart, HLA (1963), *Law, Liberty, and Morality* (Stanford, Cal, Stanford University Press)

——(1968a), *Punishment and Responsibility* (Oxford, Oxford University Press)

——(1968b), 'Negligence, *Mens Rea*, and Criminal Responsibility', in HLA Hart, *Punishment and Responsibility* (Oxford, Oxford University Press) 136

——(1994), *The Concept of Law*, 2nd edn (Oxford, Oxford University Press)

Heffernan, WC and Kleinig, J (eds) (2000), *From Social Justice to Criminal Justice* (New York, Oxford University Press)

Hirst, M (2003), *Jurisdiction and the Ambit of the Criminal Law* (Oxford, Oxford University Press)

Holtug, N (2002), 'The Harm Principle', 5 *Ethical Theory and Moral Practice* 357

Home Office (1996), *Review of Extraterritorial Jurisdiction: Report of the Interdepartmental Steering Committee* (London, HMSO)

Honoré, AM (1988), 'Responsibility and Luck', 104 *Law Quarterly Review* 530; reprinted in AM Honoré, *Responsibility and Fault* (Oxford, Hart, 1999) 14
——(1993), 'The Dependence of Morality on Law', 13 *Oxford Journal of Legal Studies* 1
Horder, J (1993), 'Criminal Culpability: The Possibility of a General Theory', 12 *Law and Philosophy* 193
——(1994a), 'Rethinking Non-Fatal Offences against the Person', 14 *Oxford Journal of Legal Studies* 335
——(1994b), 'Varieties of Intention, Criminal Attempts and Endangerment', 14 *Legal Studies* 335
——(1995), 'A Critique of the Correspondence Principle in Criminal Law', *Criminal Law Review* 759
——(1996a), 'Crimes of Ulterior Intent', in AP Simester and ATH Smith (eds), *Harm and Culpability* (Oxford, Oxford University Press) 153
——(1996b), 'Criminal Law: Between Determinism, Liberalism, and Criminal Justice', 49 *Current Legal Problems* 159
——(1999a), 'Questioning the Correspondence Principle—A Reply', *Criminal Law Review* 206
——(1999b), 'Between Provocation and Diminished Responsibility', *King's College Law Journal* 143
——(2000), 'On the Irrelevance of Motive in Criminal Law', in J Horder (ed), Oxford Essays in Jurisprudence, 4th Series (Oxford, Oxford University Press) 173
——(2001), 'How Culpability Can, and Cannot, Be Denied in Under-age Sex Crimes', *Criminal Law Review* 15
——(2004), *Excusing Crime* (Oxford, Oxford University Press)
——(2005), 'The Classification of Crimes and the Special Part of the Criminal Law', in RA Duff and SP Green (eds), *Defining Crimes: Essays on the Special Part of the Criminal Law* (Oxford, Oxford University Press) 21
Hörnle, T (2001), 'Offensive Behaviour and German Penal Law', 5 *Buffalo Criminal Law Review* 255
Hornsby, J (1993), 'On What's Intentionally Done', in S Shute *et al* (eds), *Action and Value in Criminal Law* (Oxford, Oxford University Press) 55
——(1994), 'Action and Aberration', 142 *University of Pennsylvania Law Review* 1719
——(1999), 'The Poverty of Action Theory', 21 *Philosophical Inquiry* 1
Horowitz, D (1986), 'Justification and Excuse in the Program of Criminal Law', 49 *Law and Contemporary Problems* 109
Hruschka, J (2005), 'Justifications and Excuses: A Systematic Approach', 2 *Ohio State Journal of Criminal Law* 407
Hudson, B (1995), 'Beyond Proportionate Punishment: Difficult Cases and the 1991 Criminal Justice Act', 22 *Crime, Law & Social Change* 59
——(2003), Justice in the Risk Society (London, Sage)
Hudson, SD (1986), *Human Character and Morality* (London, Routledge)
Hughes, G (1958), 'Criminal Omissions', 67 *Yale Law Journal* 590
Huigens, K (1995), 'Virtue and Inculpation', 108 *Harvard Law Review* 1423
——(1998), 'Virtue and Criminal Negligence', 1 *Buffalo Criminal Law Review* 431
——(2002), 'Homicide in Aretaic Terms', 6 *Buffalo Criminal Law Review* 9

Hurd, HM (1999), 'Justification and Excuse, Wrongdoing and Culpability', 74 *Notre Dame Law Review* 1551

Hursthouse, R (2003), 'Virtue Ethics', in EN Zalta (ed), *The Stanford Encyclopedia of Philosophy* (http://plato.stanford.edu/archives/fall2003/entries/ethics-virtue)

Hulsman, L (1986), 'Critical Criminology and the Concept of Crime', 10 *Contemporary Crises* 63

Husak, DN (1981), 'Paternalism and Autonomy', 10 *Philosophy & Public Affairs* 27

——(1987), *Philosophy of Criminal Law* (Totowa, NJ, Rowman & Littlefield)

——(1989a), 'Motive and Criminal Liability', 8 *Criminal Justice Ethics* 3

——(1989b), 'Justifications and the Criminal Liability of Accessories', 80 *Journal of Criminal Law & Criminology* 491

——(1992), *Drugs and Rights* (Cambridge, Cambridge University Press)

——(1995a), 'The Nature and Justifiability of Nonconsummate Offenses', 37 *Arizona Law Review* 151

——(1995b), 'Varieties of Strict Liability', 8 *Canadian Journal of Law and Jurisprudence* 189

——(1998a), 'Does Criminal Liability Require an Act?', in RA Duff (ed), *Philosophy and the Criminal Law* (Cambridge, Cambridge University Press), 60

——(1998b), 'Reasonable Risk Creation and Overinclusive Legislation', 1 *Buffalo Criminal Law Review* 599

——(1999), 'Conflicts of Justifications', 18 *Law and Philosophy* 41

——(2004), 'The Criminal Law as a Last Resort', 24 *Oxford Journal of Legal Studies* 207

——(2005a), 'Crimes Outside the Core', 39 *Tulsa Law Review* 755

——(2005b), '*Malum Prohibitum* and Retributivism', in RA Duff and SP Green (eds) (2005), *Defining Crimes: Essays on the Special Part of the Criminal Law* (Oxford, Oxford University Press), 65

——(2005c), 'Applying *Ultima Ratio*: A Skeptical Assessment', 2 *Ohio State Journal of Criminal Law* 535

——(2005d), 'Strict Liability, Justice, and Proportionality', in AP Simester (ed), *Appraising Strict Liability* (Oxford, Oxford University Press), 4

——(2005e), 'On the Supposed Priority of Justification to Excuse', 24 *Law and Philosophy* 557

——(2007), *Overcriminalization* (Oxford, Oxford University Press)

—— and von Hirsch, A (1993), 'Culpability and Mistake of Law', in S Shute, J Gardner and J Horder (eds), *Action and Value in Criminal Law* (Oxford, Oxford University Press) 157

Jareborg, N (2005), 'Criminalization as Last Resort (*Ultima Ratio*)', *Ohio State Journal of Criminal Law* 521

Jeffries, JC and Stephan, PB (1979), 'Defenses, Presumptions, and Burden of Proof in the Criminal Law', 88 *Yale Law Journal* 1325

Kahan, DM and Nussbaum, M (1996), 'Two Conceptions of Emotion in Criminal Law', 96 *Columbia Law Review* 269

Katz, L (1987), *Bad Acts and Guilty Minds* (Chicago, Ill, Chicago University Press)

Kell, D (1994), 'Social Disutility and the Law of Consent', 14 *Oxford Journal of Legal Studies* 121

Kelman, M (1981), 'Interpretive Construction in the Substantive Criminal Law', 33 *Stanford Law Review* 591

Kelsen, H (1925/1945), *Allgemeine Staatslehre* (Berlin, Springer; trans by A Wedberg as *General Theory of Law and State*; Cambridge, Mass, Harvard University Press, 1945)

Kenny, AJ (1978), *Freewill and Responsibility* (London, Routledge)

Kleinig, J (1978), 'Crime and the Concept of Harm', 15 *American Philosophical Quarterly* 32

Kristol, I (1971), 'Pornography, Obscenity, and the Case for Censorship', *New York Times Magazine* 28 March 246; reprinted in G Dworkin (ed), *Morality, Harm, and the Law* (Boulder, Colo, Westview Press) 46

Kugler, I (2002), *Direct and Oblique Intention in the Criminal Law* (Aldershot, Ashgate)

Kupperman, J (1991), *Character* (New York, Oxford University Press)

Lacey, N (1988), *State Punishment* (London, Routledge)

——(1993), 'A Clear Concept of Intention: Elusive or Illusory?', 56 *Modern Law Review* 621

——(ed) (1994), *A Reader on Criminal Justice* (Oxford, Oxford University Press)

——(1998), 'Contingency, Coherence and Conceptualism: Reflections on the Encounter between "Critique" and "the Philosophy of the Criminal Law"', in RA Duff (ed), *Philosophy and the Criminal Law. Principle and Critique* (Cambridge, Cambridge University Press), 9

——(2000), '"Philosophical Foundations of the Common Law": Social not Metaphysical', in J Horder (ed), *Oxford Essays in Jurisprudence*, 4th Series (Oxford, Oxford University Press) 17

——(2001a), 'In Search of the Responsible Subject: History, Philosophy and Criminal Law Theory', *64 Modern Law Review* 350

——(2001b), 'Responsibility and Modernity in Criminal Law', 9 *Journal of Political Philosophy* 249

Lacey, N, Wells, C and Quick, O (2003), *Reconstructing Criminal Law*, 3rd edn (London, LexisNexis)

LaFave, WR (2003), *Criminal Law*, 4th edn (St Paul, Minn, West Group)

—— Israel, JH, King, NJ (2004), *Criminal Procedure*, 4th edn (St Paul, Minn, West Group)

Lanham, D (1976), 'Larsonneur Revisited', *Criminal Law Review* 276

——(1999), 'Danger Down Under', *Criminal Law Review* 960

Law and Philosophy (2000), *Special Issue: The Moral and Legal Limits of Samaritan Duties,* 19 *Law and Philosophy* 649

Law Commission (1989), *A Criminal Code for England and Wales,* 2 vols (No 177, London, HMSO)

——(1989a), 'Draft Criminal Code Bill', in Law Commission, *A Criminal Code for England and Wales* (No 177, London, HMSO), i.

——(2004), *Partial Defences to Murder* (No 290; London, HMSO)

——(2006), *Murder, Manslaughter and Infanticide* (No 304; London, HMSO)

Lieberman, D (2002), 'Mapping Criminal Law: Blackstone and the Categories of English Jurisprudence', in N Landau (ed), *Law, Crime and English Society, 1660–1840* (Cambridge, Cambridge University Press) 139

Luban, D (2004), 'A Theory of Crimes Against Humanity', 29 *Yale Journal of International Law* 124

Lucas, JR (1993), *Responsibility* (Oxford, Oxford University Press)

Lynch, ACE (1982), 'The Mental Element in the Actus Reus', 98 *Law Quarterly Review* 109

MacCormick, DN (1990), 'Reconstruction after Deconstruction: A Response to CLS', 10 *Oxford Journal of Legal Studies* 539

Mack, E (1980), 'Bad Samaritanism and the Causation of Harm', 9 *Philosophy and Public Affairs* 141

Maher, G (2005), 'Age and Criminal Responsibility', 2 *Ohio State Journal of Criminal Law* 493

Markwick, P (2000), 'Law and Content-Independent Reasons', 20 *Oxford Journal of Legal Studies* 579

Marshall, SE and Duff, RA (1998), 'Criminalization and Sharing Wrongs', 11 *Canadian Journal of Law & Jurisprudence* 7

May, L (2005), *Crimes against Humanity: A Normative Account* (Cambridge, Cambridge University Press)

McDowell, J (1978), 'Are Moral Requirements Hypothetical Imperatives?', 52 *Proceedings of the Aristotelian Society* (Supp vol) 13

——(1979), 'Virtue and Reason', 62 *The Monist* 331

McEwan, J (2004), 'Ritual, Fairness and Truth: The Adversarial and Inquisitorial Models of Criminal Trial', in RA Duff *et al* (eds), *The Trial on Trial I: Truth and Due Process* (Oxford, Hart) 51

Mckenzie, A (2005), '"This Death Some Strong and Stout Hearted Man Doth Choose": The Practice of Peine Fort et Dure in Seventeenth- and Eighteenth-Century England', 23 *Law & History Review* 279

McMahan, J (1994), 'Innocence, Self-Defense, and Killing in War', 2 *Journal of Political Philosophy* 193

Melden, AI (1961), *Free Action* (London, Routledge)

Menlowe, M and McCall Smith, A (1993), *The Duty to Rescue: Jurisprudence of Aid* (Aldershot, Dartmouth)

Michaels, A (1999), 'Constitutional Innocence', 112 *Harvard Law Review* 828

——(2000), '"Rationales" of Criminal Law Then and Now: For a Judgmental Descriptivism', 100 *Columbia Law Review* 54

Midgley, M (1978), 'The Objection to Systematic Humbug', 53 *Philosophy* 147

Mill, JS (1859), *On Liberty* (London, Parker)

Mitchell, B (1999), 'In Defence of a Principle of Correspondence', *Criminal Law Review* 195

Moore, MS (1990), 'Choice, Character, and Excuse', 7 *Social Philosophy and Policy* 28

——(1993), *Act and Crime: The Philosophy of Action and its Implications for the Criminal Law* (Oxford, Oxford University Press)

——(1996), 'Prima Facie Moral Culpability', 76 *Boston University Law Review* 319

——(1997), *Placing Blame: A General Theory of the Criminal Law* (Oxford, Oxford University Press)

Moran, M (2003), *Rethinking the Reasonable Person: An Egalitarian Reconstruction of the Objective Standard* (Oxford, Oxford University Press)

Morgan, EM (1937), 'Presumptions', 12 *Washington Law Review* 255

Morris, CW (1991), 'Punishment and Loss of Moral Standing', 21 *Canadian Journal of Philosophy* 53
Morris, H (1965), 'Punishment for Thoughts', 49 *The Monist* 1
——(1981), 'A Paternalistic Theory of Punishment', 18 *American Philosophical Quarterly* 263
Morse, SJ (1998), 'Excusing and the New Excuse Defenses: A Legal and Conceptual Review', 23 *Crime and Justice: An Annual Review of Research* 329
Mulhall, S and Swift, A (1992), *Liberals and Communitarians* (Oxford, Blackwell)
Murphy, JG (1973), 'Marxism and Retribution', 2 *Philosophy & Public Affairs* 217
——(1985), 'Retributivism, Moral Education, and the Liberal State', 4 *Criminal Justice Ethics* 3
Nagel, T (1970), *The Possibility of Altruism* (Oxford, Oxford University Press)
——(1972), 'War and Massacre', 1 *Philosophy & Public Affairs* 123
——(1980), 'The Limits of Objectivity', in S McMurrin (ed), *The Tanner Lectures on Human Values* (Cambridge, Cambridge University Press) i, 75
Norman, R (1995), *Ethics, Killing and War* (Cambridge, Cambridge University Press)
Norrie, AW (2000), *Punishment, Responsibility, and Justice* (Oxford, Oxford University Press)
——(2001), *Crime, Reason and History*, 2nd ed (London, Butterworths)
Nuotio, K (2005), 'On Becoming a Responsible Person', 2 *Ohio State Journal of Criminal Law* 513
Olsen, F (1983), 'The Family and the Market: A Study of Ideology and Legal Reform', 96 *Harvard Law Review* 1497
Ormerod, D (2000), Case Comment on *Kebilene, Criminal Law Review* 486
——(2005), *Smith & Hogan Criminal Law*, 11th edn (Oxford, Oxford University Press)
Padfield, N (2004), 'The Anti-social Behaviour Act 2003: the Ultimate Nanny-state Act?', *Criminal Law Review* 712
Parry, JT (1997), 'Culpability, Mistake, and Official Interpretations of Law', 25 *American Journal of Criminal Law* 1
Pateman, C (1988), *The Sexual Contract* (Stanford, Cal, Stanford University Press)
Pettit, P and Smith, M (1996), 'Freedom in Belief and Desire', 93 *Journal of Philosophy* 429
Phillips, DZ (1982), 'What the Complex Did to Oedipus', in DZ Phillips, *Through a Darkening Glass* (Oxford, Blackwell) 82
Postema, G (1986), *Bentham and the Common Law Tradition* (Oxford, Oxford University Press)
Quinn, WS (1989), 'Actions, Intentions, and Consequences: The Doctrine of Doing and Allowing', 98 *Philosophical Review* 287
Rachels, J (1975), 'Active and Passive Euthanasia', 292 *New England Journal of Medicine* 78
Rawls, J (1985), 'Justice as Fairness: Political not Metaphysical', 14 *Philosophy and Public Affairs* 223
Raz, J (1979), *The Authority of Law* (Oxford, Oxford University Press)
——(1986), *The Morality of Freedom* (Oxford, Oxford University Press)
——(1987), 'Autonomy, Toleration, and the Harm Principle', in R Gavison (ed), *Issues in Contemporary Legal Philosophy* (Oxford, Oxford University Press) 313

——(1990), *Practical Reason and Norms* (Princeton, NJ, Princeton University Press)
——(1994), *Ethics in the Public Domain* (Oxford, Oxford University Press)
Rees, T and Ashworth, AJ (2004), 'Comment on *Goldstein*', *Criminal Law Review* 303
Reydams, L (2003), *Universal Jurisdiction* (Oxford, Oxford University Press)
Richards, DAJ (1987), 'Kantian Ethics and the Harm Principle: A Reply to John Finnis', 87 *Columbia Law Review* 461
Richards, P (2002), *Law of Contract*, 5th edn (Harlow, Pearson)
Ripstein, A (1999), *Equality, Responsibility, and the Law* (Cambridge, Cambridge University Press)
——(2006), 'Beyond the Harm Principle', 34 *Philosophy and Public Affairs* 215
Roberts, P (1995), 'Taking the Burden of Proof Seriously', *Criminal Law Review* 783
——(2001), 'Philosophy, Feinberg, Codification, and Consent: A Progress Report on English Experiences of Criminal Law Reform', 5 *Buffalo Criminal Law Review* 173
——(2002), 'The Presumption of Innocence Brought Home? Kebilene Deconstructed', 118 *Law Quarterly Review* 41
——(2005), 'Strict Liability and the Presumption of Innocence: An Exposé of Functionalist Assumptions', in AP Simester (ed), *Appraising Strict Liability* (Oxford, Oxford University Press) 151
Roberts, P and Zuckerman, A (2004), *Criminal Evidence* (Oxford, Oxford University Press)
Robinson, PH (1982), 'Criminal Law Defenses: A Systematic Analysis', 82 *Columbia Law Review* 199
——(1984), *Criminal Law Defenses* (2 vols; St Paul, Minn, West Group)
——(1988), *Fundamentals of Criminal Law* (1st ed.; Boston, Little, Brown)
——(1993), 'Should the Criminal Law Abandon the Actus Reus/Mens Rea Distinction', in S Shute, J Gardner and J Horder (eds), *Action and Value in Criminal Law* (Oxford, Oxford University Press) 187
——(1995), *Fundamentals of Criminal Law*, 2nd edn (Boston, Mass, Little, Brown)
——(1997), *Structure and Function in Criminal Law* (Oxford, Oxford University Press)
Robinson, PH, and Grall, JA (1983), 'Element Analysis in Defining Criminal Liability: The Model Penal Code and Beyond', 35 *Stanford Law Review* 681
Rorty, R (1986), 'Pragmatism, Davidson and Truth', in E LePore (ed), *Truth and Interpretation: Perspectives on the Philosophy of Donald Davidson* (Oxford, Oxford University Press) 333
——(1995), 'Is Truth a Goal of Enquiry? Davidson *vs.* Wright', 45 *Philosophical Quarterly* 281
Ross, WD (1930), *The Right and the Good* (Oxford, Oxford University Press)
Roxin, C (2006), *Strafrecht Allgemeiner Teil* 4th edn (Munich, CH Beck) i
Sayre, FB (1933), 'Public Welfare Offenses', 33 *Columbia Law Review* 55
Scanlon, T (1988), 'The Significance of Choice', in SM McMurrin (ed), *The Tanner Lectures on Human Values* (Salt Lake City, Utah, University of Utah Press) viii, 149
Schauer, F (1993), *Playing by the Rules* (Oxford, Oxford University Press)

Scheid, D (1997), 'Constructing a Theory of Punishment, Desert, and the Distribution of Punishments', 10 *Canadian Journal of Law and Jurisprudence* 441

Schlag, PJ (1985), 'Rules and Standards', 33 *UCLA Law Review* 379

Schonsheck, J (1994), *On Criminalization: An Essay in the Philosophy of the Criminal Law* (Dordrecht, Kluwer)

Schopp, RF (1998), *Justification Defenses and Just Convictions* (Cambridge, Cambridge University Press)

Searle, J (1978), 'Prima Facie Obligations', in J Raz (ed), *Practical Reasoning* (Oxford, Oxford University Press)

Shapiro, S (1998a), 'On Hart's Way Out', 4 *Legal Theory* 469

——(1998b), 'The Difference that Rules Make', in B Bix (ed), *Analyzing Law* (Oxford, Oxford University Press)

Sher, G (1997), *Beyond Neutrality* (Cambridge, Cambridge University Press)

Shiner, R (2003), *Freedom of Commercial Expression* (Oxford, Oxford University Press)

Shute, S and Horder, J (1993), 'Thieving and Deceiving: What is the Difference?', 56 *Modern Law Review* 548

Simester, AP (1992), 'Mistakes in Defence', 12 *Oxford Journal of Legal Studies* 295

——(1995), 'Why Omissions Are Special', 1 *Legal Theory* 311

——(1996a), 'Agency', 15 *Law and Philosophy* 159

——(1996b), 'Why Distinguish Intention from Foresight?', in AP Simester and and ATH Smith (eds), *Harm and Culpability* (Oxford, Oxford University Press) 71

——(1998), 'On the So-called Requirement for Voluntary Action', 1 *Buffalo Criminal Law Review* 403

——(2000), 'Can Negligence be Culpable?', in J Horder (ed), *Oxford Essays in Jurisprudence*, 4th Series (Oxford, Oxford University Press) 85

——(2005), 'Is Strict Liability Always Wrong?', in AP Simester (ed), *Appraising Strict Liability* (Oxford, Oxford University Press) 21

—— and Sullivan, GR (2007), *Criminal Law: Theory and Doctrine*, 3rd ed (Oxford, Hart)

—— and ——(2005), 'On the Nature and Rationale of Property Offences', in RA Duff and SP Green (eds), *Defining Crimes: Essays on the Special Part of the Criminal Law* (Oxford, Oxford University Press) 168

—— and von Hirsch, A (eds) (2006), *Incivilities: Regulating Offensive Behaviour* (Oxford, Hart)

Simons, KW (1992), 'Rethinking Mental States', 72 *Boston University Law Review* 463

——(1997), 'When is Strict Criminal Liability Just?', 87 *Journal of Criminal Law and Criminology* 1075

——(2002), 'Does Punishment for "Culpable Indifference" Simply Punish for "Bad Character"?', 6 *Buffalo Criminal Law Review* 219

Singer, R (1986), 'On Classism and Dissonance in the Criminal Law: A Reply to Professor Dan-Cohen', 77 *Journal of Criminal Law and Criminology* 69

Sistare, CT (1987), 'Agent Motives and the Criminal Law', 13 *Social Theory & Practice* 303

——(1989), *Responsibility and Criminal Liability* (Dordrecht, Kluwer)

——(1995), 'In the Land of Omissions: An Opinionated Guide', 14 *Criminal Justice Ethics* 26
Smith, ATH (1978), 'On Actus Reus and Mens Rea', in PR Glazebrook (ed), *Reshaping the Criminal Law* (London, Stevens) 95
——(1984), 'Error and Mistake of Law in Anglo-American Criminal Law', 14 *Anglo-American Law Review* 3
Smith, JC (1989), *Justification and Excuse in the Criminal Law* (London, Stevens)
Smith, KJM (1983), 'Liability for Endangerment: English Ad Hoc Pragmatism and American Innovation', *Criminal Law Review* 127
Smith, P (1999), 'Social Revolution and the Persistence of Rape', in K Burgess-Jackson (ed), *A Most Detestable Crime: New Philosophical Essays on Rape* (New York, Oxford University Press)
——(2003), 'Omission and Responsibility in Legal Theory', 9 *Legal Theory* 221
Solomon, R (1993), *The Passions: Emotions and the Meaning of Life* (Indianapolis, Ind, Hackett)
Solum, L (2003), 'Virtue Jurisprudence: A Virtue-Centred Theory of Judging', 34 *Metaphilosophy* 178
Spencer, JR (1989), 'Public Nuisance—A Critical Examination', 48 *Cambridge Law Journal* 55
Sprack, J (2006), *A Practical Approach to Criminal Procedure*, 11th edn (Oxford, Oxford University Press)
Stanton-Ife, J (2006), 'The Limits of Law', in EN Zalta (ed), *The Stanford Encyclopedia of Philosophy* (http://plato.stanford.edu/archives/spr2006/entries/law-limits)
Stephen, JF (1873/1967), *Liberty, Equality, Fraternity* (ed RJ White; Cambridge, Cambridge University Press)
Stone, CD (1974), *Should Trees Have Standing?* (Los Angeles, Cal, Kaufmann)
Strawson, G (1986), *Freedom and Belief* (Oxford, Oxford University Press)
Strawson, PF (1962), 'Freedom and Resentment', 48 *Proceedings of the British Academy* 1
Sullivan, GR (2005), 'Strict Liability for Criminal Offences in England and Wales Following Incorporation into English Law of the European Convention on Human Rights', in AP Simester (ed), *Appraising Strict Liability* (Oxford, Oxford University Press) 195
Sypnowich, C (2000), 'The Civility of Law: Between Public and Private', in M d'Entrèves and U Vogel (eds), *Public and Private: Legal, Political and Philosophical Perspectives* (London, Routledge)
Tadros, V (1999), 'No Consent: A Historical Critique of the Actus Reus of Rape', 3 *Edinburgh Law Review* 317
——(2002), 'The System of Criminal Law', 22 *Legal Studies* 448
——(2005a), *Criminal Responsibility* (Oxford, Oxford University Press)
——(2005b), 'The Distinctiveness of Domestic Abuse: A Freedom-Based Account', in RA Duff and SP Green (eds), *Defining Crimes: Essays on the Special Part of the Criminal Law* (Oxford, Oxford University Press) 119
——(2006a), 'Rape Without Consent', 26 *Oxford Journal of Legal Studies* 515
——(2006b), 'The Homicide Ladder', 69 *Modern Law Review* 601
——(2007), 'Rethinking the Presumption of Innocence', 1 *Criminal Law and Philosophy* 193

—— and Tierney, S (2004), 'The Presumption of Innocence and the Human Rights Act', 67 *Modern Law Review* 402
Tapper, CF (1999), *Cross and Tapper on Evidence*, 9th edn (London, Butterworths)
Taylor, C (1989), 'Cross-Purposes: The Liberal-Communitarian Debate', in N Rosenblum (ed), *Liberalism and the Moral Life* (Cambridge, Mass, Harvard University Press) 159
Taylor, P (1986), *Respect for Nature* (Princeton, NJ, Princeton University Press)
Thomson, G (1987), *Needs* (London, Routledge)
Thomson, JJ (1987), 'Causality and Rights: Some Preliminaries', 63 *Chicago-Kent Law Review* 471
Turner, JW (1945), 'The Mental Element in Crimes at Common Law', in L Radzinowicz and JW Turner (eds), *The Modern Approach to Criminal Law* (London, Macmillan) 195
Ullmann-Margalit, E (1983), 'On Presumption', 80 *Journal of Philosophy* 143
Uniacke, SM (1994), *Permissible Killing: The Self-defence Justification of Homicide* (Cambridge, Cambridge University Press)
University of Pennsylvania Law Review (1994), 'Symposium, Act and Crime', 142 *University of Pennsylvania Law Review* 1443
Urmson, JO (1988), *Aristotle's Ethics* (Oxford, Blackwell)
von Hirsch, A (1985), *Past or Future Crimes* (Manchester, Manchester University Press)
——(1993), *Censure and Sanctions* (Oxford, Oxford University Press)
——(1996), 'Extending the Harm Principle: "Remote" Harms and Fair Imputation', in AP Simester and ATH Smith (eds), *Harm and Culpability* (Oxford, Oxford University Press) 259
——(2002), 'Das Rechtsgutbegriff und das "Harm Principle"', 149 *Goltdammer's Archiv für Strafrecht* 1
—— Garland, D and Wakefield A (eds) (2000), *Ethical and Social Perspectives on Situational Crime Prevention* (Oxford, Hart)
—— and Jareborg, N (1991), 'Gauging Criminal Harm: A Living-Standard Analysis', 11 *Oxford Journal of Legal Studies* 1
—— Roberts, J, Bottoms, AE, Roach, K and Schiff, M (eds) (2003), *Restorative Justice and Criminal Justice: Competing or Reconcilable Paradigms?* (Oxford, Hart)
Waldron, J (1999), *Law and Disagreement* (Oxford, Oxford University Press)
Walgrave, L (2001), 'Restoration and Punishment. On Favourable Similarities and Fortunate Differences', in G Maxwell and A Morris (eds), *Restoring Justice for Juveniles* (Oxford, Hart) 17
Walker, N (1969), *Sentencing in a Rational Society* (London, Allen Lane)
——(1980), *Punishment, Danger and Stigma* (Oxford, Blackwell)
——(1982), 'Unscientific, Unwise, Unprofitable, or Unjust', 22 *British Journal of Criminology* 276
Wallace, RJ (1994), *Responsibility and the Moral Sentiments* (Cambridge, Mass, Harvard University Press)
Watson, G (1975), 'Free Agency', 72 *Journal of Philosophy* 205
——(2001), 'Reasons and Responsibility', 111 *Ethics* 374

Weale, A (1998), 'Needs and Interests', in E Craig (ed), *Routledge Encyclopedia of Philosophy* (London, Routledge; available at http://www.rep.routledge.com/article/S040)

Weigend, T (1988), 'The Legal and Practical Problems Posed by the Difference between Criminal Law and Administrative Penal Law', 59 *Revue Internationale de Droit Pénal* 67

Westen, P and Mangiafico, J (2003), 'The Criminal Defense of Duress: A Justification, Not an Excuse—and Why it Matters', 6 *Buffalo Criminal Law Review* 833

Widerker, D and McKenna, M (eds) (2003), *Moral Responsibility and Alternative Possibilities* (Aldershot, Ashgate)

Williams, B (1973a), 'Deciding to Believe', in B Williams, *Problems of the Self* (Cambridge, Cambridge University Press)

——(1973b), 'Morality and the Emotions', in B. Williams, *Problems of the Self* (Cambridge, Cambridge University Press) 207

——(1973c), 'A Critique of Utilitarianism', in JJC Smart and B Williams, *Utilitarianism: For and Against* (Cambridge, Cambridge University Press)

——(1981a), 'Moral Luck', in B Williams, *Moral Luck* (Cambridge, Cambridge University Press) 20

——(1981b), 'Internal and External Reasons', in B Williams, *Moral Luck* (Cambridge, Cambridge University Press) 101

——(1985), *Ethics and the Limits of Philosophy* (London, Fontana)

——(1993), *Shame and Necessity* (Berkeley, Cal, University of California Press)

——(1994), 'The Actus Reus of Dr Caligari', 142 *University of Pennsylvania Law Review* 1661

Williams, G (1955), 'Police Control of Intending Criminals—I', *Criminal Law Review* 66

——(1961), *Criminal Law: The General Part*, 2nd edn (London, Stevens)

——(1982), 'Offences and Defences', 2 *Legal Studies* 233

——(1983a), *Textbook of Criminal Law*, 2nd edn (London, Stevens)

——(1983b), 'Convictions and Fair Labelling', 42 *Cambridge Law Journal* 85

——(1988), 'The Logic of "Exceptions"', 47 *Cambridge Law Journal* 261

Wilson, W (2002), *Central Issues in Criminal Theory* (Oxford, Hart)

——(2003), *Criminal Law: Doctrine and Theory*, 2nd edn (London, Longman)

——(2007), 'What's Wrong with Murder?', 1 *Criminal Law and Philosophy* 157

Winch P (1960), 'Nature and Convention', 60 *Proceedings of the Aristotelian Society* 231

——(1972), 'Moral Integrity', in P Winch, *Ethics and Action* (London, Routledge) 171

Wohlers, W, von Hirsch, A and Hefendehl, R (eds) (2003), *Die Rechtsgutstheorie* (Baden-Baden, Nomos Verlagsgesellschaft)

Wolf, S (1987), 'Sanity and the Metaphysics of Responsibility', in F Schoeman (ed), *Responsibility, Character, and the Emotions* (Cambridge, Cambridge University Press) 46

Wolfenden, J (1957), *Report of the Committee on Homosexual Offences and Prostitution* (The Wolfenden Report) (Cmnd 247, London, HMSO)

Wood, AW (2000), 'The Final Form of Kant's Practical Philosophy', in M Timmons (ed), *Essays on Kant's Moral Philosophy* (New York, Cambridge University Press)

Young, JO (2001), 'The Coherence Theory of Truth', in EN Zalta (ed), *The Stanford Encyclopedia of Philosophy* (http://plato.stanford.edu/archives/sum2001/entries/truth-coherence)

Zedner, L (2003), 'Too Much Security?', 31 *International Journal of the Sociology of Law* 155

——(2004), *Criminal Justice* (Oxford, Oxford University Press)

——(2005), 'Securing Liberty in the Face of Terror: Reflections from Criminal Justice', 32 *Journal of Law and Society* 507

Zimmerman, MJ (1988), *An Essay on Moral Responsibility* (Totowa, NJ, Rowman & Littlefield)

Index